Lowcountry Hurricanes

Lowcountry

Three

Centuries

of Storms

at Sea

and Ashore

Hurricanes

WALTER J. FRASER JR.

The University of Georgia Press

Athens and London

A WORMSLOE
FOUNDATION
PUBLICATION

Designed by Mindy Basinger Hill

Set in 10.25/15 Electra LT Standard

by Graphic Composition, Inc., Athens, Georgia

Printed and bound by Maple-Vail

The paper in this book meets the guidelines for permanence
and durability of the Committee on Production Guidelines for
Book Longevity of the Council on Library Resources.

Printed in the United States of America

10   09   08   07   06   C   5   4   3   2   1

Library of Congress Cataloging-in-Publication Data

Fraser, Walter J.

Lowcountry hurricanes : three centuries of storms at sea and ashore /
Walter J. Fraser Jr.

    p. cm.

Includes bibliographical references and index.

ISBN-13: 978-0-8203-2866-9 (alk. paper)

ISBN-10: 0-8203-2866-9 (alk. paper)

1. Hurricanes — Georgia — History.

2. Hurricanes — South Carolina —

History. 3. Georgia — History.

4. South Carolina — History. I. Title.

QC945.F73 2006

975.8 — dc22   2006008065

British Library Cataloging-in-Publication Data available

*The satellite image of a hurricane on the half title and title pages appears
courtesy of the Cooperative Institute for Meteorological Satellite Studies.*

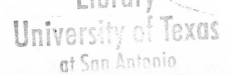

*Dedicated to those
who perished at sea and ashore
in lowcountry hurricanes,
and to my grandson, Van.*

Eternal Father, strong to save,

Whose arm hath bound the restless wave,

Who bidd'st the mighty ocean deep

Its own appointed limits keep;

Oh, hear us when we cry to Thee,

For those in peril on the sea!

"NAVY HYMN"

Contents

Preface

This is a book about hurricanes and tropical storms. More specifically, it is about how these great storms of the lowcountry have affected people and about how they have altered the built and natural environments of the Georgia and South Carolina lowcountry coasts over the last three hundred years.

I grew up near the Virginia coast, and my earliest memories are of living near the water, being on the water or in the water. Families would gather on porches on warm summer evenings and share stories far into the night. Sometimes they gave accounts of hurricanes along the Virginia or North Carolina coast that had wreaked catastrophic damages both at sea and ashore. As a youth reading David Stick's *Graveyard of the Atlantic*, I was enthralled by the harrowing narrative of vessels offshore caught in terrible storms and of the rescue of their crews and passengers from the high seas. On the Outer Banks of North Carolina in 1954, as Hurricane Hazel roared up the coast, my father refused to leave until it was almost too late. Seawater was halfway up the hubcaps of the automobile as we raced across the last bridge connected to the mainland, perhaps one of the last cars to make it off the islands. Years later, as a professional historian, I wrote histories of Charleston and Savannah — *Charleston! Charleston!* and *Savannah in the Old South* — and was surprised to learn how many hurricanes crashed into these two urban centers of the lowcountry.

It was because of these memories and experiences that I decided to write this book.

Researching and writing a book such as this is a daunting job. Thomas Jefferson said that "writing is no harder than digging a ditch." Nevertheless authors need multiple support systems: family, friends, scholars, and library staffs. My wife, Lynn, a skilled critic of style and prose, helped research and write this book. A fellow author and friend, Richard Porcher, was kind enough to share his research with me on the flora of the lowcountry and to offer advice when needed. Another friend, Ken McKenna, provided assistance in calculating the worth of money over time in current dollars. Al Sandrik, of the National Oceanic and Atmospheric Administration (NOAA), and Cary Mock, of the University of South Carolina, kindly shared their research with me. Author Buddy Sullivan provided information on storms of the lower Georgia coast. Recent books by Jay Barnes on Florida and North Carolina hurricanes were most helpful. The comments of Ed Cashin, one of Georgia's foremost historians of the state, were welcomed. The director of the University of Georgia Press, Nicole Mitchell, was enthusiastic about the project from the outset. Staff members Andrew Berzanskis, Pat Allen, and Courtney Denney, the project editor who guided the book through production, provided assistance, as did cartographers at the University of Georgia. Madelaine Cooke was the book's fine copyeditor.

The staffs of the Southern Historical Collection of the University of North Carolina, the Warren R. Perkins Library of Duke University, the South Caroliniana Library of the University of South Carolina, the South Carolina Historical Society, and the Georgia Historical Society were of great help. Administrators and reporters at the *Charleston Post Courier*, the *Savannah Morning News*, the Charleston Museum, and the Coastal Georgia Historical Society assisted me by providing photographs for this book. The interlibrary loan staff at Georgia Southern University procured microfilm accounts of old newspapers when I needed them; and librarians at the Charleston County Library, the George-town Library, Beaufort Public Library, Armstrong Atlantic University, and the Savannah Public Library (Bull Street) pointed me in the right direction for materials needed for this book. I am indebted to these few who provided so much.

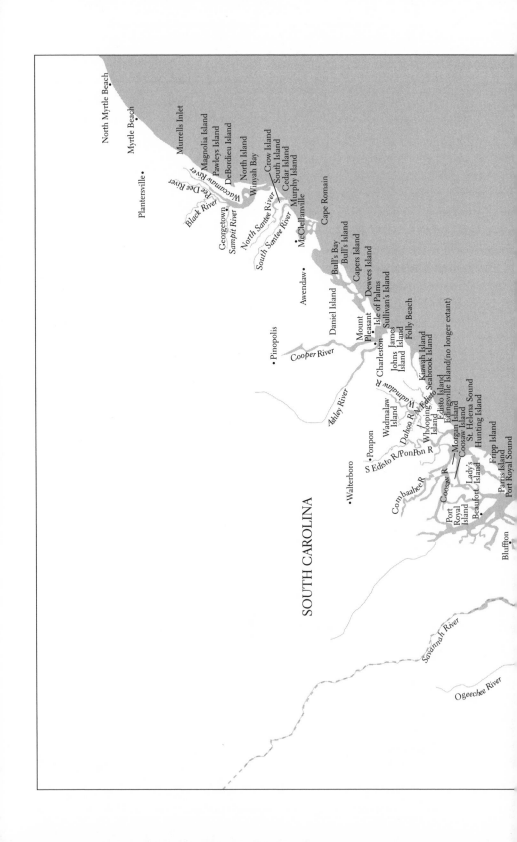

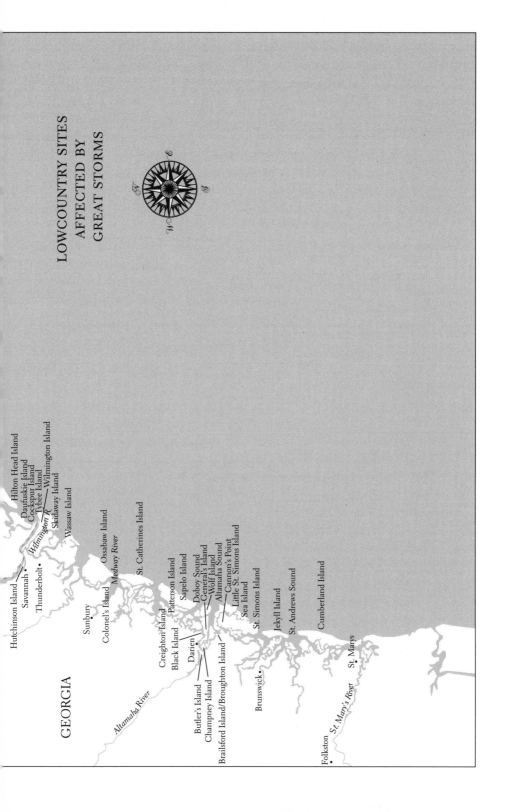

LOWCOUNTRY SITES
AFFECTED BY
GREAT STORMS

GEORGIA

Hutchinson Island
Savannah
Thunderbolt
Hilton Head Island
Daufuskie Island
Cockspur Island
Tybee Island
Wilmington Island
Skidaway Island
Wassaw Island
Wilmington R.

Sunbury
Colonel's Island
Osabaw Island
Medway River
St. Catherines Island

Altamaha River

Creighton Island
Black Island
Darien
Butler's Island
Champney Island
Brailsford Island/Broughton Island
Patterson Island
Sapelo Island
Doboy Sound
General's Island
Wolf Island
Altamaha Sound
Cannon's Point
Little St. Simons Island
Sea Island
St. Simons Island

Brunswick

Jekyll Island
St. Andrews Sound

Cumberland Island

St. Marys

Folkston
St. Mary's River

CHAPTER ONE

The Early Years, 1686–1797

Spanish Repulse Hurricane, September 1686

In the late summer dog days of 1686, high humidity, unusually intense heat, and a drought gripped the lowcountry. Colonists at Charles Town in Carolina, the heart of the lowcountry, sweltered.

In the late seventeenth century, the lowcountry, defined today as coastal Georgia and South Carolina, was a sparsely populated, unexplored subtropical wilderness. With the exception of the settlers at Charles Town, a Scottish trading post seventy miles south, planters on widely dispersed farms, and scattered tribes of Native Americans, the region was virtually uninhabited. Fearing attacks by hostile Indians or invasion by the Spanish, the colonists in 1680 had moved from their original settlement to the more defensible site at Charles Town. There on a boggy peninsula, washed on the west by the Ashley River and on the east by the Cooper, the colonists faced the open Atlantic. Contrary to the inhabitants' initial fears, the first menace to threaten them with extinction was neither Indians nor Spaniards but, instead, was a hurricane.[1]

Mariners at Charles Town, always alert to a change in the weather, may have been among the first to notice the telltale signs of an approaching storm in late August 1686.[2] Huge waves crashed along the coast. "Mare's tail" cloud formations signaled an approaching cold front. A "mackerel sky" indicated that a warm front was moving in. As the saying went, "Mares' tails and mackerel scales make tall ships take in their sails." Mariners also lived by another old bromide: "Red sky at morning, sailor take warning; red sky at night, sailor's delight." Careful observers also may have noted the curious behavior of wildlife. Swallows and bats flew lower to reduce pressure in their ears as the barometer fell, shorebirds flocked inland, and porpoises frolicked near the ocean's surface. Such behavior sometimes indicated the approach of turbulent weather.[3]

By the afternoon of September 4, gale-force winds buffeted Charles Town. Many of the inhabitants (English, Scottish, Irish, Africans, Native Americans — men, women, and children) crowded into the one hundred wooden dwellings near the tip of the low-lying peninsula. They waited and worried. Swine and cows stirred in their pens; some wandered in the dirt streets. The colonists knew that earlier fierce storms had sunk ships before sweeping ashore to their north. Local friendly Indians told them about a hurricane that had "raised the water over the tops of the trees" where the town stood. Now the air felt different, heavy, and the colonists feared a great wind, an evil spirit, which Caribbean natives called *hurracan*, or in English, *hurricane*.[4]

Near dusk, "black and menacing clouds" passed over the peninsula. A resident later told authorities in England that at daybreak, September 5, "a hurricane . . . horrid and destructive" slammed into Charles Town. The storm surge, pushed up by the shallow harbor bottom, crashed ashore near high tide. Accompanied by high winds, it swept vessels from the harbor into the streets. The high waters drowned people. Violent gusts demolished houses, killing those inside; flying debris injured many others. Driving, slashing rains soaked possessions when houses collapsed or lost their roofs. The tropical cyclone raged for five hours. Within the town and in the countryside, it "beat . . . down the corn crop, uprooted trees," and knocked over fences, and surviving hogs and cattle ran wild. For miles around "scarce one great tree" was standing. Timber fell like matchsticks. Huge trees blocked roads and paths, making travel by horseback almost impossible.[5]

Ironically, a bit of good news came from the tragedy. After the storm subsided, word arrived that the hurricane caused the Spanish to abort an invasion and turn back to Florida. Only briefly cheered, the townspeople turned to focus on their misfortunes. After surveying the number of drowned farm animals and the destruction of food crops, they worried that they faced starvation. One can imagine their despair over the enormous human and economic losses.

The hurricane of 1686 was a cataclysmic event for the early settlers at Charles Town. No storm intensity is assigned to this hurricane or to other early storms unless adequate information is provided by contemporary accounts or present-day scholars. Lack of any measuring devices makes judgments of wind speed and storm surge subjective at best; because construction techniques are often unknown, it is difficult to reach conclusions on the extent of structural damages.[6]

In the early 1970s the National Hurricane Center in Miami adopted the Saffir-Simpson Hurricane Potential Damage Scale that ranks hurricane intensity, or magnitude. Subsequently the Hurricane Center used historical records to assign a category number to hurricanes since 1851. The Saffir-Simpson Scale uses wind speed and storm surge to predict damage from hurricanes in five categories. Readers themselves may wish to speculate about the intensity of the early storms. The accounts of lowcountry residents and others who sailed offshore provide ample and compelling evidence of the horrific impact in the region of tropical storms and cyclones.[7]

Despite the carnage caused by the 1686 hurricane, Charles Town was not abandoned. The storm was the first tropical cyclone recorded by the first inhabitants of the lowcountry. Over the next three centuries many more passed offshore or made landfall on the coasts of Georgia or South Carolina. As the region and the economy developed, a small number of the inhabitants acquired vast wealth; this group exhibited a determined persistence to remain and rebuild despite gales and great storms. Others moved on. Some who might have considered migrating to the lowcountry did not because they were wary of settling in a region beset by diseases, heat, and hurricanes.

CATEGORY 1	CATEGORY 2	CATEGORY 3	CATEGORY 4	CATEGORY 5
Wind speeds of 74–95 mph, a storm surge of 4–5 feet above normal, and damage to some trees.	Wind speeds of 96–110 mph, a storm surge of 6–8 feet above normal, damage to roofing materials, and heavy damage to trees and small boats.	Wind speeds of 111–130 mph, a storm surge of 9–12 feet above normal, heavy damage to large trees, structural damage to buildings, and substantial flooding along beaches and rivers.	Wind speeds of 131–155 mph, a storm surge of 13–18 feet above normal, massive structural damage, coastal terrain less than 10 feet above sea level is likely to be flooded, and winds continue inland.	Wind speeds in excess of 155 mph, a storm surge of more than 18 feet above normal, roof failures, destruction of some structures, heavy damage to buildings less than 15 feet above sea level, and high winds far inland; a catastrophic hurricane.

Characteristics of Lowcountry Hurricanes

Tropical cyclones that approach the lowcountry form and grow in the open Atlantic when the summer sun heats the ocean's surface. Some move from as far away as the waters off the west coast of Africa.

Tropical disturbances can develop when vast quantities of water vapor rise, forming dense cumulus clouds. Rain showers and thunderstorms develop. If conditions remain favorable, the system may become a tropical depression. Barometric pressure drops, and the earth's rotation deflects air to swirl in a counterclockwise direction toward the center of the gathering low pressure area. Spiraling winds pushed by the trade winds may move hundreds of miles over warm seas, sweeping up more moisture and heat, fueling larger and larger thunderstorms. More cumulus clouds rise, sometime to a height of more than ten miles. If winds reach thirty-nine miles per hour, the tropical depression becomes a tropical storm.

As the winds around the center of the tropical storm intensify, a calm eye surrounded by spiraling rain bands becomes well defined. As the rotation becomes better organized, barometric pressure continues to fall, and if winds reach seventy-four miles per hour, the storm is classified as a hurricane. A hurricane's greatest sustained winds are located at the edge of the eyewall, a ring of thunderstorms packing high winds, and only in the northern hemisphere is the rotation of these great storms counterclockwise. Steering winds push the storm along an erratic course. Its speed may increase, and the storm may grow into an extreme hurricane that packs the destructive power of an H-bomb.

The paths of tropical cyclones are unpredictable. Some pass over the warm waters of the Gulf Stream, head toward the southeastern coast of the United States, and threaten lowcountry Georgia and South Carolina. They may skirt the coastlines and cause havoc, especially to vessels just offshore, or move onshore. If a hurricane makes landfall on the storm's right-front quadrant, or northeastern side, it is especially deadly. It is this side of the hurricane whose counterclockwise rotation brings the highest winds and the greatest storm surge.

The storm surge is born with the hurricane. The swirling winds raise a twisting column of water beneath the ocean's surface as well as a dome of water several feet above. This column of water can be a hundred miles wide, and it advances with the storm. As hurricanes approach the shallow seabed of the coast, the dome of water is pushed up — sometimes as high as twenty feet. Monstrous wind-driven waves can ride atop it. This is the storm surge — a hurricane's deadliest component.

Additional water damage comes from the spiraling bands of rain that dump six to twelve inches of water as the hurricane passes, occasionally triggering flash floods and tornadoes. In late summer the fuel of the hurricane (the ocean's warm temperature) peaks, and most great storms sweep near or over the lowcountry in August, September, or October.[8] In the lowcountry, "gale" came to describe anything from a strong wind to a hurricane.

Southern Distinctiveness

"Let us begin by discussing the weather," a historian of the South wrote, "for that has been the chief agency in making the South distinctive." More recently another scholar wrote that "climate may not be the key to human history, but climate does matter . . . [and in] the American South, it matters a great deal." Indeed, "the South remains a land apart—a land that still owes much of its distinctiveness to climatic forces."[9]

It is readily acknowledged that such diseases as yellow fever and smallpox flourished in the South's moist subtropical climate, and with the South's devotion to agriculture and slavery, there was little opportunity for white immigrants. These factors slowed population growth and retarded economic development. However, anxiety over the South's weather, certainly the scorching summer heat but also the fear of gales and hurricanes, hampered growth of the coastal South as well. Local residents, sea captains, travelers, and newspapers spread word of the horrific impact of hurricanes—the death of humans and the destruction of the built and natural environments. From the beginnings of settlement, wide publicity was given to the fatalities and damage at sea and ashore caused by the frequent great storms near or within the coastal zone of lowcountry Georgia and South Carolina. But more often than not, boosters of the region touted the climate as a means of promoting the South and ignored the effects of diseases and hurricanes that frequently swept the lowcountry.[10]

Today the region is populated by over one million people, more during the hurricane season, June 1 to November 1. The lowcountry extends 10 miles inland and stretches about 280 miles south from Myrtle Beach, South Carolina, to St. Marys, Georgia. It is part of the Georgia Bight, or Atlantic Embayment, which curls westward from the Outer Banks of North Carolina ("the graveyard of the Atlantic") to Florida's Cape Canaveral. The westward curve of the coast has lulled many into thinking that the great storms have caused little damage or death in the lowcountry and, hence, that it is unlikely that destructive ones will occur in the future. However, this unprotected low-lying region—rarely as high as twenty feet—is located on the northwestern edge of a significant hurricane "corridor" that begins above the equator. The lowcountry has been swept by numerous hurricanes during the recorded history of the region.

Lowcountry Immigrants

The first settlers of the lowcountry likely sailed part of the way with the Gulf Stream, usually about seventy miles off much of the Georgia Bight, taking advantage of its northward-flowing current of more than one knot. After the settlers turned west, their first landfall usually was the wide white sandy beach of a sea island. These low-lying erosion-remnant islands, or barrier islands, are constantly changed by winds, tides, and storms. They provide the mainland some protection from ill effects of waves rolling in from the ocean. Just beyond the beaches, the settlers saw wind-sculpted sand dunes held in place by sea oats. Standing on a dune and looking landward, a colonist would first have seen low-growing yucca, prickly pear, yaupon holly, then wax myrtles, stunted live oaks, and cedars bent by the prevailing southeast winds. Beyond these, the subtropical heat nourished an almost impenetrable jungle of palmetto trees, larger live oaks, towering pines, dense undergrowth, and brackish ponds. Inlets, bays, sounds, and sometimes a dense marsh webbed with tidal creeks separated the sea islands from one another and from the mainland. Like the barrier islands, the mainland was low-lying and vulnerable. Once on the mainland, the settlers discovered a half-dozen deep natural harbors dotting the lowcountry's coastline. Usually in the vicinity was one or more of a dozen major rivers that meandered across the region and flowed into the harbors and on to the sea. Thick marsh grasses, lime green in summer and saffron in the autumn, flanked the rivers. On the banks and in the swamps beyond grew palmettos, huge pines, gum, willow, red cedar, sweet bay, tupelo, and cypress. Giant live oak trees flourished, their gnarled branches hung with gray moss and resurrection fern; saw palmettos provided dense undergrowth. Creeks wound through the marshes. An occasional tree and brush-covered islet, or hammock, rose from the rich, dark marsh mud. Beyond the salt marshes, colonists found vast savannas thick with tall pines garnished in the early spring with yellow jasmine and wild Cherokee roses. Close by were freshwater swamps covered by a dense canopy provided by the leaves of maple, sweet gum, hickory, dogwood, and bay trees. Here colonists cleared the trees, ferns, and broom grass; dug ditches; built canals, dams, and floodgates; and turned the swamps into fields of waving rice, which in time became the staple of the lowcountry.[11]

Early promoters of the lowcountry made extravagant claims. They told prospective immigrants that the very air gave "a Strong Appetite and Quick Digestion," that men found "themselves . . . more lightsome," and that "the Women [were] very Fruitful"; other boosters extolled the region as "the most Amiable Country of the Universe," where there was "no Excess of *Heat,* or *Cold*" and where "boundless wealth" easily could be extracted from the soil.[12]

Of course the lushness, size, and number of plants and trees astonished early settlers from urban England or Europe. They were equally awed by the abundance of game, finfish, shrimp, blue crabs, oysters, and clams that flourished in the rivers or along the dark, rich banks of the marshes. Wild ducks and geese rafted offshore and in the rivers; deer teemed in the thickets; ivory-billed woodpeckers and clouds of passenger pigeons and Carolina Parakeets nested deep in the swampy floodplains along with wood ibises the size of turkeys, varicolored herons, snakebirds, white egrets, and wood storks.

But to some the region did not live up to the claims of the publicists. Diseases imported with the immigrants — yellow fever, malaria, smallpox, and typhus — flourished in the subtropical climate of the lowcountry. Deadly epidemics frequently swept the towns and countryside, striking most frequently in the warmest months, August through November, "the sickly season." Many lowcountry colonists died of infectious diseases before reaching the age of forty. In western Europe, Charles Town acquired a reputation as "the great charnel house" of America. English officials considered relocating the settlement. Judith Giton, who arrived in Charles Town in 1685 and apparently survived the hurricane of the following year, told her family that she had been "exposed . . . to sickness, pestilence, famine, poverty, and the roughest labor." Not so fortunate were the first immigrants to Savannah, Georgia, where more than one-quarter died within a year.[13]

Chiggers, ticks, clouds of sand gnats, wildcats, and panthers became almost constant companions of the early settlers. Snakes and, especially, alligators terrified them. One surveyor appointed by General James Oglethorpe — the founder of Georgia at Savannah — disliked working during the hot months "for fear of snakes." To overcome the colonists' fears of alligators, Oglethorpe had a twelve-foot alligator hauled to town, where "the Children pelted and beat him to Death."[14] Nevertheless hurricanes remained one of the most persistent fears of lowcountry inhabitants.

David Ramsay, an amateur historian and a Charlestonian who knew some of the earliest immigrants, declared that "pestilence in the city, common fever in the country, . . . [or] an expected hurricane . . . at the close of every warm season" left lowcountry residents "in a painful state of anxiety" about where to go.[15] Such was likely the case in the year 1700.

The Rising Sun Hurricane

On September 14, 1700, Charlestonians, recovering from epidemics of small-pox and yellow fever, were rebuilding the town's fortifications following a dev-astating fire. That same day, thick lowering clouds, heavy rains, and increasing winds warned of a tropical cyclone before it swept the peninsula. Waves that had traveled great distances at sea rose higher in the shallow coastal waters and crashed into and overflowed the town. The immigrant Edward Hyme saw trees "torn up by [their] roots," "many Houses blown down," and several washed away. Luckily, Hyme said, the winds shifted two hours before high tide; if they had not, he "thought the best & greatest part of [the] town would have been washed down into . . . [the sea]."[16]

Good fortune did not prevail in the harbor. Wind and waves shredded sails and tore off masts of vessels riding at anchor. The storm turned others "bottom upwards" and sent several ashore where they "broke all in Pieces." An eighty-ton brigantine was blown onto what is today White Point Gardens, knocking down a gallows used recently to hang pirates. Outside the harbor and more exposed to the sea, an eight-hundred-ton Scottish ship of sixty guns, the *Rising Sun*, dragged its anchor. The ship had lost its masts in a great storm off Florida, and Captain James Gibson was waiting with crew and passengers — Scottish immigrants — to come up to Charles Town for refitting. The hurricane battered the ship, bruising and terrifying those aboard. When the anchor failed to hold the vessel, it was driven by the winds toward sandbars. Most likely the big guns and the "Gold Silver & rich goods onboard" shifted as huge waves crashed over the decks and the *Rising Sun* foundered. Its captain, passengers, and crew of about a hundred spilled into the waves and "miserably perish[ed]" by drown-ing. Bodies washed ashore on a nearby island, which was then given the name Coffin Land, later renamed Folly Beach. Waves pushed wreckage of the *Rising Sun* and many corpses onto James Island. Scavengers salvaged what they could and buried the Scots on the islands.[17]

The same hurricane swirled north, most likely perpendicular to the main-land. The destructive power of its right side wreaked havoc on the natural environment. Where Georgetown, South Carolina, was later founded the tropical cyclone sliced a new entrance into Winyah Bay.

Beset by disease, fire, and hurricanes, some settlers "lament[ed]" their losses and abandoned the town. Some may have gone to Pennsylvania, after hearing that it was a prosperous settlement and one safe from the sea. But many decided to remain. Nevertheless the Charles Town settlement was acquiring a checkered reputation in America and abroad.[18]

Most likely the tropical cyclone of 1700 ranked with the previous hurricane in terms of wind velocity and storm surge. A few Charlestonians perished, though the full extent of the shore damage is unknown. The highest death toll was offshore. The value of the *Rising Sun* and its cargo was estimated at £50,000 ($5,040,222).[19]

A Great Storm, September 16–17, 1713

Within a few years Charles Town resumed its vigorous export-import trade. By the end of the first decade of the new century more than a hundred sea-going vessels cleared the port with naval stores and Indian slaves and arrived with consumer goods and African slaves. Blacks soon outnumbered whites in the Carolina colony of ten thousand inhabitants. Some merchants prospered. The people enjoyed casual dancing and singing in the taverns. The town itself became crowded with some four thousand people and their livestock. Mud and sand streets were filled with filth, animal and human waste. The settlers routinely became sick and died during epidemics of yellow fever and smallpox. New fortifications went up around the town. The Anglican Church became the established religion of the colony, and a new brick building was begun for St. Philip's to replace a cypress structure, but another hurricane interrupted its construction.[20]

The tropical cyclone grazed the settlement at Port Royal some seventy miles south and came ashore north of Charles Town on September 16, 1713. Although the most damaging winds struck to the north, the high winds swept a cresting tide into the town. Charlestonians scrambled to higher places, and witnesses described a sudden "inundation from the sea, to such a . . . height that a great many lives were lost"; during the twelve hours that the hurricane raged, it was "miraculous how any of us came to escape," a survivor recalled. The winds and the storm surge drove vessels into the marshes or the town and washed away many dwellings with people in them. The house of the minister of the Independent Church at White Point was "carried away by the overflowing of the Sea." The surging waters undermined the new walls and fortifications encircling the town; winds blew down the newly built, eighty-foot lookout tower on Sullivan's Island. To the north of Charles Town, where the hurricane came ashore, the damage was worse. An Anglican priest reported that the countryside for miles was "thick" with felled "large trees." At least seventy people in town and beyond perished. Later estimates of the damage from the tropical cyclone reached £100,000 ($11,833,564). The human loss and the extent and range of damage to the built and natural environments suggest that the hurricane of 1713, like the earlier two, was extremely destructive. It was remembered as the "great storm."[21]

With an outbreak of war with the Yamasee Indians and their allies in 1715, hundreds of settlers in the lowcountry fled into Charles Town for protection. The Carolina militia fought a long and costly war with the Indians while Charlestonians engaged pirates off the coast and overthrew the proprietary government for a royal one in a bloodless revolution. With more inhabitants in the already crowded town, diseases took a toll higher than ever. The rebuilding and repair of Charles Town slowed to a crawl, and additional natural disasters threatened the lowcountry.[22]

Some years later, in mid-September 1722, a major storm moved north from the Savannah River and up the coast. By now the colonists were making efforts to predict the violence of storms: one that "thunders much . . . is soon over," but a storm that "comes in sudden[ly] . . . with calm intervals [is] dangerous" and does "considerable damage," one hurricane survivor remembered. Such was the storm of 1722.[23]

The Coastal Hurricane of 1722

For three days and nights in mid-September "violent," incessant rains pounded the lowcountry. September 19–21, waters flooded the region, and the Savannah River spilled its banks. Mark Catesby, the renowned botanist, who was in Charles Town, heard that the nearby "hurricane" was so severe and the waters so high that "the Deer were found frequently lodged in [tall] . . . trees." "Panthers [and] bears" suffered the same fate when the storm blew into the upcountry. The storm pushed inland, and at the fall line of the Savannah River, floodwaters crested far above normal. Undoubtedly the hurricane and floods caused an ecological disaster. Though there is a paucity of information on human losses and the effects on the built environment, reports by contemporaries indicate that it was a fiercely destructive storm.[24]

The Gale of 1724

Two years later, on August 28, 1724, a tropical storm brushed the lowcountry coast but did little damage. By now Charles Town's fortifications had been rebuilt, bridges constructed, and the repairs and construction of St. Phillip's church completed. With its four hundred communicants, St. Phillip's testified to the growing wealth in the town, as did the dwellings of the well-to-do merchants whose homes, residencies above and stores below, went up on Bay Street's western side. The town of five thousand was nearly evenly divided between blacks and whites.

The Blow of 1728

Townspeople thought it "uncommonly hot" in the spring and summer of 1728. Produce wilted, pools of water evaporated, hogs and cattle died, and an epidemic of yellow fever was spread across the town by mosquitoes. Farmers fearing contagion refused to bring fresh produce to town, food prices spiked, people went hungry, and business ceased. By late summer townspeople began worrying about the likelihood of a devastating tropical storm. Their worst fears became justified when one came ashore near flood tide on August 13 at 10:00 p.m. southwest of the port but with its center near Charles Town. Anyone asleep immediately awakened to what Charlestonians called "a very Violent Hurricane, the wind . . . north-northeast to east . . . and continuing for about six hours." The wind then shifted to the east-southeast "still blowing violently" until noon on August 14.[25]

Huge waves crashed over the fortifications, carried away bridges, inundated cornfields, and destroyed a fruit orchard owned by John Laurens. Legend has it that Laurens's son was born during the gale. The boy, James, was the brother of Henry Laurens, one of the wealthiest men in the colonies. Trying to escape the rising waters, townspeople raced to the roofs of their dwellings. Several perished from falling debris; others died by drowning. High winds and water drove ashore twenty-three vessels (schooners, brigantines, ships, and a snow) tied off at wharfside or anchored in the harbor. Eight were total wrecks; the others were salvageable. Some 1,530 barrels of rice went down with the vessels, and another 500 barrels washed out of warehouses. Boats, boards, and staves littered the streets of Charles Town. Thousands of trees fell in the coastal zone and beyond. The damage was horrific. Though no estimates were given, it appears that the magnitude of the storm may have equaled those of 1686, 1700, and 1713.[26]

The tropical cyclone and its terrible effects received wide publicity in the *New York Gazette*, the *Boston Gazette*, and the Boston *Weekly News Letter* and were probably reported by the British Press.[27] It is likely that the news did not encourage voluntary immigration to the lowcountry. Nonetheless a trickle of European immigrants continued — English, French, Scots, Irish, German, and Welsh. Some came to escape religious persecution, whereas others sought meaningful work and a better life. Involuntary immigrants included black slaves and white indentured servants.

Voluntary and Involuntary Immigrants

A tropical cyclone brushed the lowcountry in 1730, but apparently it stayed offshore and caused little damage along the coast. By then Georgetown, South Carolina, had been founded on Winyah Bay, some sixty miles north of Charles Town, and Beaufort, to the south on the Beaufort River, had become a deep-water port and trading outpost. In 1733, some forty miles away from Beaufort by creeks and rivers, General James Oglethorpe founded Savannah for the Trustees of Georgia as a buffer between the Carolina colony and the Spanish to the south.

French-speaking Huguenots, fleeing religious harassment in France, and German-speaking Salzburgers pushed up the Cooper and North and South Santee rivers in South Carolina and the Savannah River that separated Georgia and South Carolina. Rice was fast becoming the major moneymaking crop in the lowcountry. Within a few decades nine of the ten richest men in British North America lived in South Carolina and owned vast rice plantations worked by African slaves. The large number of slaves seen in South Carolina led observers to declare that the colony "looked more like a Negro country." Initially, black slavery was forbidden in the Georgia colony.[28]

In the 1740s the Spanish threatened to attack the flourishing Carolina colony. In early July 1742 General Oglethorpe encountered a superior Spanish army on St. Simons Island under the command of General Manual Montiano. After a fierce firefight at the Battle of Bloody Marsh stymied Montiano, British warships appeared on the horizon. Fearing the reinforcements and the possibility of a hurricane, the Spanish retreated. This was the last major effort by Spain to oust the English from the southern frontier.[29] In this case the threat of a hurricane was fortuitous. Two hurricanes that swept along the South Carolina coast in the 1740s and about which little is known evidently were not.[30]

During the late 1740s and early 1750s, Charles Town grew to over six thousand inhabitants, becoming the fourth-largest city in British North America. However, unlike that of Boston, New York, and Philadelphia, its population was still almost equally divided between blacks and whites. The Spanish and French threatened to invade again, a fire burned part of the port, and yellow fever swept the town. Pigs and cattle still strolled through the port, and its streets remained filthy with human and animal waste. A theater opened, and musical life increased as a tiny elite grew wealthy in the export-import trade.

Though winds during the hurricane season battered and wrecked sailing vessels along South Carolina's entire coast, mariners especially feared the shallow shoals some miles off Georgetown at Cape Romain, latitude 33° north. Here were some of the most treacherous waters along the coast. Lowcountry Georgians knew about these fierce storms, hazardous both at sea and ashore.

In late summer 1748 an educated German-speaking pastor and recent immigrant to the new, struggling colony of Georgia confided to his diary, "At the end of August and the beginning of September . . . travelers on water here are full of fear of the great storm winds which are called hurricanes in the English language and have been described to be most terrifying." Georgia's new immigrants did not have long to wait to experience the natural phenomenon unknown in Europe.[31]

The Great Hurricane, September 1752

Oddly the prevailing southeast winds of lowcountry summers became northeasterly during August and September 1752. Blown southward when they attempted to enter the port, vessels stacked up off Charles Town's bar waiting for a change in the wind. Daily temperatures rose to 90 degrees and for twenty successive days stayed between 90 and 101. Lowcountry residents remembered it as a time of "Great Drought" and "violently hot" weather. Dogs in Charles Town stopped wandering the streets and could only "lie panting with their tongues lolling out." Even old-timers did not recall such intense, persistent heat.[32]

The unusual heat extended far offshore and into the warm waters of the Gulf Stream, which nourished a low-pressure system of growing winds and rain between the Bahamas and Florida. It grew into a tropical depression and then a tropical cyclone. By Monday, September 11, the hurricane was gathering strength off St. Augustine, Florida.[33]

Tracking northward just off the coast, winds of hurricane force pushed great waves over Cumberland Island, Georgia's southernmost and largest barrier island. On the island's southern tip, Fort William, an English strongpoint of sand and wood with a lookout tower, was battered into "a ruinous condition" by the wind and waves. On Jekyll Island, Major William Horton's tabby dwelling was nearly flooded by the storm surge.[34]

It was September 13 when the hurricane caught up with the ship *Africa* several miles off Savannah. Apparently a slave ship, it was bound for Charles Town. What certainly must have happened to this ship, happened to many others:

> The hurricane . . . shut down completely on the ship and the men on it. Drunkenly buffeted, half-drowned, hardly able to see, unable to hear, each in the strangeness and the terror was alone. The increasing sea had been a nightmare of waves since before the wind had built up to . . . screaming. . . . The dark green, wind-carved, rain-pitted swells had turned black, had swollen, fretted and tumbling with . . . white sheets . . . that made the speed of the wind visible in lightning blasts of foam. Men clung as they could to something . . . holding as the decks lifted and dropped and yawed and came bucking up to meet smashing tons of water. . . . What work there was to be done, in hope of keeping some puny order in irresistible chaos, came as a fragment of an order screamed in a man's ear. . . . The order was carried out painfully, by a man crawling and clinging under the wrench of exploding water, slow as a cripple in the agonized shocks of the ship.[35]

The *Africa*'s master, Captain John Dorrington, tried to steer into the heavy sea. Fierce winds shredded his sails, tore his rigging to pieces, and knocked down the masts. He lost all headway.

Ships can minimize the impact of heavy seas during winter storms by steering into swells that come from only one direction. However, in the chaotic seas of a summer hurricane, when winds shift rapidly from one compass point to another it is impossible to maintain control as waves come from myriad directions. One large swell rides atop others, creating enormous waves. And it was this type of sea that Captain Dorrington attempted to navigate to save his ship, crew, and cargo of slaves. All aboard must have thought the ship was going down at any moment. Huge waves battered a side of the *Africa* and threatened to capsize it. As the ship wallowed dead in the water, waves swept its decks of small boats and washed "four white seamen" and a "Negro" overboard to their deaths; amazingly the *Africa* remained afloat.[36]

Those watching the weather along the lowcountry's mainland saw the skies turn "cloudy and boisterous." By the afternoon of September 14 they observed the telltale signs of an approaching storm: the roar of heavy surf crashing along the coast, a wild and threatening sky, and heavy windblown rains. Early the following morning the tropical cyclone roared ashore north of Savannah and just south of Charles Town. Strong northwesterly winds buffeted Savannahians who witnessed "incredible damage . . . to the trees" but little to houses or vessels in the harbor. Fortune favored lowcountry Georgians. The hurricane only grazed the upper Georgia coast as its highest winds remained offshore. Charlestonians did not fare as well. At Charles Town it was a major hurricane.[37]

The hurricane made landfall near Charles Town on a lunar high tide from the southeast. During the early morning hours the winds and rains became "violent." Anyone moving about outside was blown down. Rain mixed with the spray of waves crashed around the peninsula and drenched the town. It was the height of the export-import season, and the storm battered the many sailing craft in the harbor. Captains ordered sails reefed and extra anchors thrown over. About 9:00 a.m. the storm surge, a seventeen-foot wall of water, filled the harbor and smashed into the vessels. It swept men into the roiling sea and, with their anchors dragging, pushed "all the vessels . . . ashore." More than fourteen vessels plunged into the marshes, and five crashed into the town. A brigantine was blown up Vanderhorst's Creek — Water Street today — shearing off a corner of the new Baptist church. Winds damaged vessels far up the Cooper and Ashley rivers and blew others off stocks in shipyards close by. The hurricane completely wrecked or damaged at least forty large vessels. Waves hurled smaller craft into the wharves, warehouses, and dwellings along East Bay Street. A house near the corner of Lodge Alley was nearly "torn to pieces." Seawater poured into homes, and some residents saved themselves only by swimming to safety. As the water rose in the large white house of Colonel Charles Cotesworth Pinckney at the corner of Ellery Street and French Alley, he saved his family by commandeering a ship's yawl.[38]

Water cascaded over and undermined the "strong brick wall" serving as a fortification that ran the length of East Bay Street. At the bastions on the extremities of the wall, the waves tore off cannons and floated away their wooden gun carriages. Debris became airborne missiles. Winds blew down the new "Negro School," collapsed chimneys of substantial brick dwellings, and tore off tile and slate roofs, exposing the interiors and their contents to drenching rains. On South Bay, waters swept across White Point, floating away wooden houses. Torrents of seawater rushed down the nearby narrow streets.[39]

Some inhabitants fled to their rooftops to escape floodwaters. In their home on Church Street, near the Heyward-Washington House today, the Bedon family waited too long to leave, and the rushing, swirling torrents of water sucked under and drowned Mrs. Bedon, her three children, two white servants, and five black slaves. A ship with German immigrants was blown into the marsh of James Island. The continuous rolling of the vessel from the wind and waves tumbled the passengers in the hold from side to side, breaking their arms and legs and injuring them so badly that twenty died. Three other people perished when the waters flooded James Island and destroyed Fort Johnson.[40]

Meanwhile, just across the harbor on Sullivan's Island, Artemas Elliott and fourteen others crowded into the quarantine station for safety as the great storm approached. The "wind rose very high" during the night of September 14, making the structure shake and its inhabitants tremble. The following morning the sea surged across the island; waves battered the structure until it collapsed. The dwelling and its occupants tumbled into several fathoms of a boiling sea. After Elliott hit the water he expected to drown at any moment. As he struggled to stay afloat someone grabbed his foot, threatening to drag him under. But Elliott kicked out. His "stocking came off" in the hands of a drowning victim. Some occupants scrambled onto what was left of the quarantine station. The debris and those clinging to it were tossed about by crashing waves, and one after another person was knocked from the wreckage into the turbulent waters. Pushed by tide and winds up the Cooper River, Elliott, three white men, and "a negro" survived to come ashore at Hobcaw Point. The other ten occupants of the quarantine station, including at least one slave, Prince, who belonged to the Elliott family, perished. Artemas Elliott, profoundly affected by the experience, told his daughter, Polly, "how good ye Great God has Been to me, in keeping my Sperits up, and Sending me Safe to Shore, after having nothing but Death before my Eyes, for Severall hours."[41]

South of Charles Town, on Kiawah Island, William Mathews, his wife, and about forty-seven people saved themselves from fast-rising waters by crowding into an old corn house that stood on posts high above the ground. In the coastal zone to the north, on farms between Pon Pon and the North and South Santee rivers, dozens of "Negro Houses" and outhouses were being "blown down."[42]

By 11:00 a.m. several feet of water covered most of Charles Town, and high tide was still two hours away. Suddenly the wind shifted and blew from the southwest, and the water in the town fell rapidly. By 3:00 p.m. the winds had died. Survivors left their places of refuge to discover streets littered with the ruins of some five hundred houses, "wrecks of boats, masts, timber, barrels, staves, shingles, [and] household goods." They saw bodies of the victims, both human and animal, positioned grotesquely where the swirling waters deposited them. Royal Governor James Glen called out the militia to prevent looting. The government promised to arrest and prosecute anyone taking "Advantage of the Calamity" caused by the "dreadful Hurricane," especially those found "picking up, purloining and plundering, the Goods, Wares, . . . Household Furniture, Sails, Masts, Rigging . . . and other Things, carried away by the Violence of the Wind and Waves" and strewn about Charles Town. All slaves and other "Negroes" found stealing property would be sent to the work house and punished.[43]

The coast was strewn with the wreckage of vessels. The *Africa*, which had encountered the storm east of Charles Town, continued to be blown northwestward. Finally the ship was pushed into the breakers and sandbars off the North Edisto River. Captain Dorrington and his first mate remained aboard to oversee the removal of five blacks and the rescue of his remaining crewmembers. Dorrington and his first mate finally abandoned the *Africa* when rescued by the ship *Cunliffe*.

For thirty miles around Charles Town the storm destroyed dwellings, livestock, and crops. It flattened thousands of "the best and largest trees," especially pines. Many others had been split, or "heart-shaken," and rendered unfit for lumber. Plantation owners and Charles Town merchants suffered huge financial losses. One colonist, Mr. Beresford, lost over £20,000 ($2,177,376) in trees destroyed. Roads around the town remained impassable for weeks until cleared of trees. The export of tar declined over the next several years. The total economic costs again are inestimable; obviously they were considerable. In terms of human losses at sea and ashore, estimates of deaths ranged from ninety-five to two hundred.[44]

Another Terrible Hurricane, September 1752

While the debris was still being removed around Charles Town, another great storm grazed the port on Saturday, September 30. Charles Town's *South Carolina Gazette* reported that "another terrible hurricane" had struck the town with heavy rains and high winds from the northeast and blown hard for three hours. Compared with that of the initial hurricane, the damage was light in town but greater to the north and south. At sea thirteen vessels encountered the storm; one two-masted, square-rigged snow was "beat to pieces" off St. Helena Island. Another snow from Bristol, England, went aground on the bar off Edisto Island; a ship was driven ashore at Kiawah Island, and a sloop at Port Royal. There was "greater damage" at Port Royal from flooding by the second hurricane than by the first. The tropical cyclone was "severely felt" at Georgetown and continued up the coast to devastate southeastern North Carolina.[45]

Along the South Carolina coast damage to crops was so widespread from the two September hurricanes that officials worried that "Corn, Peas, and . . . Rice" would be insufficient to feed the inhabitants. The government at Charles Town responded by prohibiting the export of these crops for twelve months.[46]

Accounts of the hurricane appeared in Boston, New York, Philadelphia, Maryland, and Virginia newspapers, and in the *Gentleman's Magazine* in London. Charlestonian Peter Manigault, a student in London, was alarmed and anxious about the "distresses occasioned by the Devastation of the . . . Hurricane." In December he wrote to his father, Gabriel Manigault, one of the richest men in British North America, and reflected "with Pity . . . upon the poor unfortunate Condition of the Sufferers in Carolina."[47] Reports of frequent tropical storms and devastating hurricanes along the coasts of South Carolina and Georgia were widespread.[48]

The lowcountry recovered slowly from the twin hurricanes of 1752. The export-import trade collapsed, and it took years to rebuild Charles Town's wharves, warehouses, and defenses. The fortifications had been "entirely destroyed." Four years later, in December 1756, work was still going forward "at great expence" to reconstruct the defenses. But even then the Charles Town government was unable to defend the place due to "want of . . . Cannon . . . other warlike stores" and experts in weaponry. Miles Brewton, the largest trader in black slaves in South Carolina, and Thomas Drayton, a member of the royal council of the colony, joined prominent English merchants to petition the king to grant "Protection" for the "defenceless state" of the provinces of South Carolina and Georgia.[49]

Henry Laurens and Others on Lowcountry Hurricanes

While Charles Town was being rebuilt, tropical storms and hurricanes followed a familiar path, buffeting the Georgia and South Carolina coasts and battering vessels caught offshore.[50] Owners of these sailing craft included such prosperous lowcountry merchants as Henry Laurens and his business associates. In the mid-1750s the sloop *Enterprize*, owned by a trading partner of Laurens, was caught in a fierce storm off South Carolina's coast. Winds blew away its sails, and the vessel wallowed in a mountainous sea. Though "almost dead with fatigue," the captain and his crew fought for hours to keep the vessel afloat. The *Enterprize* took on so much water that "both Pumps were required to keep her" from sinking. The sloop finally reached Charles Town. There Laurens oversaw the repair of his associate's sloop for £90 ($10,807), "tho we went the cheapest way to work that we could think of."[51]

The following year, during the hurricane season of 1756, the ship *Tryton*, carrying sugar from Jamaica northward, was caught in a huge storm off Florida and Georgia. It finally limped into Port Royal, South Carolina, with three feet of water in its hold and its pumps working without letup. Eventually the ship reached Charles Town. Henry Laurens again invested time, trouble, and money to repair a vessel for a business associate.[52] Laurens also worried that without warning hurricanes might sweep in from the sea to devastate his dwellings, lands, and rice crops. To an overseer who was new to the lowcountry he said,

About the middle of August begin to be much upon your Guard about tempestuous Weather. I caution you because you have never seen a Hurricane, you shd have

Bars of strong Wood ready to fasten in all your Windows, keep every Article liable to Damage six Inches off your Floors, and nothing so low as the common Surface of the Earth in the Cellars, these you must expect to be brim full, your House and Outhouses overflowed your fences blown down . . . prepare against the worst while The Weather is fair. Save all those Cypress Boards near the Counting House and in the Yard for repairing Fences and in case of Disaster send for [the slaves] Burnet and Sam.[53]

Like Laurens, a member of the privileged class and rich in land and slaves, permanent residents of the lowcountry became acclimatized to the weather and were willing to take their chances with the diseases, heat, and hurricanes. Newcomers, however, though they might be politically prominent and wealthy, were less tolerant of the region's weather. For example, Henry Ellis, the royal governor who arrived at Savannah in 1757, must have found the fledgling town a desolate place. The population of several hundred individuals lived in dilapidated wooden houses. A vast forest pressed in on three sides. He soon came to believe that in the summers the inhabitants of Savannah "breathe a hotter air than [do] any other people on the face of the earth." He noted that "the weatherwise of this country say [the temperature] forebodes a hurricane; for it has always been remarked, that these tempests have been preceded by continual and uncommon heats." His remarks appeared in the *Gentleman's Magazine* published in London and must have made at least the literate wonder that Georgia may be unlike the Garden of Eden promised by promoters. Ellis soon asked to be relieved of his duties so that he could return to London "for the recovery of [my] . . . health." Before he departed, Ellis must have witnessed or received reports of a hurricane that swept the coastal waters of Georgia and made landfall in South Carolina during a heat wave in late August 1758.[54]

The many black and white inhabitants of the lowcountry who did not have the freedom or wherewithal to leave in the face of intense summer heat or hurricanes remained profoundly concerned over the violence and frequency of great storms. John Bartram, the botanist, exploring the lowcountry in the 1760s, found residents "terrified & fearful" of storms since they might signal the approach of a hurricane.[55] About the same time, Captain Martin, an English ship master who apparently knew the lowcountry well, put into verse an unflattering yet somewhat accurate description of Charles Town:

Black and white all mixed together
Inconstant, strange, unhealthful weather
Burning heat and chilling cold
Dangerous to both young and old
Boisterous winds and heavy rains
Fevers and rheumatic pains
Houses built on barren land
No lamps or lights, but streets of sand
Everything at a high price
But rum, hominy, and rice.[56]

Captain Martin, like some visitors, must have recalled for others his views of the lowcountry, especially its weather, diseases, and storms. Surely such oral and written accounts influenced some potential voluntary immigrants to avoid the region. For even though colonial Charles Town became the largest urban center south of Philadelphia and Savannah continued to increase in size, both towns remained about half white, the remainder being predominantly black slaves. Furthermore, the population growth of these two trading centers of the lowcountry remained far behind that of Boston, New York, and Philadelphia.

Ships in Offshore Hurricanes, 1760s

During the hurricane seasons of the 1760s more storms or strong gales that battered shipping skirted the coasts of Georgia and South Carolina. Their frequency and intensity increased in the latter part of the decade.

During October 1767, Robert Whitelock, master of the brigantine *Hope*, encountered hurricane force winds and waves that sank his vessel off Charles Town. A few days later the wreckage of several vessels was sighted drifting along the coast.[57]

In late August 1769, vessels arrived in the lowcountry carrying letters describing a fiercely destructive hurricane that ripped across islands in the Caribbean. The warnings arrived too late to save ships already at sea. Then in September the tropical cyclone was following a path just off the Georgia and South Carolina coasts.

On September 5–6 the high seas and winds of a huge storm wreaked havoc with over a dozen vessels along the coast of the lowcountry. Off Georgia,

Thomas Fulker, captain of the brigantine *Chance*, battled monstrous swells and fierce winds until his vessel capsized. To save the crew and the ship, Fulker ordered the mainsail cut away. Nearer Charles Town, Captain James Campbell, aboard the ship *Pennant*, and William Bright, master of the snow *Ruby*, both out of Jamaica and bound for England, struggled to keep their vessels afloat. The storm tore away the masts of both crafts. Eventually they limped into Charles Town. Nearby, other captains shouted orders to their crews above the roar of the hurricane in attempts to prevent their vessels from foundering. John Jewer, captain of the schooner *William*, from Honduras and loaded with mahogany, Peter Mellet, master of the ship *Mentor*, from Port-Au-Prince and carrying cocoa, sugar, indigo, and cotton, and James Markham, master of the sloop *Nancy*, bound from North Carolina to Jamaica, could not prevent the dismasting of their vessels. However, each made Charles Town, including the badly leaking *Nancy*. The local press feared that "many other Vessels . . . shared a Worse Fate." Captains arriving in lowcountry ports confirmed this. They reported seeing "Water-Casks, Wine-Pipes, Masts, and other Species of Wreckage . . . floating along the Coast, and in the Gulf-Stream." Veering slightly west, the hurricane went ashore in North Carolina, with devastating effects to dwellings, stores, trees, and crops.[58]

James Grant, the former Scottish military officer and first governor of British East Florida, told London officials, "Stormy weather of September [1769] has hurt our planters exceedingly, and will prevent their sending home any thing near the Produce I expected — Georgia and the two Carolinas have suffered much from the same cause." He added, "Embarkation should be avoided in September if possible, for in these Southern Latitudes we have always very Stormy Weather about the time of the Equinox."[59]

Losses and Profits from Hurricanes

Henry Laurens, the wealthy merchant-planter of Charles Town, learned of the disastrous path of the September 1769 hurricane that tore into North Carolina. He reported to business associates, "Thank God it has done this town no damage but the ripe Crops of Rice have suffer'd very much all along the Sea Coast." At one of Laurens's plantations, Mepkin, the rice fields "suffer'd by Salt Water breaking over the Banks." But as to shipping, Laurens knew that the "very heavy storm . . . destroyed some and injured a great many Vessels upon this Coast,

Seven or Eight have put into this Port dismasted and crippled." He informed William Bright in Bristol, England, that "among other shatter'd Vessels your Snow *Ruby* . . . is put into this Port." He told Bright that the vessel needed a "New Main Mast & . . . light Sails to replace such as were lost in the Storm." Laurens planned to secure all the information necessary to "give no room for complaints from the Insurers." And he promised to do all "in [his] power to refit . . . [the] Vessel for Sea with dispatch."[60]

The profits and the expenses related to shipping were high. For instance, Laurens told a business associate on one occasion that he was concerned that a schooner he had an interest in, the *Brother's Endeavour*, was long overdue from Jamaica. Laurens alone had an investment of £1,300 ($131,046) "in Vessel and Cargo . . . including the Value of two Negroe Seamen." He asked his associate to insure the *Brother's Endeavour* for £1,000 ($100,804) to protect his own interest: "I think my Interest rather in a precarious Situation," and he was "desirous of putting some part of it upon a securer footing than it seems now to stand upon."[61]

Despite the terrible financial losses suffered by some planters, merchants, insurers, and sea captains, the owner of a ship chandlery at Charles Town, William Price, apparently enjoyed a booming business following gales and hurricanes at sea. He advertised frequently in local newspapers that canvas, rigging, cordage, and "other articles" were for sale at his store on the Bay near the Vendue House.[62] In the year 1770, Charles Town's ship chandlers enjoyed another profitable hurricane season.

A Great Storm at Night, June 1770

One of the earliest hurricanes during the season for tropical cyclones followed the usual track along the Georgia and South Carolina coast. It struck vessels offshore on the evening of June 6–7, 1770. The *Dolphin*, out of Charles Town and returning from the Caribbean, was one of the first to encounter the storm. For twenty-four hours Captain David Walker battled "a High Sea" and "a Hard gale of Wind" that "carried away his jib boom" and "did him other Damage." Miraculously he eventually brought the vessel into Charles Town. That same night the hurricane also caught the schooner *Betty* off Ossabaw Island near Savannah. Captain Turner Vardell struggled to keep the sailing craft into the wind, but huge waves drove the schooner onto the island.[63]

When the tropical cyclone came ashore that same June night, it was un-expected. Inhabitants of the lowcountry anticipated great, violent storms, but not until later in the year. A writer at the time explained that after a long drought "the inhabitants having usually observed hurricanes and tornadoes to follow in autumn, they began . . . to look . . . with superstitious dread for them as that season of the year approached."[64]

Characterized by some lowcountry residents as "a great storm at night," the hurricane was violent, brief, and confined. It was said that the greatest dam-age occurred at sea and wharfside. Nine schooners tied up in Charles Town at Beresfords Dock on the Cooper River or anchored nearby were battered by winds and waves. One loaded with lime sank. The *Savannah Packet* also went down; another vessel carrying a cargo of rice was "beat to pieces" as were two others, the *Dorchester Packet* and a craft tied off White Point on the tip of the peninsula. The *Experiment*, a forty-five-ton schooner out of Bermuda, was "overset"; and the sloop *Dove*, loaded with cargo for Jamaica, was driven ashore and numerous small craft "totally destroyed."[65]

The New Lowcountry Gentry

Henry Laurens, perhaps the wealthiest colonist in British North America, was thankful his crops were undamaged by the early June hurricane's winds and tides, which could have pushed saltwater up the rivers and into rice fields, killing the "Carolina gold." Laurens now owned thousands of acres of rice lands stretching across the heart of the lowcountry, from the Cooper River near Charles Town to the Altamaha River south of Savannah, worked by several hundred slaves. Like other great planters, Laurens remained apprehensive as the peak season for strong gales and great storms approached. In August and September 1770 he informed business associates, "Our Crops of Rice are in great Forwardness . . . but the Hurricane Season which is between us and Har-vest may work a great Alteration. Nothing but a very sudden and violent Storm can prevent our Crops of Rice from being very large indeed."[66] Again, Laurens was lucky.

Frequent hurricanes and epidemic diseases continued to sweep across the lowcountry in the early 1770s. Nevertheless trade and commerce grew. Hun-dreds of vessels cleared the ports of Charles Town and Savannah annually. The sandy streets of both towns became more littered with filth. The first suburbs emerged. The populations of the two urban centers reached twelve thousand and thirty-five hundred, respectively, each population about equally divided between black and white. The remaining population of the lowcountry was scattered on small farms and isolated rice plantations from the North Carolina line to St. Marys, Georgia, where in some counties black slaves made up 60 percent of inhabitants.

A tiny elite grew rich in land and slaves. They built brick homes in Charles Town and Savannah, where they dominated political life and enjoyed concerts and fancy dress balls during the social season. The emerging gentry numbered about 7 percent of the population and owned 75 percent of the real and personal property. Those who owned such a stake in society had little interest in leaving the region. Many among the rest of the residents — poor whites and black slaves — were unable to do so.[67]

The lull in hurricane activity along the Georgia and South Carolina coast and the end of colonial wars contributed to the general prosperity of the lowcountry through the mid-1770s. However, the outbreak of the American Revolution in 1776 and a resurgence of hurricane activity ended the commercial and agricultural boom.

Hurricane Winds, August 1778

In August 1778 a tropical storm gathered force off the coasts of Georgia and South Carolina. High winds and rains lashed the lowcountry. On the morning of August 10 a violent storm out of the northeast swept Charles Town, driving ashore a ship on Morris Island and ten schooners and a sloop on James Island. Another sloop, the *Joseph and Benjamin,* loaded with rice and tobacco and tied off the dock of the Exchange Building at the foot of Broad Street, was damaged. Hurricane force winds knocked over trees, fences, and the charred walls of numerous buildings still standing from the conflagration that destroyed over 250 homes seven months earlier.

The powerful storm eventually came ashore between Georgetown, South Carolina, and New Bern, North Carolina. Its rains and winds reached as far west as central North Carolina near Winston-Salem.[68] It caused extensive damage to vessels and crops in lowcountry South Carolina, but the costs remain unknown.

The Lowcountry in the American Revolution

Determined to take the war into the southern colonies, the British launched a combined sea and land attack against Savannah in late 1778. Outnumbered three to one, the defenders put up a brief fight before being overwhelmed. The British now occupied much of the lowcountry and Georgia.

An American and French plan to retake Savannah failed in the autumn of 1779. The way lay open for seizing Charles Town, the South's major port, and a combined British naval and army force successfully laid siege to the city in 1780. It was the worst defeat for American arms in the Revolution. The British now occupied most of Georgia and South Carolina, but fighting continued across the region. Agriculture and commerce virtually ceased.[69]

Hurricane Angst

The possible destruction of their respective fleets by great storms in American waters troubled both British and French commanders. In the late 1770s the British Royal Navy lost fourteen vessels during a hurricane of "irresistible fury and violence" at Pensacola.

Indeed, the return of frequent hurricanes bedeviled the fleets of the two combatants. Soon after the attempt to retake Savannah failed, the French admiral, d'Estaing, encountered a severe hurricane at sea. Some French ships went down, and the British attacked and seized others.

The year 1780 was one of the deadliest in hurricane history. Eight roared over the Caribbean, Gulf of Mexico, and Atlantic. Thousands perished on islands in the Caribbean, and the ships of several British fleets — in the Caribbean and off Florida, Cape Hatteras, and Rhode Island — went to the bottom.[70]

Commodore Hyde Parker, commander of the British fleet, which had assisted in the successful invasion of Savannah, aboard his ship HMS *Phoenix*, was caught in a fierce hurricane in the Caribbean. Lieutenant Archer, a young naval officer aboard, graphically described the effects of hurricanes on warships at sea:

> At eight in the morning I came up . . . found it blowing hard from the east-northeast with close-reefed topsails upon the ship, and heavy squalls at times. . . .

At twelve, the gale still increasing. . . . In the evening . . . secured all the sails; Squared the booms; saw the boats all made fast; new lashed the guns; saw the carpenters had the tarpaulins and battens all ready for hatchways; got the top gallant mast down; jib boom and spirit sail . . . fore and aft. . . .

The poor devils of birds . . . came over the ship [and] dashed themselves down upon the deck . . . and . . . endeavoured to hide themselves from the wind.

At eight o'clock a hurricane. . . . Went to supper; bread, cheese, and port. The purser frightened out of his wits. . . . The two marine-officers as white as sheets. . . . It seemed as if the whole ship's side was going at each roll. . . .

At ten o'clock I thought to get a little sleep; my cot was full of water. . . . At twelve . . . went upon deck; found Sir Hyde [Parker] there. "It blows damned hard, Archer." "It does indeed, Sir. . . ." [U]pon deck . . . a total darkness . . . the sea, . . . running as it were in . . . Peaks . . . the wind roaring louder than thunder . . . the poor ship very much pressed, . . . shaking her sides, and groaning. . . . Sir Hyde upon deck lashed to windward! I soon lashed myself alongside of him . . . glad it was . . . near . . . daylight. Another ugly sea. . . . [H]alf-way up the quarterdeck . . . the ship lying almost on her beam-ends [sides]. . . . I said to Sir Hyde, "Shall we cut the mainmast away?" "Ay! as fast as you can. . . ." [I] went into the chains with a pole-axe, to cut away the lanyards; when a very violent sea broke right on board of us, carried everything upon deck away, filled the ship with water, the main and mizzen-masts went, the ship righted, but was in the last struggle of sinking under us.

As soon as we could shake our heads above water, Sir Hyde exclaimed, "We are gone at last, Archer! Foundered at sea!" "Yes, Sir, farewell; and the Lord have mercy upon us!"

I thought I heard the ship thump and grinding under our feet; it was so. . . . [T]hat unmerciful sea lifted and beat us up . . . high among the rocks.[71]

The hurricane's winds blew the HMS *Phoenix* ashore, and it was wrecked on the coast of Cuba at the cliffs of Cabo de la Cruz. Many of her several-hundred-member crew perished.[72]

The flurry of hurricane activity in coastal Georgia and South Carolina continued into the 1780s. Some British naval officers and men occupying Charles Town experienced their first great storm in 1781.

Once more a long drought gripped the lowcountry in the spring and summer of 1781. Permanent residents of the region knew that such weather might signal a late summer gale. Their prognostications proved correct.

A tropical storm gathered strength in early August and tracked north off Georgia's coast. Charlestonians and British troops noticed a strengthening wind and blowing rain from the northeast on Thursday evening, August 9. The storm increased in "violence" throughout the night. The captains of British vessels in the harbor ordered their sails top reefed. By the afternoon of August 10 the wind was blowing "a hurricane," first from the east-northeast then from the southeast, indicating that the storm came close, but to the west of Charles Town. Vessels in the harbor dragged their anchors and went aground; HMS *Theis*, a frigate of thirty-two guns under the command of Captain R. Linzees, was blown over and sank near the wharves; the ship *London* went down at Eveleigh's Wharf. An account of the storm and the damage to British vessels appeared in the Philadelphia press on September 5.[73]

The concern of British commanders over the possible impact of great storms on their ships in North American waters was warranted. Hurricanes devastated their fleets. The great storms of October 1780 scuttled so many of Britain's fighting ships, drowning their sailors and soldiers, that the British military advantage at sea was severely reduced. Such disasters and their costs also most likely diminished the government's enthusiasm for the war.[74] By the end of 1782 the British had withdrawn their troops from the lowcountry. A treaty soon ended the conflict, bringing it to a successful conclusion for the American revolutionaries.

Postwar Storms, 1780s

Postwar social and economic disorder plagued the lowcountry. A prominent Georgian spoke for many in the region when he declared, "This Cursed War has ruin'd us all." The war devastated the lowcountry. The British decimated livestock and carried away horses. Agriculture was in disarray. The planting of rice and other crops was nearly nonexistent. The Reverend Archibald Simpson wrote of the area around Beaufort, South Carolina: "All was desolation. . . . Every field, every plantation shows marks of ruin . . . nothing but wild fennel, bushes, . . . briars to be seen."[75]

Labor was in short supply. In Georgia alone nearly ten thousand of Georgia's fifteen thousand prewar population of slaves ran away, joined the British army, departed with the Loyalists, or died. Parts of the two major trading centers, Charles Town and Savannah, were in ruins, the poor went hungry, and black and white thieves robbed and murdered on roadways in the countryside. Civil order seemed to be breaking down as an economic depression settled over the land. Meanwhile hurricanes contributed to the economic malaise.[76]

Reports of storms to their south in late summer 1783 possibly made the residents of coastal Georgia and South Carolina uneasy. A "severe gale" at St. Augustine blew sailing craft ashore.[77]

On Tuesday, October 7, 1783, a storm moved along the South Carolina coast near Charleston (an act of the new city government had changed the name from Charles Town). Throughout the day winds blew hard from the northeast. Their velocity increased around midnight and persisted into the next morning, October 8. A witness observed that it was "a most violent storm of wind, accompanied with incessant rain." Winds apparently reached hurricane velocity as waves smashed wharves to pieces, damaged and destroyed vessels, and toppled fences and trees, and seawater rushed into warehouses ruining the rice crop stored there. Residents scrambled to save themselves as waters streamed into houses along South Bay and around the peninsula. Then suddenly and "happily," at the "height of the storm," wrote a survivor, "the wind shifted from northeast to northwest . . . which kept the tide down." A reporter observed that if the wind had "shifted to the east or south east, in all probability the city would have experienced all the horrors and destruction of September 1752." Luckily for lowcountry inhabitants the storm did not come ashore. But after moving away to the northeast, the hurricane slammed into Wilmington, North Carolina.[78]

The 1783 storm was perhaps the first lowcountry hurricane to be described by an aspiring and well-educated poet. Several days following the storm the local *Gazette* published his verse under the heading, "Written on the Storm, on Tuesday 7th October, 1783, at Charleston, South Carolina." The eyewitness reported the unfolding disaster this way:

In strict obedience to the Heav'nly power
At early dawn the clouds began to lour;
All nature seems to wear a gloomy face,

Destruction now approaches every place;
Rough Aeolus his quarter thus has chose,
And from his north-east seat in anger blows;
Whilst Neptune mounts his fatal, wat'ry car,
And quick dispatches Triton from a-far;
High on the seas, the Trident-bearer soars,
And bends his way to shew his power with all his might;
Whilst rains most rapidly in torrents fall,
And num'rous ills present themselves to all.
How shall I paint the sad, distressful day,
And tell how supportively the seas did play?
Alas! 'tis horrid for myself to think,
Of vessels that I saw begin to sink:
One at a wharf, careening as she lay
Became a sad remembrance of the day!
Others, at anchor, met an equal doom;
And for succeeding wrecks, as quick made room.
A schooner next, when mooring near the shore
Did, with her bowsprit, spurn a little store;
Sorrow and fear appears in ev'ry face,
She carries now the house quite out of place.
I saw soon after that, eye witness me,
Three smaller vessels found'ring in the sea,
'Twas by a wharf, where fish have oft been spar'd,
And fishermen in losses too have shar'd.
But oh! How sad and lamentably great,
Must be the tales that others will relate!
May Heav'n ordain, that this has only been,
The real loss which we ourselves have seen.[79]

Some ships battered at sea made it to port. When winds knocked over the ship *Betsey*, Captain Francis Swinburn, who recognized that his ship "was in great danger of perishing," ordered the crew to cut away the masts. Hacking away with axes as waves broke around and over them, the crew severed the masts and the ship righted. Somehow the sailing craft survived the turbulent gale-whipped seas. After twenty-one days out of Hampton, Virginia, the *Betsey* finally limped into Charleston "quite disabled."[80]

The economic losses from the 1783 storm remain unknown. As to people drowned or killed by flying debris, one witness wrote, "Happily we hear of very few lives being lost" in and around Charleston.[81] Luckily in Georgia and South Carolina the hurricane had just grazed the coast. The following year another threatened the lowcountry and its economic life.

The next year, 1784, was a busy one for tropical cyclones. Eight severe hurricanes battered islands in the West Indies. But it was not until September 23–24, 1785, that a hurricane roared far off the coasts of Georgia and South Carolina. At sea sailing craft were caught unawares. In early October their hulls, debris, and cargoes were washing ashore and littering the shorelines. The hurricane did not move inland until it pushed into North Carolina. Once more the lowcountry escaped a significant storm.

Two years later there was again extensive hurricane activity in the Caribbean. On September 19, 1787, one of these storms may have come close enough to the lowcountry's coastline to create a storm surge that caused twenty-three deaths, extensive flooding, and crop damage from Savannah to Georgetown.[82] Tropical storms continued to brush or cross the lowcountry's coastline with some frequency until the end of the century.

The Latest-Arriving Storm, October 30–31, 1792

Many along the lowcountry's coast thought the season of terrible storms was over when the late October 1792 gale struck — likely the storm system that punished Cuba.

Drenching rains began falling along the coast on Tuesday morning, October 30. Winds increased throughout the day. In the evening an observer at Charleston watched the wind blow "with great violence." About 3:00 a.m. it shifted from northeast to southeast and "blew a severe gale." By this time the storm was just east of the harbor. It created panic in the city. Some residents feared "inundation" by the sea, but fortunately the tide was ebbing, which minimized flooding. There was "considerable damage" to the wharves; two small craft went under, and most other vessels in the harbor sustained damage to rigging and sails. Several buildings collapsed, and roofs blew away. One resident thought it "one of the heaviest gales . . . felt [in] many years."[83]

Although the storm remained offshore, it caused extensive damage along the coast. An account of the storm, likely a hurricane, appeared in the Charleston press and was reprinted in northern newspapers.[84] Within several years another October storm came ashore in the lowcountry.

End-of-the-Century Storms

The summer of 1797 was a busy one for tropical storms. One in particular was of interest to Savannah merchants trading in slaves. On September 8 the armed New Providence ship *General Nichols*, bound for the port of Savannah with a cargo of more than 150 slaves, encountered a "heavy gale" off the upper Florida and lower Georgia coasts. Because of the violence and suddenness of the storm, Captain Michael Morrison was unable to save the ship. The *General Nichols* "foundered" almost immediately.[85]

The crew barely had time to launch "the long boat and yawl" but not time enough to save the slaves. The ship "went down with 122" men, women, and children, who remained chained together below decks. Five whites and thirty-five "negroes" jumped into the longboat. Captain Morrison, six whites, and five blacks scrambled aboard the yawl. In the turbulent sea, the yawl "parted company . . . immediately with the long boat." Those aboard the longboat survived in the storm-swept ocean for twenty-four hours without food or drink before picked up by the schooner *Exuma*, which sailed into the Savannah River with the survivors on September 12. Apparently, the occupants of the yawl never reached land.[86]

A month later another storm came out of the West Indies, moved across Cuba, turned northwest, and tracked along the Florida and Georgia coasts. The storm enveloped Captain Christopher Lee and the schooner *Flying Fish* off Florida. Lee ordered close-reefed sails. Several days later in shipping lanes off Georgia, latitude 31° north, longitude 69° west, the schooner encountered a more severe storm. It upset the *Flying Fish* so quickly that seven of the seventeen crewmen and passengers drowned before they were able to get out of the schooner's cabin. The survivors somehow climbed onto the upturned hull. At daylight some swam beneath the vessel to the submerged masthead, cut away the rigging and mainmast, and the schooner righted. But the sailing craft had shipped so much water that it was nearly awash in the sea. Spars were lashed across the forecastle in an attempt to steer the wreck. Within a week one of the passengers aboard died, and shortly afterward a heavy sea washed off two other passengers and a crewmember. Now only Captain Lee, the mate, three sailors, and the cook remained aboard the slowly sinking hulk. After nearly two weeks adrift, Captain Carsten Meyers of the *Derdaurhafft*, out of Hamburg, Germany, sighted the wreckage of the *Flying Fish*. As mariners are obliged to do, Captain Meyers came about to see if anyone was alive. He found six men clinging to life and what was left of the *Flying Fish*. Meyers rescued them and Savannahians soon knew of this disaster. Again Savannah was lucky. The hurricane remained just off the Georgia coast.[87] South Carolinians were not so fortunate.

The storm that battered the *Flying Fish* at sea off Savannah soon reached Charleston. On Tuesday, October 17, the weather there turned dirty. Gale-force winds with accompanying rains out of the northeast howled through the city. On October 19 the wind shifted to the east. Then in the early morning hours of October 20 the wind came from the southwest. The storm came ashore near Charleston.[88]

For two hours a witness heard and watched as the cyclone, most likely packing hurricane-force winds, raged with "a dreadful degree of violence." Waves pounded and cascaded over the docks. At Roper's Wharf the ship *Winyaw* tore loose from its moorings and collided with other vessels before washing ashore. A sailor was blown off Geyer's Wharf and drowned. Within the town, winds made missiles of roof tiles. Gusts bowled over several houses under construction, one owned by Mr. Newton and another by Mr. Vardell.[89]

Sixty miles north of Charleston the large hurricane spawned a tornado near the small port town of Georgetown, South Carolina. In the early morning hours of October 20 it awakened Allard Belin, a well-to-do planter and slave owner of Belmont Plantation.

Belin heard "a violent and destructive tornado pass . . . through." It ripped up huge trees by their roots and twisted off "the . . . tops of most others" along a fifty- to sixty-yard swath. In his overseer's dwelling, two young slaves hunkered down with the overseer. A male and female slave huddled in a separate kitchen terrified by the storm. When the twister swept up both the house and the kitchen, it "carried" them "nearly 100 yards" and threw them "down with such violence that the structures were [smashed] to pieces, as were the bedsteads, tables, chairs, etc. in them." The bodies of the overseer and "two very fine Negro boys . . . were . . . much mangled." In the kitchen the male slave was bruised by the falling chimney while the "wench . . . most miraculously escaped unhurt."[90]

Belin, in his own house — "seated on a high hill" above the river, and elevated on five feet of brick work, heard one of his own chimneys collapse. Nearby, his kitchen and washhouse were lifted from their foundations and their roofs "carried away." High winds scattered stacks of rice already harvested and carried some into the river. Winds died, apparently when the eye of the storm passed, then "suddenly" sprang up again from the west. A surging flood tide in the river leapt its banks and "came rolling up incredibly rapid" to "inundate the fields" with rice-killing saltwater.[91]

After the tornado and storm passed, Belin looked over his land and found it "impossible . . . to paint the devastation and shocking spectacle which the whole plantation, now covered with ruins, exhibits." He was, however, "thankful to the great governor of all things" for sparing his family and himself. Belin found it "impossible to make an accurate estimate of [his] loss." His overseer and two young slaves were killed.[92]

At the very least fifteen people died at sea and ashore in the hurricane of October 1797.[93] The cost of the hurricane and tornado in economic terms is inestimable.

Monetary losses to merchants, captains, shipowners, planters, farmers, fishermen, and slave traders from the numerous tropical storms and cyclones between 1686 and 1797 are unknown. The many storm-related deaths are known only to kith and kin. What is certain is that coastal Georgia and South Carolina frequently experienced terrible storms that exacted an enormous toll on the natural and built environments. The human suffering, the deaths and those unaccounted for, brought great anguish and sometimes poverty to the surviving families.

The recurring devastating hurricanes that exacted such a fearsome toll most likely gave pause to rich or poor alike who weighed their opportunities in relocating to the lowcountry. It certainly led others to reevaluate their continuing residence in this coastal region so frequently ravaged by natural disasters.

CHAPTER TWO

First Storms

of the

New Century,

1800–1804

By the early nineteenth century, lowcountry rice planters of South Carolina
and Georgia had recovered from the economic catastrophe of the American Revolution. Along the seacoast small trading and fishing villages such as
Georgetown and Beaufort in South Carolina, and Darien, Brunswick, and St.
Marys in Georgia served sea island and mainland rice and cotton planters.
Charleston and Savannah remained the major urban economic and cultural
centers of the lowcountry.

The expansion of rice and cotton planting along the coast, and the high prices
commanded by these commodities, fueled the lowcountry's longest sustained
economic boom. To meet the soaring demands of planters for slave labor, the
merchants and speculators rushed one boatload of Africans after another into
lowcountry ports to sell at huge profits. The export-import merchants, planters,

ship owners, and captains plowed their earnings into land, slaves, and luxuries. Tailors, silversmiths, and cabinetmakers migrated from Great Britain to meet the demand for material possessions. A building boom in the construction of private and public buildings gathered steam.

Rice and cotton came to be the principal exports from Charleston and Savannah. The value of the two commodities together leaving Savannah in 1800 reached some $2,000,000 ($28,169,014) annually. Primary imports included sugar, molasses, salt, and wines. Some four hundred oceangoing vessels sailed in and out of Savannah's port annually; more entered and departed Charleston. By 1800 South Carolina's major port had a population of twenty thousand, still about equally divided between black slaves and free whites. Savannah's population in 1800 was only slightly more than five thousand, and like that of Charleston, about equally divided between slaves and whites.[1]

The economic foundation of the lowcountry was a plantation economy built on agriculture that required a huge slave labor pool. A small elite of wealthy white planters and merchants dominated the lowcountry economically, politically, and culturally.[2]

Lowcountry residents had frequent reports of natural disasters sweeping southern coastal waters. The brig *Eliza*, under Captain Bunker, sailed out of Savannah in early September 1800 bound for New York and jammed with cotton bales. Caught in a strong gale Bunker attempted to steer the brig into the storm, but it was quickly and "entirely dismasted." As the vessel wallowed helplessly in the sea, huge waves carried overboard two crewmembers, the cotton bales, and the water supply. The *Eliza* drifted for days, the sailors "destitute" of food and water. Finally Captain Rogers, master of a Swedish brig, sighted the *Eliza* and supplied Captain Bunker and his remaining sailors with beef, bread, and water. Rogers took the disabled vessel in tow toward a safe harbor.[3]

About a month after the *Eliza* incident, a tropical storm, which grew to hurricane strength, swept up the South Carolina coast. On Saturday, October 4, rain and high winds came out of the southeast and "blew with some violence" throughout the day in Charleston. Near "high water" around 9:00 p.m., winds and waves battered the city's wharves, sinking twelve to fourteen crafts tethered there. A "valuable cargo of dry goods" preparing to sail for Georgetown was driven into New Street off East Bay Street and "beat to pieces." It appears that around midnight the wind "chopped around" to the southwest, blew with great violence, and spawned a tornado that swept through the northwestern part of the city. Its twisting winds smashed the home of the Christburg family who resided in Cannonsburgh. The dwelling collapsed on Mrs. Christburg, killing her instantly. Her husband and children, though severely bruised, survived. The storm tore roofs off houses, knocked down chimneys across the city, and toppled trees and fences. A storm surge swept over most of Sullivan's Island, destroying the homes of Captain Ormond, Mr. Hunter, and Colonel Morris, whose family barely escaped.[4]

The hurricane apparently caught some seamen unawares. Offshore a sloop out of Georgetown owned by Captain Addison was passing near the dangerous shoals of Cape Romain. The master, Captain Ross, saw and heard "all her sails split to pieces," and he was unable to control the vessel. It was blown onto shoals, and amid crashing waves the schooner broke up. Both Captain Ross and Mr. Thompson, a Georgetown merchant, perished. The black sailors on the schooner somehow reached shore.[5]

The local press called the storm the most "tremendous and destructive . . . experienced in this city and harbor . . . for nearly 20 years" (most likely referring to the October 7–8, 1783, hurricane).[6] But the worst was yet to come. Four years later a major hurricane, the first seen since 1752, ravaged the coasts of Georgia and South Carolina. It was one of three major hurricanes of the early nineteenth century to strike the lowcountry at sea and ashore.

A Major Hurricane, 1804

During late summer 1804, violent weather off the Georgia and South Carolina coasts may have warned of things to come. The ship *Alexander,* at one time a packet between Charleston and New York, was sailing east of the Gulf Stream off Savannah at latitude 32° north, longitude 56° west, when on the afternoon of August 18, the weather turned nasty. Around 6:00 p.m. the ship was "struck with a very severe squall." Captain John E. Coop put the ship into the weather and ordered the crew to "let fly tacks, sheets, and halyards." But the *Alexander* capsized "in an instant," and the sea poured into open hatches and filled the hold. The crew cut away the weather lanyards, but the ship failed to right itself. Coop ordered the stern boat lowered, but it had been damaged in the storm and filled quickly with water. Other dinghies could not be reached as the ship was lying on its lee side.[7]

The crew clung to the ship as waves swept over the wreckage. Within three hours the foremast, mainmast, and mizenmast broke away, and the *Alexander* righted itself. At morning the crew took to the small boats now above water on the lee side of the ship. They bobbed close to the wreckage without water or provisions. On August 20 "a violent sea" swamped their small boats, and they swam back to the wreck. Nearly exhausted, all the crew reached the ship except Mr. Hoyt, the supercargo, and an apprentice boy who went to a "watery grave."[8]

As huge waves crashed over the *Alexander*, Captain Coop, first mate Uriah Hanford, and members of the crew lashed themselves to what remained of the mainmast. "Famished" for lack of water and giving up hope of rescue, they languished for five long days after capsizing. Then at dawn they sighted a vessel. "To our inexpressible joy," Captain Coop exclaimed, Captain Josiah Richards aboard the *Olive* came alongside the wreckage and saved the crew. Captain Coop and his seamen praised Captain Richards and his crew with "unfeigned gratitude" and hoped that when placed in a similar situation, they could provide "the relief we experienced."[9]

On August 29, 1804, a week after the surviving crew of the *Alexander* was rescued, a "violent hurricane" swept across Jamaica. It was the beginning of one of the most severe hurricane seasons in decades for both the Caribbean and the lowcountry. The first *great* storm of the new century crashed into Antigua, St. Kitts, and St. Bartholomew on the morning of September 3. It raged for over twenty-four hours. At St. Kitts every ship in the harbor (about a hundred) was "entirely lost." Deluges of rain swept houses into the sea. The huge storm sank fifty-six of the fifty-eight vessels in the harbor at St. Bartholomew and fifty-eight at Antigua and destroyed twenty-six of twenty-eight lying in the bay at Dominica. Wreckage of vessels littered the beaches of the Windward Islands.[10]

Fueled by warm waters, the massive hurricane moved west-northwest. It crossed the western end of Puerto Rico, sinking numerous vessels there, swept by Turks Island, and brushed the southeast Bahamas on September 4.

Two vessels far offshore encountered the storm, the *Olive Branch* and the *Freedom*. The *Freedom* was so badly damaged that it drifted for fifteen days in shipping lanes before being spotted. Both vessels eventually reached Charleston after sailing through a sea of wrecks.[11]

The sloop *Ranger*, captained by Moses Andrews, at latitude 28° north, longitude 30° west, far to the east and south of the *Olive Branch* and the *Freedom*, was swept by the same storm on the same day, September 6. The storm was so "severe" that Captain Andrews was forced to take down his sails and "lie under bare poles." A huge wave carried away the boom, the binnacle, two small boats, hen coops, water casks, the flying jib and jib boom, the larboard shrouds, and two deckhands. Swept overboard, the two seamen somehow "happily got in again." Suddenly the cargo shifted and the vessel went over, "half full of water and still taking water fast." Fearing that his vessel was at any "moment . . . going to the bottom," Captain Andrews saw that it was "indispensably necessary to cut away and clear the wreck." Lanterns were relit. Hands frantically bailed out the cabin with biscuit kegs. The crew cut away the rigging in the water and repaired the pumps that began working again by daylight. The vessel bobbed upright. Captain and crew had saved themselves and their vessel, and they celebrated. When the wind and sea abated, Captain Andrews ordered a foresail run up, and "under a fair wind blowing from the southeast," the *Ranger* "stood for Charleston."[12]

The tropical cyclone gained strength and curved toward the American coastline. High winds lashed St. Augustine, Florida, on September 6–7, leaving afloat only one of the ten vessels in the harbor. With gusting winds and low scudding clouds, the hurricane moved nearer the lowcountry. Crashing waves along the beaches sounded like cannon fire. By Friday, September 7, the immense tropical cyclone was still miles offshore, but it soon simultaneously enveloped large portions of both Georgia and South Carolina.

After crippling and sinking dozens of vessels far offshore, the hurricane closed over those sailing near the mainland. On that stormy Friday it found the schooner *Betsey* of Charleston, Captain Grant in command, in the Gulf Stream to the east and south of Savannah. Unable to control his vessel, Captain Grant was helpless. The waves and high winds took away her deck cargo, foremast, sails, and bowsprit. Ship and crew survived. That afternoon off Tybee Island, Georgia, Captain Baker, aboard the coastal schooner *Phoebe* out of St. Marys, ran up a creek for the safety of his passengers and crew. Those aboard the schooner *Liberty* were not so lucky.[13]

The evening of the same day, some leagues north of Tybee Island, between Charleston and Kiawah Island, Captain Benjamin Sweetzer was fighting to save the schooner *Liberty* and the lives of his crew. The schooner, recently built at Egg Harbor, New Jersey, had sailed from Philadelphia for Charleston on August 29 loaded with rum, soap, and "Negro cloth" for merchants. But the storm pushed the *Liberty* southward, and by Friday evening she was caught in the full fury of the hurricane. With rigging, sails, mast, and spars torn away, the vessel finally capsized. Driven keel up into the beakers of Kiawah Island, the sloop was destroyed. To those who found the wreckage and salvaged the contents, it was "a painful certainty" that everyone aboard perished.[14]

Captain Mood's schooner *Patsy*, out of Norfolk, bound for St. Marys, battled fierce east-northeast winds fifty miles off Charleston until it was knocked over. Huge waves swept away two hands, William Dabney, "a white man," and John Planter, a black man. Surprisingly the schooner righted itself. Not far away, Captain Miller, in command of the *Experiment* out of Edenton, North Carolina, and returning from Jamaica loaded with rum, encountered the storm just off the South Carolina coast. It overturned, and the sea poured into the schooner. The crew clung to the sinking wreckage. Captain Mood, aboard the battered *Patsy*, found what was left of the *Experiment*, rescued the crew off Bull's Island, South Carolina, and set a heading for Charleston, a short sail away.[15]

All along the coast of the lowcountry, skies were overcast. A stiffening wind blew from the northeast. Word of the damaged vessels and deaths at sea had not yet reached the mainland. Residents able to read the predictions in the *Georgia and South Carolina Almanac* for 1804 anticipated "fresh northerly winds" that would provide "temperate, pleasant weather," a relief from the summer heat. But by the afternoon, residents along the Georgia and South Carolina coasts became concerned about the rising winds and tides. Major Pierce Butler's home, Hampton, a cotton plantation, was located on St. Simons Island, which was about twelve miles long and two miles wide. Major Butler's guest on Friday, September 7, was the vice president of the United States, Aaron Burr, who was hiding from federal authorities. They had warrants for his arrest for the murder in a duel of the first treasury secretary, Alexander Hamilton. Two young slaves had rowed Burr across Jones Creek to visit John Couper at his nearby plantation on Cannon's Point. In the early evening Burr found himself unable to return to Hampton because of high winds and tides. St. Simons Island was in the direct path of the hurricane. The deteriorating weather frightened Major Butler's slaves working on Little St. Simons Island, owned by Butler. Whites and blacks alike on Cumberland Island, Georgia's southernmost and largest sea island, anxiously watched the rising winds with increasing alarm. Up the coast at Tybee Island, eleven members of the well-to-do Bolton family and their five slaves listened to the winds and crashing waves and worried. The family had come to Tybee from Savannah for a summer outing at the Bolton's beach home. At Fort Greene on Cockspur Island in the mouth of the Savannah River, Lieutenant William Piatt, the commanding officer, noticed the worsening weather. Nevertheless he decided to accompany a rowboat upriver to get freshwater. Late afternoon winds and a flooding tide made it impossible for him and his crew to return to the fort.[16]

After nightfall that evening and for the next twenty-four hours, the massive tropical cyclone lashed coastal Georgia and South Carolina, apparently making almost simultaneous landfalls at Cumberland, Jekyll, and St. Simons islands, Darien, and Beaufort. The hurricane then moved west of Charleston and Georgetown.[17]

On St. Simons Island on Saturday, September 8, Aaron Burr, stranded at John Couper's plantation, watched and listened as the wind increased. Above the noises he heard horses scream. Water was rising across the plantation. Burr and the men, women, and children hunkered down inside the big house at Cannon's Point feared for their lives. Winds shook and rocked the substantial dwelling and carried away a portion of the piazza. Windows blew in, a chimney collapsed, and most of the trees around the house crashed to the ground. As the Hampton River spilled over its banks, water began pouring into the home. Worried for the safety of his family and friends, Couper ordered everyone to run for a storehouse about fifty yards from the main dwelling. Abruptly, in the afternoon, the wind died as the eye of the hurricane passed over. During the lull Burr decided to return to Major Butler's home. While slaves rowed him across Jones Creek, the winds from the hurricane began howling again. Though windblown and apprehensive, Burr did reach Hampton, and Butler's plantation, safely. Here he remained as the winds continued to blow. By then seawater was sweeping over all the nearby islands.[18]

As the sea crashed high up the beach into the interior of Cumberland Island, Caty Greene, the widow of General Nathanael Greene, gathered family and friends at Dungeness, her solidly built four-story tabby home. Whites and black slaves fled there for safety as the hurricane bore down directly on the island. Trees went over, the shutters at Dungeness rattled, glass windows blew in, but the dwelling, with four-foot-thick walls, withstood the hurricane. All taking refuge there survived.[19]

The crashing sea inundated most of Jekyll Island and swirled around Horton House, the plantation home of Christophe DuBignon, whose tabby dwelling had survived the last great hurricane in 1752. Seawater spilled over DuBignon's many acres of fine sea island cotton, destroying what a plague of caterpillars that had spread along the entire seaboard of the lowcountry during the summer had not.[20]

DuBignon, his family, and his house survived. But his losses from the hurricane and the caterpillars represented about 20 percent of his plantation's value. DuBignon was, he said, "in a very precarious situation." Planters of rice, cotton, and corn crops, like DuBignon, gambled against the weather, insects, and the markets. They hoped the good years would exceed the bad.[21]

On Little St. Simons Island, Morris, a slave and the black driver, or "headman," was working a gang of about a hundred slaves. Morris was responsible for their work and safety. As winds increased in the afternoon, Morris became concerned. With the hurricane bearing down, the slaves ran for the flatboat that had brought them to the island. They wanted to return to their cabins at Butler's Point. But Morris knew the danger. He dashed to their front, cracking the bullwhip, a symbol of his authority that he was authorized to use to enforce orders. He called on the group to stop. He warned them their boat may be swamped and they would drown if they tried to cross the river. After getting their attention, Morris ordered them to follow him to the large log house built for refuge on the island in the event of a great storm like the one now approaching. They heeded Morris and survived.[22]

For saving his human property, Major Butler rewarded Morris with a silver cup inscribed, "For his faithful, judicious and spirited conduct in the hurricane of September 8th, 1804."[23] Other slaves were not as fortunate. On Broughton Island a human tragedy unfolded.

Broughton Island was a small, low-lying island, about six miles long and two miles at its widest point, developed by Henry Laurens for rice growing. He was among the first planters to use tidal waters for irrigation. The Altamaha River separated Broughton Island from General's Island on the north; Buttermilk Sound separated it on the south from Little St. Simons Island. About three-quarters of Broughton Island was marshland, with its eastern end exposed to Altamaha Sound and the sea beyond. An embankment encircled the rice fields that were intersected by ditches. A broad and deep canal with a small bridge separated the rice fields from the plantation house and slave quarters at the western end of the island. This was also the site of a solidly constructed rice barn that was to be used as a refuge in the event of a storm.

William Brailsford purchased Broughton Island from the estate of Henry Laurens in 1802. A prominent member of Charleston's elite, Brailsford married another member of the local well-to-do, Maria Heyward. After his marriage he moved most of his own slaves and those of his wife to Broughton Island. They numbered about a hundred and were in the charge of a white overseer when the hurricane struck.

Brailsford had instructed the overseer to move the slaves into the rice barn at the first indication of a storm. For unknown reasons the overseer hesitated — perhaps, some have suggested, because he was drunk. By the time efforts were made to get the slaves to safety, ocean waves driven by hurricane winds had breached the embankment built to keep saltwater out of the rice fields. These now flooded. The wide canal spilled over its banks. There was no black man like Morris to lead the slaves to safety. Terrified, the men, women, and children tried to cross the now turbulent and boiling waters of the canal in rice flats. More than seventy drowned. Swept out to sea, their bodies were never recovered.

The human catastrophe was an economic disaster for William Brailsford and his family. He was ruined. Because much of Brailsford's fortune was invested in his slaves, he could no longer afford to live in Charleston. He moved his family into a quickly and rudely built house on Broughton Island. Unable to afford to buy slaves to rebuild the plantation and rice fields, Brailsford was forced to sell. He died impoverished a few years following the storm.[24]

During the hurricane, slaves without leaders like Morris, who exhibited great loyalty and responsibility, perished. Major Butler lost nineteen slaves by drowning. On St. Catherines Island, two slaves owned by Mr. Owens drowned.

Damage to local crops and dwellings came from high winds that drove sea-waters seven feet above ordinary high water. Saltwater flooded and destroyed the rice, cotton, or corn fields of most planters in the area near St. Simons Island, including DuBignon, Owens, Brailsford, Butler, and John Couper, whose crop alone was valued at $100,000 ($1,492,537). Couper's Cannon's Point plantation house suffered extensive damages and the hurricane destroyed the cabins for more than one hundred of his slaves.[25]

At Darien on the Altamaha River, the tanner Reuben King took shelter as winds and rain increased during the morning of September 8. By afternoon, winds reached such strength as to bowl over trees, tear roofs off houses, and knock smaller dwellings into shambles. It blew over King's tannery, and a rising tide and high waves swamped his tanning vats. The tropical cyclone carried away anything not battened down, and it terrified the inhabitants.[26]

Just north up the coast the huge hurricane smashed into the busy, small port of Sunbury at the mouth of the Ogeechee River, which empties into St. Catherines Sound. Winds and waves crashed into the bluff, sweeping away trees and three houses and creating a perfect beach. Two of the houses were new and belonged to Doctor Dryer and William Lawton. The hurricane destroyed most of the coastal vessels belonging to nearby plantations and the surging waters boiled over the crops destroying storage houses, stables, and slave cabins.

Planters such as Cubbedge, Houston, Blackfell, Maxwell, and Maurice Miller "suffered greatly." Five of Cubbedge's slaves died after being hit by flying debris or drowned. He also lost his house, its furnishings, and his horses, cattle, and hogs.[27]

Up the coast at Tybee Island the Bolton family watched waves race up the beach higher than ever before. Their bathhouse collapsed into the surf. As the tide continued to rise, waves broke against their beach house. It became too dangerous to remain in the dwelling, and the Boltons decided to hike a mile or so to the light keeper's house located at the highest point on the island. Wrapped in shawls and blankets for protection from wind and rain, they set out. The blowing rain felt like sleet against their faces, and the wind ripped away their outer garments. The Boltons and their slaves waded through waist-deep water to finally reach the light keeper's small abode. During the day and night, crashing waves even threatened to break on the dwelling. By now the Bolton's own beach house and belongings had washed out to sea. It appeared to those on the mainland that Tybee was totally submerged. All eleven members of the Bolton family and their five slaves survived.[28] At Fort Greene the soldiers and their family members were not as lucky.

Lieutenant Piatt and five enlisted men remained stranded in Savannah on September 8 as a northeast wind pushed a rising tide across Cockspur Island. By 10:00 a.m. waves began crashing into Fort Greene, a two-story tabby and wood fortification. At noon the worst of the storm bore down on the fort at the height of the tide. Huge waves swept the island from end to end. The approaching hurricane terrified those left in the fort — a few soldiers, with their wives and children and four washerwomen. Also in the fort was Mrs. Abimael Y. Nicoll, wife of the former commanding officer, and her two sons, James, eight years of age, and Charles, an infant.[29]

The twenty-one people in the structure began moving to the second floor of the blockhouse as water poured into the fort's interior. When water continued to rise, they climbed onto the roof, only to be blinded by wind-driven rain and sea spray. Down below, powerful waves moved a forty-eight-hundred-pound cannon more than thirty feet. Around 1:00 p.m. the blockhouse collapsed. The roof drifted away with its passengers, a flotilla of terrified men, women, and children. Waves quickly pounded the roof to pieces. Some held to portions of the roof; others grabbed planks and scantling from a vessel that had broken up on the shoals off Cockspur Island. About half were swept out to sea. Seven clung to bits of flotation and eventually washed ashore on Wilmington Island. Another survived when he drifted into a treetop on the island. Rolling and crashing swells sucked others under the waves to their deaths. Seven enlisted men perished; other soldiers were injured but survived. Of the wives and children, it is known that only Mrs. Abimael Nicoll was accounted for. When Private Daniel Lacy attempted to save Mrs. Nicoll's youngest son, Charles, both drowned.[30]

The wind and waters of the hurricane washed away all the built structures on Cockspur Island and much of the island itself. Only portions of the breached ramparts of Fort Greene remained. It was never rebuilt. Atop its ruins a federal pre–Civil War fortification went up, Fort Pulaski.[31]

On Wilmington Island the well-to-do Savannah rice planter John Screven resided with his wife, Hannah Proctor Screven, and their children. When on the island, they lived at their plantation home Betz Place, on Betz Creek and the Wilmington River. The plantation house was at the east end of the island facing Wassaw Sound. Sometime in the afternoon of September 8 hurricane winds pushed huge waves across the sound, inundating Screven's crops and those of other planters on Wilmington and nearby Skidaway Island. The winds destroyed structures at both places. On Wilmington Island the storm was so violent that Betz Place collapsed, crushing Hannah and her infant son. Her husband and three other children, Emily Sophia, Martha, and James Proctor, survived. James

Proctor Screven became a distinguished Savannah physician and mayor of the city.[32] About the same time the hurricane was sweeping over Fort Greene, the full fury of the storm enveloped Hutchinson Island and Savannah.

Around 9:00 a.m. on September 8, winds from the north then northeast swept low-lying Hutchinson Island. Tides seven to ten feet higher than usual rushed in, submerging rice fields and carrying away buildings on the plantations of such prominent families as the Campbells, Olivers, Youngs, Proctors, Smiths, Telfairs, and Wards. Lives were lost. The Oxhams, caretakers of one plantation, drowned. Upwards of one hundred slaves perished because no leader emerged to save them.[33]

Winds toppled trees and unroofed private and public buildings in Savannah. The steeple of the Presbyterian Meeting House blew over, and part of the wall of Christ Episcopal Church collapsed. The courthouse sustained damage. Tiles flew off the roof of the jail, and the roof of the tobacco house collapsed. Dozens of chimneys blew over. Fearful of the high winds, Mrs. Nelson, at a house on the bay, hurried into a back room with her two children, believing they would be safer there. Tragically a chimney collapsed, burying her and her offspring. Summoned by screams, Mr. Nelson found his wife alive, but his ten-year-old son and three-year-old daughter had been crushed to death. Ironically all other rooms in the house remained intact. Nearby another chimney fell into a house occupied by Captain Webb and his wife and child. Mrs. Webb and her child escaped; Captain Webb was killed.[34]

Winds sent waves racing up the Savannah River, capsizing vessels in the harbor and sending others smashing into the wharves from one end of the city's bluff to the other. The ship *Mary* slammed into the wharf opposite Fort Wayne. The revenue cutter *Thomas Jefferson* landed on Hunter and Minis's Wharf, the ship *General Jackson* collided with McCradie's Wharf, the sloop *Liberty* sank off Howard's Wharf, and the brig *Minerva* came ashore at the Coffee House Wharf.[35]

When vessels broke apart, their rigging and hulls knocked away planking on the wharves, leaving pilings exposed. On Williamson and Morel's Wharf, the brig *Hiram* was impaled on the pilings. Some vessels were tossed so high onto the wharves that it appeared they "were built there." Other ships, sloops, and brigs sank at wharfside. Dozens of smaller creek and river craft littered the area below Savannah's bluff. The fish market, poultry market, and stores of merchants along the wharves collapsed into a shambles of wood and tabby that tumbled into the river. Their contents spilled out and washed away. Lumber, cotton, tobacco, hogsheads of rum, sugar, and produce spilled along the bottom of the bluff. After seventeen hours, the hurricane had passed.[36]

To the north, in South Carolina, the hurricane pushed tides nine feet higher than previously recorded. The May River overflowed over its banks, inundating cotton and rice crops, and swept away cotton storage houses and slave cabins on plantations close by. The massive storm overflowed islands off the coast, such as Daufuskie, where five slaves drowned who belonged to Mr. Hopkins, a plantation owner there.[37]

The hurricane slammed into the small port town of Beaufort, South Carolina, halfway between Savannah and Charleston. There a causeway linking the mainland with nearby islands had been under construction for seven years "at great expense." It was destroyed in a few hours. Surging tides carried off other small bridges and flooded roadways near Beaufort, making travel impossible. Tides rose to heights of five feet, inundating the fields of plantations and destroying cotton and food crops. Hurricane winds collapsed chimneys in the town and damaged the Baptist church. Waves accompanying the high tides carried away all the houses on Bay Point except the home of Captain John Jenkins, "which was fortunately the means of preserving the lives of all the negroe [slaves] at that place."[38]

Curiously, some of Beaufort's white inhabitants took to an open boat at the height of the storm, where they remained throughout the night. In the morning, an observer noted, they "were fortunate enough to get safely on shore." One schooner docked at Beaufort, the *Collector*, owned by Saltus and Yates, was blown ashore on Lady's Island, and another, the *Guilielmi*, went ashore at St. Helena Island. Saltwater ruined the thirty barrels of rice aboard.[39]

To the west of Beaufort surging tides and drenching rains caused streams to spill their banks. Water poured into Pocotaligo, Stony, and Huspa creeks, turning them into raging rivers. Scotland Neck was cut off and isolated. From Sheldon to Motley the creeks and rivers overflowed the rice and cotton plantations, and the saltwater ruined the crops. Roads and causeways were impassable. Animals of all kinds drowned in the flood. The stench of their rotting carcasses fouled the air.[40]

In the early morning hours of that day, Charleston too was in the grip of the storm. Northeast winds and driving rains battered the port city. Near first light, the wind shifted to the east. Hurricane-force winds swept the harbor, smashing fortifications and knocking over sailing craft. The storm destroyed the ramparts of the old and unmanned fort on James Island and smashed the breastworks and palisades of Fort Pinckney, which guarded the entrance to Charleston's harbor. It drove vessels into the marshes and wharves from Gadsden's Wharf on the Cooper River to those on South Bay. Pritchard's, Cochran's, Beale's, Craft's, and William's wharves sustained heavy damage from vessels banging into them.[41]

Sailing craft were knocked about. The sloop *Montserrat* sank; the ships *Mary* and the *Birmingham Packet*, the brig *Amazon*, and the schooner *Orange* all suffered extensive damage. Three brigs and the schooner *Mary* slammed into and damaged Governor's Bridge; two schooners hurtled into Faber's Wharf; another, *Favorite*, sank alongside; and at Prioleau's Wharf the brig *Concord*, with fifty tierces of rice aboard, filled with water. Winds blew others onto the wharf or high and dry on the shore. At Blake's Wharf a brick building that served as a counting and scale house was torn from its foundation when the ship *Lydia* plowed into it. The African slave ship *Christopher* sank at Geyer's Wharf, and the slaves below were "taken out with much difficulty." Vessels went ashore on James Island; in the Ashley River a canoe capsized and four slaves drowned.[42]

By noon the tide had crested three feet higher than during the great hurricane of 1752. Seawater covered the wharves. Stores at wharfside washed away or blew down, spilling their contents of rice and cotton into the water. A breakwater off South Bay was battered away, and seawater pulled down the nearby home of William Veitch recently built on fill. Veitch's falling chimney killed a black man.[43]

In the lower stories of some homes, the water rose to over a foot. Fearing for their lives, residents on South Bay evacuated their dwellings. Crashing waves breached places along newly built East Bay Street. As the sea poured through the breaches and into Lamboll and Water streets, residents fled. Waters rose to a depth of two feet on Meeting Street. High winds unroofed houses, uprooted trees, and blew down fences; a resident saw slates blowing from roofs that "flew in every direction like grapeshot."[44]

North of Charleston, on Sullivan's Island, the hurricane destroyed or washed out to sea fifteen to twenty houses. The suddenness and violence of the storm prevented saving their contents. Dwellings that survived the tropical cyclone did so because huge dunes of windblown sand that surrounding them served as protective ramparts. The sea covered almost the entire island and breached it from Fort Moultrie to the Cove. Some people saved themselves by taking refuge in the lazaretto, distant from the front beach. Women and children who were alone in houses at the time of the storm were saved from drowning by several men on the island. Remarkably, the press reported, only one black child perished.

The dwellings knocked over on Sullivan's Island included those owned by the Middletons, Manigaults, Ogilvies, Coffins, Stevenses, Courtneys, Little-johns, Ramages, Brailsfords, Wraggs, Halls, Watsons, Chamberses, Hunters, Calders, and Greens. Had the tide continued to rise, speculation was that not a building on the island would have survived.[45]

Up the coast, between 3:00 a.m. and 4:00 a.m. on Saturday, September 8, about the time it was coming down on the rest of the lowcountry, George-town was beginning to experience the immense storm. The schooner *Perseverance*, owned by Thomas Shubrick of Charleston, was sailing to that port from Georgetown when it was blown ashore and wrecked on South Island. The northeast wind threatened to push the brig *Augusta* onto the dangerous shoals of Cape Romain. To prevent sailing into them Captain Davidson ordered the sails reefed. But with the *Augusta* drifting closer to the shoals, Davidson ordered his crew to throw overboard the one hundred bales of cotton he was carrying from Savannah. Within three and a half leagues of the shoals the wind subsided, and Davidson added enough sail to narrowly clear the breakers. The brig eventually limped into Charleston, but not before losing its anchors. That same afternoon the English schooner *Fame* was knocked over in a heavy sea. A black man washed overboard but miraculously saved himself by grabbing a rope. The crew cut away the foremast, the schooner righted, and the schooner and its crew survived.[46]

On Saturday evening at Georgetown the winds peaked. About 8:00 p.m. Captain Cully, on the schooner *Favourite*, fought to keep his vessel from going aground on the shoals of Cape Romain. But when the cargo of corn in the hold shifted, the *Favourite* went over, broke up, and quickly sank. Captain Cully, his mate, three crewmembers, and four passengers — Mr. and Mrs. Groves, Mr. Steward, and a black slave — were on the vessel as it went down. It appears that everyone perished except Mr. Groves and Wallace, a crewmember. They battled huge waves to reach and grab a floating hen coop. Seaman Wallace held on for about four hours until he became exhausted, lost his grip, and went under. Groves managed to cling to the hen coop in turbulent seas for twenty-two hours until he was spotted and rescued by Captain Smith of the *Venus* out of New York. A few other vessels went ashore in the vicinity, but most of the crew and the sailing crafts survived.[47]

That evening Captain George Bunker, aboard his schooner *Ino*, battled the hurricane until he lost his deck boats, sails, and masts. Unable to navigate the vessel, Bunker somehow avoided the Cape Romain shoals and drifted onto the beach. Meanwhile Captain Webb, of the brig *Consolation* with twenty-one passengers, was battling the storm when a huge sea slammed into the brig, carrying away both masts and everything on deck. The vessel rolled over. One sailor washed overboard to his death, and passengers and crew below deck sustained severe injuries. The vessel drifted ashore, where the crew erected a tent and tried to save part of the cargo. For three days the survivors were without water. The *Consolation* was a complete loss.[48]

Waters rose throughout the day. The Pee Dee and Black rivers poured over their banks. Tides driven high up the rivers submerged Georgetown's wharves and flooded its streets and stores on the bay. Enormous quantities of corn, salt, and other merchandise were lost. Left behind when the tides receded were the bodies of turtles and fish. A canoe paddled by two slaves attempted to cross the roiled Sampit River; it upset, and the passengers survived by swimming to the river's bank. Two other blacks who tried to swim the river drowned.[49]

Surging tides and winds destroyed the homes of the Allstons, Thurstons, and Crofts, prominent families living at North Inlet. No family members perished, but one planter survived a harrowing experience. When his house blew away, the planter and fourteen family members found themselves stranded on a small hill about ten feet square. Waves broke around them, and with no other land in sight for nearly a mile, they expected momentarily to be "swept into eternity." At what seemed the last possible minute, the tide fell, and all members of the family waded through chest-deep water to reach high land. There they stayed exposed to the storm Saturday and Sunday.[50]

High tides and torrential rains sent water cascading over and through embankments to inundate the rice fields and ruin the equivalent of ten thousand barrels of rice about to be harvested around Georgetown. Extensive damage was done when the hurricane stalled near Georgetown for twenty-four hours. Not until Sunday, September 9, did the great storm move away from the low-country.[51]

The horrific destruction along the coast was apparent when residents emerged from their homes on Sunday to survey the damage. At Savannah they saw smashed wharves and eighteen vessels sunk or blown onto the wharves. They observed many smaller vessels "cracked like egg shells." One reporter witnessed "the hopes of merchants scattered among the fragments of the buildings or floating in the river." At the bottom of Savannah's bluff were carcasses of "serpents, turtles, [and] marsh-birds" that had washed up. From Hutchinson Island across the river came the piteous cries of surviving slaves "screaming for assistance, and for the loss of their drowned companions."[52] Throughout the town, trees, fences, and some houses were down. Estimates of damages in the city alone reached as high as $500,000 ($7,475,610).[53]

The storm was equally devastating at Charleston. A merchant there, Seth Lothrop, told his brother that the "dreadful distress occasioned by this hurricane throughout the city & country is out of my power to describe in a letter."[54] Some residents believed that the storm was more violent and continued longer than the storm of 1783. However, others thought the hurricane of 1752 had been more "dreadful," though the loss of property from the current storm was greater. Estimates for property losses across the city were reported to be as high as $1,000,000 ($14,951,220).[55]

Planters on the sea islands and in the countryside and their black slaves suffered greatly. The hurricane destroyed the money and food crops of rice, cotton, potatoes, and corn. It swept away fences and livestock, leveled lime kilns, and drove ashore and into fields schooners, sloops, and smaller craft owned by planters. Around Beaufort the value of cotton lands and black slaves fell 30 percent. One planter opined that the storm was "more destructive to the planters on the sea-shore than any preceding within the recollection of our oldest inhabitants." He speculated that the "injury done and losses sustained . . . can only be repaired by time and great industry."[56]

A Charleston merchant speculated that the "crops will be very much injured[;] perhaps not more than one third of a crop will be made this year." During the following winter, it is likely that some people went hungry. For weeks land travel between Charleston, Georgetown, Savannah, and St. Marys was impossible owing to washed out bridges and downed trees.[57]

Human suffering and loss on the sea islands and the lowcountry's coast were staggering, given the sparse population. It is estimated that along the coast more than five hundred people drowned — this does not include those who died because of falling or flying debris or the deaths at sea. The loss of life among the lowcountry slave population perhaps accounted for as many as 90 percent of all deaths at sea and ashore. Some owners personally saved their slaves from drowning. When high tides threatened to sweep away his dwellings along the coast, wrote one Georgia planter, "I removed my family and negroes to a house some distance from the sea shore; they were taken from my door in a flat."[58] But other planters and slaves did not have this option or foresight.

Large sea island planters such as Pierce Butler and John Couper lost some slaves but owned so many others that they were not ruined. Other planters, like William Brailsford, all of whose slaves perished, were ruined financially. The planters on Hutchinson Island faced destitution when their slaves drowned. In South Carolina losses were also staggering. Immediately after the "dreadful storm," Frederick Rutledge wrote to John Rutledge from Sullivan's Island about conditions on their lands: the hurricane "tide rose to an alarming height. Many hands were pulled into the sea . . . there was a great loss of crops and buildings . . . and negroes."[59]

For weeks after the hurricane sea captains spotted the wreckage and cargoes of vessels offshore. The debris included the half-submerged hulls of ships, an abandoned schooner of about seventy tons so low in the water the name was obscured, the quarterdeck of a vessel of about a hundred tons, bulkheads, a ship's binnacle, a seaman's chest, a new horse cart, barrels of apples, flour, beef, and pork, a box of soap, pipes of brandy, and a vast number of cotton bales.[60]

It appears that the death toll of more than five hundred people at sea and ashore was the highest from a hurricane along the lowcountry's coast up to that time. The deaths of black slaves far exceeded those among the white population. Because owners viewed slaves as investments, it is unlikely that they were unconcerned about the safety of their property. But with ample evidence of deteriorating weather conditions that forecast a violent storm, one wonders why so many slaves drowned. Were their deaths due to inadequate supervision by owners or overseers? Were refuge sites available? Perhaps it was a failure to anticipate the ferocity of the storm itself.

The major hurricane of 1804, like that of 1752, was a devastating event. Except for the contemporary estimates of the physical damages in the two major urban centers, Savannah and Charleston, it is again impossible to put a dollar value on the lives, crops, structures, vessels, and cargoes lost in the great storm of 1804. Surly it would reach well into the tens of millions in present-day dollars. It is difficult to imagine that this storm, like others, did not have a negative effect on economic development in the lowcountry.

Most wealthy merchants and planters recovered from the terrible storm. They remained in coastal Georgia and South Carolina and gambled on having more good years than bad. Some less prosperous residents, devastated by the hurricane, may have left the region forever. Detailed accounts of the tropical cyclone appeared in northern newspapers and in the London *Times*.[61] The horrific details of the catastrophe likely gave pause to any white immigrants who were considering relocating to the lowcountry. Future storms certainly caused some to leave, especially the new cycle of terrible storms like those that began in the 1780s and continued to lash the coasts of Georgia and South Carolina during the first decades of the nineteenth century.

The Dotterer home in Charleston was destroyed by the tropical cyclone of 1885.
Courtesy of Charleston Museum.

LEFT East Battery, Charleston, following the hurricane of 1885. Courtesy of Charleston Museum.

BELOW Sloops blocking the entrance to Chisolm's Causeway, wrecked by the Charleston cyclone in 1885. Courtesy of South Carolina Historical Society.

ABOVE The *Freeda A. Wyley* caught fire during the Great Sea Island Storm. Its charred remains were uncovered by a later hurricane. Courtesy of Jack Thompson. All rights reserved.

LEFT Hurricane damage to the Charleston docks, 1885. Courtesy of Charleston Museum.

The Great Sea Island Hurricane of 1893 caused extensive damage in Charleston.

LEFT Debris of docks and warehouses at the Atlantic Wharves.

ABOVE TOP The remains of the new Ashley River Bridge.

ABOVE BOTTOM Smashed sailing craft and a side-wheeler remain where they were hurled into Boyce's Wharf.

LEFT Damage at the corner of Southern Wharf and East Bay.

These four images are from *Harper's Weekly*, September 16, 1893, courtesy of Hargrett Rare Book and Manuscript Library, University of Georgia Libraries.

BELOW Newcastle Street, the heart of the
business district, Brunswick, Georgia, flooded
during the hurricane of 1898. Courtesy of
Coastal Georgia Historical Society.

LEFT East Battery in Charleston, looking northeast, showing heavy flagstones unearthed and tossed about by the 1893 hurricane. *Harper's Weekly*, September 16, 1893, courtesy of Hargrett Rare Book and Manuscript Library, University of Georgia Libraries.

ABOVE Residents viewing the wreckage along Council Street in Charleston, 1893. *Harper's Weekly*, September 16, 1893, courtesy of Hargrett Rare Book and Manuscript Library, University of Georgia Libraries.

High and dry at Thunderbolt,
Georgia, just south of Savannah,
August 27, 1893. *Harper's Weekly*,
September 16, 1893, courtesy
of Hargrett Rare Book and
Manuscript Library, University
of Georgia Libraries.

Major Gilchrist's Beach House, Sullivan's Island, almost
totally destroyed by the Great Sea Island Hurricane of 1893.
Harper's Weekly, September 16, 1893, courtesy of Hargrett
Rare Book and Manuscript Library, University of Georgia
Libraries.

CHAPTER THREE

A Cycle

of Hurricanes,

1806–1824

The Rose-in-Bloom

The hurricanes that had swept the lowcountry in 1800 and 1804 ushered in a cycle of storms. Nearly every two years, on the average, from 1800 to 1824, tropical cyclones battered the region. Their frequency and destructiveness sorely tested the resilience of all castes and classes.[1]

In the early years of the nineteenth century, cotton, timber, tobacco, naval stores, and especially the cultivation and export of rice to a worldwide market remained the engine fueling the plantation economy of the lowcountry. The small number of wealthy, white rice planters and their merchant factors in the port towns prospered. They poured their wealth into land and slaves. Rice crops were grown almost exclusively in a small region encompassing numerous sea islands and a mainland only 280 miles long and 10 miles wide. The subtropical climate, so ideal for rice production, was a nursery for disease and insects. Another danger of the region was its exposure to violent hurricanes. The well-to-do who continued to live in the lowcountry gambled yearly on the weather odds — they knew a violent storm could devastate their fortunes. Some wealthy lowcountry residents may have thought about these odds when they boarded the sailing ship *Rose-in-Bloom* at Charleston for New York on August 16, 1806. It was the height of the hurricane season.

Most of the passengers knew one another and likely chatted amiably as they boarded the vessel. The passenger list included the lowcountry's elite; among these was John Rutledge Jr., a forty-year-old congressman whose father was South Carolina's Revolutionary War governor. Mr. Rutledge had married into a prominent South Carolina family, was the father of six children, and owned a large plantation and over three hundred slaves. Two years earlier, his name had been associated with a local scandal when he discovered Horace Senter, a prominent physician, paying "clandestine visits" to his wife. Rutledge challenged Dr. Senter to a duel and mortally wounded him. Also boarding were General McPherson, his daughter Miss Eliza McPherson, and a servant; Mr. Thomas Tait; Dr. Ballard and servant; Mr. D. Crocker and servant; Mr. D. Botifeur and servant; and Mr. James Miller Jr. All told, the crew and passengers, including six "men of color," numbered forty-nine people.[2]

Jammed with cotton and passengers, the *Rose-in-Bloom*, under Captain Stephen Barker's command, sailed out of Charleston's harbor on Saturday afternoon, August 16. A fair wind blew from the southwest. No one aboard could have known that a powerful hurricane was gathering strength just north of the Bahamas Islands, the first of several that devastated shipping off the east coast of North America over the next six weeks.[3]

The hurricane quickly curved northwest, fueled by the warm ocean surface of late summer. It became known as the Great Coastal Hurricane of 1806. Though the massive storm remained offshore, by August 22 its outlying winds reached Georgia's southernmost coast. Offshore from St. Marys, the hurricane slammed into the schooner *L.T.* The wrecked vessel began sinking rapidly. Captain G. Geere ordered the seventeen passengers and crew into a lifeboat. But as they scrambled aboard, Maria Osborne, the "amiable" daughter of Judge Henry Osborne of St. Marys, lost her footing, was washed overboard, and drowned. Keeping the crowded lifeboat afloat in the hurricane-tossed sea was a challenging ordeal. Without oars or sails there was no way to pilot the small craft. The passengers were at the mercy of the winds and currents. When the sea moderated, only the wide ocean surrounded the small boat, and it drifted aimlessly. Days passed, and the occupants of the boat saw neither land nor sailing craft. Finally after eleven days on the open sea without food its half-starved passengers sighted a vessel. They were picked up on September 2 by Captain Hubble of a brig headed for Charleston. Amazingly, sixteen of the seventeen passengers survived the harrowing experience.[4]

The same hurricane that sank the *L.T.* off St. Marys caused flooding at Jekyll Island; it was well offshore when it swirled past Savannah without incident. Its northwesterly track brought it closer to Charleston on that same Friday, August 22. Rains whipped across the city, and strong northeast winds uprooted trees and blew vessels out of the harbor into the marsh. The "storm was violent . . . from the moment of its commencement," a Charleston resident remarked. Another told a friend two weeks later, "We have been tossed about . . . ever since the calamitous 22nd of August."[5]

Moving northeast, the hurricane slammed into Georgetown, blowing down the lighthouse on North Island at the entrance to Winyah Bay. Nearby a plantation owner on the North Santee River watched as the wind increased to a velocity "twice as hard as the [1804] hurricane." It uprooted trees in his yard and "completely ruined, twisted and smashed all to pieces" his cotton crop. He did not "expect to make ten bales out of 94 acres."[6] Other planters in the region suffered equally devastating crop losses.

After cutting through the extreme southeastern tip of North Carolina, the hurricane curved into the open Atlantic on Saturday, August 23. Behind the path of the great storm a trail of sunken or battered vessels stretched across the Atlantic from Eleuthera in the Bahamas to Bermuda, Georgia, and the Carolinas. It was about to claim more victims.

The hurricane enveloped the brig *Venus* off South Carolina, shredding its sails, knocking down the masts, and capsizing the vessel. Captain Wasson, crew, and passengers eventually righted the vessel; though everyone aboard was "very much bruised," no one perished. Close by, the sloop *Nancy*, with a cargo of gin and flour, was damaged but made it to Charleston under jury masts. Likewise the brig *Ann*, far off Charleston, fought "tremendously severe" winds. Eventually the *Ann* was knocked over, its masts torn away. It took Captain Cory and his crew two hours to right the vessel. Miraculously no one was lost overboard, but the cargo was "damaged." Under jury masts, the *Ann* reached Charleston. En route there, outside the Gulf Stream, Captain Cory spotted the wrecks of three dismasted ships, seemingly abandoned.[7]

In the same vicinity but to the north, Captain Renshaw expended all his resources trying to keep his ship, *Thomas Chalkely*, afloat in a "tremendous gale blowing from" the northeast. Huge waves broke over the vessel, and water poured into the hold. With the Chalkely's sails shredded, Captain Renshaw worried that his ship would founder as he navigated past the dangerous shoals of Cape Romain. To reach Charleston, he enlisted a pilot.[8]

Fighting the same hurricane in the same latitude of 33° north, the 150-ton brig *Lucinda* fared not so well. Despite the efforts of Captain Shove, the brig was driven into the breakers of Great and Little Murphy Island near Cape Romain. Here the *Lucinda* foundered and was dashed to pieces. Miraculously no one perished, and evidently the specie aboard—gold and silver—was saved.[9] Meanwhile, further offshore and to the north, near the eye of the hurricane, Captain Stephen Barker was fighting to keep the *Rose-in-Bloom* afloat.

The weather deteriorated soon after the *Rose-in-Bloom* departed Charleston. Early Friday, August 22, "a storm of great violence" enveloped the ship. It terrified the passengers and even the "stout mariners" aboard. Within four hours the wind ceased—apparently as the eye passed over. Then near nightfall, winds began "blowing very violently" from the northeast and continued throughout the night and Saturday. With sails shredded by the wind, Captain Barker feared the fast-drifting ship might end up ashore. He ordered his crew to reef the foresail in "hopes of the vessel clawing off" the land. The ship labored into Sunday, August 24. Finally, battered by the storm from latitude 34° north to 40° north—from the Carolinas to off New Jersey's coast—the *Rose-in-Bloom* capsized.[10]

The sea cascaded over the deck, rushed through the hatches and into the hold; it swept through the companionway and began filling the cabin where passengers huddled. John Rutledge hurried the daughter of General McPherson up the stairs through the rushing water. Other passengers followed. Unable to get out of the cabin before it filled, two prominent lowcountrians, Thomas Tait and Henry Bowering, drowned. Without an exit way, other passengers smashed through the cabin's skylight and fell into the sea. General McPherson was among them. He shouted "Save my daughter, Save my daughter" until he disappeared from sight. Other passengers embraced one another on the wreckage until waves swept them away to their deaths. With the *Rose-in-Bloom* lying on its side, some passengers and crew became entangled in its cordage; others struggled to hang on to masts, yards, and rigging. A few brave souls labored to cut away the masts in hopes of righting the ship. Crashing waves and the buoyancy of the cotton in the hold helped efforts to break away the masts and bring the ship upright. But with water flooding the hold, the stern was barely above water and the sea cascaded over the deck.[11]

Survivors, mostly from the lowcountry, made their way to the stern, where they lashed themselves to the weather railing. Nearly naked, without food and drink, exhausted, stung by a cold wind, and bruised and battered, they pressed close for warmth. Four died during the afternoon. At night the sky cleared, and the sea moderated. Around 3:00 a.m. the survivors thought they saw a ship's light in the distance but soon recognized it as the morning star. After daybreak the sun's heat, welcomed at first, became almost intolerable. Several bales of cotton and a trunk containing a bag of biscuits bobbed to the surface. The survivors shared the water-soaked biscuits to keep "soul and body together." When a sail came into view on the horizon, John Rutledge wanted to ensure that those lashed to the stern of the *Rose-in-Bloom* were rescued. Promising a reward, Rutledge induced two seamen to climb aboard a spar and paddle in the direction of the sail. The *Rose-in-Bloom* was soon spotted by the British brig *Swift*. Its commander, Richard Phelan, an Irishman, quickly took aboard his vessel all survivors, who praised him, saying that he "did everything possible to make [us] comfortable." Captain Phelan saved what he could of the passengers' possessions and then scuttled what remained of the *Rose-in-Bloom*. The *Swift* disembarked the surviving passengers and crew at New York on Wednesday, August 27.[12]

The loss of twenty-three of the forty-nine passengers and crew who boarded the *Rose-in-Bloom* in Charleston was the single greatest tragedy of the Great Coastal Hurricane of 1806. A full account of the disaster was published in papers throughout the country.[13]

News of loss of the *Rose-in-Bloom* and its victims reached Charleston by a sailing vessel on September 9, and word of the human loss spread quickly. Many of the privileged lowcountry families were affected by the sad news. One

Charlestonian told a friend, "I will always bewail the fate of those who perished and most sincerely condole with their bereaved families." Another noted that everyone was distressed "over the melancholy account" of General McPherson. John Rutledge became a local hero. Mrs. McPherson's "gratitude [knew] no bounds" for "his gallant exertions" to save "the life of a beloved daughter." Family and friends consoled Rutledge for the "scenes of horror" aboard the *Rose-in-Bloom*; others congratulated him for surviving "fourteen awful hours clinging to a wreck in the middle of the ocean."[14]

News of the tragedy also touched the lowcountry's black and poor white communities. The slaves of General McPherson and Dr. Ballard perished with their masters; D. Botifeur and D. Crocker survived while their slaves drowned. Of the six other "men of colour" aboard, Babtiste Hajadie, John Murry, Henry Davis, John Trusty, Adam Knott, and Harry Kid—the latter three drowned. Six whites listed as steerage passengers or crewmembers also drowned.[15] The rash of gales and hurricanes at sea and ashore persisted.

Storms, Hurricanes, and a Tornado

In late summer 1810 a tropical storm battered the lowcountry's coast. At Tybee Island it drove ashore the British schooner *Union*, at Savannah, the *Pizzaro*, and near Edisto Island, the rice-carrying schooner *Munroe* under Captain Hefferton grounded. High winds and torrential rains swept through Charleston on September 11–12, 1810. Several small vessels sank at wharfside, seawater spilled into the streets, and a few trees went down.[16] But this was only a prelude to the hurricane and tornado of 1811.

In early September 1811 a tropical storm lashed the Leeward Islands in the West Indies and with dizzying speed curved inward, northwest, toward the lowcountry. Captain Cox aboard the schooner *Cornelia* reported "a very violent storm" off Georgia's southeastern coast. On Sunday, September 8, just below Savannah, winds near hurricane force blew ashore the ships *Levi* and *William Dearborn*. Reports reached the cities that cotton planters on the sea islands and rice planters along the rivers had "suffered severely" from the gale sweeping into the lowcountry.[17]

Far offshore that Sunday the schooner and pilot boat *R.J.* of Charleston, commanded by Captain Hilliard, encountered "a very severe gale." Apparently the *R.J.* was near the eye of the hurricane. Captain Hilliard "was obliged to scud for several days." Battered by huge waves, the *R.J.* sprang a leak. Seawater soon poured into the schooner. The crew manned two bilge pumps around the clock, used anything they could find to bail, and threw cargo overboard. But seawater flooded in faster than it went out, and Hilliard ordered his crew of four, a first mate and "three negroes," to abandon the sinking vessel for the twelve-foot lifeboat carried aboard the *R.J.* They loaded the small boat with "20 pounds of bread and 8 gallons of water." Hilliard himself barely had time to grab his quadrant and compass and abandon the stricken *R.J.* before it went under near the Gulf Stream, far to the southeast of Charleston at latitude 29° north, longitude 78° west. The five men in the small boat feared certain death in the heavy sea. Hopes soared when they sighted a schooner scudding under a foresail. They signaled but were not seen. When the sea moderated they rigged a sail. Captain Hilliard set a heading for the coast many sea miles distant.[18]

On the day Captain Hilliard ran into the hurricane at sea, the storm's outlying northeast winds (possibly of hurricane force) hit Charleston. Water came down in torrents, and the wind "blew with increasing violence" into Tuesday morning, September 10. Around noon the wind shifted to the southeast, spawning a tornado. Just before the whirling winds touched down, witnesses heard a loud "rumbling noise," and the tornado shot pass them with "the rapidity of lightning."[19]

Sixty to one hundred yards wide, it cut a swath of destruction and death across the city, from Bay Street on the southeast to Boundary Street on the northwest. The tornado roared across Church Street, into Meeting Street, across Tradd Street, up King to Broad Street. It crossed Queen Street and then sped up Mazyck Street, leveling some houses and sending roof tiles and slate spinning through the air like missiles. It was over in minutes. Leaving the city, the tornado whirled down Boundary Street into the countryside, knocking over trees and fences. Some people, buried when houses collapsed on them, died instantly — a young woman, a French-born physician, a German-born grocer, three mulatto children, and two mulatto men. Others died later from their injuries. The tornado claimed over twenty lives. The *Charleston Courier* regretted that it was again its "painful duty to detail the awful effects of a dreadful visitation upon [the] ill-fated city."[20] Estimates of the damage in the city reached $300,000 ($4,027,007).[21]

Leaving Charleston, the storm hugged the coast, damaging crops, sweeping past Georgetown, and nearly upsetting vessels off Cape Romain. It then recurved out to sea and died in colder waters. Captain Hilliard and his crew of four in their small open boat had cheated death. After nine days at sea, the last two without food or water, they finally reached Charleston on September 19, "enfeebled" and "in the utmost distress." One can only imagine how deliriously happy they must have been to have survived.[22] A little more than two weeks later, in early October 1811, other storm victims were not so fortunate.

In 1811 the United States was on the brink of war with Great Britain. For years, as the Napoleonic wars raged in Europe, the British repeatedly seized American ships on the high seas. Feelings for war intensified in the country, especially in coastal Georgia and South Carolina. In an attempt to avoid war, the American Congress passed embargo acts prohibiting the export-import trade. The embargo and retaliatory restrictions by the British and French affected all classes. Well-to-do planters and merchants alike watched cotton pile up at wharves, while the price fell sharply from forty cents per pound in 1804 to eighteen cents in 1811.[23]

As British ships persisted in harassing American vessels and impressing seamen along the coast or on the high seas, American hostility increased. The lowcountry's privileged classes felt threatened, and local governments at Savannah, Beaufort, Charleston, and Georgetown authorized the construction of fortifications and the drilling of militia, and they asked Congress for gunboats to protect the coasts.[24] It was one of these U.S. gunboats that was caught in a storm off Cumberland Island in early October 1811.

U.S. gunboat No. 2 sailed from Charleston for St. Marys on September 29 under the command of Lieutenant John J. Lippincott. The vessel, staffed by four midshipmen and twenty-nine crewmembers, carried one civilian passenger, Mrs. R. Smith, who was to join her service-connected husband. The schooner-rigged gunboat reached Cumberland Island on Friday morning, October 4. Unable to enlist a pilot to navigate the tricky local waters, Lippincott "stood off" the island in view of a "high sea" and watched the weather turning "very bad." By morning the wind was from the northeast and "increasing to a heavy gale," likely near hurricane force. With part of the crew below deck, Lippincott ordered all hatches secured and a trysail rigged. He then headed the gunboat east into the wind in an attempt to stabilize the vessel in the turbulent sea. But with the wind and seas still rising, the vessel was unable to maintain headway, and Lippincott ordered the trysail reefed. The vessel wallowed helplessly. Within minutes a "heavy sea broke on board" and knocked it over. To right the gunboat, Lippincott ordered the mast cut away. Terrified and afraid of drowning, the crew below "forced open the hatches" secured earlier and the "Gun-Boat instantly filled [with water] and went down," taking with it those who opened the hatches. Those aboard who were lucky enough to be pitched into the heaving sea "tried to save themselves from instant death" by clinging to the great sweeps or oars, spars, or rigging. But after "struggling a while with the waves," they too "shared the fate of those who went down with the vessel."[25]

Crewmember John Tier, who had managed to grab and hold to a large oar, soon found himself alone in a rolling sea. He clung to the oar for twenty-nine hours until rescued by Captain Gould of the schooner *Dolly* out of Rhode Island. Tier was the sole survivor of thirty-five aboard gunboat No. 2. The sinking ranks as one of the greatest sea disasters off Georgia's coast.[26]

As for John Tier, it was the second time in a year that he cheated death. Remarkably he had survived a shipwreck five months earlier when U.S. gunboat No. 157 went aground on the Charleston bar and was beaten to pieces by waves.[27]

"Tremendous Gales of Wind," 1813

In 1812 the United States declared war on Great Britain. The following year over a dozen hurricanes ripped through the West Indies. Apparently two of these curved toward the continental United States — one in late August 1813 and another in September.[28]

On August 25 a hurricane just offshore bore down on the cotton-laden sloop *Polly* out of Sunbury and bound for Savannah. Captain Stewart was unable to control the vessel. It was knocked over and hurled into Romerley Marsh of Skidaway Island, where it sank. About the time the *Polly* capsized, the two-hundred-mile-wide storm caught a Spanish brig, *San Francisco*, commanded by Captain Juan Querbo, south of Cape Romain and drove it into Dewees Inlet. The brig was a total loss. A warning went out that persons found taking cargo or parts from the vessel illegally would be prosecuted.[29]

Near Beaufort, also on August 25, the British war sloop *Colibri*, attempting to reach the open sea from the Broad River, was driven into the breakers and smashed to pieces. A sister vessel, the war sloop *Moselle*, rescued the crew. Captain Hussey of the sloop *Mahala* sailing from New York for Charleston encountered the hurricane near Cape Romain on August 26. His vessel was driven into six fathoms and nearly went aground. Hussey called it the "most severe [gale] which he ever experienced in the many years he has followed the seas."[30]

At sea the hurricane struck with such suddenness and destructive power that some vessels and crews remained unaccounted for. Off Charleston's bar, the captain of the sloop *Little-Mary* spotted "much wreckage . . . and top masts of . . . vessels." The "water for many miles from the [Charleston] bar was as red as blood."[31] Passing across Georgia's coastal waters, the storm was about to come ashore.

As the storm curved inward, northwesterly up the coast, outlying winds and drenching rains brushed Savannah. Near Beaufort, winds blew small craft ashore and damaged crops of rice and cotton. Otherwise damage remained slight. But as the hurricane moved closer to the coast, residents of Edisto Island, Charleston, and Sullivan's Island were directly exposed to the sea. They knew a storm was on the way. One remarked, "The unsettled state of the weather . . . and the uncommon roaring of the sea" on the beaches was "an unerring indication" of an approaching great gale. And on the evening of August 27 the hurricane came ashore from Edisto Island to Georgetown.[32]

Torrential rains and winds had already damaged the cotton and food crops when the ocean "rose to an unusual height" and rolled over Edisto Island. Near the front beach, the sea rushed under homes along "the Bay," and their inhabitants fled in terror and in fear of drowning. Water undermined houses across the island, and others sustained significant damage from the wind. There was no injury or loss of life, but it was reported that "the loss of property . . . [was] immense." When fences went down, farm animals either drowned or roamed free. "Torn up by their roots," trees fell across roads, making them impassable for horse-drawn vehicles from Edisto to Charleston. The cotton crop was wiped out, and most likely not enough of the corn crop remained to prevent people from going hungry. Longtime residents of Edisto claimed "that it was the most severe gale which they [had] ever experienced . . . everything presents a most dismal appearance." Prospects were "very gloomy and much depresse[d] the spirits of the planters." Rice planters northward toward Charleston, along the Stono River, also "suffered" a similar fate.[33]

On the same evening that the hurricane battered Edisto it was coming ashore at Charleston and Georgetown. For several days Charlestonians had noted the "roaring of the sea" and anticipated a strong gale. But it was stronger than they expected. By mid-afternoon, Friday, August 27, the wind came "very fresh" from the northeast and brought torrents of rain. In early evening it increased to "a strong gale," and from around 9:00 and for the next six hours, it blew "a complete hurricane." The driver of the mail stagecoach from Georgetown barely escaped injury to himself and his horses as trees crashed around him. The speed and extreme violence of the storm "beat to pieces" or sank boats, coasters, sloops, schooners, and ships at Charleston. Four slaves owned by James Brown were washed overboard from their raft and drowned. The storm wrecked the sloop *Necessity* in the harbor and capsized and sank the schooners *Cornelia* and *Sally* and the ship *Canton*. Only two vessels in the harbor, two schooners of the U.S. Navy, *Nonesuch* and *Carolina*, guarding Charleston against a British invasion, rode out the hurricane unscathed.[34]

At the city's wharves, winds and waves severely battered a Spanish schooner and the ship *Phoenix* tied off Pritchard's Wharf. Both sank. The ships *Florida*, *Commerce*, and *Morning Star*, moored at Johnson's Wharf, were driven up into the streets. At William's Wharf the ship *Retrieve* was driven from her moorings and left high and dry. Other vessels, large and small, sank or were thrown onto wharves. Almost every wharf along the Cooper River was either torn apart or washed away. Waves sent tangled masses of logs, timbers, and planks (once a wharf structure) along with crushed shallops, hogsheads, and spars into the streets and beyond. The debris crashed against stores and warehouses on Bay, Hasell, and Wentworth streets, ruining structures and property stored therein. A tidal surge of twelve feet flooded Charleston. Water was neck-deep in places. The surging water carried away four hundred yards of a new bridge over the Ashley River, and all of Cannon's Bridge came down. Undermined houses were easy prey for winds to topple. Chimneys collapsed, and slates, tiles, window shutters, signs, and anything not tied down blew in every direction, causing further damage. A blacksmith's shop was leveled. The top of Ross's windmill at the head of Tradd Street was blown off. Portions of the stone wall below the gun battery on East Bay collapsed.[35]

Fort Johnson on James Island, protecting the southern entrance to the harbor, was partially destroyed by the hurricane. Fortunately the women and children who sought safety in the men's barracks were rescued before the tidal surge swept the barracks into the sea. At the opposite end of the harbor, on Sullivan's Island, where Fort Moultrie was located, the ocean surged over the sand dunes and covered the island in four to five feet of seawater. Swirling waters swept furniture out of dwellings. Fierce winds knocked over twelve houses that were carried away into the ocean. Fort Moultrie was the only place of refuge that was not awash or threatened with inundation. Soldiers hurried to save families in danger of being swept away. But they could not rescue everyone needing assistance. Nineteen people drowned, among them five of six young white women in one house and "seven or eight negroes." The bodies of some were strewn among the wreckage of homes, furniture, and small boats. They provided "an awful remembrance of the horrors the [survivors] had escaped." Deaths on Sullivan's Island and in the city reached at least twenty-three, but this was only a "reckoning" of the *minimum* number of fatalities from the tropical cyclone at sea and ashore. The damage to real property in Charleston and to the shipping there alone was estimated at $2,000,000 ($22,156,626). Near Charleston, at Goose Creek and along the western branch of the Cooper River, trees and fences went down, and rivers, spilling their banks, ruined rice crops. The wind shifted westward after midnight and "blew with much force until daylight." Then it died. The hurricane was moving fast.[36]

Residents at Georgetown felt "the violence of the Gale." It smashed into some wharves and drove ashore "two schooners, a Sloop, and the hull of a brig." Fort Winyaw, guarding the entrance to Winyah Bay, was so battered that it was rendered "almost useless." A barge commanded by Captain Lord guarding North Island and South Island was blown ashore. Freshets broke through earthen banks surrounding rice fields, and planters feared losses of "five thousand tierces of rice"—about one-third of the local crop. Waters ruined cotton and corn crops. Winds uprooted trees, and swollen rivers carried away bridges and ferries. The hurricane moved quickly by Georgetown, headed northwest, and eventually passed through central North Carolina.[37]

In sum, the number of deaths and the damage to property and crops throughout the lowcountry cannot be reckoned. Gordon Dunn, at one time the U.S. Weather Bureau's chief meteorologist and director of the National Hurricane Center, labeled the 1813 tropical cyclone making landfall on South Carolina's coast an *"extreme hurricane."* The scholar David Ludlum called the hurricane one of "Charleston's major disasters."[38]

Even before the damage from the August hurricane was cleared, a storm packing hurricane winds battered Amelia Island, Florida, and then slammed into nearby St. Marys, Georgia. Dr. William Baldwin was one of the first to experience its ferocity.

A native of Pennsylvania and graduate of the University of Pennsylvania Medical School, Baldwin migrated to Georgia for his health in 1811. When war erupted the following year, the thirty-three-year-old physician was appointed to the post of surgeon in the U.S. Navy at St. Marys. In mid-September 1813 Baldwin was visiting a seriously ill patient on Amelia Island, just twenty miles from his post, when the hurricane struck. A high wind came from the northeast, and torrents of rain swept in from the sea at night and smashed into the house — "considered the strongest on the island" — where Baldwin was staying. He and the other occupants found their situation so "precarious" that they fled to a lower structure, the kitchen, just before all the windows and doors of the house blew away. The storm died as the eye passed, but the wind came again. This time it blew from the southwest with "redoubled fury." Baldwin tried to prop up the kitchen that was on the verge of collapsing. What happened next indicates the fury of the storm that by now was enveloping Georgia's furthermost southeastern coast:

> I was blown off . . . to be carried before the wind, until I got hold of some wood [pilings] that had been driven into the ground. . . . It was with the utmost difficulty that I could maintain my hold, and prevent my face from being lacerated with the sand and shells that were driven by the wind in horrible confusion. The rain all the time came down in torrents and was driven in such a manner as to resemble the waves of the sea. It was impossible to retreat and I remained in this situation for about an hour.[39]

While Baldwin was trying to survive the hurricane at Amelia Island, the fierce storm swept over St. Marys, Cumberland Island, Jekyll Island, and St. Simons. Around 10:00 p.m. the hurricane blew all the vessels out of the harbor at St. Marys. They came to rest in the marshes or in the town. Winds and waves sank the U.S. gunboat *No. 164*, and twenty crewmen perished. The federal revenue cutter also went down, with the loss of two men. On Cumberland Island residents watched and listened as the storm came upon them with a vengeance. One resident witnessed the wind blowing from the northeast. It "attained an alarming degree of violence," and the "sea beat on the beach with a weigh that shook the whole island." The tide surged higher than it had in the hurricane of 1804. Four ships were driven ashore on the southern tip of the island where "much [was] cut away" and the "destruction . . . almost as complete as any event but annihilation." At 1:00 a.m. the wind suddenly "ceased and a dead calm ensued." Then an hour later "the wind . . . sprang up from the southwest, increased to a fury greater" than before, and continued "blowing with unremitting violence till daylight." Across the island the "sturdiest live oaks were twisted up by the roots . . . the pine barrens all laid flat . . . fruit and cotton crops all destroyed." The storm wrecked slave cabins and peeled the "copper off the roof" of Dungeness, the plantation house of General Nathanael Greene's widow and her new husband. The losses at Dungeness reached $10,000 ($111,111), but neither slave nor free perished on the island.[40]

Before recurving back to sea just below Darien, the hurricane swirled northwest across Jekyll Island, St. Simons, and the Altamaha River. It devastated the rice and cotton crops nearly ready for harvest. After the hurricane blew past Amelia Island, Dr. Baldwin saw only wrecked houses around him. His return trip to St. Marys on horseback was harrowing. He carefully picked his way along a road blocked with "thousands" of downed live oaks and magnolias. Frequently he dismounted to move around the "prostrate" trees, to cut his way through wild grapevines and briars, and to wade his horse through water that reached to the saddle. He feared what he might find at St. Marys.[41]

Located on a bluff just below Cumberland Island and on the north side of the St. Marys River, Georgia's southernmost river, St. Marys was built on a thriving trade in lumber. Residents lived in fifty or sixty wooden houses close to the river. When Dr. Baldwin reached St. Marys, where "all his hopes and fears were centered," he found a "scene of destruction" similar to what he had witnessed on Amelia Island. He was saddened by the deaths of the men aboard the gunboat and the revenue cutter. "The oldest inhabitants," with whom Baldwin talked, told him "that this gale has not been paralleled since their memory, even in the land of hurricanes."[42]

The hurricanes of August and September 1813 are ranked as very destructive and damaging to the economy of the lowcountry. Scholars have called the September storm that devastated the lower Georgia coast a major hurricane.[43]

Victims of Storms

The dead were the ultimate victims of the hurricanes of 1813. Families and friends of the dead suffered emotionally and financially. Often they agonized because they could not know for weeks whether their loved ones had lived or perished. Those aboard vessels that sank at sea, those who drifted in lifeboats for days, and those onshore in the direct path of the hurricane all suffered trauma as a result of their experiences. Survivors of such disasters perhaps never fully recover. The property of many sustained such devastating blows that they never recouped their losses. Fearful of such storms, some left the lowcountry. Others thought about leaving the coast but did not. Accounts of the great storms no doubt gave pause to those who might have migrated to coastal Georgia and South Carolina.

The cycle of fierce tropical cyclones and storms frightened even longtime residents of Charleston. A few days after the August hurricane, while the city was cleaning up, the *Courier* editorialized, "Again we have been visited with one of those disasters, which have . . . [recently] so frequently desolated our city and seaboard." It was "one of the most tremendous gales . . . ever felt upon our coast."[44]

Fear of these great storms was palpable. Major General John Floyd, a tough Indian fighter and commander of the Georgia militia during the War of 1812, was in the field and did not hear for weeks if his wife and twelve children residing in the lowcountry had survived the hurricane of August 27–28, 1813. He agonized over their safety. It was more than a month after the great storm that Floyd received a letter from his daughter Mary. He opened it "in haste and perused [it] with fearful anxiety. I was much relieved . . . to find that you had all been spared." His reply to Mary reflected his real fear of lowcountry hurricanes: "You may . . . imagine my anxiety . . . to hear from you, after seeing the account of the distressing effects of the late hurricane in the latitude which everything dear to me was embraced." Although General Floyd "was extremely anxious to hear" about his family, he "dreaded the receipt of . . . [any] melancholy intelligence."[45]

After the war, Floyd returned with his family to a plantation in Camden, one of Georgia's coastal counties, where before the war he had accumulated considerable wealth in the business of building boats for navigating Georgia's waterways. He invested his profits in land and slaves, served eight years in the state legislature, and in 1827 was elected to the lower house of the U.S. Twentieth Congress. Floyd maintained his residence in coastal Georgia until his death in 1839.[46]

Like Floyd, most of those persisting lowcountry residents enjoyed substantial stakes in property and society and were loath to move elsewhere. They simply lived with their fears and threats from destructive gales and hurricanes.

The winds and rains of the September hurricane of 1813 wiped out any hope for planters to realize a profit from rice and cotton crops that were nearly ready for harvest on Cumberland Island, Jekyll Island, and St. Simons and along the Altamaha River. Roswell King, the manager of Pierce Butler's vast plantations in the region, complained: "The cotton is as dead as in the month of January. What an unfortunate man I am to be born to see such destruction."[47]

Christophe DuBignon on Jekyll Island, whose property and crops sustained damage in the hurricanes of 1804 and 1806, again suffered losses in 1813. Despite these disasters, DuBignon initially planned to remain. He and his family, like others of their class, had an abiding interest in the island as both an investment and their family home. Once more his slaves hauled away the storm's debris, cleared the land, and replanted. But short of capital, he was forced to sell his house in Savannah. Adding to his road to financial ruin was the continuing slide in the price of cotton and the invasion of Jekyll Island twice by the British. They shot DuBignon's livestock, burned the cotton gin, ransacked his home, humiliated him, and lured away twenty-eight of his slaves. Within a few years, DuBignon and Pierce Butler, who also held a large stake in property, offered their land for sale. They found no ready buyers.[48]

Unlike the acclimatized slaveholding and propertied class, more recent migrants to the lowcountry, with little stake in property and society, quickly became alarmed over the weather and thought about leaving soon after their arrival. Such was the case of the Reverend Martin Luther Hurlbut.

Born in Massachusetts and a graduate of Williams College, Hurlbut, a kind and slightly built young man, was a Congregational minister who enjoyed a successful ministry until he became ill. By chance he learned that Beaufort College in Beaufort, South Carolina — a town of some six hundred residents, black and white — was seeking a new president. Hurlbut applied, was elected in 1812, and took over what was more an academy than a college. The student body was composed of about forty boys, ages nine to twelve, the sons of local cotton and rice planters. Over the next two years Hurlbut enjoyed a few successes as president, but he longed for "northern society." He believed that the heat and humidity of Beaufort was damaging his health, and the frequent hurricanes frightened him. Following the "tremendous gales" of August 1813, Hurlbut found it impossible to remain, he remarked, "in this land of storms" and torrential rains. The hurricane of 1813 passed close enough to Beaufort to have "ruined . . . planters of cotton and rice." Hurlbut realized that losses for the perpetually debt-ridden planters would affect support for Beaufort College. He resigned as president of the college in 1814 and moved with his new wife, a Connecticut Yankee, and child to Charleston, where he became a successful headmaster. Eventually, however, he left the lowcountry and relocated his family to Philadelphia.[49]

Joseph Bennett of Charleston worried about the prevalence of disease locally and also had a deep distaste for the climate. Several years after the devastating hurricane of 1813, a virulent outbreak of yellow fever brought business to a standstill in Charleston. Bennett wrote to an acquaintance, "The lamented occurrences of the summer . . . and the conviction that my family cannot habituate themselves to this climate induce me to think sincerely of changing my place of residence."[50]

Tropical Storms and a Hurricane, 1815 and 1817

On July 1, 1814, a strong tropical storm spawned a tornado at Charleston, but apparently damage was not significant.[51] Seven months later, in February 1815, news reached the lowcountry that a treaty had been signed ending the war with Great Britain, a conflict some called the Second War for American Independence. It ushered in a few years of national economic expansion that lowcountry merchants and planters participated in despite the disease, insects, and the weather, especially the gales and hurricanes. With the reopening of the export-import trade with Great Britain by the summer, British merchant vessels faced the menace of Atlantic hurricanes.

At least nine hurricanes swept through the West Indies in 1815. One curved northwestward toward the coastlines of Georgia and South Carolina in August. After midnight August 31, the "severe gale" caught the 140-ton British brig *Spring*, out of Liverpool, near the dangerous shoals of Cape Romain and drove the *Spring* aground on Raccoon Keys. Wave after wave crashed into the stranded vessel. When it began breaking up, Captain John C. Smith ordered the crew into a longboat and amidst foaming seas charted a course for Charleston. The *Spring* and its "valuable cargo" were lost, but Smith and his crew reached port safely. They saved nothing but "the clothes they were wearing."[52]

Far off the lowcountry on August 31 at latitude 35° north, longitude 10° west, the sloop *Brutus*, under the command of Captain J. Shaw and twelve days out of New York headed for Charleston, was knocked over. The ship lost much of her rigging and the main boom. The cargo of cheese and potatoes suffered water damage, but the *Brutus* made it to port safely. The great storm remained off the coast, but its outlying winds blew violently from the northeast for several days. Off Savannah on September 1, high winds carried away the foremast of the schooner *Richmond Packet*, out of Madeira with a cargo of wine. The huge waves crashing over Charleston's bar prevented sailing craft from entering the harbor. Anchors did not hold. Winds and waves took vessels south; one went ashore on James Island.[53]

As the hurricane moved closer to the coast, it flattened cotton crops, drove saltwater far up creeks, and burst through earthen dams surrounding rice fields along the Cooper River, ruining the crops. Once again a tropical cyclone did "much injury to the planters." On September 3 this hurricane of "*great* dimensions" roared across extreme eastern North Carolina, smashing coastal towns and shipping. It then recurved northeastward, where the great storm bore down on vessels at sea.[54]

When reports of the tragic loss of seamen and numerous sightings of the wreckage of sailing craft — masts, planking, smashed bulwarks — reached the lowcountry, an editor of the *Savannah Republican* was moved to poetry:

alas! What must be the feelings of them
whose barks had to yield to the storm! The
loud winds, mingled with darkness above,
whistling over the foaming wave,
and nothing beneath save the fathomless
deep — how must the seaman have felt when
he grasped for a hold, and the flying spume
passed between his fingers! And how doleful
his cry when "heard along the deep!"[55]

During August 7–8, 1817, a tropical storm with high gusting winds smashed into St. Marys, sending vessels in the port into the marshes and uprooting trees in the town. As the storm moved inland, its winds buffeted Savannah and Charleston as it continued northward as far as Canada.[56] Another storm ripped into the lowcountry two years later, continuing the cluster of storms that began in 1800.

September Gales and Hurricanes, 1819 and 1820

The vagaries of the weather, especially hurricanes, were never far from the thoughts of Thomas Spalding, a planter on Georgia's Sapelo Island. He knew that the local weather could change rapidly: "great booming thunderheads, now fluffy and snow white in the sunlight, now dark and threatening." Spalding was a student of the weather and was alarmed that the great storms had become more frequent in the early nineteenth century. The son of the prosperous trader and planter James Spalding of St. Simons Island, Thomas Spalding had an abiding fear and appreciation of hurricanes that could sweep in suddenly and devastate the crops and property of the sea islanders. After traveling in Europe with his new bride for several years, Spalding purchased the south end of Sapelo Island. Here, overlooking the Atlantic Ocean, he designed a plantation home to withstand the most ferocious storms. Constructed by slave labor under the watchful eye of Roswell King, who also managed Pierce Butler's plantations in Glynn and McIntosh counties, the home was built between 1807 and 1810. To offer less resistance to hurricane winds, South End House was constructed low to the ground, with recessed columns, square-hewn timbers, and three-foot-thick tabby walls. At the same time, cabins for the Spalding slaves went up behind the big house and fields were cleared for planting. South End House was to withstand several fierce storms. One of the first struck Sapelo and Darien in late August 1819.[57]

The storm was apparently localized. It most likely devastated all of Spalding's crops and then swirled onto the mainland, knocking over a two-story house in Darien and flattening the crops in nearby Liberty County. In the Darien *Gazette* a local "poet" described the tropical storm in verse:

The rain fell in tub fulls, and beat down the corn,
Pea, pumkin and tatoe vines matted were borne,
Like cobwebs in autumn, while sapling and tree
Were popping and nodding like waves on the sea.[58]

Within a year another storm came ashore in the lowcountry.

On the evening of September 10, 1820, "a smart gale" out of the northeast and drenching rain squalls swept northward past Charleston, bringing down trees and a few buildings. It came ashore north of Georgetown, on Winyah Bay into which flowed the Black, the Pee Dee, and the Waccamaw rivers. A northeast wind had blown "tempestuously" throughout the day, pushing the tides to the height of the great hurricane of 1804. Water flooded the streets of Georgetown. After dark the wind blew harder. People fled their houses fearing rising winds and tide. A church was knocked from its foundations. Around 11:00 p.m. the winds started back to the north, occasionally "blowing . . . in squalls of incredible violence" with "floods of rain." Residents from battered houses across the town said it "was one of the most violent hurricanes . . . [ever] experienced" in Georgetown. By the morning, the hurricane was recurving to the northeast where it passed over Cape Hatteras and out to sea.[59]

The frequency and number of tropical storms or tropical cyclones that struck the lowcountry in the first quarter of the nineteenth century and their proclivity to strike in September led some to coin the phrase, "September gale." These words came to define acts of nature, sometimes with hurricane-force winds, that came to be expected and feared each year.[60] Two gales came ashore in the early 1820s that came to rank with the lowcountry's most devastating.

Catastrophe in South Carolina, September 27–28, 1822

"Unsettled and agitated" weather, scudding clouds, rain showers, booming swells along the beaches — all these troubled some lowcountry residents during the waning days of September 1822. Despite such warning signs, white property owners made no effort to move their families, real property, or slaves from the low-lying sea islands, river deltas, or coast. Living where they did, the planters gambled against the insects and the weather, and this year was no exception. They were betting that the September gale of 1822 would remain offshore. It did not. The approaching "gale" was actually a powerful tropical cyclone. It became a catastrophe at sea and on land.[61]

On September 27, vessels far offshore encountered the fierce winds of a hurricane that was moving toward the South Carolina coastline. The schooner *William*, southeast of Savannah, at latitude 31° north, longitude 40° west, was in its path. Captain Richard Allen at the helm of the *William* had sailed from St. Marys for Philadelphia on September 25 with a cargo of lumber. Two days later the hurricane slammed into the vessel, sweeping the decks of everything, knocking it over, and washing overboard seaman John Vines. Captain Allen ordered the lanyards cut away, which relieved the weight of the masts, and the schooner righted. But water in the hold and damages to the rigging prevented the schooner from making headway. It was slowly sinking. For ten days the vessel drifted. The crew subsisted on a few pounds of raw salt pork and a shark hooked on a baited line. Not until October 7 was their wreck spotted by the schooner *Eliza and Polly*. Captain Allen and his crew of six, including Frederick, "a black boy," escaped the sinking *William*. Their abandoned vessel washed ashore near the Charleston lighthouse on October 11.[62]

Though Captain Allen and his crew were rescued, the pilot boat *Hunter* was still missing. It had sailed out of Savannah with four pilots aboard unknowingly into the teeth of the hurricane. The vessel and the pilots were presumed lost.[63]

Off Georgia's northeastern coast on September 27, the hurricane crashed into the schooner *Mary Ann*, from Havana and bound for Charleston, loaded with fruit, sixty-five hogsheads of sugar, six hogsheads of molasses, and $4,000 ($60,295) in gold and silver. High winds and waves carried away the masts and bowsprit, stove in the bulwarks and lifeboat, and knocked the schooner over. The wreck of the *Mary Ann*, with fruit floating around her, was spotted drifting off Tybee Island in twelve fathoms. Captain Coleman of the schooner *Colonel George Armistead*, whose own rigging and sails had been shredded by the "severe gale," found "no one on board." The captain and crew must have perished at sea. The remains of the *Mary Ann* drifted over the bar and onto the beach at Hunting Island, South Carolina, where waves beat it apart.[64]

On the evening of September 27, Savannahians briefly experienced gale winds as the hurricane spun past Savannah churning toward South Carolina waters. About thirty miles off Charleston the wreckage of a ship with white sides was spotted; only its bowsprit was visible. Another vessel, a schooner, had gone down nearby bow-first; only its stern showed above water. No survivors were found on or near either vessel. On shore Primus Swain, a free black and owner of the Charleston pilot boat *Lucy-Anna*, feared that his boat and its two crewmen were lost at sea.[65]

Offshore from Charleston, at latitude 31° north, longitude 76° west, on the night of September 27, the hurricane winds and seas slammed into the brig *Alonzo*, sweeping the deck of cables, blocks, a small boat, the aft rail, and quarter rails. The waist of the vessel (the deck between the quarterdeck and forecastle) washed into the ocean with three crewmembers. Somehow the men got back aboard, and the *Alonzo* made its way to Norfolk for repairs. One schooner, *Fame*, ran before the storm for three terrifying hours and escaped damage.[66]

Moving from sea to land, the hurricane approached South Carolina's coastline after nightfall on September 27. It smashed dozens of boats just offshore. The smack *Aurora*, a small pleasure craft from New London, Connecticut, was caught off Charleston's bar and knocked over. Waves rolled it onto the beach at Long Island (the Isle of Palms today) bottom upward. Captain Winthrop Sawyer and his crew of four perished. The body of one washed ashore on Sullivan's Island. Not far away, high and dry, was the schooner *Mark Time*. When the brig *Sea Gull* capsized, its mate drowned. The schooner *Colonel Simons* overturned and drifted into the breakers off Sullivan's Island.[67]

The tidal surge drove small boats into the marsh around Charleston's harbor and onto the oyster rakes at Castle Pinckney, a fortification at the mouth of the Cooper River. A mulatto boy named July, belonging to Edwin C. Holland, drowned in the cabin of a sloop washed into the marsh. Eighteen-year-old William Young and a black crewman stayed aboard the coaster *Cotton Planter*, which overturned. Both were found drowned inside the cabin when the boat blew ashore at James Island. Three other "negro" crewmen perished when washed overboard. A "drogging sloop," owned by Isaac Ball, master of many slaves on the family's Cooper River rice lands, was battered by the great storm, and a crewman, Bengal, of Limerick Plantation, drowned. At the height of the hurricane, Joseph Clarke, owner of two Sullivan Island packet boats, tried to save his boat, the *Eagle*, from being dashed to pieces at its dock. When the hawser rope unraveled, winds drove the vessel toward James Island, where it foundered. Clarke and two others, a black man and a black woman, went over the side to try to reach shore. All drowned. The tropical cyclone came in along the upper South Carolina coast at low tide, which lessened damages to Charleston's wharves and the vessels tied off there. Nevertheless, sails shredded, bowsprits broke, and winds drove the craft into the wharves and one another. The schooner *Benjamin*, at Gibbs and Harper's Wharf, was dismasted; when its stern tore apart, the vessel was reduced to a complete wreck.[68]

Downpours of rain, towering clouds occasionally split by lightning, and high winds from the northeast swept ashore in South Carolina around 10:00 p.m.

Steering winds pushed the tightly wound storm at a rapid pace. The energy and the "violence" of the winds increased, eventually shifting to the northwest. By midnight the full fury of the "West Indian" hurricane enveloped the coast from Charleston to Georgetown. The storm's right-front quadrant packed the most damaging winds. The "height" of the tide at Georgetown and the "havoc" caused in Charleston were without parallel "in the memory of the oldest inhabitants."[69]

In both towns the cyclone raged between midnight and 2:00 a.m. All the more terrifying because it arrived in the pitch black of night, the storm smashed window glass, uprooted trees, and knocked down fences and chimneys. Violent winds unroofed stores and homes, smashing some to kindling. Torrents of rain saturated dry goods and furnishings in the unroofed structures. Houses rocked and trembled on their foundations from a wind that some said "resembled the shrieks of a demon of the air." People fled to the lowest stories of their dwellings. One of Charleston's most socially prominent residents, Mary Lamboll Beach, had retired early. She was awakened by a sudden rising wind between "one and two o'clock" that filled the family with "terror," and they all rushed downstairs. It was "the most awful [hurricane] . . . in my memory. . . . we all looked for instant death for some minutes," Beach declared. When the hurricane passed, she felt that her family had been saved because "the Lord was stretched out over our guilty Land."[70]

Beach's choice of words is interesting. She may have been alluding to another terrifying event in the city that summer that kept many white residents on edge. Catherine McBeth, a prominent Charlestonian, spoke of the event — an insurrection allegedly led by the free black Denmark Vesey: "Our minds were kept in continual agitation as regards the Insurrection which was to take place among the Negroes."[71]

Substantially built dwellings in the city and their proximity to one another made them better able to withstand the high winds. These were the homes of the well-to-do. At Alice Izard's on South Bay, one of the city's most prestigious addresses, only "a glass window" on the staircase was "blown in and destroyed." Catherine McBeth wrote "thank God my House in town is not at all injured & no lives lost."[72]

Good fortune did not favor those living in jerry-built dwellings in the city's poorer neighborhoods. A kitchen on King Street, near Line Street, collapsed, killing a black child. Jacint Laval's new wooden house in Hampstead, near the Cooper River and more exposed to the high winds, buckled into a jumble of timbers, killing six people — Laval's wife, her two small children, "a negro wench and her child," and a lodger, the butcher John Wilson.[73]

Winds blew windows out of the customs house, damaged the chapel of the Charleston Orphan House, and unroofed several churches, the tobacco inspection house, and the Livery Stables. The South Carolina Cotton Company's house was demolished. The shops of the tanyard and a blast furnace toppled. Structures with slate roofs were "much more injured than those that [were] shingled," one resident observed. Debris was everywhere, making many streets impassable. Around the city so many trees went down that they blocked roads out of Charleston for weeks. On Daniel Island, the hurricane damaged the cotton gins and homes of planters and knocked down slave cabins. Two slaves died of injuries. Here and on James Island, winds stripped away both the leaves and pods of cotton plants.[74]

Many of the well-to-do summering on the eastern end of Sullivan's Island went to bed early on the evening of September 28, among them, Lewis Morris, his wife (a member of the prominent Vanderhorst family), and their children. At the time a strong, steady breeze was coming out of the southeast, but no one suspected "that any violent storm was about to take place." After 11 p.m. the wind shifted from the southeast to the north and west, and witnesses soon heard "a dreadful blast" sweep over the island. Morris awakened when his house began "shaking violently." It was one of the largest and safest dwellings on Sullivan's Island. In fact, the structure was among the first that mariners saw coming into the harbor.[75]

Morris roused his family, had them dress, and gathered everyone except his wife in the dining room. Mrs. Morris was ill and could not easily be moved. When winds suddenly knocked down the front piazza, Morris sent his slave Roger to find others to help carry Mrs. Morris and the children out of the house. A few minutes after Roger left, the back piazza collapsed. When Roger and the other slaves he rounded up returned, they were unable to get into the house. As they tried to figure out a strategy for getting inside, the house collapsed in the high winds and rain, burying all its occupants. Mrs. Morris was crushed by "an immense beam." Her twelve-year-old son died, the French tutor, Mr. Dargence, was "dreadfully mangled," a young male slave died of injuries, and a female slave suffered multiple fractures. Lewis Morris, Charlotte (his daughter), and four younger sons survived.[76]

Not far away Thomas Middleton and his wife Mary were guests at the home of Judge D. E. Huger. As winds increased in the pitch black of the night, Middleton, his wife, and a daughter of Judge Huger fled the home for the safety of Colonel I'on's dwelling. In the howling wind, torrential rain, and blowing sand, Middleton became separated from his wife. Overwhelmed by "the horrors around her," Mary lost her way near the beach, was knocked down by the wind, and was blown into high waters where she drowned.[77]

The D'Burney "ladies," staying in Colonel Johnson's house on the island, feared that the house was about to collapse and ran out the door. Their slave girl died near the threshold. The D'Burneys wandered into the night, nearly driven off their feet by the fierce winds, until they found a log large enough to huddle behind. They remained there for three hours until the storm abated. John Middleton's family left their large "lofty" main house for the kitchen, a "low building" they thought safer. Part of the kitchen collapsed on Mr. Middleton; he and his family "were considerably bruised" but survived. The Boyce family residing in John Magrath's home narrowly escaped injury when a portion of their dwelling was blown apart. Winds and waves knocked houses off their foundations and blew some "several miles" or destroyed them where they stood. Among the summer homes were those belonging to members of Charleston's propertied class: A. Tunno, W. Mason Smith, Alexander Robinson, Thomas Flemming, and L. Fraser. The storm so damaged the residencies of the Prioleau, Horry, Brailsford, Gaillard, and Whilden families that they "appeared hardly worth repairing." Winds took off roofs, knocked over chimneys, and blew away piazzas. The hurricane smashed the market and unroofed the Planter's Hotel, the Point House, and Jackson's Hotel—island hostelries catering to the carriage trade.[78]

At Fort Moultrie, Major Byrd, the commanding officer, Lieutenant Washington, and other officers gave shelter and protection to all who fled there to escape the "violence" of the storm. They dispatched troops to guard the property of the well-to-do who feared "being plundered." A reporter observed that protection was needed from "foul weather birds who are ever abroad in the storm and ready to steal the property of the unfortunate and distressed." No doubt some poor whites and black slaves took advantage of acts of nature to salvage property—some might have felt they had earned this right through their service and labor.[79]

"W," a poet on the island, composed "lines written at Sullivan's Island" during the hurricane. It described graphically the natural disaster and in part read:

> While midnight darkness spreads around,
> While pelting rains incessant pour,
> And howling winds convey the sound
> Of naught but ocean's dreadful roar;
> The wretched seaman's cries are lost,
> And all his feeble efforts vain;
> As on the mighty billows tost,
> He ne'er shall meet his friends again.
> And we, surrounded by the flood,
> Whose trembling houses soon might fall,
> Are we prepar'd to meet our God,
> If now we heard the solemn call?
> O shouldst thou give the dread command,
> For winds and seas thy voice obey;
> How quickly could this strip of sand
> Be wash'd by raging waves away.[80]

Just beyond Sullivan's Island, on small Capers Island, the sea came ashore several feet higher than any gale in the preceding twenty years. The outbuildings of William Price Jr. blew down, and two of his slaves nearly drowned. Some thirty miles to the northeast of Capers Island, the U.S. revenue cutter *Gallatin* sought refuge in Bull's Bay but found little protection there. The vessel was just a few miles from Cape Romain when the hurricane came ashore. Enveloping the *Gallatin*, hurricane winds blew the cutter's sails to ribbons, carried away the rigging, snapped the fore-topmast, and stove in the *Gallatin*'s launch. Breaking waves fore and aft threatened to sink the vessel. Wind reached such a peak near midnight that crewmembers were unable to go from one end of the cutter to the other without crawling. Three anchors did not hold. Around 2:00 a.m. the vessel went aground on an oyster bank, damaging the rudder. Hands were stationed at the remaining masts with axes to cut them away should she be blown over. Suddenly the wind died, and it became calm for about ten minutes. The eye passed, and as suddenly as the wind had ceased, it began to roar again with "more violence," pushing the vessel higher up into the marsh. The storm drove other sailing craft into the marshes. After daybreak, one vessel, the *Favorite of Columbia*, the people aboard screaming for assistance, drifted over the marsh grass close to the *Gallatin*. Her anchor luckily took hold, and the vessel rode out the rest of the storm with sails shredded and oars, rudder, and most of her deck cargo gone. Those aboard the revenue cutter now observed their surroundings — three houses were down, livestock was drowned, and the sea had cut entirely through the southwest end of Bull's Island.[81]

While the crew of the *Gallatin* tried to keep afloat, a few miles northeast, just below Georgetown, a catastrophe was unfolding. The dangerous right-front quadrant of the fierce hurricane was sweeping the low-lying islands in the mouth of the North Santee and South Santee rivers, where plantations and summer homes served as health resorts for rice planters.

Fierce wind-driven swells crashed into Murphy Island at the mouth of the South Santee. They rolled over the Pinckney Horry plantation, knocking over slave cabins and drowning fifty of the fifty-five slaves owned by Mrs. Horry. Miss Sarah Beuchet, who was on the plantation, was carried to sea and drowned. Her body was later found on the beach. The overseer, a Mr. Johnson, was the only survivor among his family. At Cedar Island, midway between the North Santee and the South Santee, the sea rushed over the plantation of John Middleton, drowning three of his slaves. Middleton's overseer was washed into the marsh, where he was "picked up alive," but his wife perished. Damaging winds slammed into Middleton's home and rice mills, and a fire ignited one range of the slave cabins. A barn containing a thousand pounds of rice was destroyed.[82]

On North Island, exposed to the open Atlantic at the mouth of the Waccamaw River, the ocean rushed in to land, then swept away to sea white gentry and black slaves indiscriminately. Witnesses saw houses "almost crushed to atoms." Some homes simply disappeared without a trace. Mrs. Botsford, widow of Reverend Botsford, was crushed and drowned in bed; her female slave who slept beneath the bed also died, as did another slave, Bella, and her child. The sea washed away the summer home of James McDowel, a rice planter, with him and his family inside. The last he saw of his wife and children they were struggling in the huge waves surging through North Inlet. McDowel survived when waves swept him ashore. The house of Dr. Levi Myers, a beloved local physician, was wrenched off its blocks and swept into the ocean. Myers and fourteen members of his "family" drowned. He, his wife, three daughters, ages twenty-two to seventeen, and a son, age thirteen, received worshipful obituaries in the local paper. Other members of his "family" who perished—eight of his slaves—received no mention. It was noted only that his slave March survived. The home of Robert M. Withers on the northern end of North Island "crumbled to pieces like an eggshell" and was carried away with all its occupants. A family at their summer home on DeBordieu Island watched the Witherses' dwelling slip into the sea, its lighted lamps still illuminating the interior. Withers's wife, four daughters, a son, Withers Shackelford, Mr. Wish, a carpenter, and nine slaves perished. Robert Withers found himself floating in the ocean clinging to "a piece of lumber" or log with his slave Cudjo. He spoke to Cudjo, then heard his own son, MacQueen, call out, "Hold on father . . . we may be saved." A wave drove the wreckage of a house into them, and he never heard or saw his child again. Ocean swells washed Withers and Cudjo into the marsh grasses. Lieutenant Levy of the U.S. Navy, who was staying on nearby DeBordieu Island, waded in neck-deep to help them ashore.[83]

The hurricane moved rapidly over the islands, crashed into Georgetown, and then rolled over the plantations along the rivers emptying into Winyah Bay. In Georgetown the roof of the bank blew off, windows and doors of the sheriff's office exploded inward, and the four chimneys of the jail collapsed. At the courthouse, records in the clerk's office were destroyed. The room over the market used by the town council was damaged, as were private dwellings. Some described the town as "a scene of ruin and desolation."[84]

Along the Santee delta, the hurricane pushed a surging sea far up the North Santee and South Santee, the Sampit, the Pee Dee, the Black, and the Waccamaw rivers. The rivers heaved over their banks and smashed into the earthen dams surrounding the rice fields. The waters swept away flimsy slave cabins and drowned the occupants. The winds took roofs off plantation homes and barns. Recently harvested rice, stored or in the fields, was scattered. A family at Long Bay on the Waccamaw River, living in a substantial plantation home, experienced the terror of being engulfed by the hurricane:

Between 12 and 1 o'clock [in the morning, September 28] the wind became very high; we got up, secured the doors and windows . . . but the wind increased . . . it was a hurricane more violent than any that we had ever before witnessed. . . . Conceive the agony, the terror that seized us upon hearing the tremendous crash of the roof falling in and both piazzas torn away! The first impulse was to run out, but where could we run to? The water was upwards of three feet deep at the back piazza and in front the waves were breaking over the hill upon which our house stood. We remained in the house until it appeared to be giving way, when we rushed out upon the Sand Hills, but the wind was so violent that it was with difficulty we could stand our ground; after a while, when the wind had abated a little, we got into an outhouse, where we remained until morning. The tide fell about 3 o'clock—had it continued to rise one hour longer, the whole Island must have been swept away.[85]

On the South Santee River, the losses of Elias Horry reached $40,000 ($602,950), and those of the Rutledge family were "immense." The plantation of Colonel Vanderhorst was "in a state of ruin": the dwelling house unroofed, the barn and corn house blown over. Twenty-one of twenty-six slave cabins were destroyed, and water covered the harvested rice. The waters swept in and then away (down the North Santee River to the sea) twenty-three of ninety slaves on Hume's plantation and ruined three hundred acres of rice. At the Horry plantation, forty slaves lost their lives. Charles and Thomas Huggins, on a plantation located between the South Santee and North Santee, lost thirty-eight of forty-three slaves. Many other slaves working plantations along the rivers no doubt perished.[86] Ralph Izard of Charleston informed his mother in Philadelphia that along the "Santee very many lives have been lost and immense quantities of rice destroyed. Near Georgetown almost everything has been destroyed."[87]

The devastation and deaths on the low-lying islands and the destruction of plantations along rivers of the region attest to the violence of the winds in the right-front quadrant of the storm. The hurricane knocked trees down for forty miles along the Great Road running north from Georgetown. It took weeks to clear the way for carriage traffic. Estimates of loss in rice in the Georgetown area exceeded more than one-quarter of the crop. A contemporary estimated that on the islands, in Georgetown, and along the rivers damage to property alone reached $500,000 ($7,536,885). Three hundred people perished.[88]

To some, this estimate of human loss seemed low, especially as time passed. Years later in the popular mind it was remembered that thousands drowned in the "great hurricane" of 1822. One writer—who as a child of eleven was terrified by waves crashing against his family's house on the coast near Georgetown in 1822—recalled in his autobiography that thousands drowned, "mainly slaves," along the South Carolina coast.[89]

Immediately after the hurricane, the devastation moved one lowcountry author, known only as "M.P.," to describe it in a poem entitled, appropriately, "The Tempest":

Oceans of rain oppress the earth,
Or swell the sources of their birth;
Disdainful of the curbing shore,
Onward the foaming surges roar.
Strong barks the giant waves are lashing,
Now heav'nward toss'd, now downward dashing; . . .
By birds, ne'er vocal till the hour
Dark omens of the tempest lour [lower] . . .
To orphans and the waves we cherish'd
How, 'neath your scourge, their kindred perish'd;
A cry went up—the sound was hush'd,
As o'er the wreck wild waters rush'd.
Fallen in their pride are lofty oaks,
The dwarf-tree here our pathway chokes;
Relaxing roots lose their cement,
The shelter of the dome is rent; . . .
Now glancing beams of morning-light
Reveal the horrors of the night.
Commingling voices weep and pray,
That peril e'er may pass away,
And time alone produce decay.[90]

Cedar Island, nearly washed away by the hurricane, was abandoned as a summer resort for planters. Not far away another resort was founded at McClellanville, thought to be a safer location.[91] Many planters were ruined by the great storm: their rice and cotton crops destroyed, their slaves drowned, and their net worth greatly diminished. To prevent similar tragedies in future hurricanes, planters who could afford the expense built storm towers as places of refuge for slaves along the Santee rivers and on North Island.[92]

The intensity of winds and storm surge wrought a catastrophe on the upper South Carolina coast, especially in the region around Georgetown. Coastal Georgia escaped the hurricane of 1822, but two years later a small, fierce storm tracked north from the Bahamas. The southeastern coast was only six hundred miles away, an easy distance for a tropical storm to cover in three days. Vessels in its path or those living on the southeastern coast had little warning of its approach until it plunged ashore. It was a major hurricane.[93]

Catastrophe in Georgia, September 14–15, 1824

In the first hours of September 14 the immense tropical cyclone smashed into a fleet of nine British vessels forty to fifty miles off northern Florida, Georgia, and South Carolina. Out of Honduras and bound for Cork, the vessels carried logwood, mahogany, and other goods. One of them, the *Albion*, about forty miles southeast of Savannah near latitude 31° north, longitude 81° west, was knocked over by a gale from the northeast. One seaman was blown overboard, and the vessel lost its main and mizzenmasts, boats, bulwarks, and "everything" on deck. As the *Albion* appeared to be sinking, Captain Stephenson ordered his crew to lash themselves to the poop deck. Nearby, the ship *John and Mary* encountered a "severe hurricane." Captain Laughton watched a "tremendous sea" sweep the decks and carry away the first mate, the ship carpenter, and four seamen. Also lost were the small boats, cookhouse, and both topsails. Only four hands fit for duty remained, and the ship was heavily damaged. The following day, near evening on September 15, Captain Laughton spotted the *Albion* so low in the water that the sea was making a complete breach over her. Although his own ship was difficult to maneuver and a heavy sea was running, Laughton ordered his ship's lines made fast to the *Albion* and its fifteen crewmembers rescued. Captain Stephenson and eight crewmembers were hauled aboard the *John and Mary*, but the first mate lost his grip on the lines, fell, and drowned. Soon it became too dark to take the remaining six crewmembers off *Albion*, and the two ships parted.[94]

As the *John and Mary* drifted away in the dying light, the survivors on the *Albion* retied themselves to the poop deck, realizing they might not live to tell their harrowing tale. With the ship flooded and with no way of getting food from below deck, the crew caught rainwater. But as one day passed into another without food, they killed their pet monkey, Jacko, and ate the meat raw. Within five days the *Albion* drifted ashore off St. Catherines with its crew of "six poor fellows" who were then safe.[95]

The ship *Martha Forbes* of Boston, fifty to sixty miles southeast of Savannah, also battled a hurricane in the early part of September 14. Waves washed five crewmen overboard and upset the ship, making it "a complete wreck." Only its stern was visible above water. Captain Carman, apparently injured during the hurricane, and another surviving crewman lashed themselves to the taffrail. On the same evening and in the same vicinity, the hurricane bore down on the ship *West Indian*—another of the nine British ships in the fleet headed from Honduras to Cork. Huge waves and high winds took away all masts, its small boats, and the bowsprit. To stay afloat, Captain Mathews ordered part of the ship's cargo heaved overboard. Somehow the *West Indian* remained upright. Three days later, on September 17, Captain Mathews sighted the battered *Martha Forbes*. The surviving crewmember was taken off, but Captain Carman, still lashed to the railing on the upper deck, had died. He was buried at sea. Despite the efforts made by merchants at Charleston who had a financial stake in the *Martha Forbes* to have the vessel towed ashore, she eventually went aground on the shoals off Cumberland Island. Salvagers took off some cargo and sold it in St. Marys. The hull and the cargo of the battered *West Indian* were auctioned off: 120 barrels of coffee, 31 hogsheads of sugar, 6 barrels of ginger, and 54 tons of logwood.[96]

The brig *Wilding*, another vessel in the British fleet sailing from Honduras for Cork, carrying logwood and mahogany, took the hurricane in twenty-two fathoms of water off Charleston. The brig "sprang a leak," and seawater poured in faster than the pumps could discharge it. Within a few hours the *Wilding* became "waterlogged" and "fell over on her side," drowning two seamen and the cabin boy. The remainder of the crew clung to her sides until the vessel righted. Without her masts, which had torn away, the *Wilding* was "level with the top of the water," and the sea broke over her. The crew constructed a raft and abandoned the sinking brig. The pilot boat *Friends* picked up the survivors at sea and brought them into Charleston. Twenty-five days after the hurricane struck the fleet of nine British ships bound for Cork, eight were accounted for—six sank or became floating derelicts, and two reached port safely. The ninth was unaccounted for.[97]

As the hurricane approached the lowcountry's coast on Tuesday, September 14, the weather, "heavy and threatening" for days, deteriorated. Winds increased until they "blew a hurricane." In the morning hours of September 15 the center of the "small, savage hurricane" crashed ashore near St. Simons Island and Darien.[98]

It drove vessels just offshore onto beaches and battered those in the rivers and at wharves. The wreckage of a brig and a bottom-up schooner came ashore on St. Catherines Island. Slaves from a neighboring plantation cut a hole in the schooner's bottom and took away a quantity of goods.[99] Just below Savannah, along the river, "very severe" winds drove two schooners onto Cockspur Island and blew the schooner *Jane* and the brig *Caroline Ann* into one another, damaging both. The schooner *Maria* was cut in two by a sloop and "entirely lost." The ship *Emperor*, out of New York, collided with a brig, and the pilot boat *Vexation* was driven up Stile's Creek. Another brig, *Governor Hopkins*, was carried into a rice field. A yawl with the markings "Bush, New York" was found on the beach; the discovery of pieces of another yawl indicated that "all on board perished." A vessel was spotted on the South Edisto shoal with only her mast showing above water, and another wreck was seen south of Charleston's lighthouse, near Folly Beach. Just off Bull's Island, around midnight, the schooner *Hunter* "shipped a heavy sea" and was knocked over into the breakers. With waves breaking over the schooner, Captain Lee of New Bern, North Carolina, ordered the crew to abandon ship. They survived, but the *Hunter* grounded on sandbars, severely damaging its hull.[100]

The hurricane, like the one of 1804, devastated the low-lying islands of the Altamaha delta—St. Simons, Jekyll, Wolf, and Sapelo—as well as others nearby and the port of Darien. Throughout the early evening of September 14, high winds drove booming waves onto the sea islands. Around 1:30 a.m. the winds subsided briefly as the eye passed and then blew hard again from the southeast head-on against the beaches with torrential rains. At Jekyll Island a storm surge of six feet flooded into the fields and ruined Christopher DuBignon's cotton crop, drowned his cattle, and uprooted live oaks. The scale of the devastation to DuBignon's property exceeded that of the three previous storms he had endured. Winds and seawater so battered his buildings that it took months to repair the damage.[101]

On Little St. Simons Island a hundred sheep drowned. Creeks burst their banks. Pushed by high winds, the water raced over St. Simons Island to cover the island, drowning eighty-three people.[102] Slave cabins collapsed and were swept away or left uninhabitable. Carriage houses caved in, crushing carriages, wagons, and carts and killing and maiming horses. Winds unroofed or damaged dwellings of planters and their families—the Coupers, Butlers, Grants, Hamiltons, Demeres, Pages, Matthewses, Hazzards, and James Goulds. Water, in places four feet deep, covered crops of cotton, rice, and corn. At John Couper's Cannon's Point plantation, the sea swamped the entire point, sweeping away buildings and ruining gardens. Couper's entire cotton crop was ruined—six hundred bales worth $90,000 ($1,638,713). Rains, winds, and waves damaged all the buildings at the village of Frederica on St. Simons and carried away those of the Blounts, forcing the family into an open field for preservation. The village of St. Simons was wrecked. Only the lighthouse and the dwelling there survived the surging ocean. Mrs. Page and her family were at Retreat Plantation when the sea itself crashed around them and their dwelling. Waters carried away the slave hospital, storehouse, carriage house, and cotton and corn houses as well as livestock. On Wolf Island a tidal surge smashed in one of the beacons and swept off the light keeper's house. The keeper and his family ran for safety to the lantern of the brick beacon, where they remained for thirty-six hours without food or water. They survived. A six-foot-high wall of water swept across Sapelo Island, and high winds smashed in the lighthouse lantern. Thomas Spalding was on the mainland as his wife huddled in a darkened room of South End House with an infant, three daughters, and "trembling guests." Because the plantation house was "low, massive, thick-walled and flat-roofed," everyone inside survived; other people in less-protected cabins on the island did not. The ocean also drowned Spalding's 250 cattle, 27 horses and mules, and his sheep, and saltwater covered all his crops. The losses for Spalding reached $50,000 ($910,396). On nearby Black Island, just east of Darien, the hurricane destroyed Spalding's crops and slave cabins. Some of his slaves saved themselves by climbing trees. The hurricane also destroyed the crops on Champney Island, Butler's Island, and Brailsford Island.[103]

The high winds raking St. Catherines Island destroyed the slave cabins and the entire cotton crop of George Waldburg. In the neighborhood around Darien in the Altamaha basin, the fierce storm destroyed crops and smashed into plantation homes on low-lying Patterson and Creighton islands. Five miles northeast of Darien on Crum's Creek, William Carnochan, a migrant from Jamaica, at his plantation, The Thicket, saw his profitable sugar mill and rum distillery destroyed. Carnochan did not rebuild. He died a year later. Most of his slaves saved themselves by taking refuge in the lofty cane-pressing mill.[104]

While the great storm was destroying buildings, farm animals, and crops, great human tragedies occurred. The grandson of Captain Demere, twenty-year-old Raymond Demere, and five slaves attempting to return from Darien to St. Simons during the storm drowned when their boat capsized. On Sapelo Island, Mr. Gould saw two of his children dashed from his arms and carried into the sea. Here too, on Thomas Spalding's plantation, the sea drowned six slaves and the overseer's two sons and father.[105]

On the seaboard near Darien, a planter and his family watched sheets of rain and "wild clouds" move in from the sea. Upon nightfall "the heavens . . . blackened," and "the wind began . . . blowing a gale from" the northeast. Its "violence became alarming" as it turned into "a perfect hurricane with constant beating rain intermixed with the salt sprays from the river . . . desolation and ruin pressed upon every mind. Trees, fences, chimnies . . . were . . . crushed and prostrated." "All that we had," the planter later related,

[was] swept away including . . . crop[s] except our dwelling houses, kitchen, and two or three negro houses. At this time fearful that our house would go, I attempted to secure a way of retreat, but in this I was baffled, for the rolling tide had already surrounded us, and flowed full two feet around our dwelling; thus situated, we assembled all in one small part of the house, the most dry and there, without a murmur, committed ourselves, our lives, and all that we had, to Him who "Rides upon the whirlwind and directs the storm" [which] about 11:00 o'clock changed to [southeast] and the tide began to recede . . . and our apprehensions gradually subsided. The balance of the night, still filled with anxiety we passed in anxious expectation for ourselves . . . until the dawn . . . revived our . . . almost despairing minds, and the returning sun soon enabled us to leave our "Storm beat ark" to view our desolation — and now the gale has passed, the danger's o'er.[106]

At J. Snow's plantation on the seaboard, seven miles from Darien, the hurricane brought a tidal surge that carried the slave cabins and the plantation house into the Altamaha River. Five slaves drowned. The occupants of the plantation house struggled to keep their heads above water. Rufus R. Merrill, engaged to Miss Carolina Harrison, reached to save her but came away with just a piece of her clothing, and both drowned; Miss Harrison's younger brothers, Samuel and Independence Harrison, also perished, as did Mr. Snow's youngest child. Mr. Snow survived by clinging to a tree until the waters receded; his wife held on to wreckage and floated safely to a neighboring plantation. The tidal surge on Patterson Island drowned a widow, Mrs. Lafong, twelve of her slaves, a Mrs. Chase and her young child, and two slaves. Two young Irishmen working on the island cheated death by swimming creeks and wading through the marshes to the mainland, where they were "liquored extensively." Nearby on Captain Hudson's plantation eleven slaves drowned. On Creighton Island, at John Miller's plantation, Thomas Miller, about seventeen, and another hand working the plantation, the overseer, and five slaves died by drowning or when the dwelling house collapsed on them. Dozens more perished or remained unaccounted for near Darien.[107]

In the town itself, the hurricane destroyed King's, G. Atkinson's, and H. T. Hall's stores along with several houses and most fences and trees. The sloop *Two Friends*, tied at the dock on Darien's waterfront, "went to pieces," and another was blown ashore. The tile roof of the rice mill blew off. Also unroofed was the sawmill; its sheet lead gutters weighing five hundred pounds were carried about forty feet away. One resident observed, "Nothing appears around us here but a scene of destruction." Surprisingly, in Darien no one died. However, estimates of those who perished on the islands and along the seacoast in the neighborhood of Darien ranged from eighty-three to more than a hundred. Financial losses in the vicinity of Darien alone were estimated to be $1,000,000 ($18,207,920). Many said the hurricane was worse than the one of 1804, and a bill was introduced in the legislature seeking relief for the sufferers along the entire Georgia coast.[108]

The storm moved inland but continued wreaking havoc northward along the coast. At Sunbury the wind and sea devastated crops and smashed carriages, outbuildings, and chimneys. Horses drowned. The Sunbury Academy building was "nearly torn to pieces," and the spire knocked off the meeting house. On nearby Colonel's Island, the surging waters from the river drowned Edward and Philip Bacon, and two slaves died in the same neighborhood. Closer to Savannah, at Ossabaw Island, wind and water destroyed the crops, barns, and slave cabins of the Morel and the N.G. Rutherford families. On Burnside Island, most of the houses belonging to R.F. Williams, along with his crops, were swept away. At Skidaway Island the seawater submerged the entire cotton and corn crop as well as the garden and swirled around the "fancy trees" on R.M. Goodwin's plantation.[109]

In Savannah, when the weather became "threatening" on the afternoon of September 14, it was thought prudent to evacuate slaves, women, and children from Hutchinson Island to the city to prevent a recurrence of the many drownings that had occurred there during the hurricane of 1804. Indeed, that night when hurricane winds began driving the Back and Savannah rivers together over the island, many of the male slaves remaining on the island struggled to escape drowning. Floodwaters and winds severely damaged plantation houses and stores and the rice crop on low-lying Hutchinson Island. "It was an awful night" for Savannah's residents. The ship *Augusta* at wharfside capsized, vessels collided, and the Union Ferry Wharf washed away. The crashing noises of hundreds of the ornamental trees in the city — "our summer friends" — could be heard at the peak of the storm. Winds blew over several houses at Yamacraw and tore slate from the roofs of the county jail, warehouses, stores, and dwellings — the J. Davenport and T.N. Morel houses especially suffered. Chimneys fell through roofs of some houses. Four miles from the town, at Elba Island, in the middle of the Savannah River, floodwaters at the Shad family's plantation swept away the cotton house, gins, slave cabins, kitchen, and crops. Slaves survived by climbing into the loft of the overseer's house. At plantations of the well-to-do — the Elliotts, McLeods, Bonds, Habershams, Screvens, and Daniells — along the banks of the Ogeechee and Savannah rivers, slave cabins collapsed, crops washed away, and some "valuable negroes" drowned. Other slaves saved themselves by clinging to wreckage until the waters subsided.[110]

The hurricane knocked over trees outside the city, and raging rivers tore away bridges to the north and south as the cyclone moved as far inland as Augusta and within fifteen miles of Louisville, "where the ravages [were] very visible." Communications with the world beyond Savannah were temporarily cut off. No estimate of the damage was attempted, but it was assumed by the local press that the hurricane caused "considerable pecuniary distress" to the community. Damage to the pride of India trees was so complete that workers hauled away over 1,680 wagon- and cartloads of trunks and limbs. Happily the press reported two days after the hurricane that there was as yet "no loss of life" in the city. It was a major hurricane on the Georgia coast.[111]

Just across the state line and into South Carolina, winds, rains, and flooding from the May River in the Beaufort District combined to destroy unpicked corn and cotton crops. In the town of Beaufort there was damage to the wharves, and crops in the vicinity were underwater from rains accompanying the "violent" gale. On Edisto Island a planter saw "stalks of cotton stripped bare of leaves and pods." He thought that planters would lose half their crop. Freshets tore away bridges at Tulifinny and Pocotaligo. Every bridge went down between the Combahee and Purysburg.[112]

At Charleston winds from the hurricane increased throughout the evening hours until they reached maximum force on September 15 around 2:00 a.m. At dockside the schooner *Burrows* carrying lumber sank, and the stern of the schooner *James Madison* was "stove in" when winds drove it into Fitzsimons's Wharf. Damage to shipping was "trifling," one reporter witnessed, because the highest winds of the hurricane struck on a low tide. Winds ripped slates off roofs and felled trees in the city. But as reports eventually came in from south of the city, Charlestonians recognized that the great "violence" of the hurricane came at the expense of those southward.[113]

To the north, Georgetown witnesses claimed that a tidal surge rolled over North Island at the mouth of the Waccamaw River equal to that of 1822. Waters were high enough in Georgetown to paddle a canoe along Bay Street. Hurricane winds and freshets ruined crops along the North Santee and South Santee rivers, and it was feared that the rice crop in the region might "be entirely destroyed." Some believed that the 1824 hurricane caused "total destruction" to the crops in southern Georgia. In South Carolina it was predicted that the crops would "fall far short of what had been anticipated." One reporter reckoned that planters on the "immense plantations in the swamps and low grounds, which have been totally covered with water," would lose their "entire crop." Planters also suffered huge losses in farm animals. One witness reported that while paddling through the swamps in a canoe, he saw the "floating dead bodies" of cattle and hogs and blamed planters for neglecting to move their livestock to higher ground.[114]

The enormous human and economic toll of the hurricane of 1824 in the low-country was incalculable even for contemporaries. Certainly the captains and crews of sailing vessels lost at sea and the loss of people ashore must have exceeded 150. The hurricane, unlike that of 1822, when the most damaging winds slammed into South Carolina's Santee delta, crashed into Georgia's Altamaha delta. Georgia planters, like those of coastal South Carolina two years earlier, lost their families, slaves, homes, livestock, crops, livelihoods, and lives.

After twelve hurricanes came ashore between 1800 and 1824, an average of one almost every two years, planters along the lowcountry coast began reevaluating their lives. They wondered why they persisted in planting. For various reasons some gave it up. Others decided to stay.

CHAPTER FOUR

Last Storms

of the Cycle,

1825–1837

A Time of Reckoning

The tropical storms and cyclones that battered the lowcountry during the devastating cycle from 1800 to 1824 ruined and embittered some planters who had given up rice and cotton cultivation. Others who declared bankruptcy remained to plant again. They had their reasons. After the 1824 hurricane, a planter in South Carolina's Santee River delta sounded defeated when he declared, "freshets have overwhelmed us. We shall be ruined. I had prospects a fortnight ago of reaping the toils of years of labor, but they are all blasted."[1]

Hurricanes tested the faith of some. A disconsolate planter on St. Simons Island described the aftermath of the 1824 storm: "[a] horrible devastation and ruin that has cast a general gloom on our land, despoiled our homes and disappointed our hopes. . . . [We are] now alas! wrapt in desolation and ruin. Gracious God! 'How mysterious are thy ways.'"[2]

Even among the ruins, other planters found hope and consolation in their religion. A Georgia planter on Hurd's Island, whose land was devastated by the hurricane of 1824, lost all his wooden buildings save one, his crops, poultry, and cattle, his store and his still. Indeed, when he and his sister attempted to take refuge in the mill house, the hurricane's wind and water prevented them going forward or backward, and they nearly drowned. The only reason his slaves did not perish was because he had moved them into the sturdiest house on the island, the only one left standing. But then he wondered in an open letter to the Savannah press:

What a serious, ruinous business this is for we unfortunate seaboard planters — was I not inured to disappointments, I should be more depressed I believe than I am, although this almost renders me hopeless, so far as relates to pecuniary matters, yet I still see great reasons to be thankful its no worse and so resigned. We must try again, but I fear some of us will have the means wrested from us, but as Burns says, "Lord be Thanked. I can plough."[3]

A Darien planter also found comfort in his religion. He and his family huddled together as waves beat against their home. They waited "with humble resignation the will of our Father in Heaven . . . whether to live or die." And then all their "lives [were] . . . saved through God's own power. . . . Oh may our hearts be filled with . . . love to Him who rules below, and reigns supreme above."[4]

John Couper, who owned vast cotton and rice lands worked by several hundred slaves at Cannon's Point plantation on St. Simons and at Hopeton Plantation above Darien, suffered enormous crop and property damages in the 1824 hurricane. The following year caterpillars devoured his cotton crop, and the price of cotton dropped sharply. Land values plunged by one-third, as did the price of slaves, who now sold on average for about $225 ($4,017). In 1827, at age fifty-two, Couper wrote, "I was . . . without a dollar to support my people or family." Facing bankruptcy, he was obliged to surrender Hopeton — worth over $160,000 ($2,829,231) — and 380 slaves to his principal creditor. He retained Cannon's Point and one hundred slaves. By satisfying his debts in this manner,

Couper told his brother, "neither my standing in society, nor my mode of living have suffered any change."[5] Couper may have had additional reasons for continuing to plant on a sea island subject to devastating hurricanes, but certainly important reasons were the prestige accorded him as a large planter — he retained a continuing stake not only in the land but also in the lifestyle that went with it.

Despite the catastrophic damages that Thomas Spalding suffered in 1824, his reason for returning to plant again and again on Sapelo and Black islands was love of place. He found that the climate and indefinable atmosphere of the sea islands carried "more men into old age, than any other [he knew] of; [on the sea islands, there had] been little change of inhabitants for 100 years . . . the son clinging to the home of his childhood, and to the grave of his father." Coastal Georgians, Spalding believed, were "less anxious after change . . . than their countrymen."[6] Of course, Spalding like other planters gambled: "The weather to the planter . . . was the great unknown; his prosperity or ruin rested on the weather. No other occupation was such a gamble."[7]

Christophe DuBignon gambled too. He had survived three hurricanes on Jekyll Island, but the one of 1824 was the most devastating to his property and crops. For five years he had tried unsuccessfully to sell his homeplace and island. At age eighty-five he was tired. Within a year he died. Other cotton planters were defeated for the same reasons — volatile prices, caterpillars, and hurricanes.[8]

In the early 1820s the golden age of the lowcountry's rice lords was ending. Labor costs had increased as competition grew from Southeast Asia's rice producers in the major markets for rice. At the same time, a relative decline in the region's population was accompanied by declines in output, trade, and wealth. But the rice lords remained single-mindedly devoted to a plantation economy based on the cultivation of rice. With 50 percent of the lowcountry's wealth invested in human capital (slaves), there was precious little left to invest elsewhere. Furthermore, the fragile, sickly area of swamps, bogs, and sea islands was not thought conducive to other crops. Because the lowcountry's major ports were only satellites of northern ones, no interests developed in investing in manufacturing locally. Another factor that affected the region's prosperity was the lack of in-migration. Those who did come to the lowcountry usually came from abroad. Undoubtedly they knew less about the diseases, climate, and hurricanes than did the residents of neighboring states whose migration to Georgia slowed.[9] Lowcountry boosters, however, tried to counter any negative publicity about the region following the disastrous hurricanes of 1822 and 1824.

Local papers touted bright prospects for the future and even attempted to lure immigrants. The Savannah press boasted that the export-import trade was booming and that trade was increasing with the interior of the state. "These things augur well for the prosperity of our city," local editors projected. The *Darien Gazette* portrayed Darien as a growing export center where "stores and dwellings are daily multiplying . . . which would do credit to any of the Northern cities. Here the emigrant would find every encouragement to settle and the adventurer a ready market to vend his good."[10] Yet boosterism could not gloss over the facts: tropical storms and cyclones continued to sweep out of the West Indies and along a path toward coastal Georgia and South Carolina, sometimes inflicting vast destruction.

A rare early June tropical storm, with gusts perhaps reaching hurricane force, followed a familiar path in 1825. It apparently came out of the West Indies, struck the Florida coast near St. Augustine about June 3, and swirled up the coast. Captain Pitcher of the schooner *Magnolio*, en route to Savannah, navigated "tremendous seas" off the Florida coast, where damage was "severe." He saw large seabirds, unable to use their wings, blown great distances through the air and dropped into the sea. Far offshore, southeast of Savannah, the hurricane wrecked the schooner *Samuel Smith*. It was damaged so severely that the crew jammed blankets, mattresses, and tarpaulins into the shattered hull to prevent its sinking. Directly off Savannah the captain of the *Jane* spotted a schooner of sixty to seventy tons about six miles away with its foremast gone and apparently sinking, as it soon disappeared without a trace.[11]

Outlying winds of the storm swept St. Marys and Cumberland Island without causing major damage. But on the afternoon of June 3 northeast winds reached gale force at Tybee Island and blew the pilot boat *Georgia Ann* ashore on Potato Point near Cockspur Island. "Very heavy" rains and winds "considerably injured" the cotton crops in the countryside. At Georgetown, South Carolina, the "boisterous" early June weather damaged what had been "very promising" corn crops.[12]

The hurricane swept northward into North Carolina, causing vast destruction, and continued to batter the coast all the way to New England. The lowcountry had escaped mostly unscathed from this rare, very early, and very powerful tropical storm.[13]

In August 1827 a great storm smashed into St. Kitts, Nevis, the Virgin Islands, and Puerto Rico and recurved eastward after passing Haiti. For three days, August 23–25, the storm's track remained off the Florida, Georgia, and South Carolina coasts, where it bashed vessels at sea. The ship *Lavinia,* out of New York and loaded with merchandise and produce for New Orleans, was caught in a "tremendous cross-sea." Captain Waterman ordered the mizzenmast cut away and then the topmast. Still the ship labored, pitching off huge waves and then wallowing in the trough of the sea while the crew tried to work its "pumps . . . all the time." Waves and high winds carried away the ship's small boats and wheel blocks and even bolts from the deck. The ship was literally coming apart. Only the dying of the highest winds saved the vessel. Waterman ordered jury sails rigged and a heading set for Charleston, which the *Lavinia* eventually reached safely.[14]

At about the same time, the ship *Brandt,* out of Charleston and bound for New York with twenty-five passengers, encountered the fury of the gale at latitude 34° north, longitude 17° west, far off the northernmost coast of South Carolina. Captain G. W. Steinhauer reported that the wind "blew a perfect hurricane" and that all his sails "gave way" until he was under "bare poles" and being swept by a strong current and winds southwestwardly. Passengers believed they "had only faint hopes of surviving." Within a day the ship was in sixty feet of water, and the ocean began breaking over it from all directions. Captain Steinhauer watched the sea "changing its colour from blue to yellow by stirring up the mud, and the force of the wind carrying off the tops of the seas." All the while "there was a continual torrent of water pouring in a horizontal direction as if 100 engines were playing on the ship — it was impossible to look to windward." The cabin boy, Stephen Smith, age fourteen, was washed overboard. With nine feet of water in the hold, all passengers and crew took to the pumps. They manned the pumps for two days, until they became too exhausted to continue. Seawater continued flooding the hold. Only a "Providential" westward shift of the wind saved the vessel. One passenger believed that another two days at sea and the *Brandt* "would have foundered." Captain Steinhauer praised his male passengers: "without [their] assistance . . . I should have been obliged to run the ship on shore." Aided by French frigate *La Circe*, the *Brandt* eventually reached the port of Norfolk, Virginia.[15]

Off Cape Romain in late August, Captain Smith, aboard the schooner *Mary Ellen* of Baltimore, spotted an "Eastern built schooner" adrift. Its foremast was gone, a piece of canvas was nailed to its mainmast, and there was no one aboard. A day later the *Mary Ellen*, loaded with corn and sailing thirty miles east of Cape Romain, was hit by a gale of wind from the north-northeast and knocked over by a huge sea. When the vessel did not right itself, Captain Smith ordered the foremast cut away, and the *Mary Ellen* came up, but its flying jib boom was gone and its foresail split. Under jury-rigged sails, the schooner reached Charleston.[16]

The schooner *Solon*, from New Orleans under Captain Tarr, encountered the fierce August hurricane off the South Carolina or Georgia coast. As the schooner fought its way, pitching and rolling through the storm, a huge sea broke over the vessel, washing overboard every crewmember except Captain Tarr and one other. After drifting for five days aboard the wrecked *Solon*, Captain Tarr and his crewmember were rescued by the schooner *Mary Eleanor* of Savannah. Having lost his vessel and all but one of his crew, Captain Tarr died a day later from "excessive fatigue."[17]

The eye of the hurricane was well off Charleston on August 25, 1827, but the wind blew "with great violence" for six hours that afternoon. Fortunately damage in the harbor, city, and environs was slight, since the winds had reached their highest velocity at low tide. The powerful August blow finally came ashore near Hatteras, North Carolina, sinking vessels off the Outer Banks. Its heavy rains and high winds and tides caused massive damage far inland until it recurved seaward and headed northeasterly, eventually reaching New England.[18]

The summer of 1830 was unusually hot and dry in the lowcountry. Occasionally, violent lightning and thunderstorms accompanied the heat. In August a hurricane tracked out of the West Indies on a path that threatened the southeastern coast of the United States. By Sunday, August 15, a "very severe . . . very violent" gale was blowing from the northeast off St. Augustine. Orange trees and fences went down in and around the city. If tides had been high, the damage would have been greater. The hurricane moved north. By Monday morning its winds and rains blew violently across the length of the lowcountry.[19]

William Ogilby, the British Consul at Charleston, who was on Sullivan's Island, recorded in his journal, "it has been blowing a severe gale, and this morning [Monday, August 16] it has increased to a complete hurricane." He thought that at any moment his "house would come down about [his] ears, for it rocked like a cradle and creaked dreadfully." He "stood all day almost at the side of [his] hall door ready to make a bolt, should anything happen." Like many who lived in or visited the lowcountry, Ogilby believed that "this is certainly not a country for anyone to come to whose nerves cannot stand the 'war of the elements.'" Meanwhile offshore, British and other vessels battled those very "elements."[20]

The hurricane crashed into the British bark New Prospect somewhere off Georgia on August 15–16. Bound from Jamaica to London with a "very valuable cargo" of sugar, coffee, and rum, the vessel was so badly damaged that it began to sink. It was rescued sixty miles off the Charleston light by the schooner Wade, another vessel that sustained damage from the hurricane. Twenty crewmembers and passengers were taken off, and the New Prospect was abandoned. Subsequently it was boarded at sea by salvagers, pumped out, and towed up the Savannah River to Savannah to be sold. The Wade transported the crew and passengers of the New Prospect to Charleston, where William Ogilby met them, furnished clothes, and arranged for their accommodations. Several days later Captain Miller and Lieutenants Griffith and Henderson of the New Prospect dined with Consul Ogilby on Sullivan's Island, where he "gave them lots of Champagne and Madeira, and sent them off in very good spirits."[21]

The ship Empress, sailing twelve days out of New York for Charleston with merchandise and more than sixty passengers aboard, encountered the hurricane in the early morning of August 17 off the southeastern coast of North Carolina. The great storm shredded the ship's canvas, swept the decks of cargo and small boats, and knocked it on its larboard side. The ship lay with its sails in the water for over two hours. Miraculously, no one was lost, the vessel eventually righted, and its commander, Captain Sinclair, continued for Charleston. En route, Sinclair spotted "a large quantity of wrecked material . . . such as planks, and spars" and passed several vessels "in distress."[22]

Near Bull's Island, South Carolina, a vessel out of Baltimore, thought to be the schooner Ranger, was dismasted and generally wrecked. It was abandoned when found by the pilot boat Friends out of Charleston. Only a few personal items were discovered aboard: "a lady's linen and gown, a piece of ribbon, and a linen shirt with the initials M.T."[23]

Captains sailing to port passed floating wreckage from Boston to Georgia. Some claimed it was the worst hurricane they had ever experienced at sea. A Savannah newspaper observed that the "disasters at sea . . . have been very numerous . . . we much fear from a number of vessels and parts of vessels being seen, bottom up, drifting, etc. that their hapless crews have perished, as no boat could live in a tempest such as this is described to have been."[24] At some places in the lowcountry devastation to crops and property exceeded that from the hurricanes of 1822 and 1824.

The hurricane swirled across the coastal waters of Georgia. Even though it remained off the coast, the winds blew violently at Savannah, first from the southeast and then the northwest on August 15–16.[25] Houses were unroofed, and shade trees went down. Tides crested several feet above normal, and seawater covered most of Hutchinson Island. Saltwater broke through banks surrounding the rice crop, ruining two-thirds of it. On the basis of past experience, slaves were evacuated from Hutchinson Island plantations to Savannah for their safety. It was the first time in twenty years, the press noted, that "the river was salt at the city."[26]

From Darien to Charleston about one-fifth of the rice crop was lost, and one-half of the sea island cotton crop was destroyed. The *Georgian* observed that before the gale planters had predicted "a profitable reward to their labors" and the "cheerful prospect of repaying to some degree the disappointments and losses of last season when but half a crop was made." Afterward the sea island cotton crop presented "a hopeless prospect."[27]

As the hurricane moved closer to the mainland, the destruction of crops increased. A writer at Beaufort, South Carolina, declared that the Monday gale "prostrated the hopes of the Planter. Many experienced planters compute the loss at two-thirds of the [cotton] crop." From planters on nearby St. Helena Island came word: "[The] cotton is ruined by the gale. Scarce a green leaf is left, and what remains, bears the appearance of a field, that after caterpillars, or a heavy frost, had passed over it." Another wrote, "the cotton is so battered and bruised that my expectations are less by two-thirds than what they were the last week." And as for other crops, it was said, "The corn is all prostrate and the potatoes much blighted." The destruction was the same on other sea islands: Hilton Head, Lemon, Parris, Daw's (Dataw), and Lady's.[28]

To the west, separated by a causeway from Edisto Island, tiny Edingsville Island faced the open Atlantic. For fifteen hours it was pounded by the hurricane. When the ocean threatened to spill over Edingsville, its residents fled their beach houses in "carts, gigs, and carriages." Men accompanied "a bevy of ladies" on foot "through mire" and the "peltings of the pitiless storm" to dwellings on higher ground. The islanders believed that they "experienced a storm in violence but little inferior to the destructive one of 1813." More than a century later Edingsville would face a more deadly and fierce hurricane.[29]

Nearer Charleston, on Johns and James islands, "the storm was very violent," and the damage to the crops, fences, and out buildings was extensive. A planter on James Island said that two-thirds of the cotton and corn crops were destroyed. "Happily," no lives were lost.[30]

At Charleston the winds blew hard out of the southeast for two days and then increased in force on Monday, August 16. The wind blew "violently" after daybreak but moderated as the eye passed far offshore, and then hurricane-force winds resumed from the northeast, then from the northwest, and continued until 4:00 p.m. At the height of the storm "the sea was breaking over the wharves in every direction" and causing "disasters among the shipping." At Gibbs Wharf the ship *Rasselas* broke its fasts and smashed into and sank the brig *Atlantic*, which was loaded with two hundred pounds of sugar. Both the *Atlantic* and its cargo were a total loss. The ship *Washington* broke loose from her anchorage in the Cooper River and crashed into Kiddell's Dock. The schooner *Experiment* foundered at Chisolm's Wharf, and the Spanish brig *Carolatta*, loading at Edmundsons's Wharf, broke her fasts and was propelled into a brig, carrying away its starboard bulwarks. Other schooners, sloops, and smaller craft suffered damages. Some sank with their cargoes. The ship *Othello* and the brig *Pocahontas* sustained heavy damage when wind and waves drove them onto shell banks. As in other storms, high winds downed trees and blew slate from house roofs. Flying debris injured some, but no deaths or serious injuries occurred. Charleston, like Savannah, escaped significant damage, because the hurricane stayed miles off the coast. Georgetown and its nearby plantations were to take the brunt of the storm. For the third time in less than a decade, 1822, 1824, and now 1830, a hurricane swerved inland close to South Carolina's northernmost port town.[31]

Heavy rains and high winds from the southeast began buffeting the region around Georgetown about an hour before daybreak on Monday, August 16.

A planter on Crow Island, near the mouth of the North Santee River, watched drenching rain showers come and go throughout the morning; by noon the wind was blowing "a hurricane," and it increased on Monday night: "The tide rose higher than I ever saw it; my rice is entirely lost. You cannot imagine the destruction; my fields of rice that looked on Saturday as flourishing as I could wish them, are today perfectly red from the effects of salt water and the wind. The tide was over all my banks in every direction; . . . my neighbors have all fared as badly as myself; every vessel on the river is blown ashore."[32]

Off Georgetown, waves crashed over the beach at North Island, but no houses were washed away or lives lost as in the previous hurricanes. The storm came ashore north of Georgetown, with its highest winds coinciding with peak high tide. Blowing first southeast then southwest the winds pushed the flood tides into rice plantations on Winyah Bay and along the North Santee, South Santee, Waccamaw, Black, Pee Dee, and Sampit rivers. Water "as salt as the ocean" rushed up the rivers, breaking through embankments surrounding the rice fields and flooding them up to four feet. The devastation was so complete that twenty rice plantations on Winyah Bay made little more than seed. Planters on the rivers, the Georgetown press observed, "will not make more than half a [rice] crop and some not more than a fifth." Damage to the rice was greater than that during the fierce hurricane of 1822. Wooden rice trunks (tide gates in the fields) were washed from the embankments of rice fields and into Winyah Bay. Cotton and corn crops were also ruined.[33] About the major cash crop, a writer in the *Southern Agriculturist* at Charleston wrote, "the destruction of the [rice] crop would exceed anything of the kind within the recollection of the oldest inhabitant."[34]

Georgetown's paper, the *Winyaw Intelligencer*, hoped that the planters had learned something this time from the terrible experience:

Perhaps some good may come out of this evil. It may turn the attention of our planters to the best modes of making and *protecting* their [earthen] banks, and to *investigating* whether something better than the present rude and artificial system may not be adopted. We must express our belief, that with a small comparative expense of time and labor, a great portion of the present devastation might have been avoided. The use of fascines, and on an *advanced* protection to the banks in exposed spots, is becoming every year more necessary.[35]

Planters, however, continued to plant and cultivate rice in the fashion of their fathers.

The costs of the financial catastrophes at sea and ashore in the hurricanes of the late 1820s and 1830 are again unrecorded. The latter storm took many lives on the open ocean. Ashore damage to cotton and rice crops and falling prices most likely caused some smaller planters, especially those on the sea islands, to abandon cotton and rice growing. Besides the continuing threats from hurricanes, short-staple cotton was now being grown over vast reaches of upcountry Georgia and South Carolina, creating new competition with the long-staple variety of the sea islands. Only four years after the hurricane of 1830 destroyed the crops around Georgetown (and just as they were recovering), another devastating storm came ashore in the same area.

On Thursday, September 4, 1834, the gale struck Georgetown. Punishing winds at a flood tide drove ashore the schooners *Maria* and *John Stoney*, the sloop *Exchange*, and the brig *Francis Ann*. The schooner *Comet*, carrying forty hogsheads of coffee and sugar, sank at wharfside. Seawater crashed over the port's wharves and flooded warehouses along the river.[36] The tides pushed inland as far as "the eye could reach, [and] the fields were covered, and but for the appearance here and there of a tree . . . , we could not have known that valuable plantations lay under the overwhelming waters," the editor of the local paper wrote. Compared with the hurricanes of 1804 and 1822, he told readers, the recent "gale is unparalleled . . . for duration and loss of every sort, except life."[37]

In mid-September 1835 a storm came out of the West Indies, smashed into South Florida, and meandered into the Gulf of Mexico. The storm eventually recurved to the northeast, spun across West Florida, and began a path northward and inland. Over the next week its center moved across Georgia, South Carolina, and far into New England. From September 15 to 18, southeast and northeast gale-force winds and rains lashed shipping off the coast of the lowcountry and crops ashore.[38]

The brig *Frances Sophia*, with a cargo of lumber, encountered fierce winds in the Gulf Stream off South Carolina on September 15. The vessel sprung a leak, and Captain Cannon ordered crewmen to keep two pumps working. But the incoming water gained on that being pumped out, and the vessel was "completely at the mercy of the winds and waves." To save his crew Captain Cannon grounded the vessel at Sandy Point near Cape Romain, South Carolina; they abandoned the vessel for small boats and safely made the mainland.[39]

Off Tybee Island the "great gale" ripped into the ship *Newark*, crammed with passengers sailing from New York to Savannah. It blew her "to pieces," and as the ship drifted fast and dangerously close to shore, some "expected . . . the loss of all on board." Later, passengers praised the extraordinary seamanship of Captain Bennett and his crew for saving the ship and their lives. In Savannah rains flooded the streets. High winds took away the decayed branches of the chinaberry trees injured in the hurricane of 1824 and tore away limbs from recently planted trees, the "beautiful . . . ornaments of our city." Saltwater tides inundated rice fields on the Hutchinson Island property of the Sapelo Island planter Thomas Spalding and flooded the fields of the Shad plantation on Elba Island. It came ashore as a tropical storm, likely with even higher gusts. In some areas the storm caused significant damage to the cotton crops. A planter in Liberty County, Georgia, thought the cotton "seriously injured" and estimated half his crop lost. There was at least one human casualty of the storm near Beaufort. The mail boy and his horse drowned at the height of the winds and tides at the Port Royal Ferry.[40]

High winds out of the southeast struck Charleston on September 18, knocking down the beacon light on Morris Island, damaging vessels and wharves, and uprooting trees. Bathers had used Fraser's Bath House on East Bay at the east end of Laurens Street on the Cooper River for sixteen years. During this blow it was "almost entirely destroyed" and declared "beyond repair." At plantations up the Cooper River winds knocked down rice crops, and the tides broke through the surrounding banks to inundate and ruin the rice with the salty water. One planter declared, "[The] tide was higher than I have ever seen it here. . . . The destruction is too bad to think of."[41] That same evening, September 18, the "violent gale" blew in Georgetown for six hours. There was little damage in the port, but again rice crops in the region suffered. Accounts of the destructive storm were widely circulated in newspapers along the east coast.[42]

A "Most Stormy and Destructive" Season

Eleven hurricanes came out of the West Indies in 1837. Eventually two came ashore in the lowcountry. At the beginning of August a reporter for the *Charleston Courier* characterized the summer of 1837 as one of "fervid heats" and persistent drought. The recent high winds, cloudy, rainy days, and lower temperatures brought "pleasant relief." But the reporter also added a warning — the recent weather, he said, gave an "appearance much like that of the equinoctial storm time of September."[43] And indeed it did. A large storm was gathering to the southeast.

Ships at sea and along the coast from Florida to South Carolina felt the first effects of the disastrous gales of the long hurricane season, encountering winds and rains on Sunday, August 6. The powerful storm dismasted vessels offshore that eventually made it to Savannah or Charleston under jury-rigged sails. A schooner with a black bottom washed ashore on Cumberland Island. Personnel of the pilot boat *Eliza and Emma* found an abandoned fully rigged brig twenty-five miles off Tybee Island. It was "full of water, masts and rigging all gone." Inscribed on her stern was *Providence*.[44]

In the Gulf Stream, far off St. Marys, Georgia, the hurricane knocked over the brig *Anna and Minerva*. To right the vessel, the captain ordered the topsails cut away. During the maneuver, a huge wave crashed over the vessel, carrying overboard the second mate, three seamen, the bulwarks, and weather rails.[45]

On the morning of August 6 the tropical cyclone was making landfall between Amelia Island and St. Augustine, Florida. Hurricane-force winds were sweeping across Georgia's coastal waters.[46]

Just offshore from Jekyll Island the ninety-ton schooner ss *Mills*, bound for Charleston with fifteen passengers and crew, was struck by huge waves and high winds. Knocked over in only thirty-six feet of water, the vessel turned bottom-up, trapping two black men and a white woman in the cabin and throwing others into the boiling sea. To save themselves, Captain Pellman and some crewmen climbed onto the vessel's bottom until crashing waves knocked them off. Two other men jumped into a lifeboat, but it filled with water and overturned. Only Abraham Cote survived, by grabbing and clinging to a spar. He hung on while pulling off his clothes to prevent himself from being pulled under. Cote washed ashore naked near the middle of Jekyll Island. Over the next few days the bodies and body parts of passengers and crew, including a Catholic priest and Josh H. Hickman, washed ashore. With only Abraham Cote surviving, it was one of the worst maritime disasters off the Georgia coast.[47]

That same morning winds and heavy rains swept the border town of St. Marys, Georgia, which fronted the river by the same name. Hurricane winds rose in violence over the next six hours, splintering and felling shade and ornamental trees planted along the riverbank and driving the sloop *Ann and Bolivar* far into the marsh. The steamboat *Florida* was hurled into a wharf, which crushed one side and punched a hole through its bottom. Waters from the surging tides and torrential rains flooded the streets of St. Marys to nearly six feet. Furniture floated in ground floor parlors. The winds felled homes and swept away the market house as residents fled, many "leaving in boats" just before river waters carried away their homes. The "oldest inhabitant" could "not recollect a similar occurrence." Another witness called the gale "as severe as that in 1813," saying that it had "done much injury to the place." A planter declared that it was "one of the most terrible and destructive hurricanes that ever desolated any country[;] . . . our village, which was recently so pleasant and beautiful, is now a scene of desolation." On plantations near St. Marys, water inundated the cotton crops, and winds blew down the corn and toppled fences, trees, and buildings. The "destruction in this part of the country was never before so universal. We shall scarcely recover in five years," the planter lamented.[48]

On nearby St. Simons Island a strong northeast wind was blowing at daybreak, August 6. Within five hours it shifted to the southeast and became, for a resident, "one of the most furious hurricanes . . . since 1824." On the sea islands just to the north, Hilton Head and St. Helena, South Carolina, the crops of cotton and corn were "seriously injured by the Sunday gale."[49]

A planter wrote that all along the coast of the lowcountry the crops were "severely injured." The hurricane passed over Darien, where an observer thought it "equaled . . . that of the year 1824," with its torrential rains and "very high winds . . . tearing up the oldest oaks and mulberry trees . . . by the roots" and blowing "limbs and branches in every direction." The fast-rising "water of the [Darien] river . . . covered the rice plantations so completely that they appeared to . . . form a part of the river." The rice was "greatly injured" by the salt-impregnated water.[50] A planter called the cotton around Darien "whipped," saying that it looked "as tho' fire had been through it." The scene in neighboring Liberty County was much the same. Witnesses said, "[the] hurricane . . . has torn the cotton crop into ribbons. The corn crop . . . is broken . . . and blown down, and the blades stripped into a thousand pieces." A Liberty County planter spoke for many rice and cotton planters when he declared, "Our hopes are entirely blasted."[51] The Sunday storm also pummeled the urban centers of the lowcountry.

In Savannah high winds pushed tides over the wharves, left vessels high and dry, damaged goods in stores along the riverfront, and felled trees and fences. Further north, at Charleston, a reporter observed "*unusually* high" waves crashing into English's Wharf off White Point and over the Battery and into the street beyond. Both withstood the pounding. The reporter continued optimistically, "we trust that this beautiful [Battery] walk . . . unsurpassed by any in the Union, will now stand a permanent ornament to our City."[52] Scarcely had the tropical cyclone that raged along the Georgia coast blown away than another powerful storm began punishing the lowcountry with winds and rains.

The great storm was called *Calypso* after the ship it nearly sent to the bottom east of the central Bahamas. The hurricane curved northwestward and approached northeastern Florida and the lowcountry in mid-August 1837. Its size and power were enormous. While *Calypso's* winds and rains lashed the lowcountry, the hurricane was upsetting and dismasting vessels well offshore. From August 16 to 19, vessels fought "a tremendous sea" and fierce winds. The pilot boat *Sarah M. Low* of Savannah encountered the storm ten miles off Charleston. Pummeled for twenty-four hours the vessel capsized on the afternoon of August 17. It righted only after the foremast was cut away, and a day later, under jury-rigged sails, the vessel entered the Savannah River.[53]

On August 18, huge waves and high winds overturned the brig *Oglethorpe* bound from Baltimore to Savannah. The vessel righted, but lost its masts, sails, and rigging. To keep the leaking vessel afloat in heavy seas, cargo was tossed overboard, and its pumps were kept working until it reached Charleston. Off the Georgia coast, Captain Brown, of the schooner *David B. Crane*, was fighting "a very severe wind" that carried away the foremast and bowsprit and smashed in the small lifeboat and galley. Simultaneously Captain Brown had to fight an uprising by three crewmembers — Charles Whitney, George Hinkley, and Ebenezer Carr — who had conspired "to commit mutiny." He was successful in surviving both storm and mutineers.[54]

Other vessels lost crew overboard, some craft were spotted wrecked at sea with no apparent survivors, and other vessels went unaccounted for and were presumed lost. For instance, the schooner *Lovely Kezia*, off the Georgia coast in 120 feet of water, came alongside what appeared to be a schooner, but the hull was "too far under water to" be certain. Apparently there were no survivors. The schooner *Martha Pyatt* and all hands were lost at sea somewhere off the South Carolina coast, and a craft of about 140 tons was sighted bottom-up off DeBordieu Island, South Carolina.[55] To captains and crew, the waters off the coast of the lowcountry had become notoriously dangerous during hurricane season.

Although the eye of the hurricane remained well offshore, winds and rains lashed the coast from Savannah to Georgetown. Damage on shore increased as the gale moved closer to the eastward-curving seacoast along the Georgia Bight. A planter on the Combahee River, fifty miles south of Charleston, reported that a "severe gale" blew for days in the region and that rice growers on the plantations had suffered losses from a third to a half of their crop: "[The rice crop,] which the [rice] birds will, no doubt as usual, fall heir to . . . will be very short in comparison to what . . . would have been."[56]

Thirty miles south of Charleston the storm battered Edingsville. Described by one resident as "a long and narrow sand hill," Edingsville had long been a favorite summer resort for planters. The hurricane's winds and tides ripped away twenty feet of the front beach at Edingsville, a foretaste of the devastation that would eventually come to the island. On Edisto a local planter said that he could not remember that they had "sustained as much loss from any one cause since the hurricane of . . . 1822."[57]

"Violent gusts" of wind from the hurricane reached Charleston on Thursday, August 17. Waves battered vessels at their moorings and sank smaller craft at wharfside. The following day the storm "increased to a steady and violent gale accompanied by heavy rain." In the city, winds leveled trees and stripped tiles and slates from the roofs of houses.[58]

Damage was worse around Georgetown. One resident wrote that on August 17 and 18 "the [northeast] wind blew for 24 hours violently." One-quarter of the shade trees and most fences were felled. Tides rose nine feet above their high-water mark. Again witnesses claimed that the storm was "the most destructive of Crops . . . of any that has occurred in the recollection of [their] oldest Planters." Saltwater broke through earthen dams to inundate the rice fields. Rice "in blossom" and not yet harvested made August gales more to be feared by rice planters than those in September. At least one-quarter of the crop was destroyed. The peas and the corn were also "greatly injured." Near the northern tip of the Georgia Bight, in eastern North Carolina, damage was even greater.[59]

Though the tropical cyclone of mid-August 1837 remained offshore, it was a damaging storm for coastal Georgia and South Carolina. Within several weeks a disaster at sea occurred that touched many lowcountry residents.

Crowded with ninety passengers and some forty officers and crewmembers, the steamship *Home*, one of the finest craft of its kind afloat, departed New

York City on October 7, a pleasant Saturday afternoon. Nearly one-third of the men, women, and children on the passenger list resided in the lowcountry, principally Charleston. In good cheer, many were returning from northern residences, where they had gone to escape the lowcountry's notorious summer heat. They may have reckoned it safe to return home by sea, since Carolina's hurricane season had passed. It was the third voyage for the record-setting *Home*, a sleek 550-ton craft, 220 feet long, with a beam of 22 feet. Constructed at a cost of $115,000 ($2,114,850), the vessel was captained by Carleton White, unaware that a destructive, slow-moving hurricane had entered the Atlantic shipping lanes. It was *Racer's* storm, named after the British sloop of war that first encountered it in the Central Caribbean. The *Home* was on a collision course with the storm. On Sunday, October 8, under steam and sail, the *Home* was cruising southward at record speeds. It was helped by a rising northeast wind. Passengers and crew watched as winds increased and large foam-flecked waves crashed into the vessel. By nightfall the vessel, now off the North Carolina coast, started to leak. Water in the hold was ankle-deep and rising. The next morning, Monday, October 9, a passenger observed "the sea . . . raged frightfully." The *Home* pitched and rolled in monstrous waves, its paddle wheel often grabbing air rather than water. It was in the clutches of the hurricane.[60]

Pumps failed to keep up with the water pouring into the hold, and Captain White ordered all passengers to assist the crew in bailing. Several male passengers broke into the bar and began imbibing, perhaps to calm their jittery nerves. In fear of sinking, White decided to head west and beach the vessel. But water in the hold reached the boilers, extinguished the fires, and stopped the engines before he could make headway. Now under short sail, Captain White, who had been at the wheel for hours, was soaked with seawater. He continued to navigate the *Home* through the heaving, rolling sea off Cape Hatteras, North Carolina, the graveyard of the Atlantic. Near 11:00 p.m., with "angry breakers" all around, the *Home* struck sand one hundred yards from shore. So close yet so far. By now the deck was nearly level with the water, and panic overcame passengers and crew. Thunderous waves crashed over the *Home*, carrying people to their deaths. When a female passenger's child was knocked from her grip into the sea, she leapt in to save the little one — both mother and child drowned. Moments before being swept overboard a minister was heard to say: "He that trusts in Jesus is safe even amid the perils of the sea." When the crew attempted to launch a lifeboat, it was smashed to pieces; another was put over the side with ten to fifteen people aboard, but it immediately capsized, and the passengers drowned. Two men who commandeered the only two life preservers aboard reached shore alive.[61]

Under constant battering by giant waves, the *Home* began to break up. Women and children clung to one another on the high forecastle — the portion of the ship closest to shore. There they remained helpless and terrified until the forecastle broke away, spilling them into the ocean. Few survived. Mrs. Schroeder of Charleston, who had been tied to a piece of the vessel, somehow reached the beach. Another Charlestonian, Mrs. Lacoste, portly and elderly, was lashed to a small sofa. Waves brought her close to shore but repeatedly washed her back into the surf until she was finally pulled to safety by some of the islanders. Robert B. Hussey of Charleston clung to a shattered remnant of a lifeboat and reached the beach; Andrew A. Lovegreen, also of Charleston, rang the ship's bell to signal help until the deck collapsed under him. Somehow he managed to reach shore alive. Only twenty of the ninety passengers survived. Of a crew of some forty officers and men, only half reached safety, including Captain White. Twenty of the twenty-five prominent Charlestonians who took passage on the *Home* perished.[62]

News of yet another tragedy at sea touched many families across the lowcountry. It was the second major sea disaster in 1837. First the ss *Mills* capsized off Jekyll Island, Georgia, and then the *Home*. Not since the loss of the *Rose in Bloom* had a maritime hurricane disaster of such magnitude shaken the region. The destruction of the *Home* was one of the greatest modern marine tragedies off the coasts of the Carolinas and Georgia. Once more it focused the attention of residents of the lowcountry and beyond on the death and devastation wrought by hurricanes. The *Charleston Mercury* quoted the *New York Gazette*, expressing the feelings of both communities united in their grief, though divided over the issue of slavery:

The catastrophe [of the *Home*] has . . . carried mourning into the bosom of many a family north and south . . . and united for a moment all sections of the country in a bond of sympathy and suffering [at] . . . the loss of some of its proudest, brightest ornaments. . . . The blow has fallen heavily upon families, some of them belonging to our state, some of them to South Carolina, who have drawn to themselves universal respect for their public services. . . . The old and young, useful, beautiful and bright are gone, and those who with anxious hearts were following the lengthening track of waters which separated them from home shall see them no more in this world of uncertainty.[63]

In 1838, a year after the *Home* disaster, the U.S. Congress passed a law requiring commercial vessels to carry a life preserver for each passenger.[64]

In both the West Indies and along the coasts of Georgia and the Carolinas in 1837, the effects on the natural and built environments and the number of lives lost from hurricanes most likely reached unprecedented levels. Small wonder that the *Charleston Mercury,* toward the end of the year, quoted a report out of Nassau that began: "The present season has been the most stormy and destructive . . . of any for many years past."[65]

The hurricanes of 1837 brought to a close more than three decades of frequent tropical cyclones at sea and ashore along the lowcountry. Although a brief respite came from hurricanes, the area continued to be pounded almost yearly by destructive tropical storms with wind speeds under hurricane strength.

TOP Wreckage strewn along Charleston's waterfront, hurricane of 1911. Courtesy of Charleston Museum.

BOTTOM A boat blown and washed over the wharves and onto the railroad tracks in Charleston during the hurricane of 1911. Courtesy of Charleston Museum.

ABOVE The railway bridge connecting
Mount Pleasant to Sullivan's Island,
South Carolina, battered by the hur-
ricane of 1911. Courtesy of South Caro-
liniana Library, University of South
Carolina.

ABOVE Charleston's streets flooded, 1911. Courtesy of
South Carolina Historical Society.

BELOW TOP Hurricane debris to the south of the Charleston wharves, 1911.
Courtesy of South Caroliniana Library, University of South Carolina.

BELOW MIDDLE The cottonseed-oil mill at Charleston was destroyed by
the hurricane of 1911. Courtesy of South Caroliniana Library, University of
South Carolina.

BELOW BOTTOM After the hurricane of 1911, the remains of wharves and
warehouses surround the Charleston custom house. Courtesy of South
Carolina Historical Society.

ABOVE TOP Looking south along Ocean Boulevard, Myrtle Beach, South Carolina, following the passage of hurricane Hazel, 1954. Courtesy of Jack Thompson.

ABOVE BOTTOM The beachfront at Thirty-first Avenue, Myrtle Beach, following hurricane Hazel. Courtesy of Jack Thompson.

RIGHT Destroyed beach houses at Folly Island, South Carolina, 1940. Courtesy of South Carolina Historical Society.

BELOW During the hurricane of 1940, waves crash over the Battery at Charleston. Courtesy of South Carolina Historical Society.

ABOVE Trawlers beached near Savannah by hurricane Gracie, 1959. Courtesy of *Savannah Morning News*.

RIGHT "Look both ways," warns a Savannah billboard after hurricane Gracie. Courtesy of *Savannah Morning News*.

LEFT "For Rent" at North Myrtle Beach, South Carolina, after hurricane Hazel, 1954. Courtesy of the Horry County Museum.

BELOW Hurricane Hazel damaged this fishing pier at North Myrtle Beach. Courtesy of the Horry County Museum.

Cleaning up in a now roofless restaurant, following hurricane Gracie, Lady's Island, South Carolina, 1959. Courtesy of *Savannah Morning News*.

CHAPTER FIVE

Mid-Century

Storms,

1840–1857

The Lowcountry Planter Elite

"We have had unpropitious weather for our crops, heavy rains almost without ceasing for the past five days and high violent winds," complained a planter on Wadmalaw Island near Charleston in late August 1840.[1] On August 26 Hugh Fraser Grant, a rice planter near Darien, Georgia, wrote, "rainy & very squally for several days the wind northeast and every prospect of a gale."[2] A tropical storm was washing across the lowcountry.

Many historians have overlooked the effects of the weather, especially hurricanes and tropical storms, on agriculture, class formation, economic development, and migration patterns in the lowcountry. Storms, insects, epidemic diseases among slaves, and fluctuations in crop prices led to the consolidation of coastal agricultural lands into fewer and fewer hands. It was costly and risky to do business. Only the largest planters could absorb heavy losses. Additionally the opening of new cotton lands in the west lured small farmers, some with slaves, away from the coast to upcountry Georgia, Alabama, Mississippi, Louisiana, and Texas. With this exodus, and fewer and fewer white immigrants seeing a future for themselves in the lowcountry, the largest planters, many of whom had inherited vast tracts of land, accumulated more.

Hugh Fraser Grant, one of largest and most successful rice planters in the Georgia lowcountry, inherited Elizafield Plantation from his father in the 1830s. Located on the south branch of the Altamaha, within the Altamaha River estuary, the land was close by the rice plantations of Georgia's planter elite — the Troups, Hugers, Kings, Butlers, Dents, Bryans, Bonds, and Coupers. Over the years, Grant continued to add to his holdings. At one time he owned 1,790 acres and had an estate valued at $123,000 ($2,863,253) in real and personal property, including more than two hundred slaves. By 1860 only 902 of Georgia's 62,003 planters owned more than one hundred acres, and just twenty-three planters in the state owned more than two hundred slaves. Great landholders like Grant could afford to be resilient in the face of disasters. Grant himself suffered huge losses from a deadly epidemic of measles among his bondsmen and periodic destruction of his crops when storms pushed saltwater into his rice fields. Such disasters, and Grant's love of expensive imported "seegars," Madeira, and port, often left him strapped for cash. Nevertheless he never faced the loss of his land. His less fortunate brother, Charles, did experience financial ruin and lost the property his father bequeathed him. He subsequently left the countryside and moved to Savannah.[3]

Insolvency was not uncommon among even the largest planters. Like Charles Grant, the well-connected John Fraser, who married into the prominent Couper family, was unable to avoid financial disaster as a rice planter. When he died in 1839 at Hamilton on the southern end of St. Simons (his plantation through marriage), Fraser left his wife Sarah Ann Couper Fraser and their ten children little money and large debts.[4]

Anna Matilda Page of St. Simons faced a similar situation. In 1824 she married Thomas Butler King, said to be the "stereotype of the aristocratic southern planter." But it was he who had married well. Following the deaths of Anna's parents, she inherited Retreat Plantation, slaves, cash, and bank stock. Yet by 1842, then with nine children to care for, she faced an uncertain future as a result of natural disasters, economic downturns, and her husband's financial mismanagement.[5] Distraught, Anna wrote, "Creditors have seized and taken from [my husband] . . . all his property . . . and at present Prices will probably not pay his debts." Fearing that her husband's creditors might seize Retreat, Anna asked her trustees for help in protecting "the property bequeathed in [her] Fathers will for the benefit of [her]self and children." Subsequently, U.S. marshals sold at auction 246 slaves and some twenty thousand acres in three counties to satisfy judgments against Thomas Butler King.[6]

Rice cultivation also was consolidated into the hands of a few large planters in the Savannah River region, especially in St. Peter's Parish, Beaufort District. Production here exceeded the annual crops made in Georgia's Altamaha River estuary. By the 1820s, some twenty planters produced all the rice in the region. They faced the same endemic problems of other lowcountry rice lords: disease, dramatic price fluctuations, mismanagement, competition from abroad, out-migration, and storms. Upon the deaths of the pioneering rice planters in St. Peter's Parish, their progeny often pursued other vocations, such as medicine.[7]

In the Georgetown District of South Carolina, rice production was indeed big business. By the mid-nineteenth century, just ninety-one planters, the local rice elite, had consolidated nearly all of the district's rice and cotton lands into their own hands. They produced 98 percent of the district's rice and just over 33 percent of the *nation's* rice. A dozen of these great planters and slave owners — among them Plowden Weston, John Izard Middleton, Frederick Wentworth Ford, and William Algernon Alston — each produced one million pounds an-nually. The small planter could not compete and he moved west. This out-migration led to a slow relative decline in population and economic vitality. Only the great planters could overcome competition at home and abroad, and withstand the financial losses occasioned by diseases, insects, freshets, floods, tropical storms, and hurricanes. The golden age of rice culture in coastal Geor-gia and South Carolina peaked in the 1820s, with land concentrated in the hands of a few great planters.[8] But over time even the great rice planters of the Georgia and South Carolina lowcountry did not survive. The weather, so con-ducive to rice cultivation, ironically was a major factor in its demise.

In 1841, for the second year in a row, tropical storms battered the lowcountry. During late August the coast was swept by high winds and heavy rains. Charles-ton's *Southern Patriot* reported that water was standing "nearly two feet deep" in stores on Market Street. Near Georgetown, the brig *Detroit*, loaded with merchandise out of New York, was blown onto shoals and wrecked.[9] A second and more damaging storm came out of the Bahamas in September.

High northeasterly winds from a hurricane well offshore caused flooding tides and torrential rains across northern Florida and the lowcountry from September 14 to 16. At Elizafield and other rice plantations in the Altamaha River estuary "enormous tides" broke through dikes and poured into rice fields. At Savannah tides reached heights not seen in "many years." Saltwater poured into rice fields on Hutchinson Island and others along the Savannah River. The *Savannah Republican* feared that the storm had damaged crops all along the coast. The weather at Charleston, unsettled for several days, grew worse on September 16. The "threatening weather" gave vessels in the harbor time to prepare for the worst, but in the early morning hours of September 17 the winds subsided. Near the end of the gale, a tornado roared through the west side of the city, causing slight damage.[10] The following year storms and the winds of an offshore hurricane lashed the lowcountry, making it perilous for crafts along the coasts. It was a busy season of storms.

In mid-July 1842 a great hurricane remained far off the Georgia and South Carolina coasts and curved inward to devastate southeastern North Carolina. In early August a tropical storm lashed northeastern Florida and the lowcountry. Cotton in the region had "shed" much already owing to a drought before the storm hit on August 2. Anna King, at Retreat Plantation on St. Simons Island, told her husband that the winds "did considerable damage" to the cotton. She suspected that "little will be made . . . everyone speaks gloomily of cotton crops." Further up the Georgia coast near Darien, Hugh Grant experienced a "Heavy wind & Rain from N. E. no damage done." [11] He would not say the same two months later.

In early October 1842 a devastating hurricane moved across Florida from Apalachicola to St. Augustine and into the Atlantic, where it began tracking northward.[12] Residents of the lowcountry and vessels off the coast soon felt its fury.

On Wednesday afternoon, October 4, inhabitants of Glynn County, which embraces Brunswick, St. Simons Island, and Jekyll Island, were among the first Georgians to experience the hurricane as it moved across the lower Georgia coast and coastal waters. It was the worst kind of tropical cyclone — slow moving.[13]

One resident watched high winds rise out of the southeast and on Wednesday night "increase . . . to a hurricane." It blew "with torrents of rain and great violence" for twenty-four hours. Its duration was longer than the terrible hurricanes hitting the region in 1804, 1813, and 1824. Huge trees went down, fences went over, and houses became "ruins." Plantations along the Altamaha River reported, "the water rose three feet up the rice"; "the loss and damage is incalculable"; "provision crops [are] under water" and will "rot before we can . . . dry [them]." Planters had hoped for "good crops to rescue them from impending ruin," but that "fond hope [was] snatched away . . . in one sad and disastrous night." Many could scarcely "save a pittance . . . to meet . . . calamities, necessities, and [more faced] absolute want" than the county had "ever experienced." Nevertheless, the writer concluded, "When I behold the crush and desolation around me, and yet no lives lost, I am constrained to lift up my soul in gratitude and thankfulness to 'Him who guideth the whirlwind and rideth upon the storm', that it is no worse with us!"[14] A subsequent report published in the Savannah press noted, "The injury to [Sea Island] rice is extensive, and particularly as to quality."[15]

Slowly the hurricane turned east-northeast and away from the coast. At Darien damage was far less than along the lower coast. Nevertheless Hugh Grant worried that he might lose his rice crop to very high tides. On October 5–6 Grant endured a "Heavy Gale for 36 Hours," and the "tide [came] entirely over the whole plantation." Despite his concerns, in November he shipped 1,847 bushels of rice to his factors.[16]

A weather observer at Savannah on Wednesday, October 5, noted that winds and rainsqualls in the afternoon "increased in violence." But there along the upper Georgia coast it was a tropical storm. Damage was light in Savannah, and no deaths were reported. Even though the slow-moving storm turned seaward, its effects were felt along the South Carolina coast. Mounting seas off Charleston became flecked with whitecaps. A small fishing craft east of Charleston's bar ran before the storm for port and safety. Four adult slaves, Jefferson, George, Ned, and William, and Isaac, "a negro boy," struggled to keep their boat afloat. Another sailing craft ahead of them made it through the heavy swells on the bar and into the harbor. But when the boat carrying the five black fishermen attempted to cross the bar, huge crashing waves swamped it. The boat overturned and spilled the men into the boiling surf.[17]

After the storm abated, two boats went looking for the fishermen. Exhausted from a long search, the crews returned in the late afternoon. At dockside a crowd of over one hundred black fishermen awaited news. When told that their fellow fishermen had not been found, "tears were seen on the cheeks of a number of them," a reporter noted. Several days later the missing fishermen's boat was discovered "much shattered" on Bird Key off Folly Island. Apparently the bodies of the fishermen were never recovered. It was assumed they drowned.[18]

The same day the boat of the fishermen capsized, Charleston's pilot boat *Water Witch* went to sea under the command of Captain Samuel Burrows. On October 6 it was reported missing. Four days later the pilot boat limped into Charleston's harbor, its anchors and cables lost and its sails split. Encountering the tropical storm offshore, the pilot boat had been blown as far south as Savannah. Waves from the once powerful hurricane battered the Charleston wharves. The highest tides "in many years" poured into the streets. Men rowed small boats through the streets to rescue people from their dwellings.[19]

Hurricane season was coming to a close near the end of October 1842 when a scare was thrown into lowcountry residents by a storm that came out of the Windward Islands and curved into northeastern Florida with high winds. Following a familiar track, the storm moved along the Georgia coast. The planter Hugh Grant at Darien recorded gusting northeast winds from October 29 to 31, heavy rains, flooding tides, and a break in an earthen dam. But the tropical storm's winds never reached the hurricane force that had caused the human and crop losses of the other cyclones during the season of 1842.[20]

Nearly two years later, in early September 1844, a tropical storm brushed the lowcountry.[21] But it was not until 1846 that another hurricane came ashore in coastal Georgia and South Carolina.

In early October 1846 a massive tropical cyclone was first detected south of Jamaica. It left a trail of death and destruction from Cuba to Key West and then pounded both western and northeastern Florida, especially Jacksonville. Next the massive storm moved northward.[22]

When the steamer *Mutual Safety*—a name that proved ironic—departed Charleston for New Orleans on the afternoon of October 10 with some sixty crewmen and passengers it was a pleasant day. Only a moderate breeze blew from the northeast. There was no warning of what lay offshore. Within several hours the steamer was laboring in the high seas and winds of the hurricane off the coasts of South Carolina and Georgia. A passenger observed that the storm increased "in violence" each hour. The vessel sprang a leak. Pumps driven by the engines were engaged. Passengers were called upon to bail, but they could not stay ahead of the water filling the hold. Throughout the night the steamer battled high winds and crashing waves. At daylight on Sunday, Captain James Pennoyer ordered the upper cabin, containing staterooms and saloon, cut off and thrown overboard to lessen weight. The weather deteriorated. Rainsqualls became so dense that visibility was limited to fifty yards. A council of officers and passengers concluded that the vessel might founder. It was agreed that the captain should head for the nearest coast and beach the vessel to save all aboard. Within several hours they sighted Talbot Island near Jacksonville, Florida, and there the *Mutual Safety* was grounded in heavy surf. The small boats aboard were launched, and the women were safely rowed through the surf to the mainland. The following day the rest of the crew and passengers reached shore as huge breakers demolished the *Mutual Safety*. It was a total loss. To rebut "aspersions" made against Captain Pennoyer, one passenger declared, "It is almost miraculous . . . that we have all escaped. . . . I believe we owe our preservation to Capt. Pennoyer."[23] The same tropical cyclone that destroyed the *Mutual Safety* came ashore all along the lowcountry.

Near Darien, on October 12–13, Hugh Grant watched a "very severe gale" send surging tides into his rice fields. Winds lashed Savannah and "increased in violence" on Monday evening, knocking over trees and littering the streets with branches of chinaberry trees, which a resident noted had "stood many a tempest." A brick fence was blown down; a brig was driven ashore at Tybee, and a schooner knocked over at Union Wharf. The storm reached far up the Savannah River. At Delta Plantation, owned by Langdon Cheves of South Carolina, floodwaters swept through the rice mill and ruined the rice harvest stored there. At Charleston winds raged from late Monday until Tuesday. Vessels banged into one another at the wharves, more than a dozen craft broke free from their moorings and ran afoul of others, and several packets and small boats sank. Most wharves suffered damages. Winds and waves washed away the west end of Tradd Street leading to Chisolm's Mill; South Bay's wall and sidewalk was "much broken up," and the sea breached the East Battery wall in places. "The violence of the wind" tore off part of the roof of Trinity Church on Hasell Street and deposited it in the graveyard.[24]

"It was the most severe gale we have experienced for some dozen years past," the *Charleston Courier* reported. Some believed "Divine Providence" had intervened to prevent "greater destruction of property and . . . loss of life." A low tide and winds from the southeast also helped minimize damages. The paper did "regret" that "a negro fellow," a slave of J. M. Dwight and "patroon" of his wood boat, drowned. But it was the consensus that the city had dodged the terrible catastrophe that had swept Cuba and parts of Florida, which had recently joined the Union.[25]

The summer of 1848 was hot and dry. A drought gripped coastal Georgia. While ministering to sick slaves as well as her own children and overseeing the crops of Retreat Plantation on St. Simons Island, Anna King watched her crops wither. She wrote to her husband, who seemed always away, and to her son, describing plantation affairs: "The weather is so intensely hot — & *ruinously dry* — the cotton *crop is seriously injured by it*. . . . You would be surprised to see how parched up everything is."[26] Most likely by the time rains from a storm out of Florida brought relief, the crops had withered.

It was again an October storm. It smashed into the Tampa Bay area, moved eastward striking Tallahassee and Jacksonville, and then curved northward along Georgia's coast, bringing with it heavy rains. On October 12 Hugh Grant at Elizafield, just above St. Simons Island, endured what he called a "Pretty severe Gale. Water entirely over the Plantation"; the following day he saw "Tides over the Land at Low water." The high tides opened eight breaks in dikes around his rice field.[27]

On October 12–13 northeast winds at Savannah were at or near hurricane strength. The *Savannah Republican* characterized the storm as "a severe gale blowing with almost unremitting violence . . . accompanied . . . with copious rain." Surging tides swept over the wharves and overflowed rice fields along the Savannah and Ogeechee rivers. Winds blew down some of the "prettiest shade trees" in the city.[28] The storm continued its erratic course. Many gales hitting the upper Georgia coast usually affected South Carolina, but on October 14 it appears that this storm recurved eastward and into the open Atlantic.

Damaging winds, perhaps even reaching hurricane velocity, swept the Georgia coast on August 23, 1851. At St. Marys the storm was "severe, blowing down several houses." Up the coast in Savannah "the storm was extremely violent . . . tin sheeting from the roofs of houses was . . . whirled into the air like sheets of tissue paper . . . walls of . . . new buildings were thrown down . . . tops of chimneys . . . blown off . . . and a sash from the Exchange . . . whirled down the Bay like a wagon wheel."[29]

In late August 1852 a tropical cyclone off the coast brought torrential rains to the lowcountry. The rains worried Thomas Benjamin Chaplin. Thirty-two years of age, Chaplin inherited rice lands and slaves from his mother's family, and cotton lands and slaves from his father's. Adding to his wealth was his wife's dowry of stocks and bonds. He was the owner of Tombee Plantation on St. Helena Island in Beaufort District, South Carolina, where as a large land and slave owner, he hobnobbed with the local social and political elite.[30] Chaplin wrote in his journal on September 8, "Rain. Rain. No cotton picked this week." The following day he wondered, "When will this rain stop? It is ruining the cotton . . . much cotton beat down in the dirt. . . . What is open in the pod is mostly rotten." He had his slaves picking cotton, but what "they pick look[s] very bad."[31]

A tropical storm battered Jacksonville in late October 1853. It gathered strength, reached hurricane force, and took a familiar track northward over the warm coastal waters of the lowcountry. At sea its winds dismasted vessels; from Brunswick, Georgia, to Charleston, South Carolina, it blew ashore small craft. In the town of Brunswick damage was widespread. Huge waves destroyed the new, stoutly built railroad wharf that collapsed and floated into the harbor. Winds knocked over the engine house of the Brunswick Railroad Company, a blacksmith shop, and a large cotton shed and damaged other buildings.[32] It was but a precursor to a powerful hurricane the next year.

A Major Hurricane, 1854

Northwest of Abaco Island in early September 1854 the crew of a brig, *Reindeer*, watched a brisk northeast breeze gradually rise to the winds of a tropical cyclone that threatened to overturn their vessel. For five days they endured the great storm. By the time it approached the coast of the southeastern United States it was a large, slow-moving major hurricane.[33]

"As far out as the eye could see, a perfectly white mountainous sea presented itself, while the wind moaned and whistled with awful fury," observed a passenger aboard the steamer *Star of the South*, out of New York, on Thursday, September 7, and far off Savannah. That evening, winds shredded and tore away the sails. Huge waves broke on the vessel, and water poured into the hold. The passengers became alarmed. Captain Marks assured them that the pumps were working and that "the gallant and noble ship" was behaving "most bravely." But the next morning, Friday, September 8, the water in the hold reached the boilers, extinguished the fires, and "the passengers despaired." One believed that their "destruction seemed inevitable." As the hurricane worsened, they "expected every moment to be [their] last." Waves cracked the rudder, and the "ship was left to the mercy of the waves." Captain Marks, assisted by his first mate, Mr. Teal, and crew, used cabin furniture to brace the rudder. This allowed crewmen to navigate the vessel again. Eventually the ship reached the port of Charleston in a "crippled condition." Passengers declared that the *Star of the South* was "saved" owing to the "coolness and masterly seamanship of Captain Marks and Mr. Teal." [34]

About the time the *Star of the South* was battling wind and waves to stay afloat, the brig *Mary Ann*, out of Charleston and bound for Abaco Island, ran directly into the hurricane. Far off Savannah it was up to the first mate to navigate through the hurricane. Its captain, John H. Johnson, had died at sea the previous day. The first mate had set a course for the Georgia coast when huge waves suddenly capsized the vessel. Luckily another heavy sea "put her afloat again" upright but with water in the hold. As the ship neared the Georgia coastline, off Tybee Island, winds shredded the sails, brought down the mainmast, and again knocked the vessel over. This time the *Mary Ann* did not right; she was sinking, and the crew abandoned her. Insured for $6,000 ($125,386), the brig was a total loss. In the same waters, the captain of the bark *Alice* was sailing before a southeaster with reefed topsails when, on September 8, he too was enveloped by "a perfect hurricane." Unable to "get a piece of canvas to stand, [he] had to heave the ship to, the sea running to an immense height and making a clean breach over the vessel." Eventually, the bark ran through the great storm without sustaining serious damage. [35]

Winds, sometimes from the southeast, sometimes the northeast, then northwest, created a turbulent cross-sea of huge waves that hammered vessels closer to shore. The schooner *Angenett*, off Savannah and loaded with timber, was upset, and a seaman, William Toohey, a native of Ireland, was lost overboard. The masts were cut away to prevent her from going to the bottom. Not far away, the schooner *Edward Kidder* lost its mainsail, and everything movable on deck was swept off by huge waves. The schooner *Dirigo*, loaded with lumber, was overtaken and upset by the hurricane just off Savannah, about 5:00 p.m. on September 8. The food and water of the crew were washed overboard. Cutting away the masts righted the schooner, but not before it filled with water. The dismasted schooner drifted helplessly northward for six days. When a passing ship rescued Captain Augustus Gordon and his crew, they were famished and exhausted.[36]

On the South Carolina coast the ship *Delia Maria* was dismasted. Passengers and crew took to small boats to reach safety on Hilton Head Island. Up the coast, off Dewees Island, a vessel was spotted bottom-up; nearby a schooner grounded and sank off Capers Island. Further north the hurricane drove ashore the French schooner *Les Amis Reunis* at Lavender Point on Bull's Island. Here it "went to pieces." The captain and three crewmen perished; only the mate, a sailor, and the cabin boy survived. The *Caroline Hall* was blown into the marsh off Bull's Island. Close by, the schooner *Jane* was dismasted and floated helplessly at sea. At the entrance to Bull's Harbor only the tips of the topmasts of a ship were above water; also visible were the stumps of the three masts of a bark mostly submerged. Just off Georgetown's bar, Captain Henry Latchicott, of the pilot boat *Margaret Davis*, rescued Captain Burrington and several crewmen of the brig *E. Hinds* at the height of the storm. The rescue was imperiled by waves banging the pilot boat into the sinking brig. One crewman refused to leave the *E. Hinds* and was at first presumed to have "sunk into a seaman's grave." He later drifted ashore on a plank and was "safe though badly chafed and bruised," the press reported.[37]

Up and down the coast of the lowcountry, amid other wreckage, vessels floated bottom-up. Abandoned vessels without crews eerily floated upright with the currents. U.S. Navy lieutenant W. A. Bartlett, of the steamer *Atlantic*, declared, "During twenty-one years of trials incident to a sea life, I have not before met a gale of greater severity, and in no instance have I known the wind to blow a hurricane gale for so many consecutive hours." Captain G. P. Adams, of the schooner *Aid*, who also survived the hurricane in the open ocean, sailed through what he described as "the heaviest sea ever experienced during the 25 years he has been at sea." Near the Charleston bar, he sighted a large vessel with its mizzenmast in shambles. He "passed within 20 feet of her, and no hail or signals were made from her." Captain Adams concluded she had been abandoned and was a derelict. The schooner *Mary D. Haman* was sighted eighteen miles northeast of Pawleys Island waterlogged. It was "feared all on board perished."[38]

The hurricane approached the coast, driving the schooners *Cotton Plant, James and Augustus,* and *Company* into the marshes of Skidaway Island near Savannah. Off the Charleston bar the schooner *Mary D. Scull,* out of Philadelphia and loaded with merchandise for Charleston shops, was slammed by the hurricane's northeast winds on Thursday, September 7. For thirty-six hours Captain Thompson fought the hurricane in his schooner, stripped of its sails, with smashed bulwarks and a hole in its hull. While the schooner battled the great storm off Charleston, the huge, dangerous, and slow-moving hurricane was coming ashore across the lowcountry.[39]

Northeastern gales from the hurricane brushed Jacksonville, and then the cyclone turned north-northwest and made landfall between Brunswick and Savannah. Most welcomed the first brisk winds that brought relief from an unusually torrid summer. But by morning, September 7, outlying winds of the hurricane were felt at St. Simons Island.[40]

As the storm rose over Retreat Plantation, Anna King, feeling especially anxious, wrote her long-absent husband. Running the plantation was taking a toll on her: "At times I feel worn out with anxiety & desire to see you. . . . my heart urges me to implore of you to come home at any risk." Then she wrote, "This is in truth a stormy day — high wind — some rain and very high tide." The weather deteriorated: "The wind is so high & so jerks this house I find it hard to write."[41] It worsened.

That same morning, at Elizafield Plantation, Hugh Grant watched a storm building, and he confided to his journal: "Blowing a gale from N. E. tides very high but no damage yet — Look for trouble this night." Just up the coast Dr. Charles C. Jones, the well-educated Presbyterian minister and owner of over one hundred slaves and thirty-six hundred acres on three plantations in Liberty County, warily watched the developing cyclone. It came out of the northeast, Jones noted, "with scuds of rain and thunder and heavy puffs of wind — a sure evidence of an approaching gale." In the evening, Jones worried that the full moon was destined to bring high tides. At the same time, Thomas Chaplin eyed rising winds over Tombee Plantation: "Commenced blowing from the east, and got to be a very heavy storm, or hurricane of wind & rain."[42]

Winds increased throughout the day and night of September 7. By the next day the winds of the major hurricane ripped across the sea islands. On St. Catherines Island, off Georgia's coast, winds and waves tore away the wharf of Jacob and George Waldburg, slammed into their houses, and "destroyed" their sea island cotton crops.[43]

On the mainland, Hugh Grant described September 8: "Dreadful Gale. Everything under water. Break in [dikes] 16, 22, 18. . . . Every [rice] stack in the field blown and washed away. Lost entire 110 acres of rice and 6,000 bushels."[44]

The Reverend Dr. Charles C. Jones watched and listened as winds increased over Maybank, his seven-hundred-acre cotton plantation. It was the family's "healthful" summer residence in Liberty County, located at the mouth of the Medway River on the northwestern end of Colonel's Island. Surrounded by salt marshes, Maybank had St. Catherines Island to the east and was connected by a causeway to the mainland on the west. By daybreak, September 8, Dr. Jones was unable to see "a spear of marsh [grass]. . . . A clear rolling sea all around us . . . the whitecaps keeping it a foam and the driving spray and mist shutting the distant shores from the sight." He watched a wood ibis as "the wind catches him . . . and he falls with the rapidity of a stone right into the trees . . . killed no doubt by the fall." Winds toppled "trees in the yard," and the "rain drove into the house under the shingles, through the plastering." The "servants" brought "tubs swabbing up the water as it pour[ed] into the entry and rooms." Suddenly the wind veered to the northwest, and "it blows a hurricane!" Another tree went down, and the "top of the grand old hickory is off!" The shutters "of the two large windows opening into the front piazza . . . suddenly blown to . . . shivering many panes of glass in each. . . . Aunt Abby for a moment much frightened." Sheets were "crammed in [the windows] and water shut out." Pride of India trees fell, two "poplars snapped off . . . three locust trees torn up," and the "old cedar" came down. "How the wind roars! The trees are in an agony. Their limbs are torn and twisted off. The earth is strewed with leaves and twigs and boughs." The causeway bridge was washed away, and the causeway itself was "cut deep and wide by the tide flowing over" it. By Saturday morning, September 9, the hurricane had passed. Reports came in that the storm was "terrible" in the countryside: "destruction of houses, crops, and timber . . . very great." Dr. Jones told his family, "Personal losses in crops and expenses in repairs will be heavy, so we must make economy the order of the day." Always the Presbyterian minister, Dr. Jones concluded, "The storm is a great calamity. . . . May we profit by it, and learn not to trust in our uncertain possessions, but in the Living God, who gives us all things richly to enjoy."[45] The "calamity" extended into the upper Georgia coast and South Carolina.

A yellow fever epidemic raged in Savannah as the first winds from the hurricane were felt in the city on Wednesday, September 7. Northeast winds slowly increased in velocity on Thursday as the hurricane began a slow curve northeastward, putting Savannah on the dangerous right side of the great storm.

Around midnight Thursday, the winds blew a gale, and "the wind became more and more violent," until Friday afternoon the winds peaked. An editor of the *Savannah Republican* was trying to get out the paper, and he provided readers a firsthand account: "As we go to press . . . , a terrific hurricane, exceeding in violence and the amount of property destroyed unlike anything we have ever witnessed, is sweeping over Savannah from the Northeast." In the streets the "rushing, roaring wind, [is] bearing limbs of trees, pieces of slate and tin and boards . . . as if it were lighter than chaff." Rain and river water flooded the wharves and lumberyards, and he could see that Hutchinson Island and its rice fields were under four to six feet of water. Many of the cattle there drowned. The *Republican's* editor wrote, "[It is] impossible to leave our office, so terrific is the storm . . . which now shakes the building in which we write . . . [and] is unroofing the town, prostrating trees and chimneys, and destroying vast amounts of property . . . slate, tin, . . . shutters, and sign boards whirl through the air, rendering it a rather perilous undertaking to venture out doors." The editor concluded that the hurricane was a display "of the mighty power and awful grandeur of the Deity." The editor's story was picked up and published by the *New York Daily Times*. The account may have given pause to readers in the northern states who considered seeking their fortunes in the lowcountry.[46]

So many branches and trees went down across Savannah that streets were impassable even on foot. Five hundred trees had been planted following the hurricane of 1824, and about 250 were lost. The four rows of trees on Broad Street were either defoliated or knocked down. The city's famous squares were wrecks filled with roof slate and boards. Winds and rains heavily damaged public buildings: the stained glass windows of St. John's Episcopal Church blew in; portions of the roof tore away from Trinity Methodist Church, the Exchange Building, the Medical College, the theater, and every commercial building along River Street. Nearly every private home in the city with a tin or copper roof was fully or in part unroofed. Windows exploded inward, and shutters wrenched away. Gaslight posts blew over. The waterworks were unable to provide water to customers as saltwater surged up the Savannah River contaminating the city water. On the waterfront the steamer *Jenny Lind* was a complete wreck, the steamer *Sam Jones* was broken to pieces, and the steamer *Oregon* a total loss. The shipyard owned by Henry Willink Jr. and several cotton presses were heavily damaged. Near the city the lighthouse on Fig Island collapsed. The outer lighthouse on Tybee Island was blown down. Amidst the devastation, the yellow fever epidemic continued in Savannah. Within several days of the hurricane, the disease claimed 47 lives. Before the epidemic ran its course, 954 whites and 106 blacks died from the bite of the *Aedes aegypti* mosquito.[47]

Planters along the Ogeechee and Savannah rivers lost three-quarters of their rice crops either because the fields were flooded or because the flooding rivers carried away the harvests. On the Carolina side of the Savannah River at Laurel Hill Plantation, the Savannah River spilled its banks and carried away three hundred acres of cut and stacked rice, at Taylor's two hundred acres, at Izard's six hundred acres, and at Smith's two hundred acres. To the north, in South Carolina, the Pon Pon River was covered with floating rice, and the Combahee River so completely submerged the rice fields that no dikes could be seen, and the fields gave "the appearance . . . of an angry ocean," a witness declared.[48]

Word reached the press from the isolated hamlet of Bluffton, South Carolina, that planters there "experienced . . . the severest gale . . . ever witnessed. . . . [Before the storm the cotton crops] looked full of rich green leaves and snowy fibers; to-day they look as if they had passed through the snows of Siberia." Pine trees, "whipped into tatters, . . . wear the hues of mid-winter." The cabins of blacks on the plantations were blown down and crushed. However, planters seem reconciled to their losses "by the fortunate escape of their slaves" from injury or death.[49]

Up the coast a correspondent at Port Royal, South Carolina, remarked, "Never in my life have I seen such havoc in the countryside." For twenty miles around, one-half of the rice crop was gone. Cotton growers who expected to make sixty to seventy bales saw their crops "almost entirely destroyed." The local expression was that the cotton crop "has gone to the devil."[50]

A correspondent at the small port town of Beaufort told the press that the hurricane "swept away" one of the town's wharves and its storehouse while the town's other wharf was "much broken up." The breakwaters on the Beaufort River were gone, trees were uprooted, and fences were carried away by the wind. The walk along the bay protected by its fine "concrete wall" collapsed. Two schooners looked out of place sitting high and dry. A house on Bay Point fell down, and others sustained severe damage. There was no loss of life in town, but it was believed that "one or two negros" had been drowned at nearby Pocatalico.[51]

At Tombee, Thomas Chaplin watched yet another hurricane sweep in from the sea and over his plantation: "Tremendous gale. . . . Trees & limbs flying in every direction, fences all down. . . . I never saw such a storm in my life. Crops are all ruined. The water is 2 feet deep in my yard. . . . cotton corn & potatoes were under water. . . . marsh carried off. All the large bridges on the Island gone."[52]

Edisto Island residents watched what some said was "one of the most terrifying hurricanes" ever known. It "burst" on them on Thursday night, and the following morning the ocean surged across Edingsville Island. The sea rushed under the piazzas of several houses on Edingsville, and residents concluded that this vulnerable strip of sand was no longer safe as a summer resort. For thirty-six hours the storm raged, felling trees, destroying fences and bridges, and "thrashing or flattening" the cotton crop on Edisto. Three-quarters of the crop was declared a loss.[53]

Charleston, like Savannah, was in the midst of a yellow fever epidemic as the outlying winds of the hurricane began to waft over the city. It was a time of grief and mourning from mid-August to mid-November, when 627 people died in the epidemic.[54]

Now residents faced lowering clouds and rising northeast winds from a major tropical cyclone. In the afternoon of Thursday, September 8, winds reached hurricane force in Charleston. Waves pounded wharves along East Bay Street, damaging most of them. Damages alone to the privately owned wharves totaled between $250,000 ($5,224,432) and $300,000 ($6,269,318). Although vessels had time to prepare for the approaching storm, sailing craft were slammed against the wharves by breaking waves. The brig *Eureka* broke her moorings at Southern Wharf and banged against the stonework of the Battery, crashed into and damaged a bathing house there, and finally drifted into the Ashley River, where she lay a "complete wreck" near the mouth of Wappoo Cut. Two steamers of the Mount Pleasant Line, the *Massasoit* and *G. W. Coffee*, were blown ashore west of the Ashley River. They were relocated with great difficulty. Winds sank numerous small craft at their moorings. Seawater flooded low-lying sections of the city, pouring into warehouses and stores and destroying merchandise. A causeway at the end of Tradd Street was washed away. The area south of Broad Street and west of Logan Street, including most of Franklin and Smith streets, "was one uninterrupted lake."[55]

The Charleston Hotel suffered heavy storm damage. Built in the Greek Revival Style to boost Charleston as the "Queen City of the South," the hotel could accommodate three hundred lodgers. The elegant structure first opened in March 1838 but was consumed by fire a month later. Quickly rebuilt, it opened again in 1839. Now a storm peeled back its tin roof and blew over four chimneys, exposing the hotel's interior, which was flooded by torrential downpours, ruining plaster, wallpaper, and furniture. Downpours also soaked interiors of large houses on East Bay when their roofs blew away. A "complete breach" of the Battery by crashing waves and the destruction of its stone facing along with other damages to city property were estimated to be very costly to repair.[56]

Beyond Charleston, along the Cooper River, waters surged over banks and broke through one or more rice dams on nearly every plantation. Rice cut and stacked in fields bobbed in the water as it was carried away by the flood tides. Rice yield was expected to be far below its usual annual production of twenty thousand tierces of rice from the Cooper River plantations.[57]

Families on Sullivan's Island awoke on September 8 to see "terrific, great waves" dashing up the beach, demolishing bathhouses, and sending waters swirling around their dwellings. They recognized that they had "nothing now between [them] and the wide ocean but God's Mercy."[58] Edmund Ravenel watched as seawater swept over the entire island, and he "passed through the most awful storm that [he] ever saw. Such a scene of devastation you have never seen."[59]

Sullivan's Island was cut off from communications. The fate of those there was unknown until the storm abated. When vessels did reach the island, an eyewitness declared that the hurricane had altered the natural environment: "The character and general aspect of the Island have been . . . essentially changed." The former shoreline had disappeared along with the "ramparts and embankments that had been reared for its security." Though the built environment on Sullivan's Island was also battered, no deaths occurred. The storm was so slow-moving that people had time to evacuate low-lying areas. Some one thousand islanders found refuge in Fort Moultrie and the brick Presbyterian Church, which saved many from drowning. Refugees to the fort praised the "soldierly courtesy" extended them by the garrison.[60]

Evidence of the storm's fury and the power of the pounding waves and winds that swept the island could be found in the missing landmarks — the Old Point House, the government wharf, the Mount Pleasant ferry wharf. Water surrounded the Moultrie House, a hostelry, which was nearly carried into the ocean by waves crashing against its foundations. Seawater broke through the first floor. The hotel withstood the pounding, but after the waters receded it was noticeably lower in the sand than before the storm. Witnesses saw houses east of the Moultrie House "entirely destroyed — some of them not leaving a . . . vestige to mark their former site," by then "a smooth beach." The few remaining dwellings still standing near the Moultrie House — the homes of Gen. W. E. Martin, H. R. Banks, and Henry Horlbeck — appeared on the verge of collapse.[61]

Up the coast at Georgetown, the *Pee Dee Times* called the hurricane the *"longest continuous blow in the memory of any inhabitant."* The surging tides did "great damage" to some of the wharves in the town, but it was along the Pee Dee, the North and South Santee, and the Waccamaw rivers that the hurricane exacted its heaviest toll. The rice harvest had just begun, and the damage was "immense." Adele Petigru Allston, wife of the great rice planter Robert F. W. Allston, wrote that on plantations along the rivers "not one head of rice was to be seen above the water . . . [nor] any appearance of the land. . . . It was one rolling, dashing Sea, and the water was Salt as the Sea. Many persons had rice cut and stacked in the field, which was all swept away by the flood."[62]

The hurricane was a disaster for mariners and the planters of the lowcountry. The cost in human lives was high at sea while ashore the lives lost were few because the inhabitants had many hours to seek shelter before the highest winds and tides swept through. In terms of damage, residents of Georgetown thought it was the most "severe" gale since the hurricane of 1822; Savannahians remembered it as the most destructive since 1824; Charlestonians recalled it as the worst hurricane since the blow of 1804. They noted that it had occurred to the day, September 8, and was of the same duration as the tropical cyclone of exactly fifty years before. The 1854 hurricane also followed closely the track of the tropical cyclone of 1804: it crossed the Georgia coast at an angle as it began its slow curvature north-northeast along a track paralleling the coastline of the lowcountry.[63]

The Central America

During the late 1850s, tropical storms continued to regularly lash the Georgia and South Carolina coasts.[64] In September 1857 a hurricane remained far off-shore the lowcountry but battered more than fifty vessels in its path. One of these was the *Central America*, a sturdy, three-masted steamer and side-wheeler 280 feet in length with a 40-foot beam.

On Tuesday, September 8, 1857, the *Central America* departed Havana, Cuba, for New York under clear skies with 572 crew and passengers, most of whom were returning from the California gold fields. There was $1,324,497 ($27,764,462) aboard in gold. On Wednesday officers aboard reported a "fresh breeze," or in mariner's terms, whitecaps and a wind of twenty knots. Wave heights rose with the wind, and the weather deteriorated. Far off the coasts of Florida and Georgia, on Thursday, September 10, the *Central America* experienced winds that increased to sixty knots and drove rainsqualls sideways into the ship. Huge seas broke over the bow and crashed into the cabins. The *Central America* had encountered a powerful tropical cyclone. Friday dawned gray, and the ocean "ran mountains high." The side-wheeler was taking a beating 175 miles east of Savannah. The ship sprang leaks until it appeared that the whole hull was leaking. Water came in faster than the pumps could return it to the sea. By midday, rising waters in the engine room extinguished fires in the boilers, and the engines shut down. Without steam power, Captain William Herndon ordered sails unfurled, but they were quickly shredded. The captain and his officers were unable to keep the ship headed into wind. The vessel wallowed in the trough of waves that rose high above it and broke over the steamer "in avalanches," one passenger observed. Most were thinking the worst. The captain quickly organized an all-male bucket brigade, but like the pumps, buckets were no match for the water seeping in. Captain Herndon was well aware that his vessel was likely to sink. Nevertheless, he remained calm and steady, shouting encouragement to the bucket brigade, and comforting the women and children assembled in the main cabin. Outlying winds from the powerful hurricane were felt ashore, some 150 miles to the west along the coast of the lowcountry. At both Charleston and Georgetown the weather was "stormy"—rain with high winds—that sometimes reached "gale" force on September 11–12.[65]

Aboard the *Central America* on Saturday morning, September 12, Captain Herndon directed the crew to construct rafts from the furniture, doors, and boards of the ship itself. Ironically the winds and waves were moderating. Hopes soared when the brig *Marine*, itself battered by the hurricane, was sighted. The brig maneuvered close enough to begin picking up the women and children sent over in lifeboats from the *Central America*. When all female passengers and their children were safely aboard the *Marine*, male passengers began to be ferried over until it grew too dark to continue. By nightfall, more than one hundred people had been evacuated from the *Central America*. Captain Herndon ordered the distribution of life preservers to all crew and passengers remaining aboard his ship. Shortly thereafter, around 8:00 p.m., Saturday, September 12, the *Central America* went down stern first. Some crew and passengers spilled overboard from the deck were sucked under as the ship spiraled into the deep sea; others, thrown clear, grabbed anything floating. They saw Captain Herndon and second officer James Frazer at their posts in the wheelhouse as the ship sank.[66]

About 1:00 a.m. Sunday, September 13, the Norwegian bark *Ellen* passed near the scene of the sinking. During the storm the bark lost its sails and foremast and shipped water in the hold. But hearing cries of men in the water, Captain Anders Johnsen ordered his crew to search for and take aboard all survivors. Second officer James Frazer was plucked from the water along with some forty-eight others. Nine days later three more survivors were spotted in a lifeboat and rescued. Various vessels brought survivors into Savannah, Norfolk, and New York. Only 149 crewmen and passengers survived the sinking of the *Central America*, 423 perished. At the time, it was the single greatest maritime disaster involving an American commercial vessel attributed to a hurricane. Captain Herndon was not among the survivors. A few years later officers of the U.S. Navy erected on the grounds of the Naval Academy at Annapolis a granite monument commemorating the captain's heroism and inscribed with the words "Forgetful of self, mindful of others, his life was beautiful to the last."[67]

By the 1850s new men no longer entered rice planting in the lowcountry. The great planters controlled the rice lands, but even their ranks were being thinned by death. Entry to the rice culture came only by inheritance or marriage. It was costly and labor-intensive work to repair and rebuild dikes, to dig out ditches and canals, and to restore buildings on rice plantations damaged so frequently by tropical storms and hurricanes. Competition abroad continued to threaten the rice culture. Well aware of these threats, some planters experimented by planting wheat on former rice lands. The rice kingdom was in decline.[68]

In April 1861 shore batteries around Charleston fired on a U.S. ship attempting to resupply government troops occupying Fort Sumter in the harbor. President Lincoln called for seventy-five thousand volunteers, and the Civil War began. Four years of blood and treasure were expended by the North to save and by the South to leave the Union. But even as the maelstrom of war swirled around them, the thoughts of hurricanes and the sea were never far from the minds of a coastal and a religious people.

The Reverend Paul Trapier, a former U.S. Navy officer, wrote *The Hurricane* in 1862, a pamphlet that was distributed by the Charleston Female Bible, Prayer-Book, and Tract Society. While it described a terrible tropical cyclone at sea, it was also an essay about a powerful and wrathful God. Trapier himself served aboard a naval vessel enveloped by a great storm. From his experience he wrote the following account:

The hurricane came down . . . a crashing blow, and, . . . the brig reeled, staggered and laid over on her beam ends—a low-decked, deep-waisted vessel, carrying a heavy battery of guns, with yard-arms ten feet under the water, a sailor knows, doth seldom again ever "right." The brig deep-buried beneath the waves, seemed settling fast. The slide of the lee companion-way . . . having been left open, the sea poured in, filling her below, and added greatly to the danger. The roar of the hurricane, the awful towering waves, the blinding spray, the sinking vessel, the despairing creatures, gasping for life. . . . [But] Slowly and with great effort the brig began to "right" and, obedient to her helm, fell off before the wind. [Now] . . . began our desperate encounter with death. The first plunges of the brig into the boiling sea that rose before her, completely smothered us. The pressure of the wind drove her bows entirely under, and it was evident she could not swim unless lightened. . . . the anchors were cut adrift. . . . The battery next . . . overboard. . . . The violence of the hurricane was now terrific beyond description. The sea . . . piled up in wildest confusion — pyramids of immense base, whose tops, immediately as they rose above the general level, were cut off, as by a scythe, and scattered in broad sheets of spray. We could not see twenty yards in any direction. Suddenly . . . the wind shifted . . . and before it we scudded along. . . . The hurricane was at its height. How could we escape when the reefs were reached, and the brig thrown headlong among the breakers? . . . all for the last time committed themselves to God's mercy and protection. . . . [Then] . . . tremendous crests of the breakers were seen looming through the mist like mountains of snow. . . . we were borne onward, and uplifted . . . into the foaming breakers we plunged. The sea dashed over us, burying the brig deep beneath the waters. Again she struck [the reef], and again the sea swept over. Again and again she struck. . . . we instantly expected her to break in pieces. . . . But . . . He guided . . . us . . . through the boiling sea . . . [until we were] at last in[to] smooth water, and were safe! Of eighty souls, not one even injured. . . . We had passed through the dark valley.[69]

The essay by Trapier was likely aimed at transient sailors who patronized Charleston's bars and brothels. But its appeal was wider. The essay would have resonated with those lowcountry natives who made their living on or near the sea and who frequently experienced great storms out of the tropics.

CHAPTER SIX

Another Cycle of Tropical Storms and Hurricanes, 1865–1885

The Planting Class

The Civil War was a disaster in blood and treasure for the nation, but especially the South. Across coastal Georgia and South Carolina, slaves deserted rice and cotton plantations and fled to Union lines. Some planters moved their bondsmen inland. Those who continued to plant did so with reduced numbers of slaves. Production declined, and the Union blockade of the coast prevented shipments abroad. Runaway slaves vandalized or destroyed rice mills, dikes, and trunks on the Savannah River rice plantations.

The war winnowed the ranks of lowcountry planters and their sons. Langdon Cheves II of Delta Plantation on the Savannah River was killed at Battery Wagner during the siege of Charleston; Captain Henry Lord Page King, son of Thomas and Anna Page King of Retreat Plantation, St. Simons Island, was killed at Fredericksburg, Virginia. The planter ranks also dwindled as some died of natural causes, and others grew too old or too weary to face another season of work and uncertainty. Those who continued to base their fortunes on rice and cotton needed a workforce; to find laborers, they began negotiations with newly freed slaves. Though the social climate presented unfamiliar challenges, the usual vagaries of lowcountry weather were all too familiar.[1]

Offshore and Inshore Storms

In late October 1865, the *Petit*, offshore from Savannah, was battered by a "very severe gale" for fifty-six hours; the brig *Alice Franklin*, at latitude 31.4° north, longitude 78.6° west, overturned in a "terrific gale" and remained on its side for twelve hours before righting. In the same vicinity the steamship *Republic* encountered the tropical storm, perhaps a hurricane. The ship was bound from New York for New Orleans. A former blockade-runner for the Confederacy, the *Republic*, upon capture by Federal troops, became a warship in the Union navy. The two-masted 210-foot-long vessel was powered by steam and propelled by side wheels twenty-eight feet across. It carried fifty-nine passengers and a valuable inventory of gold and silver coins.[2]

Shipping tremendous seas that poured into the hold, water soon extinguished the boiler fires and drowned the pumps. Unnavigable and taking on water, the *Republic* went down some one hundred miles southeast of Savannah in seventeen hundred feet of water on October 25, 1865. Passengers and crew took to lifeboats and a raft. Forty-two survived. Seventeen perished. In the twentieth century a robot armed with powerful lights, cameras, and mechanical arms discovered the *Republic*'s location. The gold and silver coins on the wreckage are estimated to be worth as much as $180,000,000 today.[3]

Storms remained offshore throughout the remainder of the 1860s. In 1870 an act of Congress established the National Weather Service that required the Signal Corps to warn of the "approach and force of storms . . . on the seacoast by magnetic telegraph and marine signals." The act created a network of observers along the Atlantic and Gulf coasts. Later, weather bureaus were established at both Savannah and Charleston. Over time these offices provided timely advice on storms threatening those at sea and ashore.[4]

When a violent gale swept the lowcountry on August 18–19, 1871, the Charleston press wrote that the storm was not "unexpected . . . as the weather reports, foretold its coming by several days, which enabled the river craft at least to secure safe moorings."[5] Nonetheless the storm's winds, which reached hurricane strength, battered vessels offshore, lowcountry crops, and everything else in its path.

The storm caught the 1,230-ton steamship *Liberty* far to the east of Savannah on August 18, enveloping the vessel in "clouds of rain and spray." The captain saw his steamship "shipping tons of water over bow and stern." The following day a "very bad cross sea . . . [came] from all directions . . . tossing, rolling, and pitching." The *Liberty* became "unnavigable" after waves smashed its rudder. With a moderating sea and repairs to the rudder, the *Liberty* reached Tybee Island, where a pilot boat guided it upriver to Savannah on August 20. The crew was lucky to be alive.[6]

The 143-ton schooner *Sabino*, of Bath, Maine, bound for Jacksonville, Florida, with a load of railroad iron, ran into the hurricane on August 19 south of Cape Hatteras. Winds tore away its sails, caused a leak in the hull, and left the *Sabino* waterlogged in a heavy sea. A day later the schooner was "in a sinking condition" when the *Mary R. Somers* came alongside and rescued the crew. It was assumed that abandoned craft, parts of vessels, and cargo littered the waters off the lowcountry.[7]

The hurricane brushed the Florida coast at Jacksonville, looped offshore, and made landfall near St. Simons, Georgia.[8] It moved north, sweeping across Savannah with high winds and rain. The local press praised the weather service in Washington that had predicted "a severe storm." Throughout Friday, August 18, winds battered and torrential rains flooded stores and houses. A reporter observed that Broughton Street, the main street in the business district, presented "a river-like appearance; boats ran through . . . the streets."[9]

The press reported no lives lost, but damage to public and private property was "immense." The cost to repair Savannah's public works alone reached $100,000 ($1,448,031). Beyond the city, rice and cotton crops sustained "great damage."[10]

Near Beaufort streams overflowed, trees smashed to the ground, and three vessels loading phosphates at Bull River were driven ashore. The lowcountry's burgeoning phosphate industry had experienced its first weather disaster. Eventually the industry would succumb owing to various factors, but devastating storms that ravaged its mining operations hastened its demise.[11]

The Charleston press reported the August 18–19 storm to have been "one of the severest . . . experienced for years" — northeast winds whipped across the city "with great violence in heavy squalls" of rain for twenty-four hours. The "unceasing" winds and rains combined to bowl over trees, damage roofs, and carve holes in streets large "enough to hold a carriage and horse." A nearly unbroken sheet of water covered the city from Broad Street to Franklin Street.[12]

Up the coast, in the vicinity of Georgetown, the hurricane did "serious damage" to the crops along the Santee and Waccamaw rivers, "especially to the May and June rice which [was] in blossom."[13]

Storms of the 1870s

The last three decades of the nineteenth century were a most active period for tropical storms and hurricanes in the lowcountry. In 1873 a powerful offshore tropical cyclone caught the schooner *Sylvan* at latitude 32.28° north, longitude 78.40° west, on October 6. Captained by Otis C. Veazie, a native of Maine, the schooner carried a cargo of lumber. Near nightfall a "heavy sea" knocked the vessel over, carried away nearly everything on its deck, tore off the two masts, and filled it with water. It righted and the crew cleared away the wreckage. But with the "gale . . . increasing in the morning" and "the sea running very high," Captain Veazie ordered his five crewmen to lash themselves to the after-house. Wave after wave crashed over the ship. Then suddenly a huge sea crashed into what was left of the *Sylvan* and broke off the after-house with the crew lashed to it.[14]

For three days they drifted without food or water until spotted and rescued by the schooner *J. H. Stickney.* The crew of the *Sylvan* — Captain Veazie, mate Henry P. Hatch, steward Emile La Blanc, and three black seamen — were nearly naked, their clothes torn from their bodies by the force of the waves. Their vessel, partially owned by the crew and now lost at sea, was valued at $7,000 ($102,984). It was not insured.[15]

September 1874 found lowcountry residents on the lookout for a major hurricane. In Charleston local convention held that "severe and disastrous" storms occur "once in every twenty years." It was twenty years since the last major hurricane in 1854. By the end of September 1874 lowcountry residents breathed a collective sigh of relief, believing they had escaped the fury of a great storm. But even as they celebrated their good fortune a tropical storm in the Gulf of

Mexico moved overland across Florida, exited near Jacksonville, and curved north, gaining strength over the warm waters. Vessels offshore from the low-country to Virginia first experienced the powerful storm. Captain Hunter of the steamship *Virginia* encountered it off South Carolina on September 28. He believed that "the gale was about as severe as is experienced on the ocean." His passengers praised Hunter and crew who, with "the blessings of Providence," saw them safely into port. Warnings from the U.S. Weather Service helped to reduce damage to coastal shipping. The hurricane roiled the coastal waters of Georgia as it approached Tybee Island from the east.[16]

High winds and torrents of rain flooded the island, washed away fifty feet of beach, and leveled sand dunes. Surging tides submerged rice plantations along the Altamaha, Satilla, Ogeechee, and Savannah rivers. Harvested and stacked rice floated away with the high tides. On some plantations the yields were cut in half; the losses were "severe." One planter calculated his losses at $20,000 ($309,076). Damage on rice plantations in South Carolina was much the same as in Georgia. Saltwater overwhelmed fresh in the Combahee and Ashepoo rivers, which surged over their banks and into the fields of rice.[17]

Increasing in strength, the hurricane created havoc at Charleston. A reporter who braved the storm on the waterfront observed:

> The sea in the harbor rolled mountain high, and the waves dashed over the piers in huge rollers. In every direction driftwood, bales of cotton, wrecked boats and debris were being tossed about. The wind whistling through the rigging of the shipping made melancholy music, and the blinding rain following in torrents rendered efforts to save anything almost useless.[18]

For four hours winds pummeled the waterfront. Wharves collapsed and washed away. Sailing craft parted their moorings. Some sank, and winds sent one vessel ashore where its bowsprit pierced the second story of a brick building, cutting the structure in two. Surging tides flooded streets and yards. Residents saved their chickens by taking "their whole poultry yard up into their rooms and piazzas." Streetcars floated in Calhoun Street. Tin roofs peeled away. A gust of wind knocked over the massive walls of a new theater under construction on Meeting Street. The storm flag hoisted by the weather service was blown away and all telegraph lines went down cutting off communications.[19]

On East and South Battery huge breakers crashed over the seawall, tearing away large flagstones and flooding White Point Gardens with four feet of seawater. The frail bridge connecting the Battery's south walk to the Charleston Bath House was swept out to sea, leaving stranded in the flimsy bathhouse the owner Michael McMamnon, his wife and two children, and a young man. Despite the winds and rain, hundreds of people gathered along the Battery to watch the drama unfold. Rocked from side to side by the waves, the bathhouse appeared on the verge of collapse. An attempt was made to rescue the occupants by some "colored fishermen," city policemen, and H. Nott Parker, a member of the elite Palmetto Boat crew. The group launched a small boat, but "angrily foaming" waves capsized them almost immediately. Some of the would-be rescuers nearly drowned before being pulled from the water by bystanders. On shore, the son of the bathhouse owner, young James McMamnon, had to be restrained from an attempt to swim to the rescue of his family. Next, Harry Hansen, from a U.S. buoy tender, tied a rope to his waist. He anchored one end to the shore, plunged into the crashing water, and swam to the bathhouse. He returned with one of the small children. With a lull in the storm — apparently the passage of the hurricane's eye — another boat was launched, and this rescue attempt was successful. Within a half-hour the wind returned with "fearful force" and brought down the structure, which disappeared beneath the waves.[20]

McMamnon lost everything he owned. The local government prohibited rebuilding the bathhouse, not because of its vulnerability to storms, but because it was located too near Charleston's main sewer which discharged the city's waste into the harbor.[21]

On Sullivan's Island ocean swells six to eight feet in height broke across the beach, overturning small bathing houses and two-room shanties on the island's east end. Waters broke over the walls of Fort Moultrie and submerged a portion of the island. The boat of Isaac Truesdale, "a colored oysterman," broke away from its mooring, and he went after it in a smaller craft, capsizing near Drunken Dick Shoals. Truesdale was seen atop the bottom of his vessel waving frantically for help. A summer resident, George F. Moffett, attempted to launch a boat to reach Truesdale, but the sea was running too high.[22]

Apparently, an islander of poetic bent who watched the storm unfold witnessed Truesdale's last minutes:

the whole ocean as far as the eye could reach was whitened with . . . whirling foam. While all eyes [watched] . . . the terrible scene . . . a dark object appeared suddenly upon the distant billows. . . . upon closer observation we discovered it to be a human being . . . hurried along to the dark shores of eternity! . . . far on the misty horizon a crested wave rose for an instant, rolled on its course but when it had vanished, the object was seen no more. . . . It was the most fearful feature of the storm. A sight I hope to never witness again.[23]

Besides Truesdale, another casualty of the hurricane was a black man who was killed near Georgetown when winds blew over a house, crushing him and a team of four oxen. In Georgetown County, crop damage was widespread. Robert J. Middleton observed that 50 percent of the rice was lost at plantations along the Pee Dee by flooding and freshets.[24]

In addition to the human casualties and the destruction of rice and cotton in coastal Georgia and South Carolina, the city of Charleston was hard hit. Early estimates of the damage in Charleston reached $250,000 ($3,863,445). Subsequently property losses in Charleston and vicinity neared $750,000 ($11,590,335). Despite the disaster, one reporter wrote, "It's an ill wind that blows nobody any good." Predictions were that "several hundred sturdy mechanics will at once find their services in demand"; two days after the hurricane "the ring of hammers could be heard" throughout the city.[25]

Optimistically one journalist suggested that since it had been twenty years since the last hurricane in 1854, "those who profess to know about the elements . . . say . . . that Charleston may breathe freely for twenty years to come."[26] Unfortunately for residents of the lowcountry a severe hurricane struck again much sooner than predicted.

Lowcountry Agriculture

A new cycle of destructive tropical storms and cyclones in the final third of the century threatened an economy built primarily on agriculture. Labor problems and new avenues for making money contributed to an end of cotton cultivation in lowcountry Georgia. Sea island cotton required a sizable force of regimented slave laborers before the Civil War; finding such workers after the war and emancipation was nearly impossible. Sharecropping and day-wage labor never effectively replaced the prewar slave labor. One scholar has recently written, "Whatever wage it might have taken to get freedmen to dig mud [for fertilizer] in the winter and haul it to the cotton lands, these planters were unable to pay."[27]

On Sapelo Island, Georgia, cotton planting ended in the 1870s when the heirs of Thomas Spalding turned to timber and cattle as sources of income. In the 1880s cotton planting ended on Jekyll Island when the DuBignon family sold the island to northern businessmen who formed the Jekyll Island Club of New York City. They planned to turn the island into a resort for one hundred of the United States' most prominent and influential families. Among the membership roster were the names of such capitalists as William Rockefeller Jr., Joseph Pulitzer, Vincent Astor, William Vanderbilt, and J. Pierpont Morgan. Likewise the heirs of Robert Stafford sold Cumberland Island to Thomas M. Carnegie. By that time only a handful of white and black farmers grew cotton on the sea islands and the adjacent mainland of Georgia. Subsistent farming, timbering, and truck farming replaced cotton. It was a like story on South Carolina's sea islands, where too there was no return to the "glory days" of cotton growing that planters had enjoyed before the war. Cotton cultivation became only "marginally profitable." In 1920 the boll weevil ended even that.[28]

In decline since the 1820s, rice cultivation experienced the same labor problems as cotton. The rice planters also faced ever increasing foreign competition, wartime destruction, shortages of capital, and a cycle of tropical storms and hurricanes in the final decades of the nineteenth century. The storms destroyed what remained of an intricate system of laboriously constructed dikes, ditches, canals, trunks, and embankments so essential to rice growing. Rice cultivation was abandoned. The old plantations were sold to wealthy northerners, to timber companies, and to the federal government.[29]

End-of-the-Century Hurricanes

Although tropical storms continued a pattern of crossing the lowcountry's coastal waters and coming ashore yearly in the mid-1870s, damage to property, crops, and shipping was minimal.[30] Then in September 1878, a hurricane came out of the tropics. After claiming hundreds of lives in Cuba, Haiti, and Trinidad, it passed up the spine of Florida, exited near St. Augustine, and moved northward just off the Georgia coast. It came ashore below Charleston on September 12. Sailing craft along the immediate coast were dismasted. Captains ordered topmasts cut away to prevent capsizing. The *City of New York* fought the hurricane for forty hours between Hatteras and Charleston. Vessels were abandoned at sea, and wreckage was strewn along the coast.[31]

The hurricane's winds swept the lowcountry at flood tide, pushing swells of seawater into the rice fields. Damage to rice crops at Butler's Island, Georgia, was so extensive that rice planting was abandoned altogether. The South Carolina press reported that "the storm . . . was disastrous to the rice crops on the Combahee and Ashepoo rivers." Almost without exception every planter "suffered from the disastrous high tides that swept over the banks of the rice fields, breaking them in . . . and flooding the fields with water." Rice already cut and stacked was swept away, and up to two-thirds of the crop was lost.[32]

According to the Charleston weather station, the center of the storm passed north of Charleston, which minimized damage in the city and harbor where some forty vessels were anchored or at wharfside. Although winds at Charleston blew for fifteen consecutive hours, their velocity was measured at only thirty-three miles per hour. On Sullivan's Island "the wind shrieked and howled [and] the tide came" flooding in, making some summer residents nervous. But damage was light compared with earlier hurricanes. The next day's paper described it this way: "Sullivan's Island still stands and bids defiance to all such second-class West India hurricanes."[33] Three years later a more powerful tropical cyclone came out of the West Indies to test the resilience of lowcountry residents and its economy.

Two Powerful Hurricanes with Similar Paths, 1804 and 1881

In late August 1881 a hurricane moved away from the Leeward Islands and toward the southeastern United States. Vessels in its path took a beating. Captain Daniel Higgins of the bark *Brunswick*, with a cargo of pitch pine and timber, encountered squalls for two days that increased in "violence." Friday night, August 26, about seventy-five miles north of Charleston a "fearful hurricane" struck the bark. A "grizzled and wrinkled" crewman, James Fisher, who had sailed the many seas for forty years, said he had never seen "a blow that could compare." Because of the roar of the storm, Fisher "could not hear a word at a distance of five feet." Winds carried off the rigging, and a heavy sea opened seams in the *Brunswick*. It began taking on water. Captain Higgins ordered thirty-five thousand feet of timber thrown overboard, and the vessel sailed "better for awhile." But by Saturday morning the *Brunswick* was listing so far to its leeward side that its sails dragged in the ocean. In danger of capsizing, the crew cut away the masts, and the bark came upright. The sea continued to "pour over her in torrents." It was "a roaring, rushing, irresistible avalanche." Theodore Shadduck, a Greek sailor, went overboard. Some saw him on the crest of a "mighty wave behind us" and thought he would be swept back to the bark, but then he disappeared.[34]

With "immense seas" breaking over the *Brunswick*, Captain Higgins ordered the crew to lash themselves to the stump of the mizzenmast or the spanker-boom. Fifty-five-year-old James Fisher told the crew it was "every man for himself. Let us die like men." As the bark went down, the crew was pitched into the heavy sea. Ambrose Mannelli, a Spanish sailor, drowned, and two others went unaccounted for. Captain Higgins and his five remaining crewmembers managed to crawl onto part of the wrecked vessel's deck. In the pitch black night the bark's cargo of lumber was hurled by winds and waves into the men fighting for their lives in the sea. A forty-foot log smashed into James Fisher's face: "[it] knock[ed] all my front teeth down my throat."[35]

For the next few days vessels passed near but apparently did not see Captain Higgins's overcoat raised as a signal flag over the men on the wreckage. They "drifted . . . hungry, thirsty and despairing." Without food or water, some crewmen became delirious. Three who drank saltwater "began to lose their minds." The "negro steward wanted to eat his hands." Weak, helpless, dehydrated, near exhaustion, and almost without hope, they were sighted after four days on the water by the pilot boat *Belle* of Savannah. On the same day, one crewman previously unaccounted for, Pat McDermitt, was sighted clinging to a piece of wreckage below Savannah at latitude 31° north, longitude 80° west. He was rescued by the bark, *Ceres*.[36]

Somewhere far off the South Carolina coast in late August, the schooner *Mary G. Fisher* of Philadelphia, carrying 210 tons of coal, also ran into the hurricane. Aboard was its twenty-one-year-old captain, Enoch Camp of Philadelphia, first mate James H. Harris, the "colored cook" Frank Evans, who was a native of Wilmington, North Carolina, and two "colored" deckhands. A cross-sea of breaking swells came at the schooner from the east and southeast. Captain Camp ordered sails reefed, and the schooner wallowed in the heaving ocean until a huge sea took away the lifeboat and caused massive structural damage.

Water poured into the hold. Another wave tore away the rudder. To save themselves, crewmembers climbed into the rigging, but crashing waves upended the vessel, and it began to sink. First mate James Harris thought of his "home, of loved ones and friends . . . and made up . . . [his] mind to die." Pulled under the water with the sinking schooner, Harris almost drowned before swimming to the surface. He pulled off his clothes making it easier for him to swim through giant swells to a white pine scantling some fifteen feet long. Captain Camp bobbed up near Harris, "nearly gone," and soon sank. Harris never saw the young captain or the three other crewmen again. It was Wednesday, and he was all alone in a rolling, breaking sea some twenty-five miles from shore. Harris clung to the pine board as waves washed over him, sometimes knocking him off. In the fading light of day he saw a large portion of the schooner's cabin and swam to it. He crawled upon it and lay full length gripping tightly to both sides. Near dark he glanced over the edge and thought, "heavens and earth . . . I was followed by a pack of hungry sharks swimming all around me." Terrified when he was knocked off his raft by waves, he managed to scramble back. Harris's teeth chattered from the cold, and rain pelted him throughout a night that was the longest of his life. He prayed for morning. When it came, the seas moderated though it was squally. He held his mouth to the sky and caught some drops of rain. On Thursday night the wind died, and the sea became smooth on Friday morning. The sharks were "still keeping [him] company"; "they are not very pleasant companions," he thought. His mouth and throat were parched. He was so thirsty he "could have drank [his] own blood."[37]

First mate Harris had not seen land or sail, but he knew the wind and sea were carrying him shoreward. On Saturday he burned all day in the brilliant sun. That night, Harris knew he "was not right in the head" and was "growing delirious." He hallucinated. Imagining he saw land, he tried to jump ashore but only sank into the water. He quickly reboarded his raft. Then he saw someone "handing [him] a pitcher of ice water," but it was like salt when he tasted it. On Sunday the sun "arose out of a clear horizon, not a cloud visible in the heavens." Harris was on his raft "but could not think how [he] got there." He remembered nothing until Monday morning, after five days on a raft, when delirious and blistered all over "dreadfully," he was picked up off Bull's Bay, South Carolina, by the steamship *Santiago de Cuba*. Taken to St. Joseph's Infirmary in Savannah, Harris praised his rescuers and prayed for their long life and for that of physician George H. Stone from whom he had received such kind treatment. Nine days after his rescue, nearly recovered from his ordeal, Harris told a newspaper reporter that he could say, with the Ancient Mariner:

> O wedding guest: this soul has been
> Alone on a wide, wide sea.
> So lonely 'twas, that God himself
> Scarce seemed there to be.[38]

As the hurricane moved closer to the lowcountry, vessels near shore encountered it. Off the lower Georgia coast, the hurricane knocked down the Norwegian ship *La Louisiana,* carried away its cabin, and smashed in the stern. Its captain and his sixteen-member crew abandoned the vessel for a lifeboat. When last seen the *La Louisiana* was sinking near latitude 31° north, longitude 78° west. The crew was rescued and brought into Darien, Georgia, by the Portuguese bark *Marianna III.*[39]

Off Savannah at latitude 32° north, longitude 78° west, in the early morning hours of August 28, the schooner *Hannah M. Lollis* was struck by the full force of the hurricane. Captained by Gardner H. Lollis (the schooner was apparently named for his wife), the vessel was laden with a cargo of lumber. High waves carried away the masts and washed overboard Captain Lollis and the "colored" cook, Caleb Bell. Waterlogged and with its cargo shifting, the vessel wallowed low in the ocean. Five crewmembers clung to the wreck for two days until rescued up by the steamship *Juniata* and brought to Savannah, where the men recovered from bruises and broken bones.[40]

The *Nettie Langdon* of Boston took on a load of yellow pine at Darien, Georgia, and sailed north off the South Carolina coast. Captain E. W. Collins encountered the hurricane on August 27; soon the vessel overturned, and crashing waves carried one seaman into the turbulent waters. After the masts, sails, and rigging were cut away, the schooner righted itself. With the lifeboat gone, some believed they faced imminent death. Another seaman washed overboard. In the early morning hours of August 28, the schooner was driven onto the shoals of Cape Romain, where the crew remained aboard without food or water for three days until rescued.[41]

A few miles north off Georgetown's beach, the schooner *Pride of the East* was found abandoned, waterlogged, and without deckhouse or masts. It had loaded mahogany at Tuxpan, Mexico, and was headed for New York. An observer characterized the fate of the *Nettie Langdon* and the *Pride of the East* as "forcible instances of the terrors of the . . . storm."[42] Dismasted vessels, their debris, and cargoes littered the waters off the lowcountry.

On Friday, August 26, 1881, the *Savannah Morning News* carried a brief article about a storm forming in the Atlantic, but the U.S. Signal Corps issued no official warning. Winds of the hurricane brushed Jacksonville, Florida, and the storm spun over warm waters headed for the Georgia coast. For several days mariners at the mouth of the Savannah River noticed that "a heavy sea was running" accompanied by "gale" force winds. They speculated that a large storm might be gathering. On Saturday morning, August 27, residents on Tybee Island saw "the rain set in thick, the gale increasing every minute." Tybee was a favorite spot for a respite from the summer heat. Like those on other emerging resorts along the east coast, cottage-owners and tourists were lured to the island by the prospect of healthful ocean breezes. To some Tybee resembled "a cozy village" of cottages and substantial houses. Visitors could find accommodations at Ocean House, a modest forty-room, three-story hotel with piazzas. A mule-drawn streetcar transferred guests from the wharf to lodging in the resort community. But on Saturday morning the streetcar was not in service. High seas had washed away portions of Tybee's wharf and forced the steamer from the city to turn back to Savannah. Only on Saturday afternoon did the chief signal officer in Washington, D.C., dispatch a telegram warning that a hurricane was bearing down on the South Carolina coast. But it was too late to warn lowcountry residents.[43]

Early that evening, the hurricane grazed Brunswick, Georgia. In Darien it unroofed houses, uprooted trees, and caused drownings. At Harris Neck, on the coast in rural Bryan County, high winds felled more than fifteen dwellings, crushing four black persons and injuring six others. The storm made landfall between St. Simons Island and Savannah, most likely at Ossabaw Island, just a few miles southeast of Savannah. On nearby Tybee Island, at the home of Colonel J. H. Estill, owner of the *Savannah Morning News*, hurricane-force winds began battering the dwelling. The Estill home was situated about eight feet above the highest tides. The residents there felt safe until around 7:00 p.m., when windows on the eastern side of the house blew in. Efforts of two men to nail boards across the openings were only partially successful. The rain and wind poured in. Suddenly the "lurid glare of fire" lit up the night.[44]

Winds had knocked over Henry Soloman's oceanfront home, acclaimed as one of the most solidly built houses on the island. When it collapsed, gas ignited, and the house burst into flames—flames whipped by hurricane winds. "Colored men" and neighbors of the Solomans ran to the burning house and pulled Mrs. Soloman and her son, Nathaniel, from the flames. One of the African Americans, Albert Page, broke his back and leg while assisting in the rescue. Mrs. Georgianna Wolf, about twenty-three, her daughter Halle, and her brother, Joshua Falk, who had fled from their dwelling to the Soloman house for safety, all perished. Crushed by the collapsing house, their bodies were also severely burned. One witness saw that "on the spot where the house had stood . . . there was not a vestige of it left." The *New York Times* carried the story.[45]

The men in the Estill house were too preoccupied to assist with the Solomans' rescue. Ocean water now rushed "under the house with the force of a Niagara." Fearing that it might collapse, Estill decided to abandon his home for one nearby on higher ground. The three men carried or led the three ladies, six children, and two servants into the night, through seawater two feet deep, with "the wind cutting like a knife, [and] the salt spray blinding" them. When they reached their destination they were alarmed to find not a dry spot inside. Using storm lanterns, the men watched the tide rise to unprecedented heights. Waves rolled under the house, slamming its underside with timbers from other fallen structures. They estimated the tidal surge to be twelve to fourteen feet above high water. A few more feet, and the house and its occupants may have washed into the sea. Luckily the water rose no farther. Some compared it to the "great hurricane" of 1804 that had followed the same track.[46]

House after house on Tybee, from King's Landing to Leary's, was washed away or severely damaged by the storm. Mrs. Pauline Heyward of Charleston, occupying one of the new Bacon and Company cottages near the beach, watched in terror the rising water and "huge live oaks and palmetto trees . . . centuries [old] torn up by the roots and whirled about like straws." With one child in arms and the maids carrying two others, Mrs. Heyward hurried out of the house and away from the ocean moments before the house collapsed. They fled into the blowing "rain and sand, which blinded [them] and pricked like needles." She was determined to reach the Blun house, the only home on the island she had noticed with a brick foundation and with brick chimneys. When she, her children, and the maids reached the Blun house, only one room was not flooded. The house "tottered and threatened" to fall into the waves swirling around it, but it stood. Mrs. Heyward remained here until the storm subsided. Her account of escape from the storm appeared in the *New York Times*.[47]

The beach was swept "as smooth as a billiard table." The wreckage of dwellings, bathhouses, dance platforms, trees, and sand dunes were washed or blown far ashore into the hammocks of pine, scrub oaks, and palmetto. Even some residents found safety there. Others took refuge in Tybee's hotel, Ocean House. But its lower floor offered little shelter when it flooded with water. On the northeast end of the island, near the lighthouse, a slue was cut, creating a long peninsula. As the ocean poured through the slue and into Beacon Pond it became one large lake. A young woman who was swept into the pond saved herself and her little sister by paddling on a log until she reached high ground and trees to climb. There rescuers found them.[48]

The storm surge over nearby smaller islands brought even greater devastation and deaths. On Long Island the sea burst through the door of the Tybee lighthouse, filling it with water and carrying away all supplies for the light and the lighthouse's residents. Theodore Morel, keeper of the light, his wife, sister, and daughter fled into the light room, about four feet square. Terrified, they waited, expecting the lighthouse to topple at any moment. For hours they were marooned, until rescued by boat. Earlier Morel had urged a fisherman, Valentine Morton, who lived on Long Island in a shanty, to take refuge in the lighthouse with his family. But Morton declined. Subsequently the storm surge demolished Mr. Morton's shanty, spilling the fisherman, his wife, and a young child into the sea. Their bodies washed ashore on Tybee.[49]

Just to the north, on Cockspur Island, residents saved themselves by fleeing into Fort Pulaski, the massive brick structure guarding the entrance to the Savannah River. Every house on Cockspur except one was swept away. Just to the west, on Skidaway Island, houses went down at its northern and southern tips, as did homes on Burnside Island. Residents on both islands spent a horrifying night without shelter, enduring hurricane-force winds and pouring rains. On Wilmington Island the storm unroofed houses, uprooted trees, scattered debris, and drowned cattle. The superintendent of the Bethesda Orphans' Home reported that the dwellings had "flooded from top to bottom"; "[one] shook so . . . I thought it would fall." He herded the boys into the parlor while trees crashed down around the home.[50]

Near the city, the Savannah River boiled over its banks, flooding the house of Addison Stokes. Fearing for his family's life, Stokes moved his wife, young son, and daughter out into the "pitchy darkness and blinding rain," leading them from his home into a nearby house he considered safer. It provided shelter until swept into the river. Mrs. Stokes and the two children drowned. Critically injured, Addison was rescued by "a colored man." Fast-rising tides surged over the islands and rice plantations along the Savannah River, carrying away former slave cabins and the black families huddled inside. Sometimes the shanties collapsed, breaking bones or crushing occupants who had taken shelter there. Bodies floated in the Savannah River. Bodies washed up on Hutchinson Island opposite the city. Bodies washed ashore on Shad, Fig, Elba, Argyle, and other smaller islands. Most were drowning victims, and most were black. The Savannah coroner was overwhelmed.[51]

Initial estimates of the dead reached three hundred. But the true numbers may never be known. Some unaccounted for were likely washed out to sea. The Savannah press observed that the "unfortunates had but a slight chance . . . as they lived in small houses upon low lands, and the tidal wave came upon them at night." The planters who "depended on [them] for regular labor . . . regret the loss of these people, many of whom were formerly their slaves, and who were descendants of those who had cultivated the same fields for nearly a century."[52] Savannahian Clara Waring told her husband that there were "sad accounts of loss of life among the negroes."[53]

Beginning early Saturday evening, northeast winds whipped across Savannah and continued for six hours. Steamers, schooners, sloops, and yachts smashed into the city's wharves, blew ashore, or sank. In the business district from East Broad to West Broad streets, the hurricane spared few buildings. On the waterfront, roofs tore away; warehouses, a rice mill, a granary, and a cotton press sustained extensive damages. Rains soaked the merchandize in unroofed stores. At the City Exchange the storm peeled away tin, blew in windows, and flooded offices of the city government. Portions of the city market collapsed. Facilities of the Central of Georgia railroad were battered. When winds took away the tin roof of the building occupied by the *Savannah Morning News*, rain poured into the composing and editorial rooms. Around 9:00 p.m. winds ripped away the roof of the U.S. Signal Corps office, smashing its instruments for measuring wind velocity. The barometer continued to fall, and it was estimated that winds increased to more than eighty-five miles per hour. Darkness enveloped the city. At churches and private homes, shutters wrenched away, windows and doors blew in, and tin roofs — more vulnerable than those of slate — rolled up. Downed telegraph wires, uprooted trees, limbs, and other debris of the storm choked city streets and sidewalks. It would take years to grow trees, the "pride of the city," to replace the huge oaks and elms that went down. To some it was a night of "blinding darkness, howling wind and fierce rain" — a storm "that brought . . . fearful desolation, woe and destruction."[54] Some put the number of deaths, mainly African Americans, on the lowlands along the Savannah River, at 335. Estimates of damage in Savannah and vicinity reached $1,500,000 ($25,780,372). The growing turpentine and naval stores business suffered heavy losses.[55]

The storm swept over South Carolina's sea islands. At Daufuskie Island the sea took away the wharf, a boat at the lighthouse, and several huts belonging to African Americans. Near Beaufort ten black laborers, who dug phosphates for the Coosaw Mining Company, joined others seeking shelter from the storm in the Port Royal ferry house. When high winds and waves demolished and swept away the structure, as many as forty African Americans perished there.[56]

At Beaufort, South Carolina, on Saturday evening, what locals described as a "terrific cyclone" slammed into the town. At high tide a storm surge of fifteen feet crashed into wharves, tearing them "to pieces," tossing vessels into the marshes, and sending seawater cascading over the seawall, into warehouses, streets, and homes. Winds unroofed retail stores and houses. On the Coosaw and Morgan rivers, the storm ruined equipment of new businesses engaged in the manufacture of fertilizer. It sank or blew into the marshes dredges and small boats belonging to the Coosaw Mining Company and damaged the Pinckney Phosphate Works on Morgan Island.[57]

Hurricane winds and waves pushed ocean water up the Combahee, Ashepoo, and Edisto rivers, which became as "salty as the sea." The rivers broke through embankments and flooded the rice plantations bearing such names as Laurel Spring, Cypress, Myrtle Grove, Rose Hill, Hobonney, Bonny Hall, and Dungannon. An observer said that the "fresh water reeds look as if they had been scorched with fire, so deadly was the effect of the salt water upon them." When the saltwater flooded the fields, "it was like pouring scalding water over the rice crops." Houses were overturned and trees uprooted. Along the rivers it was a "picture of desolation." Reports from forty-seven rice plantations, including those along the Cooper River to the north, indicated that 50 percent of the rice crop was lost.[58]

The storm moved north toward Charleston, littering the marshes with small craft. Edingsville Island, facing the open sea and frequently pounded by hurricanes, took the brunt of the storm. By early Saturday evening a howling east wind drove the tide high up on the beach, and waves crashed under the few remaining summer homes. The terrified occupants fled to the house of D. A. Stevens, considered to be the only safe structure on the island. The sea undermined and the wind blew over three houses. A correspondent there wrote, "The existence of Edingsville as a village has now ended . . . nothing remains to remind us of its former glory except a few dilapidated houses."[59]

Connected to Edingsville Island by a narrow causeway, Edisto Island flooded, destroying two-thirds of the cotton crop. One observer cautioned that, because of widespread crop disasters, "the colored people, owing to their inability to pay their debts this year and the failure of their provision crops will feel the present unfortunate state of things much more than the whites."[60] But to planters of the region, like those on Wadmalaw Island, there was also "great despondency" brought by "the severest blow [they had] had for years."[61]

When the once powerful hurricane reached Charleston its wind speed was that of a tropical storm, about fifty-four miles per hour. Shipping rode out the storm safely. Wharves and trees sustained minor damage, and several streets flooded. Waves broke over the High Battery opposite Atlantic Street, and there near sunset several young men of prominent families gathered for a "surf bath," letting the seawater break over them. Twenty-three-year-old Thomas Lesesne climbed up on the railing and took the dangerous position of putting his back to the breaking waves. Apparently he lost his balance and fell into the churning surf. Despite efforts by his friends to save him, he was pulled underwater and drowned. His body washed into the marshes of James Island. Interred at St. Philip's Church Yard, Lesesne, known as a man of "sunny temper," was mourned by "many loving friends." Three African Americans drowned. One was a crewmember of the sloop *Claudia*; the second, Fraser, died when his boat capsized; the third was the wife of "a colored man named Ned Marshall." Mrs. Marshall died when her husband's wagon was blown off a causeway near the city, pinning Mrs. Marshall under the vehicle where she drowned.[62]

At high tide the ocean surged under several houses on Sullivan's Island, undermining them and threatening to wash them to sea. Windows in the Catholic church blew in, and winds tore away a portion of the roof. Many residents rode out the storm at Fort Moultrie.[63]

Winds and tides pushed saltwater twenty-miles up the Pee Dee and Waccamaw rivers and flooded rice fields. An observer bemoaned that rice that had been "as verdant as the grass . . . in spring, now wears a garb similar to the brown stubble in autumn." The rice crop was heavily damaged.[64]

At Pawleys Island, a summer resort just north of Georgetown, waters surged over the island, taking away bridges and a causeway to the mainland. All ways to leave the island were cut off. The once powerful hurricane, now a large tropical storm, moved into the western part of South Carolina and across eastern North Carolina. The hurricane at sea and ashore drowned hundreds. One scholar put the death toll in Georgia and South Carolina at more than seven hundred.[65]

It appears that the actual number of deaths reached around 350. Damages to structures across the lowcountry exceeded $2,000,000 ($34,373,830). The rice and cotton crops in places suffered a 50 percent reduction in yield. Edingsville was so inundated by the hurricane that planters finally abandoned the once lively summer resort. It was to be reclaimed by the sea. A new slue was cut across the eastern beach at Tybee Island, where most of the built property was destroyed. One writer for the *Savannah Morning News* believed that remembrance of the great storm "will be a terror to those who wish to live where they can hear what the wild waves are saying." It was an accurate prediction. The development of Tybee as a seaside resort slowed.[66]

Savannahians now reckoned that the most violent and destructive hurricanes along the Georgia coast occurred on average about every twenty-five years. Especially memorable were the storms of 1804, 1824, 1854, and 1881. In terms of high water, wind velocity, devastation of property, and loss of life, it was decided by some that the hurricane of 1881 was comparable to that of 1804. The *Savannah Morning News*, always promoting the city, editorialized that despite the "havoc and desolation . . . and vast pecuniary loss [Savannah] will speedily recover from the effects of this blow, and her onward march in commercial greatness and prosperity will in no wise be retarded."[67]

An Offshore Hurricane and the City of Atlanta

During mid-September 1883 a large and fierce tropical cyclone raged far off the coast of the lowcountry, disabling or capsizing one vessel after another. At latitude 33° north, longitude 77° west, it ripped away the canvas of the *Louis V. Chaples*, washed a crewman overboard, and capsized the vessel. Near the same coordinates the brig *J. L. Bowen* encountered what its captain called "a terrific hurricane." A "tremendous sea" battered the vessel, damaged the cargo, and split the sails "like rotten rags." After sheathing was torn from its deck, the vessel began leaking so badly that all hands were kept at work on the pumps. The steamer *Newport*, out of New York and bound for Havana, ran into the storm off the Georgia coast. Two crewmen were washed overboard, the deckhouse was carried away, passenger cabins were smashed, and the rudder was disabled.[68]

There was no hint of a dangerous storm offshore when the steamer *City of Atlanta*, under Captain Robert W. Lockwood, left Charleston for New York on Sunday, September 9. As it left the harbor many of the thirty-three passengers with such familiar lowcountry names as Buist, Huger, and Smythe crowded the deck to enjoy a cool northeast breeze. In its hold the steamship carried twenty-eight hundred bales of cotton and a load of kaolin. Built for the New York and Charleston Steamship Company at Greenpoint, Long Island, in 1875, the vessel was 245 feet long with a 40-foot beam. Only after the ship departed Charleston did word arrive in the city that a powerful hurricane was churning offshore. A few hours out of port the ship began to roll and pitch in a stiffening northeast wind. Seasickness became epidemic. The ship's speed was reduced to fewer than two knots per hour. By Monday morning, off Cape Romain, South Carolina, the seas rose like mountains around the vessel, tossing it so violently that those aboard were unable to keep their footing. The wind reached hurricane force by noon, and the driving rain came in at angles. As far as the eye could see, a white sheet of foam covered the ocean under a dark, leaden sky. Again and again the ship rose high on one towering wave then sank with "sickening rapidity" into a trough that appeared bottomless. By late Monday afternoon the wind reached a velocity between ninety and one hundred miles per hour. To execute Captain Lockwood's orders, the crew now resorted to crawling about on their hands and knees.[69]

Seawater shipped over the bow and poured through the hatches into the hold. A leak sprang on the starboard side. By 4:00 p.m. the water reached seven feet, extinguishing the fires in the boilers. Everyone who was able was enlisted to bail to keep the bow above water. When attempts were made to hoist the steamship's sails, they "were blown to ribbons." The steamer itself was blown southward. The *City of Atlanta* listed dangerously to starboard; cotton bales floated in the hold. To relieve the list, Captain Lockwood ordered cotton thrown overboard. This appeared to bring the ship upright. Early Tuesday morning the winds moderated. The ship was now seventy miles east of Port Royal, South Carolina. Around 9:00 a.m. the steamship *British Empire* sighted the *City of Atlanta* flying distress signals, came alongside, and lay close by until seas calmed. The British ship took the *City of Atlanta* under tow on Wednesday morning and brought it to safety.[70]

Families of passengers aboard the *City of Atlanta* feared the ship was lost at sea. So when the telegraph brought news to Charleston that the steamer was "safe," lowcountry families celebrated. The passengers themselves publicly praised Captain Lockwood, attributing their "preservation" to "Divine Providence" and to the captain's "energy . . . scientific ability . . . and his officers and crew."[71]

The violence of the hurricane was dramatized when it sank or damaged more than a dozen vessels off the North Carolina coast and then roared ashore in North Carolina with sustained winds of 93 miles per hour and gusts exceeding 110 miles per hour. It destroyed homes, ruined crops, and claimed fifty-three lives—the most deaths up to that time caused by a hurricane in North Carolina's history.[72]

An "Extreme Storm" at Charleston

In late August 1885 a tropical cyclone churned past Cuba then turned northward and moved up the Florida coast. Along the coast it remained a tropical storm with winds high enough to damage structures in coastal towns. Offshore winds reached hurricane strength, and the sea from Jacksonville to Charleston became littered with dismasted or sinking vessels. Along the lower Georgia coast the Italian brig *Arago*, having taken on a load of lumber at Brunswick,

Georgia, encountered winds strong enough to shred its sails. Waves pummeled the helpless brig, and it sank low in the water. The captain, his wife, and the crew were rescued from the wrecked hulk by the British brigantine *Emma Ernst*. The *Arago* and its cargo were uninsured. In the same vicinity the tropical cyclone came down with devastating force on the German bark *Carolina Susannah*. When discovered by the *Lone Star* nothing remained except "a naked hull." The only sign of life aboard was a starving bulldog. Its crewmembers went unaccounted for. When a boarding party tried to set fire to the hulk, it was too waterlogged to burn.[73]

The Italian bark *Marianina*, engulfed by the storm off South Carolina, lost a seaman overboard. The Charleston pilot boat *John Stoddard* was found dismasted and filled with water near Edisto Island. No one was aboard, and it was assumed that the crew was lost. Captain Winnett of the steamship *Delaware*, who ran into the hurricane near the shoals of Cape Romain, thought he had never seen in all his years at sea "such a seething hell of water."[74]

At Tybee Island, Georgia, on Monday evening, August 24, wind gusts reached hurricane force, eighty-four miles per hour, driving ashore several British barks that began breaking up in the surf. The high winds and crashing waves terrified some summer visitors who expected to be momentarily carried away by a tidal wave. The blow leveled the summer residence of Charles Caroll. Mrs. Caroll, alone in the house, was lucky to escape with her life. Wind speeds reached only fifty-six miles per hour, tropical-storm force, in Savannah on Monday evening and Tuesday morning. River water washed over wharves. Small craft were driven ashore; several overturned and sank. In the city a tree blew into the Pavilion Hotel and damaged its roof. Leafy branches covered Savannah's sidewalks. The storm moved up the coast, gathering strength over the warm waters. As the press reported, Savannahians recognized that they were "fortunate" to be "on the outer edge of the cyclone."[75] It was much worse to the north.

In the early morning hours of Tuesday, August 25, a howling northeast wind and torrential rains swept along the lower South Carolina coast. Only some thirty miles from Savannah, at Bluffton, South Carolina, on the May River, the storm blew down houses and thousands of yellow pine trees — part of the vast turpentine business of Thomas Martin. His losses exceeded $20,000 ($364,156). Tracking just offshore, the tropical cyclone pounded South Carolina's sea islands. The storm blew down thirty-five dwellings and two churches and destroyed the potato and corn crops in low-lying areas on Hilton Head Island. At St. Helena Island forty-three shacks, houses, or buildings were bowled over on plantations owned by the prominent Fripp, McLinson, White, and Ward families. Betty Mack, a black woman living on Thomas Aston Coffin's Frogmore plantation of over one thousand acres, was "crushed and mutilated" by a falling house. Flooding tides and high winds destroyed a small African American village on the island, drowning all its inhabitants save one. All the standing pine timber on the St. Helena Island was bowled over and rice and cotton crops destroyed. On nearby Hunting Island the lighthouse "shook and swayed" so much that it altered the alignment of the light. Waves crashed on the beach, swirled past the light, and came to within fifty feet of the light keeper's house. This validated a critic's earlier warning that locating the light on Hunting Island rather than Harbor Island was "penny wise and pound foolish."[76]

Winds and tides again sank small boats and dredges of phosphate companies on the Coosaw River. Causeways and bridges linking the fragile sea islands to the mainland became impassable. At Beaufort the townspeople retired to bed under a bright moon and a star-filled sky. Then around 3:00 a.m. Tuesday, August 25, a howling northeast wind and slashing rains awakened them. Streetlamps shattered, and small houses toppled over. The trees newly planted after the 1881 hurricane were uprooted. Small boats in the Beaufort River crashed into the marshes along the town's waterfront.[77] Human tragedies multiplied offshore.

The fierce hurricane caught Beaufort's pilot boats in open waters. The *Walter Smith* wrecked and washed up on the Combahee Bank at the mouth of the Combahee River. Its twenty-eight-year-old captain, Henry Jennemann, an "accomplished professional," "popular with all classes," an apprentice, and three "colored" crewmembers drowned. The *John Stoddard*, captained by forty-year-old A. S. Casey, was cruising near Edisto Island. Also aboard was an apprentice pilot, a book agent from New York (invited along at the last minute for an evening cruise), and three "colored" deckhands. All drowned. Wreckage of the boat was found near the North Edisto River. Aboard the *F. W. Scheper*, off Bay Point near the harbor at Port Royal, two "veteran" pilots, J. M. Murray and Joe Rock, struggled against hurricane winds. When the pilot boat went down in twenty feet of water, Murray, Rock, and a black passenger, Kentuck, abandoned ship in a small boat. They capsized and all perished. The four persons remaining aboard, two white passengers and two black deckhands, climbed into the rigging of the pilot boat to save themselves. Here they hung on until reached by a rescue party led by young William Von Harten, who, at the "heroic . . . and imminent risk of his own life," saved them. Bodies from the pilot boats washed ashore in Port Royal Harbor, on Hunting Island, and St. Helena Island; some were never recovered. Fourteen lives and three Beaufort pilot boats were "swallowed by the sea." The town mourned.[78]

Warm coastal waters fueled the hurricane as it swirled northward. Between Beaufort and Charleston saltwater swept over crops on Edisto, Wadmalaw, and Johns Island. Kate Walpole Legare, of Mullet Hall Plantation on Johns Island, recalled "a never to be forgotten day when the wind and waters seemed to have us entirely in their power." She and her family fled to the kitchen for safety, thinking that the house would be destroyed. The house was not injured seriously, but "the loss [was] very great . . . on the island." They were "all gloomy." Even before the storm Kate and her husband Frank had thought "of selling . . . [the] place, if possible."[79]

It was the third disastrous year in five for cotton crops on the sea islands. Three-quarters of the crop was damaged. For some planters it meant the end of sea island cotton. A few black farmers continued to cultivate it, but most big landholders had already turned to truck farming. With at least one-quarter of the lowcountry's rice crop destroyed, rice planters again wondered how long they could afford to remain in the business.[80]

By Monday, August 24, 1885, Charleston harbor pilots who witnessed a "heavy sea" offshore predicted the approach of "dirty weather." That afternoon the weather observer in the city of about fifty-two thousand received a dispatch from the U.S. Signal Corps, Washington, D.C., to raise storm signals for "fresh and strong East to North winds." Charleston attorney William Miller, upon leaving his Broad Street office that afternoon, noticed "the storm signal . . . flying." He was not too concerned, telling his family, "The Weather Bureau has so often cried 'storm' when there was no storm, I gave their red danger sign but a passing glance." However, around 9:00 p.m. that same Monday evening, Miller had a change of mind "when appearances began to justify the prediction of approaching atmosphere disturbances." He noticed "clouds . . . scurrying across the moon from the East in dark threatening masses, and the wind . . . came in short violent gusts that shook the windows from garret to cellar." The conditions "excited a vague indefinable dread of something coming."[81]

In the early morning hours of Tuesday the noise of winds and rains awakened Miller and other Charlestonians, many of whom recognized a soughing of the winds that always signaled an approaching gale. A small boat in the harbor capsized, drowning one of the two white men trying to catch shrimp for the fishing fleet. Near dawn, high winds sent dense clouds scudding over rooftops, blotting out the sky, and spewing blinding rain. The center of the cyclone moved over the city on a general northeasterly line. Between 7:00 and 8:00 a.m. sustained wind velocity reached more than seventy-two miles per hour and increased over the next two hours. Locals estimated winds as high as 125 miles per hour. The gale came out of the southeast at high tide. The surface of the harbor turned into a sheet of heaving, billowing white foam. Huge waves carried ships and schooners into marshes, mud banks, and the causeway at the end of Tradd Street. The Norwegian bark *Medbor* was driven across the harbor "like a chip on a whirlpool." It became a mass of splintered timbers from stem to stern. A crewman went overboard and drowned. Thomas Robinson and two other black men set out in a small boat to recover some drifting lumber in the Cooper River. When it capsized, Robinson drowned.[82]

A "tidal wave" and high winds demolished cotton sheds, warehouses, and most wharves. This debris combined with vessels (large and small) piled into a jumble of ruins along the waterfront. City streets flooded. The storm demolished the Northeastern Railroad Wharf, ripping up two miles of track. Waves smashed the flagstones of the Battery promenade and carried away its iron railing. White Point Gardens was submerged. Sheets of water streamed through the doors and windows of the homes of the well-to-do facing the harbor. Three to six feet of seawater poured into the ground floors. Thousands of roof tiles and gray slates swirled through the air. Tin roofs peeled away and blew about like paper. One-quarter of Charleston's houses were unroofed. Brick chimneys collapsed; stout and ancient trees uprooted or snapped in half. Windows and doors blew in. Piazzas fell into the streets. Lightning flashes and the crash of thunder only temporarily interrupted the unceasing roar of the tropical cyclone sweeping through the city. Winds swayed and activated electrical wires, setting off alarm bells that rang every few minutes, adding to the anxiety of residents who feared they announced one calamity after another. Telephone and telegraph wires went down hopelessly tangled. From his home, William Miller watched pigeons attempt to fly, only to be "dashed to the ground." The tall spire of the Citadel Square Baptist Church fell, cutting through the front wall of the three-story residence at the corner of Meeting and Henrietta streets, exposing the interiors. The slate roof of St. Michael's Church was stripped away; the church's gilt ball and weathervane — the same one that had withstood 120 years of storms — was hurled to the sidewalk on Broad Street. On Hasell Street part of the Trinity Methodist Church roof was blown away, as were the windows. Rain saturated its walls and floors. Other places of worship were damaged, including the synagogue on St. Philip Street that was unroofed and a small African American church in the city that was demolished. Waters flooded dwellings of blacks in the city. Fierce winds toppled homes, especially those of the poor whose residences were often located in the vulnerable, low-lying areas of Charleston.[83]

Around 9:00 a.m. the high winds suddenly died, and the rain stopped as the eye passed over. Children went out to play, and Charlestonians gathered to exchange news about the cyclone's havoc. After about forty minutes, the eye passed, and the storm came out of the west-northwest to batter roofs, trees, wharves, and vessels, especially those along the Ashley River that heretofore had escaped the worst of the blow. The phosphate and fertilizer companies on the city's upper peninsula, an industry that contributed annually more than $1,000,000 ($18,207,920) to the local economy, suffered extensive damage. The iron steamship *Glenlivet* was driven into the nearly completed new bridge spanning the Ashley River, carrying away several hundred feet of the new construction. When the gale ended, about noon, debris jammed the streets, and water stood knee-deep in many of them. Ten thousand cartloads of "vegetable debris alone" littered the city. The city looked like a battlefield. The attorney William Miller remarked that he "walked down town and came back sick from the sight."[84]

Mount Pleasant, in Christ Church Parish to the north of Charleston though on the mainland, faced the open harbor. Waves washed away the high hills and shade trees along the waterfront. The wharf at Mount Pleasant was carried away so completely that nothing of the structure remained. The Rantowle's Ferry boat, crossing the Cooper River with two men and five women, "all colored," capsized, and four of the women drowned. Nine miles from Mount Pleasant, along the "sea beach," Philip E. Porcher's summer house was destroyed, but the family escaped unharmed. In the same vicinity John Whitesides, a forty-year-old plantation owner and Civil War veteran, and his family were at their summer residence when the cyclone struck. Though the house was built on a high knoll above the marsh, the storm surge came in, causing the family to rush to an upper story. Somehow the youngest daughter fell into the water swirling around the house. Whitesides plunged in to save her, and both drowned. Mary Bollard's house on Sewee Bay collapsed, killing her baby grandchild. A black man washed up on the beach, his chest crushed. Shell Hall, on the beachfront, used in turn as a courthouse, dance hall, and saloon, was blown down and wrecked. Some thought it was "good riddance of bad rubbish." On truck farms in Christ Church Parish, buildings blew over, and many black families were left homeless when their cabins collapsed in the high winds. The Laing School for "colored children," financed by citizens of Philadelphia, was blown off its foundations. It listed dangerously.[85]

At Sullivan's Island no red flag flew from the new storm tower on Monday afternoon to warn of the approaching cyclone. It took islanders unawares when it hit the eastern end of the island early Tuesday morning. By 9:00 a.m. the storm was howling out of the southeast. One resident saw "a sea lashed into fury and marching up from the ocean. No man could withstand the force of the wind." Rain came in torrents. A storm surge sent the ocean's waters over the entire island. A hundred guests from Atlanta, Macon, Augusta, and Charleston huddled in their rooms at the New Brighton Hotel as the building shook. Windows blew in, blinds tore away, and the sea lapped against the steps. The hotel's casino collapsed. "Frantic with fear," hotel guests fell to their knees and prayed. Some believed that at any moment they "might be ushered into eternity."[86]

At homes near the eastern end of Sullivan's Island, residents fearing for their lives rushed to the upper stories. Frank J. McGarey's home rocked so violently that his wife became "seasick." McGarey ventured outside and was blown under the house. He watched the roof blow off "and the sides laid out like so many cards." A "colored man" waded through ocean water and assisted in getting the children out of what remained of the structure. McGarey entered the dwelling and found his wife and her mother huddled together; at that instant the floor gave way and they "were all buried in the ruins." Fortunately no major beams landed on them, and unhurt they were helped from the wreckage. Winds and waves leveled other houses, broke some in half, and lifted others off their foundations. A reporter recounted the scene with this simile: "Houses melted in the waters as if they were built of sugar or salt." Such homes built on sand would continue to be swept away unless, he wrote, they were built on a raft of timbers anchored in the sand and attached to the superstructure by galvanized spikes. His was one of the earliest warnings for builders of "expensive . . . seaside cottages." Another lesson learned, he wrote, was that they "must have a sure and safe retreat from the island to the mainland," preferably by a bridge or railroad. Fortunately during this terrifying storm no one perished on Sullivan's Island.[87]

Along the coast to the north, the hurricane slammed into the resort and fishing village of McClellanville. The sea drove two schooners, a sloop, and small craft across the beach and into the yards of residents. Several prominent families sustained heavy losses: the McClellans' stables and kitchen collapsed into a mass of ruins; Dr. Horace Leland's home was blown from its foundations, forcing the family to take refuge at Captain J. H. Leland's house until it too was blown into "a heap." "Thousands upon thousands" of trees went down in the pine forests around the town. The damage to the turpentine business was "incalculable." The terrapin "crop" was swept away. Pens owned by Graham, Remfry, Sloan, and Leland housed ten thousand terrapins—all were lost at a cost of $4,000 ($72,832). Bridges linking the village to the mainland went down. Damage in and around McClellanville was estimated to be $25,000 ($455,198).[88]

The hurricane's highest winds reached Georgetown on Tuesday about 11:00 a.m. and continued for two hours. An observer described the wind as high enough to lift a man from the ground and carry him fifty yards before dropping him to the ground. Vessels at wharfside were battered, tin roofs rolled up, and the icehouse caught fire from a cookstove that ignited when the building collapsed from the winds. In the countryside, winds felled thousands of trees and brought ruin to some turpentine farmers. Little cotton was grown any longer in the county, but 20 percent of the small crop was lost. Rice planters were more fortunate. The storm came too late to harm most of the rice, which by now had reached maturity.[89]

Excluding private real estate, damages in Charleston, the lowcountry's most populous city, exceeded $2,000,000 ($36,415,840). Only four well-to-do families in the city carried storm insurance that covered their home and its contents. Even though the hurricane devastated crops, businesses, and private property across the lowcountry, it was a boon for skilled and unskilled laborers. This was dramatized in a story reported by the *Charleston News and Courier*—two "colored men" were overheard in conversation, and one expressed the situation aptly when he said, "All you got to do now is pick up a hatchet or a hammer and go on the street. The bosses don't stop to ask you where you learned your trade, or how much wages you want. They just snatch you up bald-headed."[90]

Even well-off families anticipated brighter days ahead. William Miller told his family, "Hope springs eternal in the human breast. We are all safe and with hope and energy, we can retrieve all our fallen fortunes."[91]

Officially deaths were put at twenty-one, but perhaps twice that number of people perished offshore and along the coast of the lowcountry.[92] Carl McKinley, a Charleston author, called the tropical cyclone "the most fearful storm that has ever visited our coasts within the knowledge of man."[93] Of course, he had no way of knowing that the "storm of the century" was just a few years away.

CHAPTER SEVEN

Major Hurricanes
at Century's End,
1893–1898

The cycle of tropical storms and cyclones that began in the 1870s persisted into the 1890s. In 1886 three hurricanes moved across Florida but caused little damage in the lowcountry. In October 1888 a hurricane out of the Gulf of Mexico curved up Florida's east coast, bringing tropical-storm winds of forty-eight miles per hour at Charleston. In late September 1889 the weather bureau at Charleston again raised a cautionary flag and announced that a tropical cyclone was moving up the coast from Florida. On Monday, September 23, the residents of Beaufort experienced "a gale . . . but Florida bore the brunt" of the storm. At Charleston, high southeast winds never reached hurricane strength. Perhaps Georgia and South Carolina residents were being lulled into complacency. The leading lowcountry paper reported that warnings of tropical cyclones "had been received so frequently of late . . . and Charleston had escaped so often, that little attention was paid to the warnings."[1]

But lowcountry residents were jarred from their complacency during the hurricane season of 1893 when three tropical cyclones made landfall along the coast. One became known as the Great Sea Island Storm. It was a major hurricane.

The Great Sea Island Storm

The hurricane season of 1893 was one of the most deadly in the history of the United States. It began in June when a tropical storm blew by Georgia and South Carolina. In late August a hurricane grazed the lowcountry then ripped along the coasts of Delaware, New Jersey, and New York, causing deaths and massive damages. Already another tropical cyclone from the Cape Verde Islands was crossing the Atlantic to the West Indies and moving rapidly toward the southeastern coast of the United States.[2]

On Friday, August 25, 1893 the national weather bureau in Washington, D.C., issued a bulletin stating that there were "indications of a storm center about 500 miles east of Florida, moving toward the northwest." Another bulletin in the evening warned that "a heavy swell on the South Atlantic coast has been reported." At Savannah the official weather observer cautioned ship masters "to keep themselves advised." Danger signals were hoisted at Savannah and Charleston. On Sunday morning, August 27, the Washington weather bureau reported that the "great storm" was moving northwestward and would likely strike "the coast of Georgia Sunday evening or night."[3]

Urban centers had been warned. But thousands of African Americans living on Georgia and South Carolina sea islands had no way of knowing about the approaching hurricane, and the warning came too late for vessels offshore. Only a rising northeast wind and falling barometers alerted captains at sea that "dirty weather" was approaching. Unfortunately, they had neither enough sail nor steam to outrun the storm. All they could do was lower their mainsails, hoist a storm jib, and under bare poles prepare to "ride it out." Despite the best efforts of their captains, more than seventy vessels were badly battered or lost at sea.[4]

Captain McDonnell, of the small coasting schooner *Anna S. Conants*, loaded with white pine lumber, encountered the cyclone several days out of

St. Simons Island, Georgia. To McDonnell the hurricane was "rolling before it one of the most frightful seas" he had ever seen. The crew, half-drowned by spray, held on to the weather railings for dear life. Huge waves pummeled the schooner, opening seams in the hull, knocking it over, and sweeping away the lumber on deck. The vessel took a "dizzy plunge down the slope of a mountainous roller" followed by "a crashing and wrenching of the timbers." It righted a complete wreck without a mast standing. Waves washed over the waterlogged vessel as the crew held on throughout the night "waiting for the end." At dawn they launched a lifeboat, but a huge swell "hurled it violently" against the side of the schooner, dashing the boat to pieces. As the schooner sank deeper, the crew climbed atop the deckhouse. Exhausted, the men passed another night in a rolling sea, thinking that the wreck they clung to would sink at any moment. The next day the bark *Tillid* spotted the wreckage in the distance. Initially the captain saw no one aboard the schooner and planned to sail by, but taking a last look through glasses, he saw men on the deckhouse. The *Tillid* came about and in heavy seas rescued Captain McDonnell and his six-member crew. The *Anna S. Conants* became a derelict at sea.[5]

On Sunday, August 27, the hurricane struck the 507-ton bark *Freeda A. Wyley*, loaded with yellow pine. It was sailing southeast of Savannah. Pounded by waves and winds, the bark became unmanageable in the heavy seas. Constantly shifting lumber on the deck made it too dangerous for the crew to remain there; they climbed up the masts and lashed themselves in the rigging. Its hold filling from multiple leaks, the vessel sank close to the water's edge. When the sea moderated on Monday, Captain Ichabod Willey attempted to prevent the vessel from going under by ordering the masts cut away and the deckload of lumber heaved overboard. A fire was built in a large box of sand on deck, and the crew cooked beef. On Tuesday Captain Willey and his eight-man crew were rescued off Savannah—latitude 32° north, longitude 79° west—by the schooner *Annie Kranz*. In abandoning the vessel hastily, the crew left the cook fire burning, and the *Freeda A. Wyley* accidentally was set ablaze. The burned hulk washed ashore near what is today Fortieth Street, Myrtle Beach, South Carolina.[6]

Some one hundred miles off southern Georgia, Captain Cosman struggled to keep the 1,378-ton British ship *Nettie Murphy* upright as "mountainous seas" swept the deck of its cargo of lumber, water tanks, pumps, and lifeboats. Fearing his vessel on the verge of sinking, the captain ordered his eighteen crew-members into the rigging. When sighted in the Gulf Stream by the Norwegian brig *Medea*, the *Nettie Murphy* was "lying very low in the water, the decks beginning to break up, and . . . she was listed heavily to starboard." The rescued sailors were brought into Savannah.[7]

About forty miles east of Tybee Island, Georgia, the Norwegian steamship *Banan* was enveloped by the cyclone. Captain Hansen knew immediately that he was in "the worst storm [he had] ever experienced." He tried to keep his ship afloat while its lifeboats, "skylights, doors, compasses and every movable object . . . [were] either smashed to smithereens or cast overboard." Then when "the ventilators broke in, the sea began to pour into her hold." Remarkably Captain Hansen brought the "badly damaged" ship and his bruised crew safely into the Savannah River.[8]

Another British ship, *Astoria*, loaded with yellow pine, encountered howling winds that tore through the sails off the coast of South Carolina. Huge waves swept her deck of everything. Loose timber slammed into a sailor and "crushed his leg like a pipe stem." Captain Edward Faulkner and his twenty-member crew lost control of the ship. It drifted before the hurricane a "helpless wreck." Giving up all hope of saving the ship, the crew turned to save themselves. As the storm raged, they carried the sailor with the broken leg, Captain Faulkner's wife, and the "colored" stewardess into the rigging of the mizzenmast and tied them securely. The sailors then went aloft and lashed themselves to the masts. "They almost despaired of touching land again." Here they remained for twelve hours until the *Astoria* was sighted north of Hunting Island, South Carolina, by the passenger steamer *D. H. Miller*. "Benumbed and exhausted," the crew and passengers were rescued. Most likely the *Astoria* sank soon after being abandoned. The ship was valued at $40,000 ($782,553) as was its cargo of lumber.[9]

The steamship *City of Savannah* was about fifteen miles off Hunting Island on that fateful Sunday evening, August 27. The hurricane's huge waves pounded the 2,250-ton ship, tearing away the smokestack, flooding the engine room, and extinguishing the fires in the boilers. Unmanageable and dragging anchors set by the captain, the vessel was driven onto sandbars off Hunting Island, where it began breaking up. The captain ordered its thirty passengers and crew into the rigging. There many remained through two days. Passing close to shore, the *City of Birmingham* sighted the wreck and began rescue operations. Passengers and crew were exhausted and dehydrated; amazingly no one perished. Valued at $400,000 ($7,825,531), the *City of Savannah* appeared to be a total loss.[10]

The schooner *Harold C. Beecher*, carrying a load of lumber from Brunswick, Georgia, was so battered by the storm that its captain ordered his crew into lifeboats. The schooner was abandoned somewhere off South Carolina. The schooner *Morris W. Child*, also out of Brunswick, rescued the crew. However, it was not long before the *Morris W. Child* itself appeared close to foundering, and its commander, Captain Haskell, ordered eighty thousand feet of lumber thrown overboard. Eventually a tugboat brought Haskell's vessel into Charleston.

On the way into port Captain Haskell passed a great deal of wreckage and "six men floating with life preservers . . . [who] barely had life in them." Haskell found it "impossible to rescue them on account of the high sea running and the disabled condition of [his] schooner." Apparently these six men perished.[11]

In the waters offshore and along the beaches of the lowcountry the flotsam and jetsam of the fierce tropical cyclone became apparent: vessels bottom-up, some dismasted, others sinking, cabin doors, spars, broken masts, lumber, and railroad ties. Many vessels and their crews—upwards of fifty sailors—were never seen again.[12] A week after the great storm, the *Savannah Morning News* reported, "[the] beach along the coast is strewn with the bodies of dead seamen and with wrecks of which no account can be given." At Rockville on Edisto Island, South Carolina, the bodies of twenty-one drowned sailors were buried in a common grave.[13]

The tropical cyclone proved equally devastating upon landfall. As the moon rose over the lowcountry that evening, the hurricane swirled thirty miles offshore from St. Simons Island, Georgia, and was moving closer to the coast. Winds were reported at ninety-five miles per hour upon landfall south of Tybee Island at Blackbeard or Sapelo Island around 4:00 a.m. on Sunday morning, August 27, 1893, coincident with a full moon.[14]

Some of the first casualties of the storm occurred at Sapelo Island. Noda Spaulding, his son, and three other African Americans heard and saw signs of the approaching storm. Deciding to leave the island for the mainland, they climbed into a small sailboat. But somewhere in Sapelo Sound high winds and waves capsized the craft. All five men drowned. The storm also wrecked and washed two Norwegian barks and a sternwheeler, *Mascot*, into Sapelo's marshes and blew the bark *Mary G. Reed* off her moorings. Moving slowly northwestward the storm raked St. Catherines Island and sent three schooners onto land.[15]

Rain and fifty-mile-per-hour sustained winds out of the northeast whipped across Tybee Island throughout the day, Sunday, August 27. The one hundred people on the island watched the storm. One described the ocean as "a boiling, hissing, seething sea," and the "rain, driven by the gale in blinding torrents, penetrated everything and blew against the faces of those exposed like chilled shot." The storm submerged Tybee under "six feet of water." Tybee had only recently rebuilt after the devastating hurricane of 1881.

In the evening, winds increased, and waves cut away the sand dunes in front of the houses on Tybee's beach, forcing such prominent Savannahians as the Butler, Good, and Lane families to leave their homes for sturdier structures. Charles and Henry Green, whose own house caught fire, had to swim to rescue Mrs. J. G. Butler and others before the Butler house washed out to sea. When the A. C. Ulmer family's house blew over, Mrs. Ulmer and her children fled in darkness to the well-constructed home of shipbuilder H. L. Willinik. Unbeknownst to Mrs. Ulmer, her husband was on Hutchinson Island and had drowned in the storm. The homes of Captain W. T. Daniels and Colonel J. H. Estill, which had withstood the hurricane of 1881, were wrecked. Henry Soloman's home, destroyed in the hurricane of 1881, then rebuilt, was blown forty feet from its foundations. The furnishings of some homes were found in the woods, a half-mile away. Some dwellings, undermined by crashing waves, simply floated out to sea.[16]

The water tower toppled. Social clubs were smashed, and the police station was partially destroyed. The track of the Tybee railroad was blown from the ground and stood on end along the rail line like a fence. Bridges washed away connecting the mainland to Tybee and made the future of a railroad to the island "uncertain." At the quarantine station on the north end of the island, waves wrecked one bark and washed five others into the marshes. At the storm's height, the sea knocked a dredge from its six anchors. It crashed into the home of the lighthouse keeper, Hugo Johnson, and the dwelling began filling with seawater. Johnson snatched up his seven-year-old sister and flung her aboard the dredge to safety. Somehow he managed to scramble aboard the vessel with only scratches.[17]

The Norwegian bark *Harold* went to pieces off the front beach at Tybee. To save themselves her sailors swam to the beach, leaving behind an unconscious, severely injured young crewman who drowned. An "old negro," Scott Bacon, and his son who lived in a railroad boxcar at the north end of the island drowned when their "home" blew over. On nearby Cockspur Island waves tore away the wharf and leveled wooden buildings. A surging tide poured over the casements of Fort Pulaski, covering the parade field with four feet of water. It swept into rooms, floating bedding, furniture, and cooking utensils. To the west at Wilmington Island wind gusts likely reached more than eighty miles per hour around midnight. One resident watched the barometer drop to an "incredibly low figure." Crashing waves washed away about fifteen feet of the island's bluff and carried off the wharf and every boat but one.[18]

As the tropical cyclone moved across Tybee, Cockspur, and Wilmington islands, it also battered Savannah's suburbs. Bridges connecting Thunderbolt and the Isle of Hope to the mainland went down; yachts moored at the Savannah Yacht Club were thrown into the marsh. Four miles west of Savannah four blacks drowned at Brampton Plantation on the Augusta Road. In the evening, the five-foot tidal surge that accompanied the approaching hurricane submerged the islands along the Savannah River. Whitecaps covered Hutchinson Island just north across the river from Savannah. A prominent Savannahian, A. C. Ulmer, an employee of the Central Railroad Bank for twenty-five years, had gone to the island by boat on Sunday afternoon to move livestock from his dairy farm to higher ground. Stranded after nightfall by the fast-rising waters, Ulmer and his farm employee, Fred Stewart, took refuge in Ulmer's barn. When it collapsed, the two men tried to swim to safety in the darkness. Both drowned in the high, turbulent waters. Ulmer's wife and children survived the hurricane on Tybee Island. Winds knocked over a cabin on Hutchinson Island, drowning a "colored child," Tony Holmes, whose father was also employed by Ulmer. To save himself, another African American child, Taylor Squire, climbed onto the roof of a shanty as rising waters lifted the dwelling from its foundations. It floated aimlessly until a collision with a tree knocked Taylor off the roof and into the waters where he drowned. Three adult African Americans perished on a rice plantation. Their bodies lay among the hundreds of drowned cattle, goats, and barnyard animals that covered Hutchinson Island.[19]

Savannah was saved from complete inundation, because it stood above the river on a bluff thirty feet high. Residents no doubt spent a sleepless night as they listened to the hurricane's northeast winds and the pounding rain that swept the city. At the height of the cyclone, around 11:30 p.m., the wind velocity reached seventy-two miles per hour, with even higher gusts. The barometer recorded 28.31 inches. When the eye passed over the city shortly after midnight, a dead calm followed for about an hour. Winds then came from the southwest with lesser velocity. The river covered Savannah's wharves with six to eight feet of water. Waves beat against the retaining walls of Factor's Walk. Vessels tied with chains and ropes broke loose from their moorings and crashed into the wharves. A stern-wheel steamboat, the *Abbeville*, was wrecked by the winds and waves. Pilings punched holes in the bottom of the *Fred F. Brown*, an oyster boat. River dredges blew into the marshes. Floodwaters surged into the naval stores yard of the Central of Georgia railroad and floated fifty thousand barrels of rosin and spirits as far as Laurel Grove Cemetery. Wharves along the lower river from East Boundary Street to the Savannah, Florida and Western Railroad Wharves tore away. Surging tides drove timber through the railroad company offices. The Savannah Cotton Press Wharf was badly wrecked, and the Savannah Guano Company suffered damages from floodwaters over four feet deep.[20]

On Bay and Broughton and streets to the north, winds ripped roofs from hundreds of stores and warehouses, blew in skylights and windows, and loosened chimneys and walls. A night watchman in a warehouse on the waterfront had a harrowing experience when the building he was guarding was knocked loose from its foundations and began to float. Part of the roof of the solid granite customs house was ripped off. Churches were not spared. A turret on St. John's Church was blown down, and portions of the towers of St. Patrick's Roman Catholic Church, the First Presbyterian Church, and the African Baptist Church collapsed in the high winds. Trees crashed down in the squares. Telephone and telegraph wires dangled from their poles. Lewis Gagnett died when he came in contact with one of the live wires. Debris blocked the city's sidewalks and streets.[21]

The number of dead on Georgia's low-lying islands and around the city reached more than forty. Estimates of property losses were "much more than

$1,000,000 [$19,563,829]." Two-thirds of Georgia's lowcountry rice crop was lost—about $400,000 ($7,825,532)—the "cotton badly hurt," and 25 percent of the pine trees used in the naval stores business were down. Damage to vessels driven ashore at Savannah or wrecked on Georgia's sea islands was in the "hundreds of thousands of dollars."[22]

It was a major hurricane on the upper Georgia coast and the worst natural disaster since 1804. However, drownings and damages remained comparatively low only because the right-front quadrant of the hurricane—the one packing the highest winds—remained offshore. But when the enormous hurricane, eight hundred to one thousand miles wide, swirled inland near Savannah, it exposed South Carolina to its most deadly side.[23] The results were horrific.

Official warnings of the hurricane never reached thousands of blacks living on South Carolina's isolated sea islands—a lowcountry archipelago that stretched from the Savannah River to Georgetown, South Carolina. The region, the size of Connecticut, embraced more than eighty islands facing sounds or the open Atlantic Ocean. Some of the impoverished blacks who lived here owned their land; others were tenant farmers who worked for the white owners of cotton and rice lands or truck farms; hundreds were employed by the new and burgeoning phosphate mining industry. Their staple food crops were corn and sweet potatoes. They usually lived in hovels built directly on the ground, without window glass, and at sea level. Sometimes as many as eighteen people occupied four-room shacks. The *New York Times* reported, "Along the coast the negroes live literally in droves. They are probably as near the uncivilized state as any people in this country."[24] But Ellen Murray, a white temperance worker on one of the largest islands, St. Helena, knew them best. She described the island's black farmers as "an industrious, self-supporting people, caring for their sick and aged, raising on their small farms of ten to thirty acres the provisions for their families and putting the rest of their 'force' into cotton."[25]

Despite stiffening northeast breezes throughout Saturday, August 26, 1893, white bosses of the profitable phosphate industry kept black crews working in dredges and lighters along the rivers. But when Sunday brought torrents of rain, and winds sent enormous waves crashing onto the beaches, residents—black and white—agreed that a hurricane was approaching. Having neither the wherewithal to leave nor a place to go, they prepared to "ride out" the storm. They died by the hundreds.[26]

On Sunday night, August 27, the hurricane slammed into Hilton Head and Daufuskie islands, destroying the provision crops of more than thirteen hundred families. Seawater inundated island wells, making the water undrinkable. Winds bent and twisted a tower on the Daufuskie Range lighthouse. Waves swamped the light keeper's house, and around 2:00 a.m. Monday he led his family three-quarters of a mile through waist-deep waters to safety. Daufuskie Island's seven-hundred-foot-long bluff that served as a seventy-five-foot barrier to the sea was demolished by pounding waves. One hundred feet of the bluff in front of Albert Stoddard's home, Melrose, on Calibogue Sound, disappeared, taking with it "half of his beautiful garden." Cabins of blacks flooded and collapsed. Nearby Pine Island was submerged. The "negroes" on the island passed the night in their boats, clinging to live oaks. White families deserted the island after the earlier hurricane of 1881.[27]

On the mainland in Beaufort County, at Bluff Place on the Okatie River, Elise Fripp, her family, and her home came close to being blown into the river. They fled the dwelling, and in waist-deep water held on to oak trees against fierce winds throughout the night. All around them livestock drowned. The right-front quadrant of the storm became even more dangerous as it moved over warm waters and up the coast.[28]

Forty miles north of the Fripp home winds greater than one hundred miles per hour accompanied by a giant storm surge swept out of the Atlantic Ocean. This is a region defined by "tidal rivers and creeks [that] wind through a maze of grassy marshes and sandy islands to form one of the most intricate patterns of land and water in the world."[29]

The hurricane raced through Port Royal Sound and overflowed the island village of Port Royal. It roared down the Broad and Coosaw rivers, across Beaufort, Lady's Island, St. Helena Island, and spilled over smaller islands in the vicinity. In all these locations people perished as the hurricane demolished vessels, wharves, docks, warehouses, and dwellings. It was the beginning of the end of the phosphate industry. The Coosaw River, which empties into Port Royal Sound, was the base of the phosphate mining operations in South Carolina, an industry that extracted marl from the region's rivers and turned it into fertilizer. The offices of phosphate companies and the cabins of African American laborers who worked there were located on Coosaw and Morgan islands. The tidal surge sank or drove into the marshes most of the fleet of the Coosaw Phosphate

Company: five dredges, sixty-eight lighters, forty flat boats, and numbers of tugboats. The tug *Catherine* was hurled into the top of a clump of oaks. The *John Kennedy*, a huge phosphate dredge valued at $300,000 ($5,869,149), capsized, taking with it a white engineer, Martin Hahn, and a "colored" fireman, Phinsey. On the islands of Port Royal, Parris, Morgan, and Coosaw, the tidal surge crashed into cabins where terrified occupants huddled. Eleven members of a family crowded into one dwelling perished. Seventy blacks died on Port Royal Island. On Parris Island cabins collapsed, crushing those who had sought safety there; others floated away holding on to pieces of wreckage, only to drown in Port Royal Sound. Some climbed into the trees but lost their footing in the high winds and fell to the waters below. At least twenty-four black residents of Parris Island died. On Coosaw Island sixty-five of the seventy-five cabins of black laborers were demolished, and forty-two blacks were interred there in long ditches.[30]

In the immediate vicinity of Port Royal more than one hundred African Americans died during the great storm. Whites also drowned, including fifty-seven-year-old Dr. Gowan Hazel, a former plantation owner, Confederate veteran, and greatly admired physician in the Parris Island community. Hearing the cries of two "negro" boys just off the wharf of the U.S. naval station, Hazel leaped into the water and swam toward their voices. He drowned trying to save them.

Other heroes emerged. John Densler, a white employee of the U.S. naval station, tied his cabin to a sturdy oak tree. He and his family remained inside their home until water rose to their throats. They then grabbed onto the rope and worked their way into the branches of the tree. They remained there until the storm subsided.[31]

A young boy, George Elliott, worked for a phosphate company. At the height of the storm he pushed a seaworthy boat in the direction of men in peril on the sea. He saved a "negro" cook from a tugboat, two men from a dredge, and five who had lashed themselves together on a piece of wood. By Monday morning, young Elliott had rescued fourteen men.[32]

Despite the heroic efforts of a few, the great storm became a tragedy of epic proportions. An eyewitness at Port Royal, Edward M. Averill, remarked: "No one can form an idea of the horror of this disaster who has not seen it."[33]

Just up the Beaufort River from Port Royal Sound was Beaufort, South Carolina, called by some "the prettiest island town in the Carolinas." Its population of thirty-five hundred was predominately African American, with blacks out-numbering whites about three to one. There on Sunday, August 27, 1893, wit-nesses described a rising wind that "shrieked hoarsely, driven on with relentless fury . . . till it attained the fearful velocity of one-hundred and twenty miles per hour and . . . [the] hurricane raged . . . for nearly fourteen hours." Twenty-foot-high waves on the Beaufort River tossed barks and schooners ashore like wood chips. The two wharves and three warehouses of Beaufort's largest property owner, F. W. Scheper, were lifted from their foundations and knocked into kindling. An "aged negro," Thomas Huge, and his wife drowned in the town's streets at the height of the hurricane, about 3:00 a.m. Monday. Nearly every building in Beaufort suffered damage. Some were reduced to rubble. On Bay Street nothing remained of the law library and legal offices of the Honorable W. J. Verdier except the iron safe. When the Beaufort House was unroofed, its occupants fled in terror. Awnings blew away, and gusts smashed the glass fronts of stores. The home of the enterprising merchant H. F. Von Harten was demol-ished. Debris choked Bay Street. Estimates of damage to the business section of Beaufort reached $200,000 ($3,912,766).[34]

When the tin roof of historic St. Helena Episcopal Church ripped away, drenching rains ruined the recently refurbished interior. The hurricane "com-pletely wrecked" the "colored" Baptist church. Winds pounded the Beaufort County Court House, the Sea Island Hotel on Bay Street, the Live Oak Hotel, and other public and private buildings. Magnificent oak and magnolia trees, with trunks two and three feet in diameter, snapped in the gale. In every part of town, houses were wrecked. The dwelling owned by Maria Alston, "colored," was tipped on its side. Many of Beaufort's well-to-do who lived in pre–Civil War mansions on the Point—called the "pride of the town"—fared poorly. Jut-ting out into the Beaufort River, the Point and the homes there took a fierce pounding.[35]

Susan Hazel Rice, sixty-three, once a member of the planting elite and a "highly esteemed" resident of Beaufort for most of her life, watched the great storm approach and the floodwaters rise in her house. The wind-driven rain poured through the plaster in every room. The men of the house spent all Sun-day night nailing doors and windows shut. The family lay on pallets in the sit-ting room, but "got no sleep until 4:00 a.m.," wrote Rice in her diary. With "day light came a scene of desolation. But we were better off than many others," so

Susan thought, until she was notified that her brother, Dr. Gowan Hazel, had drowned. After viewing his body, Susan wrote, "to think I never shall hear him speak again is too much for me to bear."[36]

To the north and east of Beaufort the hurricane winds and the tidal surge swept over Lady's Island (population fifteen hundred), St. Helena Island (population forty-five hundred), and numerous small islands. A fiction writer from the region later tried to recapture the experience of African Americans on these islands during the hurricane.

> Some of the negroes had fallen asleep in their cabins and knew not that the waves in the darkness were briskly at work surrounding them. . . . There was no one to warn them who understood the possibility of what might happen, they dwelt in the security of the past, which had revealed it not unto them, they trusted the water they had been friends with all their lives.[37]

The author's description of the storm was accurate. The huge waves rolled in so fast that the waters drowned blacks in their beds. Some tried to escape by climbing to the top of their modest dwellings, but unable to keep their balance in the high winds, they fell into the waters and drowned. Some climbed onto the rafters of their cabins, but when the flood undermined the structures, they floated away and then collapsed, crushing or drowning the occupants. Some lashed themselves and their children in the tops of trees and survived; the winds knocked others from the limbs into the boiling waters. Others who tried to flee in the darkness to what they thought might be places of safety perished. Whole families left their homes as the sea rushed in, moved to neighbors' houses until they gave way, and then fled on to yet others. Some failed to make it to safety, and families died washed together in heaps. On one small island 150 bodies were discovered in a one-half-mile area. Mrs. R. C. Mather, a local educator on the islands, believed that some people became too "confused and dazed" to seek shelter and wandered into the waters and drowned.[38]

Across the islands bodies of the victims lay intermixed with their meager possessions and cattle, horses, hogs, chickens, dogs and cats, and wild game. "Hundreds of corpses were strewn along the farms, unknown save to the vultures which flocked about them." The coroner swore in an army of deputies to hunt for the dead.[39]

The smell of death wafted over the land. Each incoming tide washed more "swollen, bruised and distorted" bodies up on the beaches, victims of the storm of the century. Fearful of disease, African Americans buried their dead quickly, sometimes in mass unmarked graves. Initially the death toll on the sea islands around Beaufort was reported as a few hundred, then six hundred, and then fifteen hundred, and finally, three thousand. Clara Barton, president of the American Red Cross, who relocated her office to the lowcountry to assist in relief work, estimated that of the thirty-five thousand primarily black inhabitants of the sea islands near Beaufort, "four or five thousands had been drowned." Thirty thousand, she said, "remained with no earthly possession of home, clothing, or food." The number of African Americans who drowned in the great storm or later perished of injuries or starvation was probably closer to three thousand. However, as the press finally acknowledged, the number of those who died as a result of the great storm "will never be known."[40]

Many black people in Beaufort and on the sea islands were destitute. Eighty percent of the homes had been destroyed. Homeless survivors numbered in the thousands. They huddled in improvised shelters; many faced starvation. The small plots of sweet potatoes and corn planted for home consumption were gone along with the money crops of cotton and rice. Dysentery, from "bad water," and malaria broke out. In Beaufort a disinfectant was distributed to combat diseases. Gone too was a major source of livelihood. The phosphate mining industry that employed hundreds of black laborers before the storm told survivors they need not apply for work. Nearly all the property of the phosphate companies was uninsured. Immediately following the hurricane, the mayor of Beaufort, George Holmes, declared that the commerce of Beaufort was "sadly crippled." The town had been supported by the phosphate mining business, and it was "completely swept away." The recurring and devastating tropical cyclones along the South Carolina coast in the 1880s and 1890s cost the phosphate industry dearly and was a major factor in its decision to leave South Carolina.[41]

The governor of the state, Benjamin Tillman, responded to the great human tragedy on the sea islands publicly by saying, "The people have the fish of the sea there to prevent them from starving. I hope, too, that someone will make them go to work at once and plant turnips on the islands. I do not want any abuse of charity." Tillman waited nearly a month before asking for assistance from the American Red Cross.[42]

Businessmen in Beaufort estimated that the destruction in the town exceeded $1,000,000 ($19,563,829) and that it would take $2,000,000 ($39,127,658) to repair damages on the sea islands. A local committee was formed to solicit aid nationwide, and food, clothing, and money trickled in for the homeless and hungry. Clara Barton was the most famous of all the relief workers. She and her staff provided desperately needed assistance to the black islanders for months.[43]

Joel Chandler Harris, who toured the islands for *Scribner's Magazine*, wrote, "Out of the seething depths disaster sprung, and out of the roaring heavens calamity fell. There has probably never been a counterpart of this hurricane at any previous time or in any other region of this continent."[44]

The Great Storm Rolls North

Up the coast from Beaufort, the hurricane sent drenching rains, fierce winds, and waves across Edisto, Little Edisto, and Whooping islands for fourteen hours, beginning late Sunday, August 27, 1893. Saltwater submerged nearly all crops on the islands. Dozens of sheep and cattle drowned. Bridges across creeks separating one part of Edisto Island from another disappeared. Trees went down across every road. Winds unroofed cabins, and rising waters swept away some with their contents and their occupants.[45]

Some sense of the human tragedy can be gleaned from those who died— the wife of Captain Alston, "colored," of Whooping Island drowned; eleven black persons perished on Major Julian Mitchell's plantation on Edisto Island; another eighteen went unaccounted for at the Whaley and Hanahan plantations on Little Edisto; on the Dahoo River the bodies of the four black children of William Green and Cudjo Bunnum Jr. were recovered; eight drowned in Cudjo Sr.'s home. There were heroines: on Edisto Island, Lou Montgomery, referred to in the press as a "brave and noble colored woman," saved three persons. She swam with them until they reached a place of comparative safety and tied them to trees.[46]

At a place on the island known as Cowpens Point, three white families—the Chisloms, Whaleys, and Mitchells—were surrounded by a "vast expanse of dangerous waters" and cut off from the main part of the island. "Their escape was almost miraculous." No whites lost their lives, but thirty-one African Americans perished on Edisto Island, twenty on Little Edisto.[47]

Nearby at Pon Pon, Laura Hamilton, an African American, fled to find shelter as water rapidly rose in her shanty. When the water became too deep, she tried to swim, holding her baby in her teeth. She struggled "bravely for some time" before succumbing and drowning with her child.[48]

Seawater rolled up the Edisto, Combahee, and Ashepoo rivers, over plantations, and over shanties. Whole families perished. The rushing waters swept poultry, rabbits, sheep, horses, and cows into the rivers, creeks, and canals. The saltwater ruined the rice crops and left a scene of abject desolation and ruin. On the Combahee alone, the waters submerged the food crops of fifteen hundred black laborers employed in the rice fields. Those who survived the storm had no money, little shelter, and less food. White planters saw the situation "as serious . . . and the rice plantations in worse condition than when the [Civil] war ended." It was predicted that the "demon of hunger" would soon be upon the land.[49]

Closer to Charleston, the tidal surge swept across Kiawah and Seabrook islands, carrying away the hovels of African Americans, their personal belongings, and their pets. "A colored boy" perished in one of the inlets. On Wadmalaw, Johns, and James islands rushing waters knocked over wharves and drowned cattle. At the Legare place on Johns Island, a black family of five drowned. One white planter said of the survivors "the poor negroes . . . need help badly."[50]

A red storm pennant flew in Charleston on August 25, two days before the hurricane hit. The city of sixty-five thousand, with its fine harbor, fifteen banks, three railroad lines, machine shops, gristmills, cotton presses, and phosphate manufacturers, was the first commercial city of the state and lowcountry. Residents hoped the storm would go elsewhere or that it would be less severe than predicted. Indeed, a group of Charleston yachtsmen and their families ignored the storm warnings and sailed south into the teeth of the hurricane. The E. Rhett Lewis family aboard their yacht *Winona* was among them. As winds increased they lost control of their craft and were blown into the marshes behind Kiawah Island. There they tied themselves to a tree and huddled together for hours in "deafening" wind with rain pelting them "like small shot," sustained only by "whiskey and raw eggs." The Lewis family and their fellow yachtsmen survived. On Sunday morning, August 27, 1893, high winds and drenching rains lashed Charleston. Only then did many of the city's residents believe that a tropical cyclone was bearing down on them.[51]

Huge waves battered Fort Sumter in Charleston's harbor. The keeper of the fort, Sergeant Thomas Britt, and his family survived by taking refuge in the powder magazine. By the evening, the cyclone was demolishing steamships, barks, schooners, and pleasure boats around the city. A surging tide rushed over the wharves. Only two of the one hundred piers along Charleston's waterfront survived. Waves hurled small boats into warehouses and homes near the waterfront. One vessel rammed the piazza at 107 Tradd Street. Seawater surged over the "beautiful Battery, the admiration of strangers and the pride of every son," and the spray from crashing waves leaped the rooftops of nearby houses. A huge sea tore away the iron railing running along the top of the Battery walk, and rushing tides undermined the promenade. Winds flattened the umbrella trees in White Point Gardens, the city's pleasure ground. A cove at the end of King Street, usually a snug harbor for yachts, filled with smashed boats and pieces of boats. The bathhouse disappeared.[52]

The city's finest mansions overlooked White Point Gardens and the Battery beyond. Their occupants heard shrieking winds and watched torrents of water surge down nearby streets. Waves crashed into some of the homes, streaming down stoops and sometimes flooding dwellings to the second floor. Around midnight a reporter discovered chest-high water running rapidly southward on Church and Legare Streets. Ten feet of water covered the low-lying south and west portions of the city—Rutledge, Bull, Gadsden, and Lynch streets. The waters submerged the gas meters, and the lights went out, plunging residents into inky darkness. The terrified occupants listened to the rising waters splash against their homes. To the well-to-do, "it was a night of horror." But in the tenements on Gadsden Street, African Americans started a "meeting of song and prayer." A newspaper reporter heard the refrain—"On Jordan's stormy banks I stand" as "the whistling, shrieking gale . . . wafted" over the submerged west end of the city.[53]

Winds increased to 120 miles per hour early Monday morning, wrecking the six huge phosphate works near the city and nearly destroying the new iron and steel bridge spanning the Ashley River. Limbs wrenched from trees. Winds uprooted nine hundred large trees belonging to the city and hundreds more owned by private citizens. Electric light and fire alarm wires went down. The streets were impassable. Twenty refrigerated railroad cars were hurled thirty feet into the marshes. Winds tore slate, shingles, and roofs off churches, homes, and stores. Tin roofing piled up ten feet high on East Bay Street. The interiors of public buildings and private homes flooded with rain. Cats, dogs, and chickens drowned. Amid all this devastation, amazingly, only four persons died in Charleston. Mary Barnwell, "colored," who huddled together with eight others in a house on Charleston Neck, was crushed when the chimney collapsed. An African American, Robert Oree, attempting to repair the tin roof on a dwelling at the corner of Warren and Coming streets, was blown to the sidewalk and "mangled." He died of his injuries. On Sunday evening the surging tide separated a black family in a shanty at the foot of Tradd Street. Neighbors rescued everyone except a child, James. When "a negro man," Robert Simmons, attempted to save the young boy, both drowned. The white press called Simmons a "hero."[54]

At the height of the hurricane, waves from the Ashley River broke against the walls of the City Hospital and its neighboring Pest House where "three poor, demented [female] creatures" were confined. Dr. Owens, on duty at the hospital, realized that the helpless women had to be rescued. He walked into the black night and through chest-deep waters to and from the Pest House three times to "save the poor maniacs." His peers called Owens's act "a heroic deed."[55]

The great storm swept inland. During the night of August 27–28, in the village of Summerville, some twenty miles west of Charleston, Anne Deas and her family huddled in their home listening to the "crash and rushing noise" of trees falling and "rain like hail against the . . . sides of the house." The village streets became "tangled with fallen trees."[56]

North of Charleston the rice fields along the Cooper River resembled "a sea of water." To the east of Charleston, in the village of Mount Pleasant, the hurricane destroyed breakwaters and wharves, eroded the embankment along the waterfront, and threatened to wash homes into the sea. Main avenues such as Ferry and Pitt streets became rivers. Waters rose two to three feet above the first floors in the stores of Messrs. Sharfer, Koper, Weinheimer, Schlorndorff, Lucker, Tecklenberg, and Tiencken, and their families had to be rescued and carried to higher places in the village.[57]

A witness to the hurricane on Sullivan's Island, Dr. H. Baer, an annual summer resident, recalled that it was "a big storm," that "the force of the wind was terrific." The islanders stood "in helpless impotence in the awful presence of these mighty [cyclones]." However, he said that the "velocity of the cyclone" was not as great as that of 1885. The weather observer at Charleston, Lewis N. Jesunofsky, disagreed, saying it "was more severe" than the earlier hurricane. Islanders estimated the winds at 125 miles per hour.[58]

The hurricane changed the natural environment of Sullivan's Island. It flattened twenty-five-foot-high sand dunes and redistributed the sand across the island. The houses once on Ocean Row were now in the middle of a beach that extended some three hundred yards beyond them. The ocean swept across the island to stand seven feet deep in places. The greatest destruction occurred between Fort Moultrie and the ferry wharf. Dozens of buildings were damaged or destroyed. Men on the island seized boats and rescued numbers of people from their residences. Hundreds fled to the fort for safety. Three who remained in their homes perished. A black couple, "Uncle Andrew" Bryan and his wife, Sylvia, huddled in their cottage until it floated off its foundations and into the sea. They waited too long to leave and drowned. Mrs. Ellen Pollard, a longtime resident of the island, was trying to exit her tiny cottage when it collapsed, crushing her to death. The island became littered with wrecked boats, homes, debris, and dead chickens.[59]

About twenty-five miles northeast of Sullivan's Island, the tiny fishing village of McClellanville faced the marsh and the open sea. Here the wind blew steadily all day Sunday. Then around 10:00 p.m. "the tide rose so rapidly it was thought to be a tidal wave. Great white capped waves rolled in, sweeping away fences and bridges," and inundating the village with four feet of water. Men carried women and children to places of safety as trees toppled into houses. In the village of 140 people no one died, but the hurricane caused "total destruction"—dead calves, sheep, and poultry were intermingled in the wreckage of homes. The wells filled with saltwater. Cotton fields were ruined by the inundation. One McClellanville man likely expressed the sentiments of many when he said, "I have lost . . . all I was worth in the Storm."[60]

About twenty-five miles to the northeast was the larger village of Georgetown (population three thousand). Located at the mouth of the Waccamaw River, facing Winyah Bay, the town was fourteen miles from the ocean. Its principal exports were rice, pine lumber, and turpentine. The Sampit River that emptied into Winyah Bay became "a raging sea," and the hurricane's northeast winds sent it crashing into Georgetown's wharves, sinking small boats at their moorings. The surging tide poured through stores on the waterfront, flooding Queen, Cannon, and Front streets. Storm debris—cordwood, lumber, barrels of rosin and turpentine—bobbed like corks in the waters. Winds whipped the town's foliage into tatters, prostrating Georgetown's magnificent shade trees. The tower of the city hall was smashed. A turpentine distillery was wrecked. It was the cyclone's "unparalleled and unremitting violence" that caused such destruction. A banker in Georgetown estimated the loss of city property at $10,000 ($195,638) and damage to the turpentine business in the countryside as incalculable. He noted, "Only six lives lost in the country so far as we can learn, all negroes."[61]

Rice crops around Georgetown suffered as saltwater surged twenty-five miles up the Waccamaw, Pee Dee, Sampit, and Black rivers. One witness, surveying the damage, described that as far as the eye could see, the wind lashed the waters "into angry waves" that broke over the rice fields.[62]

An observer on the South Carolina coast described the crops from Georgetown to Mt. Pleasant as "completely destroyed. The cotton, rice, potatoes are all sprouting and rotting in the field. The turpentine interest is all gone. . . . I see nothing but destitution and want in this part of the state. All business is destroyed."[63] Leaving a path of destruction, the hurricane roared inland to Charlotte, North Carolina, across Virginia, the northeastern states, and finally into Nova Scotia. Along the Georgia coast and, especially, in South Carolina, the great storm was the most massive human disaster from a hurricane in North America's history. Thousands died on South Carolina's coast, especially on the sea islands. Hundreds of African American laborers in phosphate mining around Beaufort, and another three thousand in the phosphate factories near Charleston, were now unemployed. Several thousand black workers on the rice plantations along the region's rivers also were without work, income, and adequate food. The living quarters of some were damaged; homes of others had disappeared. Visitors to the sea islands described black families living in "abject poverty" months after the hurricane.[64]

Most jobs in the phosphate industry were gone forever in South Carolina. From the Savannah River to Charleston preliminary losses in the industry were put at $5,000,000 ($97,819,145). It was a crippling blow from which the industry never recovered. Additionally, the dollar-a-ton tax on phosphate rock levied by Governor Tillman combined with the discovery of new phosphate beds in Florida assured the demise of the industry in South Carolina.[65]

The loss of South Carolina rice crops, estimated at more than $840,000 ($16,433,618), and damages to structures essential to its production placed an enormous burden on anyone involved in rice cultivation. Water and wind eroded dikes and destroyed trunks — all expensive to replace. One of the region's last great rice planters, Langdon Cheves, remarked that his losses were "Pretty bad."[66] The end of rice cultivation in the lowcountry appeared close at hand.

Property losses in South Carolina reached $10,000,000 ($195,638,290). Charleston's losses were put at $1,162,000 ($22,733,169); however, the majority of this was recovered as the city's well-off received about $1,000,000 ($19,563,829) from cyclone insurance on their homes and businesses.[67] The lowcountry was still recovering from the August storm when a second cyclone struck on Columbus Day.

"De Flagg Flood," October 13, 1893

The weather bureaus at Savannah and Charleston in early October 1893 warned mariners navigating near the coast of the lowcountry to be "very careful" because a dangerous storm out of the West Indies was moving toward the southeastern coast. By the evening of October 12–13 the hurricane was some sixty to ninety miles off the lowcountry. Its winds of forty-two miles per hour at Savannah increased to seventy-two miles per hour at Charleston — obviously the hurricane strengthened as it curved over open water and moved northwestward. It was on a collision course with South Carolina's upper coast.[68]

By the early morning hours of Friday, October 13, the hurricane reached Bull's Bay south of Georgetown where it knocked over a sloop owned by an African American, Captain Henry Williams. Every person in his five-man crew drowned. In the heavy seas Captain Williams somehow managed to swim to a small boat and pull himself aboard. When rescued he had been without water and food for three days and was lying in the bottom of the boat "waiting for grim death to seize him."[69]

Offshore from Georgetown the hurricane enveloped the *Conecuh*, a three-masted, eight-hundred-ton schooner. Losing "all hopes of life," Captain M. F. Harris and his crew lashed themselves to the rigging. For hours the sea rolled over them as winds pushed the battered schooner across the Cape Romain Shoals and onto a sandbar at the mouth of the South Santee River. The *Conecuh*, valued at $40,000 ($782,553), was declared a complete wreck. Though safe, the captain and crew had "lost everything."[70]

At daylight Friday morning McClellanville residents watched a "fierce northeast wind" push waters over the marshes into the village itself: "a wild sea raged over streets, yards and fields." The pitiful amounts of cotton and corn harvested after the hurricane of August 27 were "completely destroyed."[71]

Packing strong winds and following a path similar to that of the tropical cyclone of September 27, 1822, the hurricane came ashore a few miles northeast of Georgetown along the Waccamaw Neck, a peninsula bounded on the east by the Atlantic Ocean and the west by the Waccamaw River. There in the Indian summer of October 1893, residents had lingered at their beach homes on DeBordieu Island, Pawleys Island, and Magnolia Beach (today Litchfield Beach). Fortunately it was a sparsely settled region, because the hurricane made landfall on its most dangerous side — the right-front quadrant — inflicting terrible human and property losses for the people living in the region.[72]

The early morning hours of October 13 were stormy along Waccamaw Neck. On DeBordieu Island high winds and torrential rains beat against Anna Alston's cottage. In a dream her father appeared and urged Anna to pack her valuables as she would have to leave the island soon. At dawn, Friday 13, Anna, her sister, Charlotte, and young nieces, Mary Lucas and Mary Deas, and the black "servants" watched "mountain-high" waves break on the beach in front of their cottage. When water began streaming into the house, the women hurriedly retreated to a bedroom and climbed onto the beds. A huge cedar tree fell, shattering the front door. The sea swirled waist-deep around the occupants. They fled into an attached "storm room" built after the hurricane of 1822. It was ten feet above ground and anchored to an underground framework. Terrified they heard waves break on the roof of the cottage and watched in horror as water began to rise in the "storm room." The ocean and creek had joined to submerge DeBordieu Island. Suddenly the wind shifted to the southwest and the sea receded. The women in the Alston cottage had survived.[73]

Six miles up the coast, on Pawleys Island, the Tucker, Fraser, Lachicotte, and Freeman families fled their cottages. The tide crested fourteen feet above normal. The waters washed away large sand dunes and drowned island animals. No human casualties were reported, because the islanders had been able to climb trees and cling to limbs until the hurricane passed. When they descended from the trees, they found no sign of their cottages or belongings.[74]

A few miles away, on Magnolia Island, the Flagg family did not sleep. The sixty-five-year-old patriarch, Dr. Arthur Flagg, was worried that the family might become isolated if the tide rose too high. Dr. Flagg and his wife, Georgeanna, were entertaining their son Dr. Ward Flagg and his three nieces at their summer residence. Another son, also a physician, was nearby in his beach cottage with his wife, Mattie, their five children, and Mattie's sisters, Elizabeth and Alice LaBruce. On the beach at Magnolia Island the stinging rain came in at angles. By mid-morning it was nearly as dark as midnight. The Flaggs watched huge waves advance up the beach toward their dwellings. The Lewis Hasell family who owned a house on a high knoll at the north end of the island sent a servant to ask the Flaggs to take refuge with them. The Flaggs declined. The Flagg family soon realized the extent of the danger. When the tide did not recede from the beach or the creek behind them, they found themselves cut off from the mainland. Dr. Flagg told his sons to rip up the floor in the lower story of his house so it would fill with water and not float away. He then ordered family members to take refuge in the attic. But when winds blew away the porch roof, Dr. Flagg called for everyone to save him or herself by climbing a gnarled cedar tree in the yard. Everyone waded or swam to the tree as bricks from the chimney fell about them. The Flagg family and their servants shimmied up the tree and wrapped themselves around its prickly bark. They held on for life itself.[75]

Fierce sand-filled winds cut their faces, debris pummeled them, and breaking waves tore away their clothes. Occasionally someone lost their grip on the tree but somehow managed to climb up again. Ward Flagg pushed one young niece, Ann Weston, into the limbs of the tree but was unable to save his other two. The girls were swept away by the surging waters. The elder Dr. Flagg tried to help his wife hold on, but exhausted, he was unable to protect her. A black servant watched: "The old Cap'n see his wife turn loose, and he loose his grip and make a grab, and they lock together and down they gone. En de Cap'n, he cry, 'Miss Georgie gone! I gone too.'" When the wind sprang up from the southwest the water receded from the island and the old cedar tree. Ward, his niece Ann Weston, and several servants released their viselike holds and climbed down. "By 1:00 o'clock in the afternoon the sun was shinning and the ocean and air was as calm as on a summer day."[76]

Ward Flagg walked the beach to find his brother and his sister-in-law, Mattie. Their cottage was gone, and Ward found Mattie, who, he said, "looked like she was lying on a mattress, and her arms were stretched out like she was floating in water. I went to her, and she was drowned." The body of Mattie's infant daughter and her sister, Elizabeth LaBruce, washed ashore on DeBordieu Island. The remains of the patriarch, Dr. Flagg, were found in the marsh mud. Thirteen members or guests of the Flagg family and several of their "servants" perished. Ironically only one house — the Hasells', the home offered to the Flaggs as a safe haven — remained standing on Magnolia Island. The tragedy became known among the region's black families as "de Flagg flood."[77]

Along Waccamaw Neck, up to forty miles above Georgetown, the press reported, there was "desolation and destruction everywhere." It was argued that what happened around Georgetown in October was "precisely what happened" to South Carolina's southernmost sea islands in August. Appeals went out for assistance. Now survivors in the northeastern part of the state needed immediate supplies of food, clothing, and medicine.[78]

Leaving South Carolina, the October 1893 hurricane rolled across North Carolina, causing unprecedented flooding, numerous drownings, and severe damage to crops.[79]

The Cycle of Storms Persists

In late September 1894 a tropical storm swept along the coast of the lowcountry, causing little destruction except for the ruin of rice crops by saltwater inundation. For the fourth year in a row, planters experienced crop losses.[80] Storms and hurricanes, foreign competition, and labor problems continued to bedevil the rice planters — 1896 was to prove no different.

In late September 1896 a powerful September hurricane tracked south of Cuba and Jamaica and then came ashore on Florida's Gulf Coast. Speeding overland on a narrow, deadly, and destructive north-northeast path, the storm caught weather bureaus off guard. The hurricane's center was west of Jacksonville on September 29. There, on the right-front quadrant, damage was extensive. Sustained winds exceeded hurricane force — seventy-six miles per hour.[81]

The tropical cyclone roared into southern Georgia around 9:00 a.m. on Tuesday, September 29. At the small border town of St. Marys and in the hamlets of Folkston, Waycross, Woodbine, and Jesup winds knocked over stores, small hotels, and houses. A black barber, Tom Wright, was killed in Folkston when winds demolished his house. The grade school, constructed of heavy timbers and thought to be the strongest building in Folkston, collapsed with thirty-eight children and their teacher inside. All escaped injury. In the surrounding turpentine forests, pine trees became airborne, smashing into homes and injuring occupants. Persons who ventured into the storm faced great risk from flying timbers. A witness remarked that where once pine forests grew, there was now "a prairie-like appearance." In some places it was impossible to ride horseback through the forest because of downed trees. The press declared it "a disaster to turpentine men." Their losses in South Georgia were estimated to be about $500,000 ($10,448,863).[82]

On the coast at Brunswick, a port ranked second only to Savannah as the world's largest exporter of naval stores, damage to shipping was "terrific." Sixty-mile-per-hour winds accompanied by much higher gusts carried away masts and drove many vessels aground. The body of Martin Gatewood, most likely a mariner, washed ashore. In town, winds tore away tin roofs and destroyed buildings, killing four "colored" persons: John Jefferson and baby, A. Davis, and William Daniels. Three white persons were also injured: Mrs. M. Wiggins and child, and Mrs. Richard Purcell. "These three have their heads crushed in, but will probably recover" was the curious comment of a reporter. The Electric and Gas Light Company plant, the opera house, a wholesale grain and grocery warehouse, St. John's Church, and a school all became "total wrecks." The roof of the Oglethorpe Hotel was carried away and its windows blown in. Dozens of other businesses, churches, and private homes sustained significant structural damage. Trees crashed down across Brunswick and debris filled the streets. The press described Brunswick as "wrecked by the hurricane." It was thought that property losses locally might reach as high as $500,000 ($10,488,863).[83]

A few miles east of Brunswick, at the beach resort of St. Simons Island, the sea destroyed the ocean pier, wrecked cottages, and flooded the island's hotel. Winds wrecked most of the island's churches and severely damaged the "negro village" on the south end of the island as well as the "colored settlement" at "Jewtown." It was estimated that the damage at St. Simons would reach $150,000 ($3,134,659).[84]

Up the coast at Darien a witness described the hurricane as "the severest storm" to ever strike the port town. No building escaped damage. "Everywhere destruction and ruin were visible. Trees . . . tin roofs, all lay piled in a conglomerated mass about the streets."[85]

When the storm reached Tybee Island on Tuesday, September 29, one resident estimated its winds at 108 miles per hour. Cottages were unroofed, bathhouses demolished, the hotel damaged, and the Tybee to Savannah Railroad again was "badly injured." The storm caught Henry Simmons fishing in a small boat off Wilmington Island, and he was drowned. At the resorts of Thunderbolt and the Isle of Hope, watercraft were driven ashore.[86]

The hurricane swept up the Savannah River, driving steamships, schooners, and barks ashore and sending "smaller boats . . . in every direction." It capsized the small coasting schooner *Island Flower*, and Captain Lewis Hill, his brother, Frank, and a deckhand, the seventeen-year-old "boy" Ulysses Steel, drowned. Nearby, the tug *Robert Turner* was smashed to pieces and its captain, C. E. Murray, a crewman, and a passenger perished. Just before the storm struck Savannah the local weather observer predicted thirty-mile-per-hour winds. But around noon the weather station wind gauge blew away after recording sixty-six miles per hour. Estimates of the wind speed reached seventy-five miles per hour. Some said the storm was of greater intensity and destructiveness than that of 1893, and only the hurricane's short duration — about forty-five minutes — saved Savannah from "annihilation."[87]

High winds filled the air with flying debris, causing severe injuries throughout the city. At Southville, a "colored settlement," four African Americans died when a house collapsed. Nearly every private dwelling and public building in Savannah suffered some damage. Thousands were unroofed and others razed. Debris choked the streets. The city market was blown down. The walls of railroad warehouses collapsed. Churches, hospitals, and the armory of the Georgia Hussars were "badly damaged." Every store in the retail section of the city suffered the effects of the storm. In Forsyth Park more than half the trees went down. Savannah was a net of crossed and tangled telephone and telegraph wires. Streetcars stood motionless on tracks. Fallen buildings and trees blocked their way. In some spots, the streets were impassable even for pedestrians. At least seventeen people on the river or around Savannah perished in the brief but powerful hurricane. Initial estimates of damages in the city reached $1,000,000 ($20,897,727). It was yet another disappointing year for rice planters — 30 percent of the crop along the Ogeechee River was ruined. Savannahians blamed the weather bureau for failing to "predict the storm's course." The press ranked the hurricane "as one of the three great storms that have visited Savannah in the last twenty-five years."[88]

Around noon the hurricane knifed into the lower South Carolina coast from the southeast with punishing rains and winds. Here too the weather bureau had not predicted the severity of the blow, and people were unprepared. At Port Royal and St. Helena Island winds blew coasting vessels into the marshes, knocked over houses and shanties, and uprooted trees. Four blacks perished during the storm. Violent gusts at Beaufort lashed the bay into "foaming, dashing billows" that capsized yachts of the well-to-do, the *Osprey*, *Nellie*, and *Julia*. Water submerged wharves and poured into warehouses. Again winds wrecked stores along Bay Street, the courthouse, and St. Helena Episcopal Church. Older homes owned by prominent residents were battered so badly that tin roofs were "rolled up as scrolls and flown through the air in the shape of sweet wafers" to land blocks away. Heavy piazzas crashed down, window blinds tore away from their hinges, windowpanes blew in, and drenching rains soaked interiors. A newspaper reporter observed that the wind "toyed with the fragments it was making of timbers and roofs and shutters and branches of trees . . . as if they were straws and endangering the lives of any person along the thoroughfares. At times it was impossible to stand even upon one's feet, either to breast the storm or to drift with it." Residents of Beaufort believed they were fortunate that the hurricane came at low tide. But they were angered that it came "without [warning] from the weather bureau." Officials estimated the damage second only to the hurricane of 1893. There was "on every side ruin and devastation." Only the storm's brief duration limited the destruction. What remained of the already-crippled phosphate industry sustained further damage.[89]

At Charleston residents noticed the "ominous" red and black storm flag flying above the weather bureau. Around 11:00 a.m. a rising southeast wind filled the sky with dark swift-moving clouds. Some residents hurried home to "batten down the hatches." Within an hour the wind and rain made "walking very disagreeable," and waves pounded the South and East Battery. Yet wind speeds at Charleston never exceeded sixty-two miles per hour — tropical-storm velocity. Though the winds died in Charleston around 4:00 p.m., they accelerated over land, reaching hurricane strength at Florence, South Carolina.[90]

Just two years later two hurricanes crashed into the lowcountry. Once more the largest loss of lives and the severest damage occurred along the Georgia coast and South Carolina's lower coast.

Last Cyclones of the Century

With the outbreak of war with Spain over events in Cuba in 1898 and the sinking of the American battleship *Maine* in Havana's harbor, the U.S. government became concerned over weather events in the region and quickly established a hurricane-warning network in the West Indies. These stations gave advance notice that a hurricane was headed for the lowcountry in August 1898.[91]

Residents became "apprehensive" after watching several days of "ugly weather." By Monday, August 29, Savannahians believed that "a storm of unusual intensity was heading [their] way." At Beaufort, South Carolina, Susan Rice said, "[the] rising wind . . . distresses me."[92]

The weather forecast for the Georgia coast on August 30 was "light to fresh southerly to easterly winds." The season at Tybee Island was over, and most vacationers had returned to the city. The few who remained and the soldiers stationed there never received word that a hurricane was approaching. Flags warning that a *tropical storm* was moving toward the Atlantic coast did go up from Savannah to Norfolk about 4:00 p.m.—a few hours before the hurricane struck Tybee Island. When the hurricane hit, the island residents guessed wind speeds to be between eighty-five and one hundred miles per hour. Winds blew away the tents of the army unit stationed at the north end of Tybee. Damage to the concrete fortifications and gun emplacements was minor. On the south end of the island, winds demolished cottages, unroofed cottages, and once again blew Henry Soloman's beach house off its foundations. The windmill at Hotel Tybee blew over, and the hotel kitchen collapsed. A water tank at the South End Hotel toppled, and winds again damaged the island's two social clubs.[93]

Apparently the hurricane formed far off Jacksonville and developed rapidly over warm coastal waters. Damage to shipping was heavy. Wreckage was strewn along the beaches from Tybee Island to Beaufort. Just offshore, hurricane winds capsized barks, brigs, schooners, and smaller sailing craft, drowning mariners. The storm drove other vessels ashore on Tybee, Hilton Head, St. Helena, and Hunting islands. On the sand shoals two miles off Tybee the 512-ton Italian bark *Noe* was blown aground and was being beaten to pieces by crashing waves. Fearing they would be swept overboard, the sailors climbed high into the rigging. They fired rockets into the night sky that were seen by those on shore. One crewman, afraid that the bark was breaking up, donned a life jacket, told his shipmates "goodbye," and jumped into the boiling sea, where he drowned. When winds moderated on August 31, Lieutenant Henry S. Morgan of the U.S. Corps of Engineers, who was in charge of fortifications on the island, helped lead an expedition to save the Italian mariners. Lieutenant Morgan, born into a prominent South Georgia family, had graduated from West Point in 1897, fourth in his class and first in his military grade. He "was idolized by the men who worked with him on the fortifications at Tybee." Before climbing into the small rescue craft (a sailboat) with five other men, Lieutenant Morgan handed his West Point class ring and wallet to a bystander, remarking, "Keep these for me, one can't tell what may happen." As the sailboat approached the *Noe*, an "ugly line of breakers reared before them" along the sandbar. Someone yelled, "We had better tack." Lieutenant Morgan thought the men wanted to go back. He replied, "No, don't lets think of ourselves. Just look at those men in the rigging. We [can't] go back and leave them there."[94]

A minute later a giant wave crashed over the sailboat, filling it with water and capsizing it. As the small sailboat rolled in the breakers on the bar, the six men managed to grab the boat and hold on. To prevent being weighed down by their wet, heavy clothes, some of the rescuers quickly pulled off their outer garments. Lieutenant Morgan remained fully clothed in his wool uniform covered by a heavy mackintosh. When another breaking wave crashed into the sailboat, the lieutenant lost his grip and went under. He bobbed to the surface and again grasped the boat, but his face was "wild and staring" and "deadly white," a member of the boat crew noted. When another huge wave rolled the sailboat, Morgan again lost his grip and slipped into the "seething sea," not to be seen again.[95]

Another member of Lieutenant Morgan's rescue team, Harry Smith, climbed onto the bottom of the sailboat but was knocked off by waves and drowned. The four remaining men now thought their fate would be the same. For five hours winds, waves, and tides pushed the overturned sailboat and the near-naked men north toward Daufuskie Island. There the boat with the four men still holding to it finally bumped ashore. The men aboard the *Noe* were also rescued. Their vessel became a "useless hulk," and it too eventually drifted onto the beach at Daufuskie Island. The bodies of Lieutenant Morgan and Harry Smith, it appears, were never recovered.[96]

In the hurricane's path from Tybee to Savannah the storm unroofed houses on Wassaw Island, at Thunderbolt, on Wilmington Island, and on the Isle of Hope. Vessels from steamships to small sailboats were tossed about like corks. Heavy rains and hurricane-force winds swept Savannah from late afternoon, August 30, to the following morning. On the waterfront, cotton warehouses, fertilizer works, and rice mills were heavily damaged. Hundreds of buildings across the city were unroofed or blown down. Chimneys toppled, spilling bricks across public walkways. Street signs flew through the city; telephone and telegraph wires went down in tangles. Presses stopped at the *Savannah Morning News*, and the building swayed in the wind. The north side of the First Baptist Church was blown into Hull Street. When the roof of the city's theater came off, torrents of rain drenched the interior. There was no storm insurance on the theater, but the manager planned to add it. As the hurricane raged, thieves robbed several stores. More than eight inches of rain fell. No storm on record had dumped a greater volume of water on the city. With the ground saturated, winds uprooted hundreds of trees in the city's squares and Forsyth Park. Damage to property was estimated at $250,000 ($5,284,483). Rice along the Ogeechee and Savannah rivers was a total loss, inundated by high, salty tides. The once robust and now modest crops of cotton in the lowcountry were also ruined. In addition to the constant threat of hurricanes, the cotton planters on "the sea islands . . . [felt] more directly the effect of the large importations of Egyptian . . . cotton."[97]

North of Savannah, at Bluffton, South Carolina, the hurricane damaged nearly every house. At plantations along the May River, cattlemen reported a "big loss" in livestock. The wind speed at Port Royal reached seventy-five miles per hour, and trees that had survived the 1893 storm went down. The cyclone raged all night in Beaufort, and for Susan Rice "there was no sleeping." Windows in her house shattered and torrents of rain blew in.[98]

Flooding on some of the lower South Carolina sea islands destroyed black dwellings and food crops, and hunger was again widespread. On Hilton Head Island a committee of whites collected food and other supplies to distribute to the needy. But the *Palmetto Post* editorialized that "able-bodied colored men . . . by force of arms attacked the homes of the white committee that had gathered . . . the supplies" and demanded "their share." In turn white people "in terror . . . quit the island." In the racially charged language of the day, the editor concluded that it had "come to a pretty past when a few white people" wishing to assist the needy "should be set upon and terrorized by savages."[99]

The storm caused minimal damage at Charleston. But within a month a second and more punishing tropical cyclone swept the lowcountry. It would be the last in the cycle of storms of the late nineteenth century.

Last Storm of the Century

The hurricane formed in late September east of the Leeward Islands and headed northwest toward the southeastern coast of the United States. On October 1, 1898, the national weather bureau issued a warning of "dangerous shifting gales" to all ports from Key West to Norfolk. The warning kept some vessels in port and likely saved many lives. But the powerful tropical cyclone sank and disabled vessels already at sea. It was a major hurricane.[100]

The brig *Robert Dillon*, out of Brunswick, Georgia, was struck by the storm early Sunday, October 2. The brig's steward was washed overboard to his death, and then the vessel capsized. The remaining crew and its commander, Captain Bowen, clung to the vessel for three days until rescued by the German steamship *Macedonia*. By daylight Sunday some one hundred miles off Charleston, the fifteen-member crew of the 880-ton Norwegian bark *Safir* had battled the hurricane for hours. The bark carried a heavy load of lumber. An exhausted crew was on the deck when its master, "tall and spare . . . fifty-five year old" Captain Knudson, saw a "particularly heavy sea" approaching. The bark capsized, throwing the crew overboard. Captain Knudson reached floating pieces of the vessel, secured his legs with a length of rope, and held on. Huge waves in the violent sea quickly separated the men clinging to or trying to swim to debris from their capsized vessel. With waves breaking repeatedly over his head, Captain Knudson drifted alone in the Atlantic Ocean. Although water was all around him, there was not a drop "to cool his tongue." He did not know it, but he was drifting toward the coast. Three days after the *Safir* capsized, sixty-five miles off Charleston, Captain Gentile of the fishing smack *Herbert* sighted Captain Knudson clinging to wreckage. Miraculously he had survived, and even more miraculously he was discovered in the open sea. So exhausted he could barely speak, Knudson was pulled aboard the vessel that transported him to Charleston — the lone survivor of the *Safir*.[101]

On Sunday, about seven miles off Charleston, the hurricane slammed into a four-masted schooner out of Port Charlotte, Florida, the *Sarah E. Palmer*, burdened with eighteen hundred tons of phosphate rock. The vessel sprang a leak. In darkness the crew of nine struggled to keep the schooner upright. In fierce winds, the two-hundred-foot-long, one-thousand-ton schooner began going "to pieces," sinking as she did. Seven crewmembers "went down with her." Two black sailors, James Rowe and Joseph Meyers, managed to grab a heavy plank that tore away from the ill-fated schooner. In the rolling, breaking sea they clung to the plank for life itself. After fifteen hours the two exhausted mariners washed ashore on Edisto Island.[102]

About the time the *Sarah E. Palmer* was going down, the crew of the barkentine *Wandering Jew* was fighting to keep afloat off Charleston. Carrying one thousand tons of coal and leaking badly, the six-hundred-ton vessel foundered off the Isle of Palms. Waves crashed over the vessel, and the six-member crew climbed into the rigging to save themselves. At daylight the tugboat *John Harlin*, out of Charleston, sighted the masts of the barkentine. Only a small boat could get close enough to rescue the sailors aboard. First mate Mark Jones and Simon, an African American, volunteered. At great risk to themselves, they negotiated "mountainous seas" and rescued the six mariners from the *Wandering Jew* as it was breaking up. An observer lauded their bravery, noting that the rescuers came just "in the nick of time."[103]

It was a major hurricane when it lashed northeastern Florida on Sunday, October 2, 1898. The hurricane's towering waves and high winds devastated Fernandina Beach. The less dangerous southern side swiped St. Marys, Georgia. Accompanying it was what some called "the greatest tidal wave in [the] history" of the town. The wharf and houses along the St. Marys River washed away or broke into pieces. River water in the streets reached waist-deep and flooded dwellings and stores. St. Marys, the seat of Camden County, was cut off from the rest of the county because of downed trees and washed-out roads.[104]

Around 11:00 a.m., the hurricane made landfall on Cumberland Island, just to the east of St. Marys, as a category 4 cyclone. The "tidal wave" accompanying the storm roared ashore, flooding Dungeness, Thomas Carnegie's Cumberland Island mansion, and "badly damaged" a "magnificent yacht" owned by Mrs. Lucy Carnegie. The storm drove sailing vessels onto a nearby sandbar, drowning eight mariners. The "tidal wave" gathered strength and height as it moved north along Georgia's shallow coastal waters and sent a storm surge as high as twenty feet across Cumberland's neighboring islands and Georgia's lower coast.[105]

The tidal surge washed away the old fort and dismounted heavy cannon at the south end of Jekyll Island. Waters poured through the "millionaires' cottages" of the exclusive Jekyll Island Club, and its dock ended up on the porch of Joseph Pulitzer's cottage. Damages reached $30,000 ($634,138).[106]

The tropical cyclone moved inland following a west-northwest path similar to that of Dora (1964) and Hugo (1989). Just north of Jekyll Island, the residents of Brunswick, Georgia, endured eighteen hours of driving rain and wind before the hurricane finished raking the city Sunday afternoon. "The hurricane was so sudden. It came up and you didn't know what hit you," said Thomas Spalding Hopkins.[107]

The tidal surge appeared to sweep water out of the bay, rivers, and creeks, inundating Brunswick. Steamships, barks, schooners, and pilot boats blew ashore; hundreds of thousands of feet of lumber, hundreds of railroad cross-ties, and barrels of naval stores were swept off the city docks to disappear into the sea. Brunswick's streets became rivers. Black and white townspeople appropriated small bateaus and paddled to higher ground. Some carried or swam with their wives and children to the sturdy Mansfield Street School where they anxiously watched the rising waters. The crack of tree limbs and falling trees terrified townspeople, who feared that their own houses might collapse on them. Those who tried to escape their flooded homes sometimes found themselves pinned against buildings by the wind "as with bands of iron," unable to move until the wind subsided. The three-story "colored" Odd Fellows Hall blew over, church steeples "twisted." The surging waters poured four to eight feet deep into private dwellings, stores, and warehouses. Men armed with knives bravely swam through flooded streets to the city livery stables to cut the tethers of horses and save them from drowning. Twenty of the animals were housed in the Baptist church, one of the most "magnificent brick edifices" in town.[108]

A reporter on the scene used language typical of the era to describe damage to the shanties and the behavior of African Americans in a black settlement in the city — "Hell's Half Acre, the notorious retreat of the criminal classes, was practically wrecked" and the "inmates . . . driven from their homes." Some "began to fill up on liquor, and raised Bedlam amongst themselves." One was shot, another knifed—both died; a white store owner was stabbed. "Depraved negro men and women disported themselves in the water in the most shameful manner, and the entire gang wound up in a partial riot." Brunswick's police chief called up additional forces and began arresting the rioters. But it was difficult to hold them, since both the city and the county jails were "four feet under water." At least seven persons perished in Brunswick. The bodies of two "colored" children were found floating in six feet of water in one of the city's streets; the bodies of a white man, Captain Frank Cummings, who apparently went down with his sailboat during the height of the storm, and a black man washed up in the marsh grasses.[109]

To the east of Brunswick, on St. Simons Island, the hurricane drove vessels over sandbars and onto the beach. Some people took refuge in trees.

Horace Gould and his family, year-round residents on the island, whose home was just off the front beach, watched and worried as the winds increased and the tide rose up beyond the woods bordering the beach. Gould brought his chickens into the house for safety, and when the water began pouring into the house itself, he placed them atop the stove. As the seawater rose quickly throughout the house, Gould heard "a succession of crashes."

> The dining room windows all burst in and the water [was] up to my waist. . . . the shed rooms were going up and down like a bucking horse and the waves were striking the sides . . . like a battering ram. . . . we saw the south piazza . . . separate from the main body of the house and disappear. . . . the yard . . . looked like the ocean, great waves chasing each other across from East to West and striking the trees. . . . on all sides the air was filled with flying spray. The . . . rain striking your face and hands felt like . . . shot. . . . Frequently, the crest of a wave was taken off clean, as though cut with a knife and the mass of water was sent flying through the air, like a great sheet. . . . we could see fowls and turkeys . . . drowning. . . . Mama caught two hens as they were passing and saved them. When the water began to thump against the floor of the parlor I feared we would have to get on the roof as the safest place in case the walls fell.

The anxiety and terror that gripped the family for hours passed when the water began retreating at about 3:00 p.m.[110]

The sea covered almost all of St. Simons Island, and houses were wrecked or washed from their foundations. Gould saw ancient oaks he remembered from his childhood lying "indiscriminately" where they fell, "their limbs crossed and recrossed," and "mingled with them . . . remnants of chairs, tables, linen, crockery; everything broken into bits. Dead animals, both wild and domestic, lie plentifully around." At the rear of the beachfront, Gould saw "all the pretty cottages, bath houses, etc. . . . piled in one inextricable mass next to the woods . . . and mixed in among them are the fragments of their furniture." Only the Hotel St. Simons and the Arnold Hotel remained upright, but the sea had passed through the lower floors, washing away the verandas of one; the "parlor furniture . . . the fine piano, [was] . . . strew[n] over the beach." Apparently there were no white fatalities on St. Simons Island, because the summer vacationers had returned to their permanent residencies. However, Gould observed, "The exact loss of life among the Negroes will never be known. The rice-fields were swept and they must have been drowned by scores."[111] His observation was correct. On tiny Egg Island the sea swept in, knocking over the dwelling of Alex Stokeley and his wife. They took refuge on the downed roof until waves washed the couple into the boiling surf. Holding on to his wife and with a "desperate effort" he grabbed on to the limb of a tree and held fast until his wife apparently drowned. Crashing waves wrenched her lifeless body away from him and knocked Stokeley into a "mass of driftwood." The debris served as a raft that he clung to for three days "more dead than alive" until he reached land and safety.[112]

Up the coast the hurricane roared through the mouth of the Altamaha River, over the islands along the river, and into Darien, situated on a bluff above the river. The port of Darien was second only to Pensacola, Florida, as the largest exporter of yellow pine in the United States. From the interior of Georgia, tons of cotton flowed down the Oconee and Ocmulgee rivers into the Altamaha, ending up at Darien for export abroad. The lumber and cotton exports made Darien the state's second leading port behind Savannah. A dozen planters cultivated rice locally, though the amount produced was only a pale reminder of the quantity harvested years earlier. The hurricane surprised Darien's residents. Despite days of rising winds and driving rains, most thought it was just another early fall gale that posed little or no danger. But here, as elsewhere on the lower Georgia coast, the cyclone was especially destructive because it came in on a high tide and a full moon.[113]

The tidal surge, reminiscent of the one of 1804, again swept Butler's Island. Perhaps as many as eighty African American men, women, and children drowned. At nearby Champney Island, the Central of Georgia railroad employed black laborers in the rice fields. In the "settlement" where the laborers lived, the tidal surge reached thirteen feet, and five perished. Waters swept away every structure on the island. Pieces of the rice mill ended up on Butler's Island. Mules drowned, and the sea carried away the tools, books, desk, and tables of the white manager, John G. Legare. Surging waters broke through the dike around the rice fields and damaged all the tide gates that controlled the flow of freshwater. Saltwater covered the rice crop. On smaller islands, the tidal surge drowned an unknown number of poor black farmers who grew vegetables for urban markets. The "tidal wave" raced over Wolf Island, smashing and sweeping away quarantine facilities on the north and south ends. Caretakers of the Wolf Island Club, Sarah Cobb Poppell, her husband, and their two children, drowned when the sea demolished the clubhouse. Only James Cromley, the keeper of the light at Wolf Island, and a "colored man" survived.[114]

Opposite Darien, on Sapelo Island, Archibald McKinley and his wife, Sallie, the island's prominent white landowners, watched ocean waves crash ashore and race toward them. The McKinleys had cleared the land between the beach and their pre–Civil War house on the landward side of the island for farming, and there was nothing to stop the ocean. They saw waves "fully twelve feet high" break in their yard. The sea began rising in the house until the McKinleys stood "waist deep in water." The furniture in the house floated. Sallie watched the sea outside "beating against the house almost mountain high" and McKinley put "his shoulder against . . . [the] back door to keep the waves from bursting the door open." Waves tore away the back piazza, steps, and kitchen, and the outhouse disappeared. Sallie wondered if they "would ever live through" the hurricane; she was "expecting every breath to be [their] last." Eventually the sea retreated, but it seemed as though it took hours for the water to drain out of the house. Everything was soaked and covered with marsh mud. Sallie soon realized that they had "lost *every thing* on earth [they] had. And it is hard to start life at [their] ages with nothing."[115] But they had survived. Others on Sapelo Island and neighboring islands suffered greater losses.

Willie Jones, a young man who attempted to leave Sapelo for the mainland, drowned. The keeper of the light on the island, William Cromley, watched what he believed was a thirty-three-foot wave smash into the Sapelo Island lighthouse, rendering the light useless. As waves battered down the light keeper's house, Cromley swam first to the lighthouse with one child, then another, and lastly his wife. All survived. Exhausted and losing consciousness, Cromley was rescued by "a colored man" who tied him down in a boat and rowed him to safety. The sea submerged Black, Hurd's, Union, Cane Creek, and Doboy islands. On Doboy six members of an African American family, the Gilliards, drowned. A family on Black Island survived by climbing into trees. Some saved their houses by opening the front and rear doors to let the rushing waters pass through. The wreckage of other dwellings washed up on the mainland. About a hundred cattle drowned on General's Island, and the rice mill simply disappeared.[116]

At the town of Darien, on Sunday morning around 10:00 a.m., the wind blew furiously and increased in velocity for the next three hours. The Altamaha River became "one roaring sea, having overspread the rice-fields and wharves." Every wharf but one was destroyed at great losses to shipping agents. Some witnessed what they described as "a tidal wave" as the sea suddenly rose "ten to twelve feet higher than ever known before." Winds and waves scattered "millions and millions" of feet of timber in every direction. Residents watched the storm unroof their homes, demolish the "colored" Methodist and Episcopal churches, and bring down centuries-old trees. One resident said, "The storm simply wiped out a part of Darien."[117]

Like other lowcountry authors, Brainard Cheney, who grew up in southeast Georgia, was fascinated by the fierce hurricanes that frequently swept the region. A fictionalized account of the October 2, 1898, hurricane appeared in his novel *River Rogue*, published by Houghton-Mifflin years later.

The sky was a muddy gray. The wind smote [Ratliff's] face. . . . The boughs of the great live oaks churned angrily. . . . In the wind, in the roar about him, was a deep, giant drum-roll from the marsh, from the sea.

Suddenly, as he reached the outskirts of Darien . . . the hurricane struck him with a concussion that sent him into the air, floating, whirling — at the heart of a rising, rending howl — the roof of a house sailed before his eyes. . . .

On his belly, clawing at the palmetto roots, he inched his way into the wind. . . . He came to the lower edge of [Darien's] Bluff. . . . Below him, the masts of schooners jumped, darted, swerved . . . their hulls rose high, disappeared beneath monstrous walls of water — water that roared, smashing, foaming over the wharves, over the roofs of the depots.

[I]n the distance he saw a church steeple crumple . . . there won't be a wharf left, or a boat. . . . "The town may go!" . . . Out of the infinite gray sky, sweeping in from the gray horizon, mountains of sea rocked and rolled toward the Bluff.[118]

Winds from the major hurricane had moderated by the time it swept along the uppermost Georgia and lower South Carolina coasts. But flooding was extensive, since the storm came ashore on a full moon at high tide. At Tybee Island the sea floated away four miles of railroad ties and track and drove barks and schooners loaded with lumber into the marshes. In the Savannah suburbs of Thunderbolt and the Isle of Hope, winds and waves smashed wharves and capsized dozens of sailing crafts. At Thunderbolt, Joseph White, the African American caretaker of the sloop *Glance*, drowned while trying to swim to the yacht club. At Savannah the wind blew from forty to sixty miles per hour all day Sunday but caused only minor damage in the city. Seawater submerged the lowlands along the rivers. Most of what remained of the rice crops following the August hurricane was lost. On Hutchinson Island waters reached waist-deep in places as the Back and Savannah rivers came together. Boats evacuated more than a hundred African Americans from the island.[119]

The South Carolina coast experienced a storm surge as high as fourteen feet on the same sea islands that suffered most during the hurricane of 1893. But casualties were few by comparison; there were likely fewer than ten storm-related deaths. Planters along the Combahee, Pon Pon, and Edisto rivers again saw saltwater sweep across their rice fields.[120]

On the upper South Carolina coast, winds never exceeded tropical-storm velocities. The Charleston press called it "a storm more disagreeable than destructive." Lewis N. Jesunofsky, the local weather bureau official, reported that a high-pressure system forced the hurricane away from Charleston and the upper coast of the state.[121]

Much of the lowcountry escaped the highest winds of the major hurricane of October 2, 1898. The greatest number of fatalities and most extensive property and crop damage occurred on the lower Georgia and South Carolina coasts and offshore. Some estimates of the death toll reached two hundred; property and crop losses exceeded $2,000,000 ($42,275,862).[122]

The four hurricanes of the 1890s, an unprecedented number for a single decade, shattered the fragile lowcountry economy based on rice, phosphates, timber, lumber, and the export business—major employers of the region. The phosphate and timbering industries never recovered, and the end of two hundred years of rice cultivation appeared imminent.

TOP President Lyndon Johnson visits St. Simons after hurricane Dora, 1964.
Courtesy of *Savannah Morning News.*

BOTTOM The north end of Tybee Island, Georgia, is flooded by hurricane Dora.
Courtesy of *Savannah Morning News.*

LEFT TOP AND MIDDLE
During Dora, 1964, trees
toppled around Savannah.
Courtesy of *Savannah
Morning News.*

LEFT BOTTOM A tree
downed by hurricane
Dora in Savannah's Bacon
Park. Courtesy of *Savannah
Morning News.*

RIGHT Hurricane Dora
battered the St. Simons
Island, Georgia, beachfront.
Courtesy of Coastal Georgia
Historical Society.

BELOW Residents of Tybee
Island, Georgia, move about
by boat after hurricane
Dora. Courtesy of *Savannah
Morning News.*

BELOW TOP Tybee Island, Georgia, during the passage of
hurricane Dora. Courtesy of *Savannah Morning News.*

BELOW BOTTOM The aftermath of hurricane Dora on St.
Simons Island, Georgia, beachfront. Courtesy of Coastal
Georgia Historical Society.

ABOVE The *Mary Ann* blown into the marshes of the Wilmington River by hurricane David. Courtesy of *Savannah Morning News*.

RIGHT Phone remains on the hook after winds from hurricane David destroyed most of the Dixon Construction Company, Savannah. Courtesy of *Savannah Morning News*.

BELOW TOP Century-old oak felled by
hurricane David in downtown Savannah.
Courtesy of *Savannah Morning News*.

BELOW BOTTOM Winds from hurricane
David stripped limbs from trees in
Oglethorpe Square, Savannah. Courtesy
of *Savannah Morning News*.

LEFT The Goodyear House after hurricane David, Sea Island, Georgia, 1979. Courtesy of *Savannah Morning News.*

BELOW Boats at the Savannah Marina damaged by hurricane David. Courtesy of *Savannah Morning News.*

Van crushed by trees during hurricane David, Savannah, 1979. Courtesy of *Savannah Morning News.*

Hurricane David dashes past Kitty's Marina, Thunderbolt, Georgia. Courtesy of *Savannah Morning News.*

Hurricanes

and Gales of the

Twentieth Century,

1904–1979

Charleston's Mosquito Fleet

For unknown reasons the U.S. Weather Bureau failed to warn residents of the approaching hurricane.[1] No storm flags flew when Charleston's Mosquito Fleet, a group of African American fishermen, left their berths at the end of Market Street Tuesday morning, September 13, 1904. They sailed their smacks and sloops through the harbor into the open waters of the Atlantic. The fleet supplied the city with much of its seafood. The boats headed for the usual fishing ground twenty-five miles east of Charleston.

By the time they reached the blackfish banks a heavy sea was running. As the waves became "mountain high" and "dangerous," John Wylie, captain of the twenty-seven-foot vessel *Pride*, decided to return to port. The boat weathered the gale for a short time before it capsized, throwing Captain Wylie and three crewmen into the sea — two drowned almost immediately. Captain Wylie kept trying to reach the upturned boat, but eventually he too went under. The fourth crewmember, Abram Jones, made it to the boat four times but was repeatedly knocked back in the water by huge waves before he could get a firm grasp. Bruised and exhausted, Jones was "ready to give up," when he was miraculously rescued by another fishing boat from the Mosquito Fleet. He was the sole survivor from the *Pride*.[2]

In the same vicinity, Captain Pompey Aiken, of the *Big Ella*, and his crew of six struggled as the wind tore the sails to "tatters." Despite the condition of his vessel, Captain Aiken somehow managed to maneuver close enough to assist a boat of the Mosquito Fleet that was flying a distress signal. The *Salem* was sinking with five people aboard. Captain Aiken took off two crewmen and the boat's captain, Prince Bryan. The fishing smack *Gray Eagle*, also of the fleet, rescued the remaining crewmembers. With their charges safely on board, the rescuing crafts set a course for Charleston. After some twelve hours of navigating heavy seas, Captain Aiken reached safety in the "quiet water" of the Stono River. The smack *Gray Eagle*, its crew of six, and the two rescued crewmen were not as lucky.[3]

Battling huge waves near the Charleston Lightship, Captain William Simmons's *Gray Eagle* was close to foundering when spotted by Captain Ingram of the steamship *Huron*. Ingram offered to take the men aboard, but they refused, thinking they could save their vessel; instead they asked for a towline. But as it was being secured the *Gray Eagle* capsized, spilling the eight crewmen into the ocean. Life preservers and ropes were dropped. Three men were brought safely aboard the *Huron*. Five others drowned, including the two men rescued from the *Salem*.[4]

Once ashore the survivors of the Mosquito Fleet waited and watched hopefully for the return of the *Dora* until its wreckage was spotted near the entrance to the Charleston harbor. The three men aboard, Captain Lunne Cross and his two crewmen, were presumed lost at sea.

During the offshore hurricane of 1904, eleven African Americans of the Mosquito Fleet perished. Astonishingly more were not lost. This was likely the greatest tragedy to befall Charleston's African American fishermen.[5] The Charleston paper observed that the unexpected storm "proved fatal to some unfortunate fishermen, yet . . . should never cause serious fear to the people . . . in seaworthy ships."[6] However, in that same hurricane, far larger and sturdier vessels were uncertain they would make it to safe harbor.

The *Rebecca M. Wall*, a 150-foot, three-masted schooner, was enveloped by the same hurricane that pummeled the Mosquito Fleet. The first mate watched seas sweep the upper deck and carry away anything not tied down. He found it "impossible to walk to windward or even to stand erect," and though he had "sailed for twenty-nine years [he had] never encountered such a gale." The mate estimated wind speed at ninety-five miles per hour. Ten feet of water stood in the hold, and the crew worked the pumps as the schooner put in to Charleston for repairs.[7]

Winds from the offshore hurricane only grazed Charleston. Though some residents passed a sleepless night worried about the rising winds, the gale never reached hurricane force. The city's main damage was a few broken tree limbs and blocked sidewalks. But up the coast at Georgetown the situation became markedly different as the storm moved northwesterly: without warning the hurricane made landfall in the area from Georgetown to the village of Myrtle Beach, exposing the region to its right-front quadrant and its most powerful winds. Between 9:00 p.m. and midnight, September 13, wind velocity increased to eighty miles per hour. Georgetown's shade trees were stripped of their leaves, and many were uprooted. Saltwater pushed up the rivers of Georgetown County into the rice fields. It was readily apparent that "the rice planters . . . suffered severely."[8]

In neighboring, sparsely settled Horry County, today dominated by the resort community of Myrtle Beach, "ruin and desolation was visited on the crops and forests." Corn and cotton crops were destroyed. The pines were "smashed almost beyond recognition." Lowlands "became a sea of water," barns and stables blew over, crushing mules and horses. Logging camps were demolished. Tenant shacks were stood on end. The new bowling alley and pool hall at Myrtle Beach "went down in a wreck." Though damages on the coast reached $1,500,000 ($29,661,289), no deaths were reported on land. As the storm moved across the state, it continued its destructive path, causing extensive damage as far inland as Florence, South Carolina.[9] Two years later, almost to the day, another tropical storm came ashore on the upper South Carolina coast.

1906 Hurricanes

In mid-September 1906 the U.S. Weather Bureau again provided no warning of an approaching storm. Under criticism later, officials argued that the tropical disturbance had moved far north of the usual path of storms and beyond the range of their West Indies tracking stations. Hence the captains of vessels offshore were not expecting the hurricane when it found them.[10]

There had been nothing of an "untoward nature" at sea for Captain T. McDonald and his crew of the British steamship *Framfield*. Three days out from Matanzas and bound for Philadelphia with twenty-four thousand pounds of unrefined sugar, Captain McDonald's situation changed dramatically on Sunday night, September 16, 1906. Off the upper South Carolina coast, winds began gusting. By the next morning the ship was in "the fury of a hurricane." Eighty-mile-per-hour winds "swept high, rolling seas" over the steamer "from stem to stern." Despite its size, the three-hundred-foot, sixteen-hundred-ton vessel pitched and rocked violently. Captain McDonald watched as "high combers struck the ship with terrific force and the wild wind shrieked amid the cordage." Doors, windows, and hatches blew off. A lifeboat broke its ties and careened overboard. Waves crushed deckhouses and tossed crewmembers about. One man went down with a scalp laceration; others suffered shoulder and leg injuries. The sea poured into the ship. The *Framfield's* pumps, often clogged with its cargo of unrefined sugar, worked continuously to discharge water in the hold. Captain McDonald headed for the nearest port and eventually brought his ship safely into Charleston's harbor. His injured crewmen were taken to St. Francis Xavier Infirmary.[11]

Off the upper South Carolina coast, the 138-foot *Flora B. Rogers* and 163-foot *J. W. Belano* suffered such extensive damage when they encountered the storm that their crews were forced to abandon them. The two schooners became derelicts at sea.[12]

In the vicinity the three-masted schooner *Job H. Jackson*, with a cargo of pine, became so waterlogged that it sank to deck level. As the sea rolled over it, mountainous waves washed three crewmen overboard. The remaining crew clung to the schooner for a day before rescue. The *Job H. Jackson* also became a derelict at sea. That same Sunday night, September 16, the bark *Ethel*, carrying lumber north out of Charleston, was struck by the hurricane off Myrtle Beach.

Winds and waves ripped away her mast and the lifeboats and drove the bark close to shore. Captain J. K. Albertson gave the order to abandon ship. Eight crewmembers made it through the breakers to dry land, but Captain Albertson and the steward did not. A Dane by birth, Albertson had been in and out of Charleston for twenty years and was "very much missed among his adopted people."[13]

The 167-foot schooner *R. D. Bibber*, carrying lumber from Savannah to New York, ran into "stormy weather" soon after departure. Captain B. S. Sayres, described by his crew as "a brave, bright, and generous-hearted man," ordered his crew to "shorten sails." By Sunday night the schooner was leaking badly; pumps worked continuously, but the water in the hold was gaining. Out of nowhere a huge wave carried away the deck load of lumber and a portion of the deck itself. The schooner "turned keel up," throwing the crew into a "seething sea." One seaman drowned immediately. Captain Sayres and Anthony, a crewman, clung to a spar that was still attached to the upturned schooner. First mate Gardener Gould and three other crewmen grabbed a piece of the wreckage. They soon lost sight of their captain and the ill-fated vessel. Some twenty-four hours later the steamship *New York* rescued the four wave-tossed men. A "diligent" search was made for the *Bibber's* captain, but neither he nor the "keel up" schooner was sighted.[14]

Upturned and partially submerged vessels, spars, and deckhouses littered the sea off the South Carolina coast. Most were in the track of the coastwise trade and deemed "a menace to navigation."[15]

The September 1906 hurricane remained offshore from Charleston, and though the city experienced rains and forty-mile-per-hour winds, little damage was done. The storm headed northwest toward the upper coast. As the hurricane approached land, it overturned small buildings and shade trees at McClellanville before coming ashore near Myrtle Beach. Once the storm reached land the wind velocity dropped to about sixty miles per hour. Nevertheless the storm caused widespread destruction. On Sunday night, September 16, Georgetown plunged into darkness as electric lines went down. Ancient shade trees blew over, and winds "wrecked" the Presbyterian church, businesses, and private residencies. A "negro" drowned in the Sampit River, and a church collapsed, killing a black man who was found clutching a Bible in his arms. Northeast of Waccamaw Neck, at Pawleys Island, a storm surge of "angry waves" swept in from the Atlantic Sunday night and Monday morning. All along the beaches sand- and salt-laden winds sliced like knives into anyone venturing outside. Walking or even standing was difficult. Seawater spilled over Pawleys Island, cutting off escape to the mainland. Recognizing that anyone left on the island needed to be evacuated, a fourteen-year-old boy volunteered to accompany an older man to bring any person marooned there to safety. After reaching the island, they found it deserted. But then they found themselves in trouble. When attempting to return to the mainland through shoulder-deep water, the older man became exhausted. Only the energy, calmness, and physical strength of the youngster saved both their lives.[16]

By Monday morning, September 17, the storm had moved just west of Waccamaw Neck and was roaring toward Plantersville, a settlement in the dense pinewoods. Here rice planters had built summer homes to escape the "fatal fevers" prevalent along the rivers nearer the coast. Around 11:00 a.m. a "tornado" spawned by the storm "snapped off" pines midway to the top. Residents watched their "windows smashed, doors blown off, chimneys collapse," and trees fall onto houses. Remarkably no one was injured, but damage was extensive. Across Georgetown County hundreds of pine trees went down. One could walk from one fallen tree to another for "miles upon miles." Some thought the "destruction to the forests . . . was the worst in a century." A conservative estimate put the loss to turpentine farmers alone at $350,000 ($6,847,340); the industry was "practically wiped out." Surging rivers forced saltwater upstream into the rice fields, destroying 50 to 75 percent of the crop. Farmers of corn and other staple crops took heavy losses. Folks in the countryside called the storm a "hurricane" and described it as "one of the most disastrous visitations of the kind ever experienced in [Georgetown] county's history."[17] While people were still trying to salvage something from the devastation, another hurricane churned off the lowcountry.

The four-masted schooner *Malcolm B. Seavey* was already under shortened sails when the hurricane struck on October 18, 1906. Piloted by Captain Henry M. Dodge, the 203-foot vessel was headed for Alexandria, Virginia, loaded with nineteen hundred tons of phosphate rock. Monstrous combers broke high against the masts. Cross-seas made standing upright impossible. Winds shredded the sails, and water rose to four feet in the hold. The powerful steam-driven pumps labored to keep the vessel from becoming waterlogged. Captain Dodge and his crew survived but "were well nigh worn out" when the hurricane abated. They cheered upon sighting the Charleston pilot boat.[18]

The hurricane caught the schooners *Susan A. Bryan* and *Emma S.* in St. Helena Sound near Beaufort. Carrying thousands of bushels of rice from plantations along the Combahee River, Captain Edgar Cahoon and his crew of three aboard the *Susan A. Bryan* had only time to furl their sails as winds and waves drove their schooner miles south to St. Catherines Island off Georgia. They survived. With no word of the *Emma S.* for more than a week following the hurricane, it was presumed that Captain Henry L. Graddick and his crew of three had drowned.[19]

Only outlying winds and bands of rain from the fierce offshore hurricane reached the lowcountry on October 20, though damage was minor. Savannahians experienced thirty-six-mile-per-hour winds. At Charleston sixty-four-mile-per-hour winds blew over trees and knocked down fences, chimneys, and billboards. Live wires ignited trees, and flooding occurred in the Rutledge Avenue area. In the countryside between the two urban centers, saltwater pushed up the rivers, causing planters heavy losses.[20]

As in the past, the Charleston press tried to put the best face on things: "There is plenty of pluck here and it is being put to good use in overcoming tremendous difficulties."[21]

Winds and heavy rains from tropical storms swept the lowcountry in 1907 and 1908. In early October 1910 the national weather bureau issued an advisory that a large tropical cyclone was off Florida's east coast and headed northward. Local weather bureaus across the lowcountry raised hurricane-warning flags.[22] The alert from the national weather bureau kept vessels in port and most likely saved lives at sea and ashore.

The hurricane remained off the Georgia coast, but tides reached heights unseen for decades. Water covered the wharves at Brunswick. Tybee Island residents fearing a repeat of earlier death-dealing storms evacuated to Savannah and luckily so. The ocean surged over the resort island, swirled around the foundation of the new hotel, and washed away or covered miles of the island's railroad tracks. Fifty feet of a retaining wall at the army's Fort Screven was washed away, and the parade field flooded. Winds at Savannah and Charleston never exceeded sixty miles per hour, as the hurricane remained offshore. Damage was light. But in the countryside saltwater intrusion caused "serious" damage to cotton and rice crops in both Georgia and South Carolina. The storm and a full moon caused flood tides that devastated the intricate systems for rice cultivation, and the crop stacked in fields along the Combahee and Edisto, the only two rivers in South Carolina where significant rice planting occurred. Duncan C. Heyward, a former governor of the state and the largest rice grower in South Carolina, planted eighteen hundred acres on the Combahee. There he witnessed tides rise to an "astonishing height." Duncan called the storm the "worst disaster the rice planters of [that area had] suffered since the great cyclone of 1893." Heyward estimated that 75 percent of his crop was lost. Repair to the earthen embankments would be difficult and costly.[23]

The relentless devastation of the rice crop by storms and hurricanes was too much for the Edisto planters to bear. They gave up rice cultivation after the storm of 1910. Only Duncan Heyward and a few growers planted on the Combahee.[24] It was assumed that another "disaster" would spell the end of large-scale rice cultivation in the lowcountry. It happened the following year.

The Big Hurricane of 1911

A tropical depression formed in late August 1911 about twelve hundred miles east of south Florida and grew into a category 2 hurricane that began moving toward the southeastern United States. Like the cyclone of 1906 the storm originated far to the north of the national weather bureau's West Indian tracking stations; hence there was no early warning of the fast-approaching hurricane. Lowcountry residents read in their August 27 Sunday morning papers that "fair weather" with "light variable winds" was expected. That same day, the national weather bureau detected a dangerous hurricane off the Georgia and South Carolina coasts and issued a warning. By then the cyclone was only about a hundred miles offshore. Storm flags went up, but for those at sea the warning came too late.[25]

Around noon on Sunday, August 27, the hurricane slammed into the *Bessie Whiting* twenty-seven miles north of Sapelo Island, Georgia. Carrying 375,000 feet of yellow pine lumber, the vessel was under the direction of Captain Lawry, who always sailed with his wife, Weona, at his side. Captain Lawry ran before the storm as far as feasible and then ordered the sails close-reefed. But the jib boom and mainmast blew away, and the *Bessie Whiting* fell into the trough of the sea. Rain and huge waves swept the deck. Lawry ordered the crew to lash themselves to the deckhouse. If they had not "every soul would have been blown overboard." By Sunday night the wind howled at 130 miles per hour. Captain Lawry's concern increased as he watched his vessel "roll . . . and tumble amid the angry waves like a mere bubble in the wrath of the storm." Sixty thousand feet of lumber stored on deck blew overboard. For forty-eight hours there was neither food nor sleep for those aboard. On Tuesday morning the steamer *Ligonier* came alongside to offer assistance. Despite the pleas of Captain Lawry for his five-member crew to remain aboard to help bring the vessel safely to port, they elected to abandon the schooner for the *Ligonier*. Only the captain, his wife, and their "loyal servant" George Petersen remained. The wrecked vessel drifted helplessly at sea until Wednesday, when a tugboat provided the three aboard with food and water. The U.S. revenue cutter *Yamacraw* soon took the *Bessie Whiting* under tow into Charleston's harbor. An enterprising reporter watched from the wharves as the "dismantled schooner" came into port: "The slender girlish figure in pink on the shattered deck of the vessel . . . was Weona Lawry . . . wife of the captain . . . who apparently stared death in the face. Her dress was torn and her long hair streamed out on the wind." Captain Lawry was at her side, as was George Petersen, the steward. Both "pulled quietly at their [smoking] pipes."[26]

Other captains of vessels offshore estimated that the hurricane packed winds of 135 miles per hour. The schooner *Sarah D. Fell*, bound from Georgia to Boston with a cargo of lumber, was about a hundred miles off Savannah when the cyclone so damaged the vessel that it settled low in the water with its decks awash. The crew of eight was "at the mercy of the wind and waves" for hours. A Standard Oil steamer, the *City of Everett*, rescued the crew. The *Sarah D. Fell* was abandoned, and within two weeks drifted 225 miles north.[27]

Off the South Carolina coast the storm ripped into the *Margaret A. May*, a 458-ton schooner bound from Charleston to Philadelphia with a load of lumber. Only the vessel's stern was ever recovered. It is presumed that Master and Captain George L. Jarvis, one of the "youngest and most popular skippers on the coast," his two brothers on board as guests, and his eight-member crew all perished at sea.[28]

That same Sunday, August 27, off South Carolina, the hurricane pounded the *Malcolm B. Seavey* bound from Florida to Baltimore with phosphate rock. The four-masted schooner had survived a tropical cyclone in the same vicinity in 1906 and now felt the full fury of another. High seas washed a crewman from the deck, and winds blew the schooner onto shoals off Georgetown. Two masts fell into the water, and the stern settled deeper and deeper into a sea that pummeled the vessel from all sides. Captain Henry H. Dodge and his seven-member crew climbed up into what rigging remained. A terrific gust of wind snapped the spar Captain Dodge was clinging to, and part of it toppled into the sea. Somehow he managed to grasp a rope dangling from the spar and hold on. For hours waves repeatedly banged Dodge into the side of the schooner until the crew managed to pull him back aboard the vessel. Heavy swells stymied rescue efforts for two days. The ocean was still "running high" on Tuesday when the *Mohawk*, of the Clyde Line, sent a small boat alongside the wrecked schooner to save the half-drowned and exhausted crew. The *Malcolm B. Seavey* did not survive its second encounter with a hurricane. Stranded on the bar, the vessel was demolished by waves. Pieces of it later washed ashore.[29]

Indeed the sea off the upper South Carolina coast became littered with wrecks. Marine officials concluded, "It will be a long time before all of the wrecks are discovered and the loss of life at sea during the storm . . . is figured up." Some remained unaccounted for to this day. Federal revenue cutters assumed the responsibility of destroying hazards to shipping. Sometimes it was necessary to use explosives to sink the derelicts. When a waterlogged wreck was sighted off Cape Romain in late August 1911, it was thought to be the *Massachusetts*, a lumber-carrying schooner. The federal revenue cutter *Yamacraw* destroyed it.[30]

The Hurricane Comes Ashore

The winds of the August 1911 tropical cyclone diminished upon landfall near the mouth of the Savannah River. But it remained a robust storm with sustained winds of about ninety miles per hour.[31]

"Boisterous and gusty winds" lashed Tybee Island on Sunday morning, August 27. By late night a "violent" wind from the northwest upset cottages, tore off porches and piazzas, and ripped tiles from the roof of the new Tybee Hotel. The Inlet Hotel also lost part of its roof and its verandas. Windows of the post office blew in, and the two windmills that supplied the island with freshwater toppled over. Few structures on the island escaped the storm's "fury" that sank small boats on the Savannah River and blew others into the marshes. Alone in a rowboat J. J. Bucherer was trying to reach the city when waves capsized his boat and he drowned.[32]

Sustained winds of eighty-eight miles per hour, with gusts of ninety-six miles per hour (the greatest wind velocity yet recorded in Savannah), whipped the city Sunday night and early Monday. Electrical lines went down, plunging most of Savannah into darkness. Telephone and telegraph lines collapsed, cutting the city off from the outside world. Signs, uprooted trees, and sections of chimneys littered the city streets. Few homes and businesses were without some damage, especially from driving rains that seeped through roofs, cracks, and crevices to ruin walls and furnishings. Witnesses thought damage was less than that of previous hurricanes because winds had come from the west instead of the east, which minimized flooding. But this was small comfort to planters along the Savannah River whose rice fields were again inundated with saltwater. Little of the crop was saved.[33]

As the hurricane swept over South Carolina's coast, far greater damage occurred. On Sunday night and into Monday residents of Beaufort watched enormous swells roll up the Beaufort River, smash wharves and boats, pour over the seawall, and flood streets, homes, and businesses. A witness observed that the "wind blew as hard as he ever saw the wind blow." He was right. Wind speed reached 110 miles per hour. It rocked dwellings, unroofed houses, and uprooted trees. The storm raged for thirty-six hours, and its sitting in place caused massive damages in the countryside. Rice and cotton planters once in "high spirits" saw their crops "wiped away" by the hurricane, and they became "disconsolate." The sea flooded most of the low-lying islands around Beaufort. When the tides and winds swept the largest island, St. Helena, home to seven thousand African Americans, it took many by surprise. Ned River's shanty rocked so violently that he shimmied up a tree. But the tree shook so "hard" that he abandoned it to take refuge with others in a schoolhouse. The storm drowned horses and chickens, blew down bridges, sunk boats, and ruined cotton, the major cash crop on the island. The hurricane demolished over 130 dwellings, mostly those of African Americans. Other houses lost chimneys and parts of roofs, which meant leaks and "great discomfort." One witness to the devastation, Grace Bigelow House, wrote that the black islanders faced "a year of famine, want and suffering such as they have not experienced since the great '93 storm. Fever and sickness . . . adds distress to the situation."[34]

Now destitute, many looked to the Penn School—founded by northerners and a friend to blacks for over fifty years—for help. But it too was damaged by the storm. With total property losses in Beaufort and the islands reaching $1,000,000 ($18,575,757), African American islanders turned to Beaufort's city fathers for assistance. But local white officials decided not to seek help from the Red Cross, a "foreign, outside" agency. Although they did acknowledge that "there seem[ed] to be some suffering and . . . abject want on the islands," the white elite thought it "ill advised" to ask for such assistance: "The class of labor in this territory is absolutely dependent; hold out to them the hope of assistance without work and the problem of labor will be increased tenfold."[35]

The storm raged up the coast. Between Beaufort and Charleston hundreds of telegraph poles and an inestimable number of trees went down. Saltwater flooded rice fields.

On Edisto Island winds reached ninety-five miles per hour out of the northeast, the most dangerous side of the hurricane. Winds damaged John Townsend's two plantations, Bleak House and Sea Cloud, where all the windows on the east side of the house blew in, and its porches were ripped away. The Seabrook and McConkey plantations also sustained damages. The two-hundred-year-old Brick House that had withstood so many hurricanes suffered water damage and lost its shutters. Horses, cattle, chickens, and wildlife drowned, saltwater inundated crops, and hundreds of shanties, abodes of African Americans, blew to pieces.[36]

The tropical cyclone was a disaster for whites and especially for blacks on nearby Wadmalaw Island. Nevertheless the Charleston press, like Beaufort's, stressed that there was "no need for relief measures." There was plenty of work on Wadmalaw. White planters there wanted cotton picked quickly at sixty cents a hundred pounds, but the "negroes" were striking for a dollar a hundred. Planters said, "[black hands are] taking this attitude . . . because they have an idea that the Red Cross . . . intends to send them provisions . . . whereby they can be lazy. It is . . . well to be sensible in these matters. The people who have suffered most from the storm are the white people, not the negroes."[37]

By noon Sunday, rains and strong northeast winds enveloped Charleston, now grown to a city of sixty-five thousand. Though the storm intensified throughout the day, there was no warning from the chief local weather forecaster, J. F. Cole—he did not order ringing the fire bell twenty-four times, running up storm flags, or firing three red rockets into the air. Around midnight at Charleston the barometer fell to 29.43 mm Hg, and the anemometer recorded ninety-four-mile-per-hour winds before the weather bureau's wind gauge blew away. Lightning illuminated the city, thunder boomed, and fierce winds (estimated to have reached 106 miles per hour) continued until daylight. A pilot boat was destroyed; steamships, schooners, tugs, and dredges blew into the marshes. Almost every boat of the Mosquito Fleet tied off the wharf house was wrecked. The waterfront itself was demolished. Docks and warehouses became piles of splintered wood. The storm tide rose to nearly eleven feet, slightly less than the record set during the hurricane of August 1893. Water surged through the streets of the city, reaching five feet deep in the city market. The storm ripped flagstones from the Battery and hurled them a hundred feet away; one-hundred-pound cannon balls stacked on the East Battery spilled about "like so many marbles." The drawbridge section of the new bridge across the Ashley River was spun around like a "small flywheel," making it inoperable. Winds ripped away roofs, demolished houses, broke windows, uprooted hundreds of trees, and blew down electrical wires; lights went out across the city. The trolley system was put out of commission. Pedestrians made "hair-breadth escapes" from flying missiles and falling buildings. It was a night "of great terror" in the city, at Mount Pleasant, on Sullivan's Island, and on the Isle of Palms.[38]

The old Wappoo Mill on the Ashley River collapsed, killing five persons, some serving as caretakers of the phosphate factory. Ernest Hodge, who lived in a small frame house in Charleston with two women, Ida Morgan and Rosa Robinson, climbed onto the roof to replace tiles blown away as the storm reached its height Sunday night. Suddenly a terrific gust of wind blew the house over and bounced it around like a "rubber ball." The house was flooded by water from a nearby marsh. Hodge caught a glimpse of the two women standing on a dining room table screaming for help. Thrown into the marsh, Hodge managed to survive. The two women drowned.[39]

A board crashed through the office window of the trainmaster's office of the Southern Railroad in Charleston and killed instantly Alfonso J. Coburn, an engineer. In Mount Pleasant the town hall blew over, and a house collapsed on a "colored woman," killing her. Nearby, on the Consolidated Railway Company's ferryboat wharf, a motorman and a passenger, E. R. Smith, took refuge from the storm in the ticket office. The building collapsed, crushing both men to death. Smith's wife of four months had sent him back to the wharf to retrieve a pocketbook she had forgotten.[40]

Fascinated by the frequent tropical cyclones, lowcountry poets and authors left vivid accounts of them. DuBose Heyward, a Charlestonian with a prominent lowcountry name, left a graphic account of the impact of the 1911 hurricane on Charleston and its black community in his novel *Porgy*, the basis for George Gershwin's opera, *Porgy and Bess:*

> The stiffening eastern gale . . . filled the bay with large waves that leapt up to angry points. . . . Slowly the threatening undertone of the wind grew louder. . . . The noise [of the storm] became deafening . . . and . . . delivered its attack upon the panic-stricken city. . . . Here and there the wind would get beneath the tin [roof], roll it up suddenly . . . and send it thundering and crashing down a deserted street. . . . It would gain entrance to a room, and, exerting its explosive force . . . blow all . . . the windows out. . . . It was impossible to walk upon the street. . . . The group of negroes who had sought shelter in the wharf house fled to [Catfish] Row. . . . By bending double and clinging together . . . they were able to . . . traverse the narrow street.
>
> Porgy and Bess sat in their room. Suddenly an enormous breaker loomed . . . and smote the solid wall of the Row. . . . They saw their own door give slightly to the pressure, and a dark flood spurt beneath it. . . . Bess got Porgy to a stairway. . . . They sought refuge in . . . the mansion . . . [with] many refugees. The night that settled down upon Catfish Row was one of nameless horror to the inhabitants . . . huddled on the second floor . . . to avoid the sea from beneath, and Deafening assaults upon the roof above their heads. . . . Porgy turned to Jesus. . . . He lifted his rich baritone voice. . . . "Oh, between de eart' an' sky, I kin see my Sabior die. I gots uh home in de rock. Don't yuh see!" Then they were all in it, heart and soul. They swayed and patted, and poured their griefs and fears into a rhythm that never missed a beat . . . and that finally sang up the faint grey light that penetrated the storm, and told them that it was again day.[41]

The sea swept over Sullivan's Island. Water reached the height of a man's head on First Street. With winds reaching more than one hundred miles per hour, islanders pushed furniture against doors and windows to keep out foam-topped waves. But the residents were not successful. Dozens of beach cottages were demolished. The soldiers at Fort Moultrie formed hand-to-hand lifelines and pulled people out of deep water to the safety of the fort. Patrons of the new Seashore Hotel on the Isle of Palms, who had paid a special weekend rate of three dollars for room and board, heard a portion of the roof blow away Sunday night. A guest, Mildred A. Kuhr, said they listened to "the constant bell-ringing from a room where some recently sobered drunk was trapped because the second floor over his room had blown away and he was huddling under his mattress." Cottages, bathhouses, and the Consolidated Railway terminal lost roofs. Waves leveled the island's sand dunes. One vacationer saw "huge fish — sharks and porpoises" come in with the tidal surge and wash far into the island. Amazingly there was no loss of life on the two islands. But in and around Charleston more than twenty people died by drowning or injuries suffered during the hurricane. Damages in the city exceeded $1,000,000 ($18,575,757).[42]

Following the hurricane, the Board of Commissioners of Sullivan's Island urged islanders to "build stronger houses" to avoid recurring catastrophic damages from storms. Prominent Charlestonians, angry with the local weather bureau officials for failing to provide a timely warning, maneuvered the transfer of the bureau's chief forecaster, J. F. Cole. Of course, Cole had never received notice of the approaching tropical cyclone from the Washington weather bureau until it was nearly ashore. To appease Charlestonians, the chief of the U.S. Weather Bureau also raised the status of the Charleston station and the rank of the new officer in charge.[43]

Immediately after the devastating hurricane, boosters across the lowcountry put out the message that despite periodic storms, the lowcountry was a great place in which to do business. Charleston's News and Courier editorialized that the city had "weathered storm after storm," and "with smiling faces and grateful hearts Charlestonians will set about" moving the city toward "supremacy in commercial and industrial lines." James Sotitle, owner of the Seashore Hotel, described the Isle of Palms as having a better beach since the hurricane leveled the island's sand dunes![44] Despite such boosterism, some worried that the damage done to the rice crop along the coast might "yet prove the greatest blow inflicted by the storm."[45] They were right.

Years of relentless poundings by hurricanes and tropical storms finally exacted a toll that ended rice cultivation in the lowcountry. One of the last of the rice-planting elite, Duncan Heyward, said so: "Storms that so frequently devastated our coastal country . . . contributed in a very great degree to the abandonment of the rice culture in South Carolina and Georgia." He believed that the 1911 hurricane sounded the rice culture's "death-knell." Following the tropical cyclone of 1911, Heyward sold off several of his plantations to northern capitalists. Theodore Ravenel, the last of the commercial rice planters on the Combahee, sold his property in 1927 to E. F. Hutton of New York. In Georgia, families such as the Spaldings sold their sea island properties to northern millionaires. The rice-threshing mills on plantations along the rivers fell silent. Schooners no longer loaded rice for transport. The rice-pounding mills in the urban centers shut down forever. Some planters turned to truck farming. A historian of the region has written that the rice industry was "the low country's *raison d'etre* and, alas, a principal reason for its demise as well."[46] Another historian wrote that without an economy based on its major commodity, "Carolina gold," the "lowcountry reverted to what it had been two hundred years earlier, a semitropical wilderness."[47]

The collapse of the rice industry devastated the economy of the region. The economic life of Charleston, once the capital of the rice kingdom, continued to atrophy. First the phosphate industry succumbed to hurricanes. Sea island cotton, also relentlessly pummeled by cyclones, was in decline even before the boll weevil wiped out the crop in Georgia and South Carolina in the early 1920s. Lowcountry cotton farmers never recovered. Likewise, and for various reasons, the region's lumber and naval stores industry experienced a downturn.[48] By the early 1900s the lowcountry was "perhaps the poorest part of the poorest census region in the United States."[49]

Of course the collapse of the economy built on rice, cotton, phosphates, and timbering fell heaviest on the lowcountry's African American laborers and their families.

Thousands became jobless. The lowcountry was a hardscrabble place and the weather remained relentless.

The End of the Cycle: The Hurricane of 1916

Fierce tropical cyclones or storms pounded the lowcountry regularly from the 1880s through the early 1900s, a period of about thirty years.[50] The hurricane of 1916 marked the end of this cycle.

The 1916 hurricane season was an active one. Eleven hurricanes swept through the Caribbean and the Atlantic. On the evening of July 13, the national weather bureau ordered hurricane warnings up from Tybee Island, Georgia, to Georgetown, South Carolina. A storm of "considerable intensity" was approaching the lowcountry. Red flags with black centers went up at coastal cities, warning of its approach. At Charleston the fire alarm sounded, whistles blew, the new electric advertising sign flashed a warning, and the naval radio station broadcast an alert. Weathermen climbed to the roof of the customs house and fired rockets into the air to warn offshore vessels. When winds drove the sea high up on the beach at Tybee on July 13, vacationers evacuated the island for Savannah. At the resort of Sullivan's Island, South Carolina, some sixty people boarded the last ferry for Charleston at 9:00 p.m. In the city winds gusted at tropical-storm force, sending breakers over the Battery, and filling the streets with seawater. During the night, the storm made a beeline for the coast and came ashore north of Charleston, saving the city from the punishing right-front quadrant of the hurricane. But the storm's seventy-four-mile-per-hour wind speed sank private sailboats and motor launches along the waterfront. A black man on the sloop *Jubilee* washed overboard and drowned. Trees and telephone and electrical lines went down across the city. Harry Edwards, an African American employed by the local YMCA, was on his way home when he came in contact with a dangling light wire on King Street and was electrocuted. Up the coast there were more deaths and far greater damage.[51]

The most dangerous side of the hurricane, packing 90- to 110-mile-per-hour winds, raged along South Carolina's upper coast during the night of July 13 and into the following morning. The hurricane drove the collier *Hector*, carrying 120 U.S. marines and crewmen, aground near Cape Romain, where it broke in two. Nearby coal-carrying barges, the *Southeast* and the *Northwest*, each with five crewmembers, broke loose from the tug *Wellington*. They drifted and rolled in huge seas. Suddenly, the nine hundred tons of coal in the *Northwest* shifted. "Water rushed into the engine room and the boiler burst, blowing open the forward part of the vessel." The crew held on as waves pushed the wrecked and sinking barge aground off Cedar Island in Bull's Bay. Captain Christine Jensen and his men climbed into the rigging and "held on for life itself." Waves began breaking the barge apart and Captain Jensen ordered his men to don life preservers and swim for shore. They reached the beach in minutes. Captain Jensen, the last man to leave the barge and unable to walk, made it to dry land through the "heroic efforts" of his engineer, Martin Gundersen. Captain Thorveld Nelsen of the tug *Wellington*, while searching for his barges, sighted the *Hector* and came alongside. In a "sea running tremendously high," Captain Nelsen managed to rescue all 120 crewmembers and marines aboard who praised his "seamanship, nerve, and fearlessness." Seafaring men called his act "miraculous" in such a sea. Captain Nelsen found his coal barge, the *Southeast*, sunk in Bull's Bay. Its captain and crew had drowned. Their bodies later washed ashore.[52]

The hurricane pounded the village of McClellanville from 1:00 a.m. to 4:00 a.m., July 14. Surging seas drove boats into the streets and debris into homes. Five feet of water flooded the lower part of the village. Winds bowled over the houses of whites and destroyed more than fifty shanties and their contents owned by African Americans. In the darkness men rushed women and children to higher ground. Incredibly no humans perished. Hundreds of dead seabirds, raccoons, minks, and chickens lay under the water. Sea sedge and debris littered McClellanville. Drowned cattle and horses floated. Residents believed that the "decaying matter" threatened their health. In the countryside — from the Awendaw Bridge to the Santee River, a distance of twenty-two miles — ninety out of every one hundred pine trees tapped for turpentine blew down. So complete was the destruction in the forests that in many places of five acres or more there was "scarcely a standing sapling." The storm destroyed 97 percent of the cotton (though only a modest amount had been planted) and 75 percent of the corn.[53]

News of the approaching tropical cyclone arrived only a few hours before it struck the upper South Carolina coast. Well-to-do Edwin Kaminski, owner of the power yacht *Ulana II*, braved rising winds and waves in crossing Winyah Bay to reach Pawleys Island. He pounded on cottage doors, telling people to evacuate immediately. His warnings began "a stampede" of several hundred people summering there. They rushed across the causeway to the mainland as one-hundred-mile-per-hour winds whipped through the region leaving a trail of "devastation." On Pawleys Island, in Georgetown, at Myrtle Beach, and in the countryside, thousands of trees went down, some crashing into houses and buildings. Winds and tides destroyed bridges, cattle and horses perished, and crops were destroyed. The upper South Carolina coast was devastated. Damage was estimated at $100,000 ($1,687,156) in Georgetown and $500,000 ($8,435,780) in the countryside. No one perished. Residents of the area calculated that the tropical cyclone caused the greatest financial losses since the hurricane of 1822. "The oldest inhabitants" could not remember a more destructive storm in their lifetimes.[54]

The intense, powerful hurricane roared inland. At his large two-story home in Pinopolis, some miles west of the coast, Dr. Kershaw Fishburne listened to the rising wind in the early morning hours of July 14. As the storm increased in intensity, Dr. Fishburne noticed "that the body of the house seemed to move over several inches and then shudder back into place with heavy groans and creaks." Around 2:00 a.m. he decided to move his family to a safer part of the house. By candlelight they made their way down the stairs into the sturdy, masonry basement. Here "they sat for hours listening to the roar of the wind and lashing gusts of rain." Great pines splintered and crashed around the house. With morning light came diminishing winds and the Fishburnes' celebration that they had survived.[55]

Hurricane, 1928

Except for the usual tropical storms with winds of forty to fifty miles per hour, the lowcountry was spared hurricane-force winds for over a decade. Then in September 1928 a storm formed in the eastern Atlantic near the Cape Verde Islands. Moving westward, it devastated parts of the West Indies and struck Florida as a major hurricane, where it became known as the Great Okeechobee Flood. It was one of the country's worst natural disasters. But as it curved northward across the Sunshine State, the hurricane lost much of its fierce punch.[56]

Before it came ashore in Georgia west of St. Marys, its winds were just over seventy miles per hour. When it struck on Monday, September 17, sea captains and sailors congregating in towns along the coast offered a prediction: "We should certainly 'have a blow.'" The cyclone followed a path through the state close to the present Interstate 95. At Brunswick, Georgia, winds smashed expensive plate-glass windows and uprooted trees. Damages of $20,000 ($215,088) to the Atlantic Refining Company interrupted gas service. Electrical wires of the Mutual Light and Water Company went down, and lights went out in Brunswick for two days. Eastward, along the oceanfront at St. Simons Island, winds and waves destroyed cottages and demolished an apartment house under construction. Seawater covered the island's new Ocean Boulevard.[57]

Aware of the devastation in Florida, Savannahians fearfully awaited the approaching storm. But winds never reached more than fifty miles per hour in the city, and damage was minor: telephone and telegraph lines down, trees and tree limbs across streets. The greatest damage came from the record-setting rainfall of 11.27 inches in twenty-four hours. Flooded streets halted automobile traffic. Wobbling northward, the hurricane's right side pounded Beaufort with sheets of rain and winds of seventy-five miles per hour from midnight Monday, September 17, until daylight Tuesday. Roofs blew away, power lines and telephone poles crashed down, trees were uprooted, approaches to bridges were washed out, and water covered causeways. Some thought the storm was the "severest" to hit Beaufort since 1893.[58]

As the storm moved up the coast, it "devastated" the resort of Folly Beach just south of Charleston. When breakwaters in front of beach cottages did not hold, waves demolished the homes. Furniture floated away in the surf. Waves tore away part of the Atlantic boardwalk pavilion and carried off fifteen feet of sand along the beach. Winds at Charleston reached fifty miles per hour Tuesday morning but apparently gusted higher, as a new Cooper River bridge under construction was damaged, and waves wrecked wharves and docks and sank small boats on the Ashley and Cooper rivers. A thirty-five-foot motorboat was hurled onto rail tracks, splintering the hull, and a yacht was dashed to pieces against the Battery. Downed trees and power lines and flooded streets again challenged the citizenry. Marsh hens crippled by the winds were hunted down on the banks of the Ashley River, bludgeoned to death with sticks, tied up in sacks, and carried away for food. When the hurricane passed, damage estimates at Charleston reached as high as $100,000 ($1,075,440). At nearby Sullivan's Island damage was slight. Up the coast at McClellanville, a tidal surge inundated the town, toppled trees, and ruined the sweet potato and hay crops. Winds at Georgetown reached fifty miles per hour, and high tides covered the city docks, flooding ruined goods stored in warehouses. Damages reached $25,000 ($268,860). Moving north the winds of the once powerful hurricane had diminished to thirty-five miles per hour when it passed Myrtle Beach, then under development as a resort community.[59]

Washouts on causeways near rivers bisecting the coastal highway that passed through the lowcountry required vast sums to repair. The *News and Courier* editorialized that something had to be done to make roads more resistant to storms. Closing a major highway for a week, they said, brings "loss and inconvenience. Highways must stand up in all weather." On the matter of beach erosion, the editors cautioned that "when the beach is forced back a hundred or more feet in a season the threat is grave. Houses . . . must be placed on new foundations farther from the high water mark."[60]

A *Calm before the Storm*

Although in the years following 1928, gale-warning flags often flew along the coasts of Georgia and South Carolina, it was a period of relative calm. On October 1, 1929, a tropical storm dropped twelve inches of rain on Beaufort and pounded the town with fifty-mile-per-hour winds. The weather bureau at Charleston reported on September 5, 1933, that winds from a gale moving along the coast were diminishing and predicted that the upcoming day would be "fair." Charlestonians retired for the evening in sweltering heat. But they soon awakened to the sounds of fifty-three-mile-per-hour winds and rains that dumped a record ten inches on the city. Streets flooded quickly, and some trees went down. The storm spawned a tornado that roared across Sullivan's Island, demolishing two houses and causing structural damage to five others. It was mainly the destruction on Sullivan's Island that prompted an estimate of $100,000 ($1,414,615) in storm damages for the Charleston area.[61]

Two other tropical storms during the 1930s battered Beaufort and Charleston. It was remarkably early for the gale season when, in May 1934, a storm packing fifty-mile-per-hour winds whipped along the coast, knocking out electrical power from Beaufort to Pawleys Island. On Edisto Island during the night of May 28–29, winds unroofed houses and downed trees, and saltwater flooded fields of food crops. Breakers as high as palmetto trees crashed across the spit of sand where the village of Edingsville Beach had once stood and swirled around the foundations of houses on Edisto Island. At Folly Beach winds swept waves fifty feet beyond the high-water mark, wrecking five houses and "seriously" damaging twenty-seven others. Wind gusts at Charleston reached a tropical storm–force wind speed of sixty-eight miles per hour. Vessels of poor and rich alike suffered. Waves sank bateaux belonging to African Americans of the Mosquito Fleet and damaged the "handsome" yacht *Zapala*, chartered by millionaire Richard J. Reynolds and owned by millionaire Howard Coffin of Sapelo Island, Georgia. Up the coast at Pawleys Island the summer colony estimated their losses at $10,000 ($137,238). In 1935 a gale with winds of forty-seven miles per hour inflicted light damage at both Beaufort and Charleston.[62] For the next four years calm prevailed. Then in 1940 a hurricane ripped into the lowcountry, inaugurating another cycle of frequent tropical cyclones.

The 1940 Hurricane

In early August 1940 a hurricane tracking toward the southeastern coast of the United States came out of the West Indies. By August 10 it was off the coast of Georgia. Gale warnings went up from Savannah to Cape Hatteras. Winds at Tybee Island picked up, and by late evening a "heavy sea was running." Thousands of vacationers at Tybee Island fled inland across a single causeway. By August 11 debris and high water blocked the route. The island appeared deserted. On a high tide, winds whipped across the island at speeds of more than seventy miles per hour, tearing small boats from their moorings and roofs from houses. Roland Jones, the mayor of Tybee, made his rounds on the wind-swept island, dodging "flying objects" and crawling over fallen trees. Though the center of the hurricane came ashore north of Savannah, the city was not spared the storm's fury. During the afternoon of August 11 the weather service's barometer fell to 28.78 mm Hg, the lowest ever recorded in Savannah. Winds of seventy miles per hour, and gusting higher, ripped across the city, unroofing houses, sending bricks flying, felling power and telephone lines, uprooting beautiful oaks and sycamores in the squares, blasting out windows, and smashing plate glass in the business district. Annie Wade, described as "colored," suffered cuts so severe from flying glass that she died within hours. A security guard for the Union Bag Company, Jessie Wallace, fled to his son's house for safety, then dropped dead of a heart attack. The chairman of the park and tree commission was on the "verge of weeping" as he witnessed the damage done to the city's trees. Insurance adjusters estimated damages at Savannah as high as $4,000,000 ($52,542,856). The day following the powerful storm, news from Europe shared space in bold, three-quarter-inch-type headlines in the *Savannah Morning News*: "Over 400 Nazi Planes Attack England. Hurricane Sweeps up Atlantic Coast."[63]

Unlike Savannah, South Carolina's lower coast took the brunt of the right-front quadrant. The first hurricane to hit the South Carolina coast directly in thirty years most likely crossed the coast in the vicinity of Beaufort and Edisto Island. Hilton Head Island was "swept clean." The shanties of African Americans there were carried into the sea. On the southernmost tip of Beaufort County, at

Bluffton fronting the May River, waves rose to ocean heights, wrecking docks and cottages. Age-old trees collapsed across streets; one demolished the Methodist church. Seventy persons took refuge in the school building, the safest place in the town. At Beaufort, on its namesake river, winds exceeding seventy-five miles per hour whipped up huge waves that smashed wharves and poured into warehouses along the waterfront. It was a "scene of complete chaos," a witness said. Bridges went down, isolating Beaufort for days. Adequate warnings saved lives at Beaufort and the marine base on Parris Island, but again, warnings never reached some isolated sea islanders.[64]

A storm surge of thirteen feet rolled over St. Helena Island and Lady's Island, drowning thirty-three African Americans. A young white boy and member of the Civilian Conservation Corps, an agency of Roosevelt's New Deal, perished as he attempted to move a stalled car on a causeway, and "the tide rushed over him." Harrowing tales became part of the storm's lore. A young African American father left his house as it filled with water, cradling his three-month-old baby in his arms. He held on to the child and a palmetto tree for hours as waters rushed by. Both father and infant survived.[65]

The hurricane uprooted hundreds of pine, oak, pear, and pecan trees. It demolished shanties and drowned cows, mules, pigs, and poultry. The storm contaminated wells with saltwater or sewage and destroyed the food crops on the islands. The homeless and hungry from the hurricane numbered seven hundred, mainly African Americans on the sea islands. Damages exceeded $1,000,000 ($13,135,714). All this was inflicted "on a people who in normal times live on a slender margin of security for food, shelter, and clothing," said an officer of the Penn School on St. Helena Island. Even the school itself, which blacks looked to for leadership and help, was unroofed and its poultry drowned, straining resources "to the breaking point."[66]

Edisto Island was inundated. The ocean wiped away sand dunes, even those anchored with palmettos. Theodore Ravenel, the manager of the state park at Edisto, watched winds and waves wreck the park and destroy or severely damage more than half of the two hundred private beachfront homes. All that remained of some was the plumbing. The storm surge flooded six or seven automobiles. It ripped up both the sidewalks and the highway along Edisto Beach, once regarded "as the best beach thoroughfare in the state." If the coast guard had not assisted in evacuating the beachfront, many may have drowned. Even at the Ravenel home, located on high ground one-half mile from the beach, the ocean surged to within a few feet of the dwelling. To Ravenel "it was the sea that caused more damage than the wind, though [he believed] it was blowing ninety miles an hour."[67]

Ten miles south of Charleston, at the beachfront resort of Folly Island, winds may have reached one hundred miles per hour. The thirteen-foot sea surge washed away the entire front beach, and water covered the seven-mile-long and one-eighth-mile-wide island. Waves and winds toppled about half of the 150 beach houses. There was no trace of some, and others were damaged beyond repair. Waves wrecked the Folly Island pier and crushed the ocean side of the pavilion. Seawater reached waist-deep on the dance floor. A witness saw the "brilliantly-colored horses of the merry-go-round . . . strewn over the entire lot and water . . . standing where the Ferris wheel once stood." The island suffered more than $1,000,000 ($13,135,714) in property damages, but no lives were lost, thanks to the evacuation carried out by the coast guard and the local police. Some said that the island as a resort "was gone forever."[68]

At Charleston on Sunday afternoon, August 11, winds of eighty-five miles per hour sent huge waves crashing into wharves and small boats in the harbor. The storm demolished the African American Mosquito Fleet. Hulls of some boats were blown out of the water, landed on railroad tracks, and split open from stem to stern. To one witness the waterfront "resembled a mad game of jack straws with the wreckage of boats, warehouses and docks piled as high as a man's head." Waves tore flagstones out of the Battery, and water poured into the ground floor of the Fort Sumter Hotel. Winds blew trees across electrical, telegraph, and telephone lines and rolled up tin roofs. A tide of nearly thirteen feet poured into the streets, paralyzing Charleston. Flooding forced hundreds of people to evacuate their homes for shelter in segregated refugee centers, two for blacks and two for whites. Industrial plants on Charleston Neck alone suffered damages amounting to $500,000 ($6,567,857). When rumors spread that a second and more violent hurricane was off the coast, anxiety was rampant until clouds parted to reveal bright stars and a quarter moon.[69]

The sea surge destroyed a portion of the causeway over Cove Inlet linking Mount Pleasant to Sullivan's Island. It washed out twenty-five feet of the Breach Inlet bridge connecting Sullivan's Island to the Isle of Palms. Winds and waves leveled sand dunes on both islands, destroyed the boardwalk on the Isle of Palms, upended concession stands, and toppled the Ferris wheel. None of the island resorts near Charleston escaped the fury of the hurricane. Winds had dropped to tropical-storm velocity, fifty miles per hour, by the time it reached the upper South Carolina coast at Georgetown. Damage there was light. Nearby at Pawleys Island, the tidal surge came at high tide and destroyed huge sand dunes and roads. Winds at Myrtle Beach reached only forty miles per hour and unroofed only a few cottages. Early warnings of the storm led to a speedy and orderly evacuation from the beaches. There were no casualties on the upper South Carolina Coast.[70]

The Charleston press once again went out of its way to promote the region, saying in an editorial, "It was not the severest tropical storm through which Charleston has passed, but it was by no means the least severe. Charleston and its countryside have not been stripped of their spirit to overcome what has occurred." Nevertheless, at the very least, thirty-six people died in the Georgia and South Carolina lowcountry, and property losses reached into the millions.[71] One writer believed that disasters serve "to oil human resilience . . . to test courage . . . to remind . . . that for all man's smartness, there is an outside power before which he is as nothing." The author concluded, "Anyway, it's just as well to be philosophical about hurricanes — there's nothing else you can do about them."[72]

Better-built vessels and improved early warning systems for hurricanes offshore limited losses of life and craft. Quick response by the coast guard in warning and evacuating people along the seashore saved lives and property. However, the failure to alert and evacuate people on isolated sea islands continued to contribute to fatalities. And as the built environment increased along lowcountry beaches, so did the costs associated with hurricanes.

The War Years

A tropical storm moved offshore from Jacksonville and whipped by Georgia's coastal counties of Glynn and McIntosh on October 19, 1944, damaging the busy World War II shipyard at Brunswick, tearing roofs off houses, and uprooting huge live oaks. It "lunged" ashore at Beaufort, South Carolina, with sixty-five-mile-per-hour winds and drenching rains. Structural and flood damages reached $350,000 ($3,657,102). At Charleston the gale knocked down trees, signs, and power lines. Warned of the approaching storm, boat owners moved their crafts out of the harbor to places of safety. Losses at Charleston were minor.[73]

The coast guard, army, and local police had become more proactive in preventing fatalities from storms. In late June 1945, reports of a strong gale moving just offshore and up the coast from Florida prompted officials to call for the evacuation of some beach resorts along the Georgia and South Carolina coasts on June 24–25. The tropical storm remained off the coast, and its high winds did little damage ashore. Luckily the gale blew by at low tide, which minimized coastal flooding. At Charleston a reporter observed that "insomnia, caused by banging shutters, seemed the most prevalent ill effect of the storm in the city."[74]

Several months later a hurricane curved from west Florida east across the state. It entered the Atlantic near Jacksonville and raced up the coast. On September 17 it came ashore between Beaufort and Charleston, with seventy-mile-per-hour winds and headed inland as a tropical storm. Winds gusting at sixty-five miles per hour and a nine-foot tidal surge did comparatively little damage at Charleston, though the storm wrecked the piers of the Charleston Yacht Club and felled trees and power lines. At Myrtle Beach wind gusts reached only forty miles per hour. However, drenching rains ruined crops across the state. The president of the South Carolina Agricultural Society said, "Farmers can have little hope of harvesting any crops this fall." That same year civil defense organizations created to assist on the homefront during the war were directed by Washington to coordinate measures to prevent natural disasters and to provide relief when they occurred.[75] Their opportunity came two years later.

Tropical Storms and Hurricanes, 1947–1952

In early October 1947 a tropical depression was spotted off the Nicaraguan coast. It passed over western Cuba, gained hurricane strength, and struck south Florida with winds and flooding rains on October 11. The tropical cyclone then headed east into the Atlantic Ocean. With the hurricane safely offshore, scientists saw an opportunity to test their idea that "seeding" a tropical cyclone with dry ice could reduce its strength. The storm was seeded, then to everyone's surprise the hurricane stalled, turned around, and headed due west toward the mainland. On October 15, 1947, lowcountry newspapers reported that a "rejuvenated hurricane" packing ninety-mile-per-hour winds was headed for the

South Carolina–Georgia coast. The U.S. Weather Bureau issued an advisory for hurricane warnings from Georgia to North Carolina. On October 15–16 the tropical cyclone slammed the Georgia coast. It knocked down trees and power-and-light poles and tossed wires across the highways and byways from Darien to Savannah and for forty miles inland.[76]

Early warnings allowed an orderly bus evacuation of one thousand people from Tybee Island before surging tides destroyed access across the causeway connecting the island to the mainland. Sirens wailed throughout the night, warning of the storm. A tidal surge of twelve feet flooded the island up to four feet in places. Two cabin cruisers ended up atop the causeway, and the pavilion sustained heavy damage when the seawall gave way. Hurricane winds with gusts of one hundred miles per hour severely damaged houses, ripped roofs off businesses, and demolished old Trinity Methodist Chapel. On nearby Wilmington Island, at Safford Field, a hangar collapsed, destroying several planes. The storm passed west of Savannah, and sustained winds reached only sixty miles per hour in the city, with occasional higher gusts. Plate-glass windows exploded in the business district, trees toppled in the squares, and roofs of houses blew away. Winds wrecked hangers and damaged two C-47 transport planes at Chatham and Hunter airfields near Savannah. There were no human casualties, but fifteen hundred houses and one hundred businesses suffered damages in the coastal region. Losses were more than $500,000 ($4,123,318) on Tybee Island and $1,000,000 ($8,246,637) in Savannah.[77]

Up the coast at Folly Island, South Carolina, waves washed away sand at both ends of the island and undermined houses. At Charleston wind gusts never exceeded fifty-four miles per hour; it was flooding that caused most of the damage. In the county an eighty-four-foot pine snapped in half and fell into a cabin, crushing to death thirty-five-year old Neil McCord.[78]

During the hurricane seasons of 1949 and 1950, gales whipped across the lowcountry. A small but powerful storm began deep in the Caribbean in October 1950 and developed into a destructive hurricane. It came ashore near Miami and traveled up Florida's east coast, bringing record high winds to Jacksonville.[79]

Just across the Florida state line, at St. Marys, Georgia, the remnants of the Florida hurricane roared ashore with seventy-mile-per-hour winds on October 18–19. It knocked over trees, sheared away tin roofing, and downed power lines.

A World War II veteran, Q. E. Hooks, who had been recently acquitted in a fatal shooting, was hunting marsh hens in a creek near Brunswick when high winds capsized his boat and he drowned. Tides flooded Brunswick up to three feet in some places. Another near-tragedy occurred when Mr. and Mrs. T. E. Harrison and their fourteen-year-old granddaughter, Mary Elizabeth, walked into water that was charged with 110 volts by a downed live wire. Somehow Mary Elizabeth was able to pull away from the paralyzing current and by quick action saved her grandparents' lives.[80] Hardest hit was St. Simons Island, just across the causeway from Brunswick. Shingles tore away from the roofs of beachfront cottages, and either rain or seawater found a way into every dwelling. With the storm moving inland and west of Savannah, residents "breathed a little easier." Wind and rainsqualls buffeted the city, but the gales never reached hurricane strength.[81]

In late August 1952 a relatively small hurricane meandered along the southeastern coast threatening to come ashore from Florida to South Carolina. It was called Able by the U.S. Weather Bureau, only a year before the agency began using women's names for hurricanes. On August 31 the tropical cyclone's eye passed over Beaufort, South Carolina, causing little damage. But "the full fury" of the cyclone — winds of up to ninety miles per hour on its right-front quadrant — slammed into Edisto Island. The hurricane came ashore at night, around 10:00 p.m.; screaming winds and torrential rains terrified residents. Roofs were ripped off prefabricated army-type "hutments" that were being used as beach cottages — some were demolished; waves carried others out to sea. More sturdy frame houses lost parts of their roofs and porches. Waves washed out part of the road along the beachfront and filled it with the flotsam and jetsam from the storm. Then the storm roared inland. At Hardeeville high winds and slashing rains that limited visibility caused a traffic accident that killed two people. Around midnight, forty miles inland, the storm hit Walterboro like "a fast freight train." Even with diminished winds, scores of trees went down, window glass shattered, and gusts lifted cars, turning them around on rain-slick roads.[82]

Up the coast at Folly Beach, winds less than hurricane force whipped shingles off roofs, destroyed a section of the pavilion, and "unpeeled a hotel's circular water storage tank . . . like a candy-bar wrapper." In Charleston's harbor "haven-seeking" vessels rode out the storm safely. With ample warning U.S. Navy ships at the Charleston Naval Shipyard were moved up the Cooper River or sent to sea. There was some wind damage at the nearby resort beaches of the Isle of Palms and Sullivan's Island. Luckily the hurricane came in at low tide, or the damage along the coast would have been greater. After the hurricane passed, on hard-hit Edisto Island a customer buying a pound of bologna and a loaf of bread reflected the speculators attitude toward beachfront-property owners when he was heard to say, "Hurricanes are just a chance we have to take, but it's worth it." Damage in South Carolina reached $3,000,000 ($20,818,867).[83] With postwar beachfront construction surging, the cost of hurricane damage was rising.

"The Lady, Hazel," 1954

A fragile ceasefire in Korea, the effect of Elvis's rock and roll on their children, and Khrushchev with the bomb all concerned many adults in the southeastern United States in the 1950s. Also alarming was a renewed flurry of hurricanes. During the decade eight threatened to come ashore in Georgia or the Carolinas, and some did. The most destructive was called "The Lady, Hazel."[84]

In early October 1954 the U.S. Weather Bureau's Miami office was tracking a storm moving west-northwest over the warm waters of the southern Caribbean. Its name was Hazel. The storm passed just east of Grenada. With winds over one hundred miles per hour, Hazel slammed into Haiti, devastating the island. Quickly regaining strength after passing over land, the tropical cyclone skirted the eastern edge of the Bahamas and began following the warm Gulf Stream on a northward path toward the United States. It was difficult to predict where on the southeastern coast the hurricane might strike, so no evacuations were ordered.[85]

On the afternoon of October 14, at the tiny South Carolina fishing village of Ocean Drive Beach, later incorporated into North Myrtle Beach, the chief of police, Merlin Bellamy, read in the local newspaper that Hazel had killed hundreds in Haiti, but was forecast "to harmlessly pass out to sea." The sky along the Carolina coast confirmed this. Bellamy himself noticed that "it was absolutely a beautiful autumn afternoon." Then late that evening Chief Bellamy took a call from a forecaster at Charleston warning him that Hazel had suddenly changed course and appeared to be on a direct path to strike near Ocean Drive Beach. Landfall was imminent. With no hurricane plans, Chief

Bellamy sounded the town siren. Firefighters rushed to their station as the outlying rain bands of the storm began whipping across the beach. Bellamy and the fire chief directed the village's four firemen to fan out across town, knock on doors, awaken residents, and tell them to leave immediately. It was not until around 3:00 a.m. Friday that the U.S. Weather Bureau gave the order to fly the hurricane flag from Charleston to Wilmington, North Carolina.[86]

In the early morning hours of October 15 radio stations warned of the storm fast approaching the upper South Carolina coast. The U.S. Coast Guard joined local and state police to alert the population to the threat. Although the summer season was over, a few vacationers and a small number of permanent residents remained. The time for evacuations was dangerously short, even for several thousand persons. Trying to evacuate one hundred thousand or so permanent residents living in the region today on short notice would be next to impossible and likely to end in a disaster of epic proportions. Hazel was more than ninety miles east of Charleston when around 8:00 a.m. its outlying winds and high waves began striking North Island off Georgetown, DeBordieu Island, and Pawleys Island. The eye of the storm was coming ashore near the border of the Carolinas, with winds exceeding one hundred miles per hour, precisely at the time of the highest tide of 1954, October's full moon.[87]

At Georgetown fierce winds whipped shingles from roofs and smashed in windows; trees fell into front porches, and tides flooded the town's low-lying streets. But along the nearby oceanfront resorts stretching northeast of Georgetown for some forty miles to Wilmington, North Carolina, the damage reached catastrophic proportions. On Pawleys Island giant waves driven by hurricane winds pounded the natural environment, leveling forty-foot sand dunes and cutting a new inlet on the southern end of the island. No distinctions were made among Pawleys Island's six hundred homes—whether wooden bungalow, rambling fifty-year-old summer houses, modest concrete-block retreats, gaily painted, brick, or sheathed in weathered siding—more than two hundred simply disappeared. Some landed in the marshes, and five caught fire and burned. Of four hundred houses remaining, all suffered water or wind damage. Some that a few hours earlier had stood behind the high dunes were a few feet from the edge of the sea. The ocean end of the new fishing pier collapsed. Witnesses described Pawleys Island as "a debris of destruction."[88]

Up the coast at the village of Ocean Drive Beach Chief Bellamy and others evacuated everyone without means of transportation to a high school five miles inland. Bellamy watched from a distance "terribly high waves . . . 40 to 50 feet in the air" crash into the town; occasionally "a roof or a portion of a building" floated by. Waves washed over the village's only stoplight; houses torn from their foundations washed into the sea, where they splintered like kindling. Two hundred of the 380 cottages were destroyed; those remaining suffered heavy damage. The belongings of residents, including their refrigerators, washed inland as far as three miles. Hazel punched gaping holes in a row of post–World War II beachfront homes at Garden City, turning some to rubble and tilting others on cracked and broken foundations. It was the same all along the thirty-mile stretch of beach today called South Carolina's Grand Strand. At such resorts as Surfside, Floral Beach, Myrtle Beach, Atlantic Beach, Windy Hill, Crescent Beach, Cherry Grove, Tilghman's, and East Cherry Grove giant waves gnawed away high sand dunes and destroyed or severely damaged the cottages and homes that had been built behind them. Up to that time it was the most destructive storm in terms of property damage ever to strike coastal South Carolina. Within a few hours $27,000,000 ($184,572,000) invested in homes, inns, piers, and businesses was lost.[89]

After the storm passed and calm winds and brilliant sunshine enveloped the region, stunned residents wandered through the rubble. One woman collected an armful of kitchen utensils; a man tried to mop up water in his house, which had washed hundreds of feet inland from its original site on the beachfront. Amazingly, given such short notice of the approaching hurricane, there was only one death. Apparently Leonard Watts drowned near his cottage at Cherry Grove Beach. Other residents suffered scrapes, bruises, broken bones, and, perhaps, broken hearts. At Georgetown an enormous tree fell on a twenty-nine-year-old African American, Benjamin Johnson, fracturing his leg and spine and pinning him under it. He was rescued and admitted to a local hospital.[90]

South Carolina was lucky. Winds up to 150 miles per hour battered North Carolina, causing nineteen deaths and an estimated $136,000,000 ($929,754,643) in property losses. To date, it is the most destructive tropical cyclone in North Carolina's history. Hazel did not stop there. It swept into Virginia and the northeast, causing massive damages and more than one hundred deaths. Hazel ranks as one of the most catastrophic storms to strike the United States in the twentieth century.[91]

No sooner had the storm passed than lowcountry promoters were at work. The editors of Charleston's *News and Courier* headed the list with their blend of boosterism and southern pride — the size of the bill for damages alone along the Carolina Grand Strand, they argued, "attest[s] to the great development of Myrtle Beach and the surrounding area." A chief asset of the Carolina strand "is safety in time of storms. The flat countryside, excellent highways and ease of communication make it possible for people to get out. Even those who stay too long usually can find refuge of a safer nature than is afforded *on rocky New England shores.*" Indeed "the strand itself . . . seems not to have suffered permanent hurt. Loss of beach property is a calculated risk of the seashore." Then the supposedly educated newspaperman made this incredible observation: "*Over the years, hurricanes seldom strike the same place.* The attractions of beach life outweigh the occasional blows from wind and sea. . . . By next season, we predict, Myrtle Beach and its neighbors will be in full swing."[92]

In 1955 the lowcountry was again fortunate. Three hurricanes swept offshore past Georgia and South Carolina and slammed into many of the "*same place*[s]" in eastern North Carolina hit by Hazel, compounding the damages.[93]

Gracie, September 29, 1959

Punishing gales continued to whip along the coast of the lowcountry, but five years passed before another hurricane came ashore. Gracie organized into a tropical cyclone near the southeast end of the Bahamas island chain in late September 1959. Like Hazel it posed tracking problems for the weather bureau. Moving north-northwest it meandered along Florida's coast for several days. On September 26–27 Gracie was downgraded to a tropical storm that appeared destined to blow itself out in the Atlantic. Then on Monday, September 28, Gracie suddenly gained in intensity, changed direction three hundred miles southeast of Charleston, and headed for the mainland. The weather bureau warned small craft to remain in port and issued an emergency storm alert for an "extremely dangerous hurricane" expected to come ashore between Savannah and Wilmington, North Carolina. All along the coast storm shelters opened. Stores experienced a run on candles, flashlights, and foodstuffs. Schools closed. At Charleston, U.S. Navy vessels went up the Cooper River, and aircraft were dispatched to distant bases. Late that evening, rising winds and rainsqualls buffeted Tybee Beach and Beaufort; six-foot swells crashed on Edisto Beach, and the Beaufort County sheriff's office urged coastal residents to evacuate low-lying areas.[94]

On the morning of September 29 the hurricane knifed into the coast just north of Beaufort, South Carolina, with winds of more than 125 miles per hour and slashing rains. The storm tore live oaks from the ground and blew down 90 percent of the telephone and power lines in Beaufort. Plate-glass windows shattered in the business district. Winds destroyed eight homes and severely damaged eighty others. A few miles from Beaufort, Charles Dickey of Youngstown, Ohio, lost control of his car on a rain-slick road, overturned, and crashed into a tree, killing himself and injuring the two passengers. James Chaplin, about thirty-five, of Beaufort was killed trying to push a stalled car off a highway. Winds wrecked six homes on St. Helena Island and caused major damage to twenty-four others, sank thirteen fishing boats in St. Helena Sound, each valued at $25,000 ($157,990) to $50,000 ($315,979), and then moved on to Edisto Island, which bore the brunt of the storm. Gracie's waves tore away three-quarters of the island's fishing pier. Winds smashed, unroofed, and twisted from their foundations sixteen homes and partially wrecked sixty-three others along a two-mile stretch of beach. Luckily homeowners had evacuated before the storm hit. Power lines fell across the island's main road; garbage cans banged noisily as they blew about the island. The roof of the once-proud Ocean Villa Hotel peeled away; some roofs were blown one hundred yards inland. The superintendent of the state park, Keith Fleischman, watched waves boiling across the marsh "as high as those on the ocean." Fortunately the hurricane came ashore at dead low tide, minimizing flooding. The press concluded correctly that had it not been for "the weather bureau alerts" and evacuations on the lower coast "loss of life might have been widespread." The mayor of Beaufort estimated damages in the city at $2,000,000 ($12,639,175) and said, "We won't be the same in 100 years."[95]

The hurricane moved inland and up the coast, knocking over trees and power lines. A resident of Johns Island, Mrs. L. M. Andrews, watched white-capped waves breaking in the yard of her home, destroying barns, killing pigs, and ruining crops. At neighboring Folly Beach winds of 125 miles per hour drove the ocean ashore, tearing the roof off the Folly Beach Hotel and the pavilion.

Homes collapsed. Two hundred people who elected to "ride out the storm" were cut off from the mainland and without food until the Red Cross managed to reach them. At Charleston pounding seas destroyed the Carolina Yacht Club's dock. Winds smashed vessels at the municipal yacht basin, where the manager estimated wind speeds at 130 miles per hour. White foaming waves crashed over the Battery, flooding White Point Gardens; the Fort Sumter Hotel suffered broken windows and rain damage estimated at $65,000 ($410,773). In the city's business district, glass swung crazily from strips of tape attached to storefront windows to prevent shattering. A window broke in Charleston's city council chamber, and shards of glass scratched the treasured portrait of George Washington painted in 1791 by John Trumbull. Shingles littered neighborhoods, and trees crisscrossed streets and highways, paralyzing automobile traffic. Colonial Lake overflowed into Rutledge and Ashley avenues. The west wall of Johnson Hagood Stadium, the city's main arena for football, blew down. Damages in Charleston and Charleston County reached $4,200,000 ($26,542,267). On the upper coast, winds never reached hurricane force. A tornado spawned by the storm damaged screened porches at Garden City and tipped a restaurant off its foundation at Murrells Inlet. Roaring inland the storm left a trail of debris at Walterboro before continuing on to Columbia, where winds and rains damaged the capitol building.[96]

Hurricanes, 1960s–1970s

The flurry of hurricanes that struck the lowcountry in the 1940s and 1950s appeared to have ended in the early 1960s. Tropical cyclones Brenda, Donna, and Ginny remained miles offshore. Cleo, by the time it neared Savannah, was only a weak tropical storm. As Cleo tracked out to sea in early September 1964, the weather bureau was watching Dora, seven hundred miles off Florida. Reconnaissance aircraft reported a "well-organized and dangerous hurricane . . . that more nearly resembles a typhoon." Within days it made landfall near St. Augustine, where its wind speeds reached 125 miles per hour, causing extensive damage. The hurricane spun north up the coast. At Jacksonville the storm caused the cancellation of a concert by a sensational new group from England, the Beatles. Winds exceeding ninety miles per hour, huge waves, a thirteen-foot tidal surge, and torrential rains swept Georgia's southern coast from Glynn County to Tybee Island.[97]

The hurricane followed the same track as, and was the most devastating storm to strike along the Georgia coast since, the tropical cyclone and tidal wave of 1898. For eighteen hours Dora's right-front quadrant pounded the lower Georgia coast. At Brunswick, Georgia, a man attempting to secure a boat drowned. Hundreds of trees went down across the city. Power and phone lines lay tangled in the flooded streets. On St. Simons Island tropical-storm winds, hurricane gusts, and pounding waves smashed boats to smithereens; the tidal surge undermined beachfront homes, and four vanished into the sea. Hastily rigged dikes prevented the ocean from flooding the lobby of the King and Prince Hotel. Hurricane gusts toppled seventy-five large oak and pine trees. Despite taping, windows shattered in the business district. President Lyndon Johnson, who toured Brunswick and St. Simons following the cyclone, turned to a member of his party and commented, "It's worse than you told me."[98]

A slight jog in Dora's track may have resulted in a direct hit on Georgia's coast rather than Florida's. As it was, damages in Georgia reached $8,000,000 ($47,458,064). Early warnings prompted most residents who could to evacuate Georgia's low-lying islands. Undoubtedly this saved lives. Storm tracking and forecasting was becoming more reliable. Television permitted more coastal residents than ever to keep a watchful eye on developing weather conditions.[99] Technology had changed the way agencies and individuals monitored the weather.

It was quiet along the coast of the lowcountry during the hurricane seasons of the late 1960s. Hurricanes Alma, Abby, and Gladys passed by as tropical storms or remained far offshore. This was followed by another period of relative calm during the 1970s, when the number of hurricanes that made landfall in the United States was the fewest ever. It was not until the last few months of the last year of the decade that a tropical cyclone made landfall in Georgia. Its name was David.[100]

For the first time, in the year 1979, tropical storms and cyclones were named from an alternating list of male and female names. David developed far out in the Atlantic in the vicinity of the Cape Verde Islands. By late August it reached the West Indies, with winds of 145 miles per hour. It devastated Dominica, Puerto Rico, and the Dominican Republic, killing more than thirteen hundred people and leaving two hundred thousand homeless. The "monster storm" weakened after crossing the mountains of Haiti, but on Labor Day weekend it was headed toward Florida. On September 3 David came ashore north of Palm Beach, with heavy rainsqualls and winds of eighty-five miles per hour, and then exited into the Atlantic. Fed by the warm waters of the Gulf Stream, the storm intensified. On Tuesday, September 4, with wind gusts over ninety miles per hour, David, by then called the "killer storm," was bearing down on Tybee Island.[101]

Along the lowcountry thousands evacuated resort beaches. Tybee Island's Chief of Police, John Price, suffered knee and rib injuries while assisting in the evacuation. Some old-timers intended to ride out the storm. The police found one resident calmly walking on the beach. When warned of the approaching storm, he told them, "They scare a lot of people, but they don't usually do too much damage." Some persons, who were unauthorized to do so, took refuge in the 105-year-old lighthouse at the north end of the island. In the late afternoon David's winds, estimated at seventy to ninety miles per hour, swept across Ossabaw Island then moved west of Tybee Island and Savannah. At Tybee roofs blew off a few houses, there was flooding, signs and fences went down, but otherwise damage was light. Winds and waves battered the marina at Skidaway Island, sinking the floating docks and some of the vessels moored there, causing more than $1,000,000 ($2,533,058) in damages. Nearby, at the Bethesda Home for Boys, damages reached $100,000 ($253,305). Less-than-hurricane-force winds brushed by Savannah but not before knocking out television and radio broadcasts. Flying debris injured two workers at the Georgia Ports Authority. Trees crashed into homes and automobiles. Tree limbs, shingles, and pieces of roofs littered roads. Low-lying suburban areas flooded. On Savannah's west side an industrial building exploded into flames, but the fire department was unable to fight the blaze because power failures crippled pumping stations. For three days areas of Savannah were without electricity, and the price of ice skyrocketed. One crowd became unruly at the Savannah Ice Delivery Company. Damages in Chatham County reached $4,000,000 ($10,132,231).[102]

The *Savannah Morning News* thought the area "survived admirably" largely through the efforts of civil defense, the Red Cross, and other agencies that warned citizens of the approaching storm and helped provide shelters. But the press declared there was much to learn from David and chided radio and television stations, and the city especially, for failing to have emergency generators ready when electrical power failed. David could have come ashore on the

Georgia coast as an extremely destructive hurricane had it not taken a sudden turn to the north in the Caribbean and swept over Haiti as a category 5 storm. There Haiti's high mountains broke up the cyclone that then struck Florida as a category 2 storm. Georgia again had dodged the "big one."[103]

Up the coast Daufuskie Island, Hilton Head Island, and Beaufort sustained damage from flooding and winds but no casualties. There was significant erosion on the beaches. In and around Beaufort damage to private and public docks, businesses, homes, and Beaufort's new waterfront park reached about $2,000,000 ($5,066,116). Winds at Folly Island destroyed several houses. At Charleston, winds were under hurricane force, but trees went down across the region. On the upper South Carolina coast, David demolished thirteen homes at Litchfield Beach. Property damage reached $7,000,000 ($17,731,404) on the South Carolina coast, but again there were no fatalities. This was not the case a decade later.[104]

CHAPTER NINE

Hugo and After, 1989–2004

As in the 1960s and 1970s, tropical storms continued to lash the lowcountry in the 1980s. Then, in the last few months of 1989, perhaps the most destructive and costly tropical cyclone in South Carolina's history plunged ashore. In early September 1989 a cluster of thunderstorms formed off the coast of Senegal, West Africa. Converging trade winds in the vicinity of the Cape Verde Islands pushed the growing storms west over the warm Atlantic Ocean, and a tropical depression developed. Upgraded on September 11 to a tropical cyclone named Hugo, it grew rapidly into a powerful category 4 hurricane, with winds of 130 to 155 miles per hour. The storm slowly curved west-northwest. During September 17–20 Hugo raked islands in the eastern Caribbean, causing massive destruction and more than forty-one deaths. The "killer storm" then turned to the northwest, and a hurricane warning was issued for the southeastern coast of the United States.[1]

During September 20–21 Hugo tracked toward the Georgia coast along the same path as the destructive hurricane of 1940 that had come ashore near Savannah. On the morning of September 21, Savannahians read in their morning papers that the National Hurricane Center in Coral Cables, Florida, predicted that Hugo had a 21 percent chance of striking either Savannah or Charleston. The huge storm was only several hundred miles offshore. However, a meteorological event shifted Hugo one degree north on a track toward the central South Carolina coast. By this time 150,000 people along Georgia's coast were fleeing inland. The hurricane brushed Tybee Island and Savannah with only gale-force winds of fifty-five miles per hour. A few trees and some power lines went down. Savannahians breathed a long sigh of relief.[2]

The early morning hours of September 21 found Hugo a few hundred miles southeast of Charleston, with winds of 135 miles per hour. The category 4 hurricane was as large as the state of South Carolina. The governor ordered the evacuation of all coastal areas. From Hilton Head Island to Myrtle Beach tens of thousands of people began leaving the region's beach resorts. At Charleston, Mayor Joe Riley asked everyone living in single-story homes to evacuate the Charleston peninsula. Noon traffic on Interstate 26 west toward Columbia was bumper-to-bumper. For fifty-four thousand people with nowhere to go, emergency shelters were opened. In the late afternoon the hurricane was about 180 miles from the South Carolina coast and called "extremely dangerous." At nightfall outlying winds of the giant storm came ashore all along South Carolina's lowcountry.

Those on the south side of the hurricane experienced only tropical-storm winds. It was more like a typical summer thunderstorm on the lower South Carolina coast. At Hilton Head, Beaufort, and St. Helena a few trees went down, but sustained winds reached only fifty miles per hour. Like Savannah, these communities were lucky. However, those near the dangerous right-front quadrant of the storm — Folly Beach, Charleston, Mount Pleasant, Sullivan's Island, Isle of Palms, Awendaw, and McClellanville — were not so fortunate.[3]

Around 9:00 p.m. fierce winds began sweeping Charleston. Gas lines broke. Electrical transformers atop telephone poles exploded, filling the city sky with phosphorescent flashes. Winds continued to rise. By 10:30 p.m. sustained winds of over 90 miles per hour, gusting to 130, blew rain horizontally across the peninsula city, battering and drenching four thousand historical public and private buildings. The tin, copper, and slate roofs of such structures as City Hall, Charleston United Daughters of the Confederacy Museum, and the First Baptist Church tore away and with other debris became projectiles that smashed windows and windshields. Mayor Riley and his staff, managing the crisis by candlelight at City Hall, were able to save priceless paintings from water damage. About one-third of the distinctive older homes in the historic district sustained severe damage; there was far greater devastation in the less affluent neighborhoods of the city and suburbs west of the Ashley River. In North Charleston winds peeled away the roofs of emergency shelters, forcing the occupants to flee to other shelters. Along King Street, Charleston's shopping district, glass storefronts exploded, spilling macabrely twisted mannequins across the sidewalks. Fires erupted from natural gas leaks. Winds split open or uprooted ancient oaks and magnolias. Water rose in the streets. Utility poles snapped and crashed. Television and radio stations went off the air. The city and suburbs were plunged into darkness.[4]

Around midnight a seventeen- to twenty-foot wall of water crashed over historic Fort Sumter in Charleston Harbor. At the municipal marina the storm surge and winds tossed fifty-foot sailboats, yachts, and smaller craft into the air and into the city streets. The sea surge inundated Folly Island south of the city. Crashing waves and high winds destroyed or severely damaged about 80 percent of the homes there. Some floated away, leaving only their supporting pilings. Dean Dubai and several friends were partying in a front-beach house until "it began breaking up." One homeowner, who had brought in huge rocks on the seaside, erected a ten-foot-high fence, and filled the space between the two structures with sand, found his defenses had completely vanished. The house was split apart, its contents — mattresses, clothes, and furniture — strewn across the beach. The sea took away all signs of the old Atlantic House Restaurant except for its distinctive red roof. Mayor Bob Linville said, "All my usual landmarks are gone."[5] It was much the same at Mount Pleasant, Sullivan's Island, and the Isle of Palms.

The huge tidal surge and winds destroyed or severely damaged more than 50 percent of the hundreds of homes on Sullivan's Island and the Isle of Palms.

Hurricane Hugo tossed the *Guppy* onto Charleston's Lockwood Boulevard, 1989. Courtesy of *Charleston Post and Courier*.

Hurricane Hugo's high-water mark at the Lincoln High School, McClellanville, South Carolina. The school was used as an emergency shelter, but those seeking refuge there were compelled to climb onto tables to save themselves from drowning, as the water rose to nearly seven feet. Courtesy of *Charleston Post and Courier*.

ABOVE King Street and South Battery, Charleston, after Hugo,
1989. Courtesy of Charleston Museum.

RIGHT Looking south along Ocean Boulevard, Myrtle
Beach, South Carolina, after hurricane Hugo. Courtesy of
Jack Thompson.

BELOW Charleston's old oaks stripped of leaves, their branches downed, White Point Gardens, after Hugo. Courtesy of Charleston Museum.

Pool and resort hotel, Myrtle Beach, South Carolina, before (TOP) and after (BOTTOM) hurricane Hugo. Courtesy of Jack Thompson.

The Kingfisher Pier and Arcade, Garden City, South Carolina, before (TOP) and after (BOTTOM) hurricane Hugo. Courtesy of Jack Thompson.

TOP A man sorts through his possessions after hurricane Hugo hit Charleston. Courtesy of *Charleston Post and Courier*.

BOTTOM Nancy Swain, in her Mount Pleasant, South Carolina, kitchen with friends, clears away the debris following hurricane Hugo. Courtesy of *Charleston Post and Courier*.

LEFT A jumble of mobile homes in Charleston left in the wake of hurricane Hugo. Courtesy of *Charleston Post and Courier*.

BELOW Hurricane Hugo, 1989, blew and washed ashore boats of the McClellanville shrimping fleet. *Daddy's Girl*, a boat owned by Farrell White, is seen in the background. Courtesy of *Charleston Post and Courier*.

TOP   The Ben Sawyer Bridge, connecting Sullivan's Island and Mount Pleasant, South Carolina, blown upright by winds of hurricane Hugo. Courtesy of *Charleston Post and Courier.*

BOTTOM   Following hurricane Hugo, a sign points the way to a space where the famous Atlantic House once stood on Folly Beach, South Carolina. Courtesy of *Charleston Post and Courier.*

Some structures simply disappeared; others became "piles of firewood." Homes lost their roofs; some filled with seawater and fish and were uninhabitable. At the Isle of Palms, which was thought to have taken "the brunt of the storm," some homes teetered perilously on the remaining two or three supporting pilings. Gas leaked from smashed propane gas cylinders. Power lines and other debris clogged the roads. Luxury yachts and sailboats moored at the marina of the Wild Dunes resort were thrown like cordwood atop houses or onto a neighboring island. Every fishing pier from the Isle of Palms to Myrtle Beach — more than one hundred miles to the north — was destroyed. The concrete bridge over Breach Inlet, connecting the Isle of Palms to Sullivan's Island, was torn away; part of the steel drawbridge linking Sullivan's Island to the mainland was lifted and twisted upright by gusting winds. Disrupting vehicular traffic, both islands now were isolated from one another and the mainland. Around 1:00 a.m. the screaming winds stopped. An eerie quiet enveloped the South Carolina lowcountry. Above Charleston the sky was clear and filled with galaxies. The eye of the hurricane was passing. The calm did not last for long. Winds with renewed force came out of the west as the storm surge flooded across Charleston's peninsula.[6]

Carla Duprey, who elected to remain at her apartment in a concrete condominium facing the Charleston harbor, fled into the stairwell as the building swayed and windows blew out. "I won't do this anymore. I'd be out of here," she said, if another hurricane was on a track to hit the city.[7]

A couple on Montague Street watched a dumpster float by. How high would the surging water rise? They quickly donned life jackets and fashioned one for their dog as the water reached almost to the top stairs of their porch. Crowded together in the bathroom, they listened as pieces of houses, tree branches, and debris banged into the dwelling. Water began to seep under the door. Then it stopped.[8]

Some blocks away Gene Geer dodged glass shards as windows blew out and water rose to two feet on the first floor of his antebellum mansion at 31 East Battery, one of the city's most exclusive addresses. At a housing project near the Cooper River, Marcia Glover, a young single mother, watched water rise rapidly in her small apartment. Hours before, she had sent her children to a shelter. Marcia climbed atop her kitchen counter as her refrigerator began to float. She had only two feet of breathing space left when the waters started to recede.[9]

The wood-frame houses of Arthur McCloud and Isaiah Mack collapsed on them, and both died. Others perished on the rivers as the storm surge funneled up the Wando, Cooper, and Ashley rivers, pushing hundreds of boats upstream and smashing many to pieces. Robert Page and Harold Hutson, who hoped to pilot their forty-five-foot shrimp trawler up the Wando to safety, died when it was slammed into a bridge. On the same river, Floridians Brian and Kathleen Jackson drowned when winds overturned their catamaran. On the Cooper River, Paul Spencer died trying to navigate his thirty-foot powerboat upriver to a safe harbor.[10]

While the eye of the hurricane passed over Charleston, four babies were delivered in the city's hospitals. At Roper Hospital two maintenance workers, Daniel Dyer and David Johns, tied ropes around themselves and waded into rushing waist-deep waters to reach a diesel-fuel tank. There they hand-cranked a pump all night that sent power to Roper's intensive care and coronary care units. Dyer and Johns later received national recognition for their heroism.[11]

Shops in the business district whose plate glass windows fell out or whose doors blew off became easy pickings for looters who roamed the city streets. Police on patrol apprehended several.[12] Charleston and the surrounding countryside resembled a combat zone. The contents of stores, lumber, twisted metal roofing, entire roofs, glass, ancient oaks, palm fronds, and other storm debris blocked streets and highways; pluff mud that had been washed into the city from the surrounding marshes filled the air with its distinctive smell. Up the coast, about halfway between Charleston and McClellanville, the storm surge nearly erased the tiny fishing village of Awendaw. The home of Sam and Nan Welsh floated off its foundation. When water poured into the house, they ran to the second floor. The water rose to their waists, then chests. They climbed onto their floating china cabinet. The house rocked and creaked; "wood was being pulled off the nails." The house seemed to be coming apart. The Welshes thought they were going to drown. Hours passed, and ever so slowly the water began to drain from the room. Only then did they believe that they had survived the tempest.[13]

Near Bull's Bay, on the edge of the Cape Romain seashore, the four hundred residents of the fishing village of McClellanville prepared for the worst. With other fishermen, fifty-year-old Farrell White triple tied his shrimp trawler *Daddy's Girl* and set anchors for a bad storm. The villagers lived by the sea and knew its destructive power. Then as the eye was passing over Charleston after midnight, the dangerous right-front quadrant of Hugo roared across Bull's Bay with winds reaching 140 miles per hour. The storm surge followed close behind.[14]

The cyclone slammed into McClellanville with a vengeance. The ocean rose thirteen to sixteen feet, foam whipping off the tops of waves riding waves, picked up fifty- to seventy-foot-long shrimp trawlers, and tossed them into the marshes. The sea crushed others at dockside — the *Mary Ann*, the *Edisto*, the *Wasp*, the *Moonrise*, the *Lucky Lady*, the *Charlestonian*, and the *Sun Maid* never again trawled for shrimp or fish. To the villagers the wind sounded like runaway freight trains. Old oaks that had withstood earlier hurricanes and shaded homes for years splintered or crashed to the ground. Flotsam and jetsam from the storm flooded through the village streets: sea creatures, broken tree limbs, animal carcasses, family pets, and personal belongings. Ocean water poured through the second floor windows of some of the oldest wooden houses in the village. Houses were knocked from their foundations. The air reeked of pluff mud from the marshes inside houses and in the open. Water began to seep under the door of shrimper Farrell White's home. He and his wife, Denie, tried to sop up the water. Suddenly, the tidal surge smashed through windows, and the Whites found themselves standing in three feet of water. To escape the rapidly rising flood, Farrell led Denie, his adult son, and his daughter upstairs to the attic. Within minutes water filled the house and began rising in the attic. Farrell then led his family back down the stairs, through the seawater, and into the kitchen, where they swam through broken windows to get outside. Somehow they all managed to climb onto the roof and hold on. From here they could see lights shorting out on the automobiles floating by. The White family survived. Hugo battered Farrell's trawler. It took all of the insurance on the trawler, about $75,000 ($111,230), to repair it. Without flood insurance, the Whites had to use most of their nest egg for the restoration of their home. Soon after the storm, Farrell suffered a massive heart attack and underwent a six-way bypass. In 2003, at age sixty-four, he was still trawling.[15]

The storm surge passed through the village, through woods and fields, and over U.S. Highway 17. Just off the highway, in a twelve-room house, Juanita Middleton, principal of the St. James–Santee Elementary School, and her husband hurried into the attic as the flood approached. Water surged through the rooms below, carrying away cherished family possessions: her son's trophies, Juanita's wedding album, and *Playbills* of New York shows she had collected over the years. With daylight Juanita and her husband slowly inched their way downstairs. Fearful of electric shock, they waited for the water to recede. The couple's beautiful oak floors had buckled from the water. Juanita covered them with carpet, hoping to blot out the memory of the storm that wrecked her home. Nearby, northwest of U.S. Highway 17 and over a mile from the ocean, Barbara Singleton and her husband listened as the winds of Hugo howled. Barbara opened the back door, turned a flashlight on the yard, and found the ocean at her steps. Toilets in the house backed up. The house shook. Winds blew a man across the highway and into their front yard. Barbara and her husband saw he "was in shock . . . alive but dead. There was nothing there in his face. Blank. Nothing." Barbara panicked. Thinking she was going to die, she took her three children, sat down in the rocking chair and began to rock. She said, "If I was going to die, it would be with my children in my arms." Though helpless as the storm raged on, she "felt a sense of peace." All members of the Singleton family survived.[16]

Close by the Singletons, Lincoln High School was being used as an emergency shelter. It was jammed with residents who had rushed there for safety. The nearly new school of brick and steel was on low ground. It began filling with water. As the water covered the school's floor and continued to pour in, some of the refugees became hysterical. They scrambled onto the school's elevated stage and onto tables, lifting their young children up with them. The water reached nearly seven feet. A few men fled to the roof. All passed the night terrified as the storm raged around them. Amazingly there was only one casualty. The Reverend Steven A. Shepard died of a heart attack.[17]

Because Hugo tracked westward across the state after landfall, the storm surge was somewhat less on the lowcountry's uppermost coast. Even so, Pawleys Island was transformed: the storm surge of about ten feet wiped away several houses and in their stead opened a hundred-foot-wide channel cutting the island in two. At Garden City, Surfside Beach, Murrells Inlet, and Myrtle Beach, the beaches disappeared. Myrtle Beach — now a sprawling resort town with a permanent resident population of over twenty thousand and a summertime population of over two hundred thousand — saw the sea wash away fifty thousand truckloads of sand, or $4,500,000 ($6,673,790) of the recent sand renourishment project. Waves pounded and destroyed 110 public-access walkways to the beach, turned concrete slabs topsy-turvy along its main promenade, flattened oceanfront stores, and severely damaged several hotels and about twelve homes.[18]

On isolated barrier islands huge numbers of birds and mammals died. Hugo killed 60 percent of the endangered red-cockaded woodpecker population as the storm deforested the Francis Marion National Forest, a preserve of 250,000 acres halfway between Charleston and Myrtle Beach. Seventy percent of the trees — longleaf pine, oak, cypress, and hickory — splintered and toppled before 140-mile-per-hour winds. Approximately one million board feet of timber was destroyed. Miles from the coast, 110-mile-per-hour winds struck Camden and Florence; the full force of the storm was felt at Charlotte, North Carolina, 220 miles from the seashore. Hugo was the most costly storm ever to strike the lowcountry and the state. In Charleston alone damages exceeded $1,000,000,000 ($1,483,064,500); total damages to property and timber statewide reached $5,000,000,000 ($7,415,322,500).[19] Hurricane Hugo became a marker, a watershed, a defining moment for the people who lived through it.

Lowcountry Tropical Storms and Hurricanes, 1990s–2000s

It appears that the 1990s ushered in a new cycle of hurricanes that some predict may last for thirty to forty years. Tropical cyclones increased at a dizzying rate, especially from 1995 to 1999. According to systematically collected hurricane-activity data, Atlantic hurricanes occurred more frequently in these five years than in any previous five-year period. National Hurricane Center tropical cyclone forecasters worked twenty-four hours a day to keep track of the sixty-five named storms, forty-one hurricanes, and twenty major hurricanes that occurred during these years. The tropical cyclone season in 1999 alone produced five category 4 hurricanes, a phenomenon never before observed since reliable data collection began in 1886. Throughout the 1990s these tropical cyclones almost annually pounded, and some devastated, the coastal regions of the states of Florida and North Carolina. A few brushed the coasts of Georgia and South Carolina, causing some damage. But during most of the decade, the lowcountry was fortunate. Nevertheless whenever television or radio warned that a hurricane was moving northwestward from the Caribbean, it was a tense time for many lowcountry residents. They recalled the terror and damages brought by Hugo and hoped another one was not at hand.[20] In 1999 hurricane Floyd appeared to be just such a storm.

Like Hugo it formed off the west coast of Africa as a tropical wave. By September 10 it had grown into a large hurricane. Intensifying as it crossed the warm waters of the Atlantic, Floyd was a four-hundred-mile-wide category 4 storm with winds of 155 miles per hour as it approached the central Bahamas. On the night of September 13 the hurricane changed direction to west-northwest. From the Bahamas to Florida and up the southeastern seaboard, those who had radios or televisions listened and watched as Floyd struck Abaco and nearby islands a devastating blow. The storm turned northward. Hurricane warnings went up from Miami to Jacksonville, and more than a million people fled inland. By September 15 the storm was passing the Florida coast and headed for the lowcountry. Many in Georgia and especially South Carolina recalled the haunting images of Hugo. They became part of the most massive evacuation ever along the Georgia and Carolina coasts. Traffic crept bumper-to-bumper west along interstate highways. At McClellanville, so hard hit by Hugo a decade before, great uneasiness settled over the community. Marina owner Jack Leland, who remained in the fishing village during Hugo, vowed he would never "ride out" another one like that. "I will only see it if I look over my shoulder on the way to the mountains."[21]

Floyd remained about a hundred miles off the lowcountry. Bands of rain came ashore, sustained winds reached about fifty miles per hour, with gusts of eighty in places. Trees and power lines went down, and low-lying islands flooded. At McClellanville the power went off, winds uprooted trees, and awnings tore away. Although it appeared for a while that Floyd would be another life-changing event, a large cold front swept in from the west and pushed it away from the Georgia and South Carolina coasts. Floyd will not be remembered like Hugo. Its legacy was the bumper-to-bumper traffic leading to the upcountry from the lowcountry. Once more the lowcountry was spared. Floyd finally came ashore in the early morning hours of September 16 at Cape Fear, North Carolina. It continued along the coast into New England. The vast majority of the fifty-seven deaths caused by Floyd came from sudden floods.[22]

Gales and hurricanes continued to buffet the lowcountry at the beginning of the twenty-first century. In mid-August 2004 Charley, a tropical cyclone, blew out of the Caribbean and savaged Florida's west coast with 145-mile-per-hour winds. Charley moved eastward across the state, exiting into the Atlantic near Jacksonville. The punishing hurricane then headed north. South Carolina's governor issued a mandatory evacuation order. Those who remembered Hugo needed no prodding. More than 180,000 residents and tourists evacuated Myrtle Beach. "I'm nervous," said Bob Baldwin, a coastal resident who remembered Hugo tossing his boat a mile from its mooring. "We were expecting it to go inland, where it would lose a lot of steam not head back over water where it could gather strength again." On Saturday, August 14, Charley blew by Charleston with winds of over fifty miles per hour, but up the coast gusts reached hurricane force. Georgetown suffered some damage to its infrastructure; the storm came ashore along South Carolina's Grand Strand with wind gusts of about eighty miles per hour. At Myrtle Beach monstrous waves crashed on the beach just a few feet from shops and inns. Winds downed power lines, caused superficial damage to some structures, and sent lounge chairs into the streets. Estimated damages to the upper South Carolina coast reached $2,000,000.[23]

Once more a meteorological event saved the lowcountry from landfall of a hurricane. As Charley moved up the Georgia coast, it was caught between two weather systems — an upper level low to the west and an area of high pressure to the east. The low prevailed over the high, changing the wind direction from the northeast to west. It nudged the hurricane sixty miles offshore.[24]

In late August 2004, two weeks after Charley, tropical storm Gaston was gaining strength in the Gulf Stream some 130 miles off the lowcountry. On Saturday, August 28, it was upgraded to a tropical cyclone, and the National Weather Service issued a hurricane warning for the South Carolina coastal region. Gaston's outer rain bands and winds came ashore all along the coast in the darkness of early Sunday morning, August 29. The storm raged throughout the day. Winds occasionally gusted to seventy miles per hour, downing power lines and ripping trees from rain-saturated ground. The slow movement of the storm wreaked havoc. More than 172,000 customers of South Carolina Electric and Gas in Charleston and its metropolitan area lost power. One electric company official remarked, "There's some stuff that looks like 'Hugo' out here." Gaston came ashore at McClellanville, and high waves tore through marsh grasses to pound the docks of the Carolina Seafood Company on Jeremy Creek. Shrimpers remembered how Hugo tossed their seventy-five-foot boats around like toys and kept their engines in gear to prevent the surging tide from smashing their trawlers at their moorings. But all agreed that Gaston was no Hugo. Dan Ravenel, a Charleston resident who lived through Hugo, described it this way: "Others had World War II, or the Civil War, the hurricane of 1752, the 1886 earthquake. Each generation has its own piece of history. [Hugo] was our piece."[25]

Conclusion

"Let us begin with the weather," a historian wrote decades ago in trying to explain the South. Indeed the premise of *Lowcountry Hurricanes: Three Centuries of Storms at Sea and Ashore* is that the weather, especially tropical storms and cyclones, for more than three hundred years profoundly affected the human, built, and natural environments.

Storms terrified the earliest settlers. Their accounts of their experiences and newspaper reports of the great storms most likely discouraged prospective immigrants and slowed population growth in the lowcountry. Some moved inland where they were not threatened by the violent tempests. Those who decided to remain on the land — some generation after generation — showed a certain grit and determination to persevere. Over the past three centuries thousands of those who did stay perished in hurricanes at sea or ashore. For the survivors, the great storms became life-changing events both economically and psychologically.

During major hurricanes, far more African Americans died than whites, most likely because many blacks lived near sea level on isolated islands. Even if warned of approaching storms, their only refuge was usually a poorly built structure. Where African Americans and whites lived near one another, accounts of blacks risking their lives to save whites during hurricanes are more frequent than whites saving blacks.

Planters feared the devastation wrought by tropical cyclones and storms, yet year after year they risked their lives and fortunes in the face of tempests that sometimes drowned their laborers, ruined their crops, and damaged their homes. Following each major hurricane, the ranks of the planters dwindled. Yet for more than two hundred years the agricultural economy of the lowcountry was built on rice and sea island cotton.

Ship owners, captains, crew, and passengers provide some of the most terrifying first-hand accounts of hurricanes off the Georgia and South Carolina coasts. Losses from storms at sea of uninsured vessels, their crews, and their cargoes brought personal tragedy and economic disaster of epic proportions to owners, shippers, seamen, and survivors of the victims.

By the early twentieth century the unremitting tropical cyclones and tropical storms, coupled with other factors, brought an end to the lowcountry's rice and cotton culture and the coastal carrying trade.[1] The region's phosphate business, begun with such promise in the 1860s, was so crippled by great storms that it was virtually over in thirty years.

The end of rice and cotton planting and of the phosphate industry threw thousands of black laborers out of work and into a stagnant economy. For many and their families, life became a hand-to-mouth existence. Except for minimum-wage jobs, there was little opportunity for uneducated displaced laborers to find permanent, gainful employment in the lowcountry's twentieth-century economy — built now on tourism, military spending, and the shipping industry.

The recurring losses of lives and property and the displacement of workers as a result of the great storms encouraged out-migration, stifled in-migration, and stymied the economic development of the lowcountry. This was especially damaging in an area that was one of the poorest regions in the nation for much of its history.

Over time the built environment increased dramatically along the coasts of Georgia and South Carolina, and the costs attributable to hurricane damage soared. Villages grew and became towns and then cities such as Charleston and Savannah. Resorts such as Myrtle Beach burgeoned. Houses, high-rise apartment buildings, hotels, amusement parks, and other businesses went up along the beaches and shores of the fragile sea islands.

Since the late nineteenth century a few farsighted residents of the lowcountry, among others elsewhere, have advocated better-built dwellings sited far off the beaches. Many others who enjoy living by the sea believe that the risk of this lifestyle is worth any gamble. This speculation is encouraged by inexpensive federal flood insurance. Furthermore low-country promoters have argued that — despite the facts — hurricanes rarely strike a second time in the same place.

By the late twentieth century the damages caused by hurricanes on the coast of the lowcountry increased from thousands of dollars to billions. Though property losses have been staggering, warnings by the federal government of approaching hurricanes have sharply reduced the loss of lives at sea and ashore.

As for the natural environment, hurricanes over the years have changed the land. Islands have been eroded, new channels and inlets cut, dunes destroyed, and wildlife drowned. By the 1980s miles of sand dunes had been wiped out by uncontrolled development alone. Concerned that such threats to the beaches might harm tourism, the South Carolina general assembly passed the Beachfront Management Act, which stated that it was "economically unwise and ecologically irresponsible to develop the coast in ways that... obliterate storm buffering dunes, and impair the natural processes that create and maintain wide, attractive beaches." Then threatened by a lawsuit, the South Carolina Coastal Management Council in 1990 backed away from the act and permitted construction forward of the baseline previously set for the beachfront construction of homes.[2] All along the lowcountry, promoters have trumped prudence. Scientists, however, have introduced a word of caution.

Recent studies indicate that the Georgia Embayment offers little protection from great storms. It is usually a meteorological event such as steering winds, a high-pressure area off the coast, or a low-pressure area out of the west that nudges hurricanes eastward and keeps killer storms off the Georgia and South Carolina coasts. The probability of tropical cyclones striking the lowcountry in an average year varies by location: 2.6 percent in Darien, 3.1 percent in Savannah, 3.4 percent in Charleston, and 3.7 percent at Myrtle Beach.[3]

Meteorologists have concluded that the sea-surface temperatures, sea-level air pressure, east-west wind speeds, and rainfall in Africa, taken together, affect whether a hurricane season will be above or below average. Science also suggests that hurricanes come in cycles. To use a baseball analogy, the lowcountry may be in the second inning of a hurricane cycle that began in the 1990s and that could last for thirty to forty years. When a great storm does come to the region, the gentle sloping coast off Georgia and South Carolina makes the lowcountry more prone to a towering storm surge than anywhere else on the East Coast.[4]

Today the National Hurricane Center at Miami, Florida, uses high-altitude aircraft reconnaissance and the latest technology to forecast the movements of hurricanes approaching the country's coastlines. Predicting the landfall of a tropical cyclone has vastly improved, but meteorologists continue to struggle with assessing the intensity of the hurricane.[5]

Coordination of public and private, and local and national, organizations has improved recovery efforts following hurricanes. But sometimes coordination among the various organizations, especially federal, state, and local governments, has broken down, as in the case of hurricane Katrina, which slammed into New Orleans in 2005. People perished, and agencies responsible for recovery efforts were slow to respond.

So those who build or live near the seashore should keep in mind that "the past is prologue" and that the Atlantic Basin is likely to experience more-frequent tropical cyclones over the next several decades. They should remember too that the lowcountry throughout its history has been vulnerable to the vagaries of nature, especially hurricanes.

Chronology of

Lowcountry Hurricanes

YEAR	MONTH/DAY	CATEGORY IF KNOWN	OFFSHORE/ LANDFALL AREA	WIND SPEED (EST. MPH)
1686	September 5		Landfall near Charleston	
1700	September 14		Landfall near Charleston	
1713	September 16		North of Charleston	
1716	September 17		Center remained offshore	
1722	September 19–21			
1724	August 28		Lowcountry coast	
1728	August 13–14		Center near Charleston	
1730	?		Offshore	
1743	August 31		S.C. coast	
1747	Mid to late October		S.C. coast	
1752	September 13–15	Major hurricane	Offshore/landfall near Charleston	111+
1752	September 30– October 1		Offshore and S.C. coast	
1753	September 15		S.C. coast	
1758	August 23		Ga. and S.C. coasts	
1760	October 5–6			
1767	October		Offshore	
1769	September 5–6		Offshore/Ga. and S.C. coastal waters	
1770	June 6–7		Ga. and S.C. coastal waters	
1778	August 10–11		Ga. and S.C. coastal waters	
1781	August 9–10		S.C. coastal waters	
1783	October 7–8		Ga. and S.C. coastal waters	
1785	September 23–24		Offshore Ga. and S.C.	
1787	October 19		Offshore	

STORM SURGE (EST. FEET)	DEATHS (EST.)	DAMAGES (EST. 2003 DOLLARS)	NAME	COMMENTS
				Contemporaries called it "horrid and destructive."
	100+	$5,040,222		Cut inlet at Winyah Bay.
	70+	$11,833,564		Called a "Great Storm."
				"Deer lodged in trees."
				Especially damaging to shipping.
	95–200	One colonialist alone lost $2,177,376 in trees.		Extensive crop damage; remembered as "*the* Great Hurricane."
				Especially damaging to shipping and crops.
				Heavy damage to shipping and crops.
				Heavy damage to shipping.
				Damage to shipping and crops.
				Heavy damage to British warships at Charleston.
				A witness called it "a most violent storm of wind."
				Heavy damage to offshore shipping.
	23+			Crops damaged.

YEAR	MONTH/DAY	CATEGORY IF KNOWN	OFFSHORE/ LANDFALL AREA	WIND SPEED (EST. MPH)
1792	October 30–November 1		Offshore	
1797	September 8		Ga. coastal waters	
1797	October 17–20		Ga. coastal waters/ landfall near Charleston	
1800	October 4		S.C. coast/ landfall Charleston	
1804	September 7–8	Major hurricane	Ga. and S.C. coast	111+
1806	August 22–23		Offshore/Georgetown	
1811	September 8–10		Offshore/Charleston	
1811	October 4		Ga. coastal waters	
1813	August 25–27		Ga. and S.C. coastal waters/ landfall between Charleston and Georgetown	
1813	September 16–17	Major hurricane	Lower Ga. coast	111+
1815	August 31–September 1		Offshore/Ga. and S.C. coasts	
1819	August	Tropical storm (?)	Lower Ga. coast	
1820	September 10–11		Landfall near Georgetown	
1822	September 27–28		Offshore Ga./landfall upper S.C. coast	
1824	September 14–15	Major hurricane	Offshore/coastal waters of Ga. and S.C./landfall near St. Simons and Darien	
1825	June 3–5	Tropical storm (?)	Offshore/coast of Ga. and S.C.	

STORM SURGE (EST. FEET)	DEATHS (EST.)	DAMAGES (EST. 2003 DOLLARS)	NAME	COMMENTS
				"Winds blew with great violence" at Charleston.
	133+			
	14+			Raged with "violence" at Charleston; spawned tornado at Georgetown.
	3			Spawned tornado at Charleston; tremendous and destructive at Charleston.
	500+	$7,475,610 at Savannah; $14,951,220 at Charleston.		Huge losses in lives and property.
	23+			*Rose-in-Bloom* sinks; 23 drown.
	20+	$4,027,007		Spawns tornado.
	33			Gunboat #2 sinks; 33 drown.
12 at Charleston	23+	$22,156,626 at Charleston.		At Charleston sailing craft "beat to pieces."
19 at St. Marys	22+			Catastrophic damage at St. Marys and on Ga. sea islands.
	Sailors perish offshore			Heavy damage to vessels offshore.
				Crops ruined.
				A "violent hurricane."
	300+	$7,536,885 property damage in Georgetown area.		Immense property and crop losses.
	150+	Financial losses in Darien $18,207,920.		Vessels, crops, and farm animals lost.
				Crop losses.

YEAR	MONTH / DAY	CATEGORY IF KNOWN	OFFSHORE / LANDFALL AREA	WIND SPEED (EST. MPH)
1827	August 23–25		Offshore	
1830	August 15–16		Offshore/upper S.C. coast	
1834	September 4		Landfall near Georgetown	
1835	September 15–18		Center moved across Ga. and S.C.	
1837	August 6		Lower Ga. coast	
1837	August 16–19		Center offshore Ga. and S.C.	
1837	October 8–9		Offshore	
1842	October 4–5		Lower Ga. coast	
1846	October 11–13		Lowcountry	
1848	October 12–13		Ga. coast	
1851	August 23		Ga. coast	
1853	October 20–21		Lower Ga. coast and S.C. coastal waters	
1854	September 7–8	Major hurricane (3)	Offshore/landfall between Brunswick and Savannah	111+
1857	September 10–12		Offshore	
1865	October 24–25	Tropical storm (?)	Offshore	
1871	August 18–19		Offshore/landfall near St. Simons	
1873	October 6	Tropical storm (?)	Offshore	
1874	September 28		Lowcountry	
1878	September 12		Offshore/landfall south of Charleston	

STORM SURGE (EST. FEET)	DEATHS (EST.)	DAMAGES (EST. 2003 DOLLARS)	NAME	COMMENTS
	6+			A ship's captain said it "blew like a hurricane"; battered vessels offshore.
				Disasters at sea; enormous crop losses.
				Heavy crop losses.
				Damage to shipping and huge crop losses.
	16+			ss *Mills* sinks; shipping and crops battered.
	Offshore deaths			Offshore shipping battered; onshore crop losses.
	70+			*Home* sinks.
	5+			Slow moving; heavy crop losses.
	1+			
				Crop losses.
				"Extremely violent."
				Brunswick battered.
	Numerous deaths offshore			Slow moving; heavy damage to vessels at sea, property, and crops.
	423			*Central America* sinks.
	17			*Republic* sinks.
		Damages to public works in Savannah $1,448,031.		Shipping battered; crops destroyed.
				Vessels damaged.
	2	$11,590,335 in Charleston and vicinity.		"The sea in [Charleston] has rolled mountain high."
				Crops ruined.

YEAR	MONTH / DAY	CATEGORY IF KNOWN	OFFSHORE/ LANDFALL AREA	WIND SPEED (EST. MPH)
1881	August 26		Offshore/upper Ga. coast and lower S.C. coast	85 at Savannah
1883	September 9–11		Offshore	93
1885	August 24–25		Offshore/upper Ga. coast and lower S.C. coast	84 at Tybee Islan 125 at Charlesto
1893	August 27–28	Major hurricane (3)	Offshore/coastal S.C. and Ga./landfall south of Tybee Island	111+
1893	October 12–13		Offshore/landfall north of Georgetown	
1896	September 29		Ga. and lower S.C. coast	108 at Tybee Island
1898	August 29–31		Upper Ga. and lower S.C. coast	85–100 at Tybee Island
1898	October 1–2	Major hurricane (4)	Offshore/landfall Cumberland Island	111
1904	September 13		Offshore/upper S.C. coast	80–95
1906	September 16–17		Offshore/upper S.C. coast	80 offshore
1906	October 18–20		Offshore	
1910	October 18–19		Offshore	
1911	August 27–28		Offshore/landfall near mouth of Savannah River	100 at Sullivan's Island

STORM SURGE (EST. FEET)	DEATHS (EST.)	DAMAGES (EST. 2003 DOLLARS)	NAME	COMMENTS
15 at Beaufort	350+	Structural damages in lowcountry reach $34,373,830.		Massive damage to vessels at sea and crops; "havoc and desolation" at Savannah.
	21+	Excluding private real estate, $36,415,840 in damages in Charleston.		
	2,000–3,000	Property losses in S.C. $195,638,290.		"Six feet of water covered" Tybee Island; "hurricane raged for hours" along lowcountry; crops and phosphate industry severely damaged.
	18+			
	36+	Property damage in Savannah $20,897,727.		Brunswick "wrecked."
	3			Crops ruined.
16 on lower Ga. coast	139+	$42,275,862		Crops ruined and phosphate industry again damaged.
	11 deaths at sea	$26,661,289 on upper S.C. coast.		Vessels battered; crops ruined.
	7	$6,847,340 loss to turpentine industry.		Vessels at sea damaged; crops destroyed; turpentine farmers ruined.
				Tides at "astonishing heights" devastate S.C. rice crops.
	Numerous deaths at sea; 20+ ashore	$18,575,757 at Charleston.		Heavy damage to crops and property.

YEAR	MONTH/DAY	CATEGORY IF KNOWN	OFFSHORE/ LANDFALL AREA	WIND SPEED (EST. MPH)
1916	July 13–14		Landfall upper S.C. coast	90–110
1928	September 17–18		Landfall west of St. Marys	75 at Beaufort
1940	August 11–12		Landfall in vicinity of Beaufort and Edisto Island	75–100 at Folly Beach
1947	October 15–16		Ga. coast	90
1952	August 31		Landfall Edisto Island	90
1954	October 15		Landfall near border of S.C. and N.C.	100+
1959	September 29		Landfall north of Beaufort	125
1964	September 12–13		Landfall lower Ga. coast	90+
1979	September 4	1	Landfall Ossabaw Island and moved west of Tybee Island and Savannah	70–90
1989	September 21–22	4	Landfall upper S.C. coast	140
1999	September 15		Offshore	Wind gusts to along lowcoun coast
2004	August 14		Offshore	Wind gusts to on upper S.C. coast
2004	August 29		Offshore	Wind gusts to along lowcoun coast

STORM SURGE (EST. FEET)	DEATHS (EST.)	DAMAGES (EST. 2003 DOLLARS)	NAME	COMMENTS
	7	$10,122,936 on upper S.C. coast.		Thousands of trees down; crops ruined.
		Charleston area damage $1,075,440.		Folly Beach "devastated."
13 at St. Helena and Folly Beach	3	$13,135,714 in damages at Beaufort and sea islands; $52,542,856 at Savannah.		
12 at Tybee Island		$12,369,954 at Tybee Island and Savannah.		
		$20,818,867 in S.C.	Able	U.S. Weather Bureau begins naming hurricanes.
	1	$184,572,000 on upper S.C. coast.	Hazel	
	4	$12,639,175 in Beaufort; $26,542,267 in Charleston and Charleston County.	Gracie	
		$47,458,064 damages in Ga.	Dora	Slow-moving hurricane pounds Brunswick and St. Simons.
		$10,132,231 in Savannah and Chatham County; $17,731,404 on upper S.C. coast.	David	
17–20	8	$7,415,322,500 in S.C.	Hugo	
			Floyd	Power lines down, some flooding.
		$2,000,000 on upper S.C. coast	Charley	Wave and wind damage at Myrtle Beach.
			Gaston	Power lines and trees downed.

Notes

Chapter One. The Early Years, 1686–1797

1. Fraser, *Charleston! Charleston!* 6–8; Ludlum, *Early American Hurricanes*, 41–42; Bartram, *Diary of a Journey*, 20; Rowland, *History of Beaufort County*, 72–74.

2. According to the new-style calendar, which is used hereinafter, this would have been early September.

3. Barnes, *North Carolina's Hurricane History*, 14.

4. Barnes, *Florida's Hurricane History*, 32.

5. Ibid.

6. Ludlum, *Early American Hurricanes*, 41–42; Bartram, *Diary of a Journey*, 20.

7. Sandrik and Landsea, "Tropical Cyclones," 1–3; Sheets and Williams, *Hurricane Watch*, 155–56; Mock, "Tropical Cyclone Reconstructions"; Barnes, *North Carolina's Hurricane History*, 23.

8. Barnes, *North Carolina's Hurricane History*, 6–8, 14–25; Barnes, *Florida's Hurricane History*, 6–8, 21–30; Pielke and Pielke, *Hurricanes*, 68–73, 118–27; Tannehill, *Hurricanes*, 26–28; Scotti, *Sudden Sea*, 23, 34, 46.

9. Arsenault, "Long Hot Summer."

10. Stewart, "'Let Us Begin.'"

11. Cowdrey, *This Land, This South*, 7; Edgar, *South Carolina*, 4–5, 6–8; Fraser, *Savannah*, 1; Jordan, "Tropical Storms"; Kilgo, "Tidewater Heritage"; Sullivan, "Touring Coastal Georgia"; Smythe, *Carolina Low-Country*, 6–29.

12. Fraser, *Charleston! Charleston!* 8–9.

13. Fraser, *Savannah*, 1, 3–4, 5; Smythe, *Carolina Low-Country*, 26–29; Fraser, *Charleston! Charleston!* 449n16; Edgar, *South Carolina*, 8–10, 51, 156–59; Merrens and Terry, "Dying in Paradise"; Coleman, *History of Georgia*, 40.

14. Fraser, *Savannah*, 9–10.

15. Ramsay, *History of South Carolina*, 176.

16. Calhoun, *Scourging Wrath of God*, 3–4.

17. Ludlum, *Early American Hurricanes*, 42; Hewatt, *Colonies of South Carolina and Georgia*, 142; Jordan, "History of Storms," 17; Spence, *Guide to South Carolina*, 49.

18. Ibid.

19. Hereinafter, following each estimate of the hurricane damage at the time is an estimate of the damage in 2003–4 U.S. dollars. For conversion tables from pounds to dollars, see McCusker, "How Much Is That?"; for conversion formulas using the Consumer Price Index from pounds to dollars, 1991–2003, see McKenna, "Formulas for Estimating Cost."

20. Fraser, *Charleston! Charleston!* 16–31.

21. Ibid., 31–32; Ludlum, *Early American Hurricanes*, 42–43; Jordan, "History of Storms," 17; Bartram, *Diary of a Journey*, 20; Klingberg, *Carolina Chronicle*, 137, 159.

22. Fraser, *Charleston! Charleston!* 32–38; Rowland, *History of Beaufort County*, 95–103; Edgar, *South Carolina*, 98–108.

23. Bartram, *Diary of a Journey*, 20.

24. Ibid.; Meyers, *Empire's Nature*, 74.

25. Fraser, *Charleston! Charleston!* 37–44.

26. Ibid.; Calhoun, *Scourging Wrath of God*, 5.

27. Ludlum, *Early American Hurricanes*, 43–44; Bartram, *Diary of a Journey*, 20; Hewatt, *Historical Account*, 316; Jordan, "History of Storms," 18; Ramsay, *History of South Carolina*, 176–77; Spence, *Guide to South Carolina*, 49.

28. Fraser, *Charleston! Charleston!* 45–52; Edgar, *South Carolina*, 49–52, 63–66, 139–44, 153–63; Purvis, *Listing of Tropical Cyclones*, 7.

29. Coleman, *History of Georgia*, 32–33.

30. Mock, "Tropical Cyclone Reconstructions," 23.

31. Quoted in Tresp, "September, 1748 in Georgia," 323; Rogers, *History of Georgetown County*, 45; Spence, *Shipwrecks, Pirates and Privateers*, 13, 66, 71, 73; Rogers, *History of Georgetown County*, 254.

32. Fraser, *Charleston! Charleston!* 83.

33. *South Carolina Gazette*, September 1, 19, October 10, 1752.

34. Wood and Bullard, *Journal of a Visit*, 29; Keber, *Seas of Gold*, 205.

35. A composite of the impact hurricanes have on ships at sea by a student of hurricanes is found in Douglas, *Hurricane*, 3–4; *South Carolina Gazette*, September 1, 19, 1752.

36. Pielke and Pielke, *Hurricanes*, 118–19; *South Carolina Gazette*, September 1, 19, October 10, 1752.

37. Sandrik and Landsea, "Tropical Cyclones," 3, 9. Sandrik, Senior Forecaster, NOAA, and Landsea, Hurricane Research Division, NOAA, use the term *hurricane* to describe a tropical cyclone in which maximum sustained wind speed is 74 miles per hour or greater, and the term *major hurricane* to describe tropical cyclones in which sustained wind speed is 111 miles per hour or greater; these definitions are based on the Saffir-Simpson Hurricane Potential Damage Scale; Ludlum, *Early American Hurricanes*, 43–46.

38. Sandrik and Landsea, "Tropical Cyclones," 9; *South Carolina Gazette*, September 19, 27, 1752; Fraser, *Charleston! Charleston!* 83–84; Spence, *Guide to South Carolina*, 52–53; Jordan, "History of Storms," 18–19; Ludlum, *Early American Hurricanes*, 43–46; Ramsay, *History of South Carolina*, 177–79; Calhoun, *Scourging Wrath of God*, 5–8.

39. Fraser, *Charleston! Charleston!* 83–84; Calhoun, *Scourging Wrath of God*, 5–8.

40. Ibid.

41. Artemas Elliott to "My Dear Child [Polly Elliott]," October 16, 1752, Cochran Family Papers, Bacot-Huger Collection, South Carolina Historical Society.

42. *South Carolina Gazette*, September 19, 27, 1752.

43. Fraser, *Charleston! Charleston!* 83–84; Spence, *Guide to South Carolina*, 52–53; Jordan, "History of Storms," 18–19; Ludlum, *Early American Hurricanes*, 43–46; Ramsay, *History of South Carolina*, 177–79; Calhoun, *Scourging Wrath of God*, 5–8.

44. Ibid.

45. *South Carolina Gazette*, October 3, 9, 10, 1752; Jordan, "History of Storms," 18–19.

46. Ludlum, *Early American Hurricanes*, 48; *South Carolina Gazette*, October 3, 1752.

47. Peter Manigault to Gabriel Manigault, December 14, 1752, in Webber, "Peter Manigault's Letters," 116.

48. Sandrik and Landsea, "Tropical Cyclones," 10; Mock, "Tropical Cyclone Reconstructions," 23; Tannehill, *Hurricanes*, 244.

49. "Petition of the Merchants . . . and Others Interested in the Trade and Prosperity of South Carolina and Georgia [London] 21st December 1756," in Hamer, *Papers of Henry Laurens*, 378–80.

50. Sandrik and Landsea, "Tropical Cyclones," 9–10; Mock, "Tropical Cyclone Reconstructions," 23.

51. Henry Laurens to Peter Furnell, November 18, 1755.

52. Henry Laurens to John Knight, October 12, 1756, January 6, 1757, to Thomas Rumbold and Co., October 15, 1756, November 18, 1756, January 6, 1757, in Hamer, *Papers of Henry Laurens*, 14–15, 333–36, 338–39, 355–56, 397–99.

53. Henry Laurens to John Loveday, June 21, 1777, in Chesnutt, *Papers of Henry Laurens*, 385.

54. Ellis, "Heat and Weather"; Fraser, *Savannah*, 48, 56; Sandrik and Landsea, "Tropical Cyclones," 10; Mock, "Tropical Cyclone Reconstructions," 23; Purvis, *Tropical Cyclones*, 8.

55. Bartram, *Diary of a Journey*, 20.

56. Quoted in Edgar, *South Carolina*, 155; Fraser, *Charleston! Charleston!* 124.

57. Spence, *Guide to South Carolina*, 54–55.

58. *Carolina and American General Gazette*, August 23–30, September 13–18, September 18–25, September 26–October 2, October 2–October 9, 1769; Barnes, *North Carolina's Hurricane History*, 36.

59. Quoted in Sandrik and Landsea, "Tropical Cyclones," 11.

60. Henry Laurens to Henry Bright & Co., September 21, 1769, to John Rutherford, October 13, 1769, in Rogers, *Papers of Henry Laurens*, 140–41, 158–60.

61. Henry Laurens to Richard Grubb, September 8, 1770, in Rogers, *Papers of Henry Laurens*, 346–48.

62. *South Carolina and American General Gazette*, November 2–9, 1769.

63. *Carolina Gazette*, June 19, 1770; *Carolina Gazette and Country Journal*, July 3, 1770.

64. Hewatt, *Historical Account*, 316.

65. Spence, *Guide to South Carolina*, 55; Jordan, "History of Storms," 19.

66. Henry Laurens to Mayne & Co., August 1, 1770, in Rogers, *Papers of Henry Laurens*, 317; Henry Laurens to Richard Grubb, September 8, 1770, in Rogers, *Papers of Henry Laurens*, 348; Fraser, *Savannah*, 62.

67. Fraser, *Charleston! Charleston!* 115–34; Fraser, *Savannah*, 98–113.

68. Ludlum, *Early American Hurricanes*, 27, 49–50; Spence, *Guide to South Carolina*, 56; Fraser, *Charleston! Charleston!* 157; Jordan, "History of Storms," 19.

69. Barnes, *Florida's Hurricane History*, 41–59; Fraser, *Savannah*, 124–33.

70. Barnes, *Florida's Hurricane History*, 41–59; Douglas, *Hurricane*, 161.

71. Quoted in Douglas, *Hurricane*, 167–69.

72. Douglas, *Hurricane*, 166.

73. Ludlum, *Early American Hurricanes*, 50; Spence, *Guide to South Carolina*, 57; Sandrik and Landsea, "Tropical Cyclones," 12.

74. Barnes, *Florida's Hurricane History*, 51.

75. Fraser, *Savannah*, 134–32; Fraser, *Charleston! Charleston!* 167–75; Rowland, *History of Beaufort County*, 254–56.

76. Ibid.

77. *South Carolina Gazette and General Advertiser*, September 6, 1783.

78. Ibid., October 8, 1783; *South Carolina Weekly Gazette*, October 11, 1783; Ludlum, *Early American Hurricanes*, 50–51; Spence, *Guide to South Carolina*, 57.

79. *South Carolina Gazette and General Advertiser*, October 11, 1783.

80. Ibid., October 22, 1783.

81. *South Carolina Weekly Gazette*, October 11, 1783.

82. Jordan, "History of Storms," 20; Tannehill, *Hurricanes*, 247; Ludlum, *Early American Hurricanes*, 30; Spence, *Guide to South Carolina*, 57–58.

83. *Charleston Daily Advertiser*, November 2, 1792; Tannehill, *Hurricanes*, 248.

84. Ludlum, *Early American Hurricanes*, 51.

85. *Columbian Museum and Savannah Advertiser*, September 15, 1797.

86. Ibid.

87. *Savannah Gazette*, November 24, 1797; Sandrik and Landsea, "Tropical Cyclones," 13.

88. *Savannah Gazette*, November 3, 1797; Ludlum, *Early American Hurricanes*, 51–52.

89. Ibid.

90. *Savannah Gazette*, November 10, 1797.

91. Ibid.

92. Ibid.

93. Ibid.

Chapter Two. First Storms of the New Century, 1800–1804

1. Fraser, *Charleston! Charleston!* 178, 187–88; Fraser, *Savannah*, 152–54; Edgar, *South Carolina*, 260.

2. Ibid.

3. *Carolina Gazette*, September 25, 1800.

4. Ibid., October 9, 1800; Ludlum, *Early American Hurricanes*, 52–53; Bossak, "Early Nineteenth-Century," 37.

5. Ibid.

6. *Carolina Gazette*, October 9, 1800.

7. *Charleston Courier*, September 29, 1804.

8. Ibid.

9. Ibid.

10. *Times* (London), November 3, 5, 19, 1804; *Charleston Courier*, September 15, 1804.

11. *Charleston Courier*, September 26, 28, 29, 1804.

12. Ibid., September 13, 1804.

13. Ibid., September 14, 1804.

14. Ibid., September 28, 1804; *Columbian Museum and Savannah Advertiser*, October 7, 1804.

15. *Charleston Courier*, September 12, 1804.

16. Ferguson, *Couper Family*, 142–43; Stegeman and Stegeman, *Caty*, 183–85; Bagwell, *Rice Gold*, 4; "Hurricane of 1804—Tybee Island," 1–2, Heyward-Hawkins Papers, Georgia Historical Society; Ralston B. Lattimore, "Destruction of Fort Greene," 2–7, Savannah Historical Research Association Collection, Georgia Historical Society.

17. Ludlum, *Early American Hurricanes*, 54; Sandrik and Landsea, "Tropical Cyclones," 13; Keber, *Seas of Gold*, 204–5.

18. Ferguson, *Couper Family*, 142–44; Bullard, *Robert Stafford*, 189.

19. Stegeman and Stegeman, *Caty*, 185; Cochran, *Cumberland Island*, 10–12.

20. Keber, *Seas of Gold*, 204–5; *Columbian Museum and Savannah Advertiser*, August 29, 1804.

21. Keber, *Seas of Gold*, 204–5.

22. Lovell, *Golden Isles of Georgia*, 85–86; Bell, *Major Butler's Legacy*, 112–15, 143; Caroline S. Coleman, "The Hurricane of 1804," *Charleston News and Courier*, October 9, 1938.

23. Quoted in Bell, *Major Butler's Legacy*, 143.

24. Lovell, *Golden Isles*, 183–86; Bell, *Major Butler's Legacy*, 143; Sullivan, *Georgia Tidewater*, 173–74.

25. *Columbian Museum and Savannah Advertiser*, September 19, 1804; Ferguson, *Couper Family*, 143–44; Ramsay, *History of South Carolina*, 184.

26. Wood and Wood, "Reuben King Journal."

27. *Columbian Museum and Savannah Advertiser*, September 19, 1804.

28. "Hurricane of 1804—Tybee Island," 1–3.

29. *Charleston Courier*, September 19, 1804; Lattimore, "Destruction of Fort Greene," 2–7.

30. Ibid.

31. Ibid.

32. Screven, "Georgia Bryans and Screvens"; *Columbian Museum and Savannah Advertiser*, September 12, 1804.

33. *Columbian Museum and Savannah Advertiser*, September 12, 1804; *Georgia Republican and State Intelligencer*, September 14, 1804; *Charleston Courier*, September 15, 19, 1804.

34. Ibid.

35. Ibid.

36. Ibid.

37. *Charleston Courier*, September 22, 1804.

38. *Columbian Museum and Savannah Advertiser*, September 22, 1804; *Charleston Courier*, September 18, 1804.

39. Ibid.

40. *Charleston Courier*, September 20, 1804.

41. Ibid., September 10, 11, 12, 1804.

42. Ibid.

43. Ibid.

44. Seth Lothrop to "Dear Brother," September 18, 1804, Sylvanus Keith and Cary Keith Papers, William R. Perkins Library, Duke University; *Times* (London), November 2, 1804.

45. Ibid.

46. *Charleston Courier*, September 12, 13, 15, 1804; *Columbian Museum and Savannah Advertiser*, September 15, 1804.

47. Ibid.

48. *Charleston Courier*, September 14, 1804; *Columbian Museum and Savannah Advertiser*, September 19, 1804.

49. *Charleston Courier*, September 15, 1804; *Columbian Museum and Savannah Advertiser*, September 19, 1804; *Savannah Republican and State Intelligencer*, October 2, 1804.

50. Ibid.

51. Ibid.

52. *Charleston Courier*, September 15, 1804.

53. *Charleston City Gazette*, September 19, 1804; *Times* (London), November 5, 1804.

54. Seth Lothrop to "Dear Brother," September 18, 1804.

55. *Charleston Courier*, September 10, 11, 1804.

56. Ibid., September 10, 20, 1804; Seth Lothrop to "Dear Brother," September 18, 1804.

57. *Charleston Courier*, September 10, 20, 1804; Seth Lothrop to "Dear Brother," September 18, 1804.

58. *Columbian Museum and Savannah Advertiser*, September 22, 1804.

59. Seth Lothrop to "Dear Brother," September 18, 1804; Frederick Rutledge to John Rutledge, September [?], 22, 1804, John Rutledge Papers, University of North Carolina; Dunn and Miller, *Atlantic Hurricanes*, 294.

60. *Charleston Courier*, September 12, 15, 24, 26, 27, 28, 1804.

61. Ludlum, *Early American Hurricanes*, 55; *Times* (London), November 5, 1804.

Chapter Three. A Cycle of Hurricanes, 1806–1824

1. *Charleston News and Courier*, September 2, 2001.

2. *Georgia Republican and State Intelligencer*, September 16, 1806; Edgar, *Biographical Directory*, 1:500–502.

3. *Georgia Republican and State Intelligencer*, September 16, 1806; Ludlum, *Early American Hurricanes*, 55–56.

4. Isaac F. Arnow, "History of St. Marys and Camden County," *Camden County Tribune*, March 7, 1952.

5. Keber, *Seas of Gold*, 245; H. [Rutledge] to John Rutledge, Esq., September 9, 1806, Col. John Rutledge to Robert Lenox, Esq., September 9, 1806, John Rutledge Papers, Southern Historical Collection, University of North Carolina.

6. Quoted in Ludlum, *Early American Hurricanes*, 55.

7. *Georgia Republican and State Intelligencer*, September 9, 1806.

8. "Extract from the Log Book of ship *Thomas Chalkely*," *Georgia Republican and State Intelligencer*, September 9, 1806.

9. *Georgia Republican and State Intelligencer*, September 9, 1806; Spence, *Shipwrecks, Privates and Privateers*, 89.

10. *Georgia Republican and State Intelligencer*, September 16, 1806.

11. Ibid.

12. Ibid.

13. Ludlum, *Early American Hurricanes*, 55–56.

14. Rutledge to Rutledge, September 9, 1806; Rutledge to Lenox, September 9, 1806; Eliza Laurens to John Rutledge, Esq., September 10, 1806; Charles C. Pinckney to John Rutledge, Esq., September 10, 1806, all John Rutledge Papers, Southern Historical Collection, University of North Carolina.

15. Ibid.

16. Ludlum, *Early American Hurricanes*, 57; Spence, *Guide to South Carolina*, 61.

17. *Charleston Courier*, September 14, 20, 21, 1811; Ludlum, *Early American Hurricanes*.

18. Ibid.

19. *Charleston Courier*, September 11, 12, 14, 17, 1811; *Charleston News and Courier*, October 23, 1910.

20. Ibid.

21. A. Moubray to William Moubray, January 12, 1812, vertical file, South Carolina Historical Society.

22. *Charleston Courier,* September 14, 20, 21, 1811.

23. Fraser, *Savannah,* 179–80; Fraser, *Charleston! Charleston!* 191–92; Rogers, *History of Georgetown County,* 232; Keber, *Seas of Gold,* 206–7, 213.

24. Ibid.

25. *Anti-Monarchist and South Carolina Advertiser* (Edgefield, S.C.), November 2, 1811.

26. Ibid.

27. Ibid.

28. Tannehill, *Hurricanes,* 249–50; Ludlum, *Early American Hurricanes,* 58; Sandrik and Landsea, "Tropical Cyclones," 15.

29. *Charleston Courier,* August 30, September 1, 3, 4, 8, 1813; *Washington (Ga.) Monitor,* September 18, 1813.

30. Ibid. There is some difference of opinion as to whether the *Moselle* or *Colibri* went down in the breakers at the mouth of the Broad River and whether both sank.

31. Ibid.

32. *Charleston Courier,* August 30, September 1, 1813; *Republican and Savannah Evening Ledger,* September 2, 1813; Sandrik and Landsea, "Tropical Cyclones," 22.

33. *Charleston Courier,* August 31, 1813.

34. *Republican and Savannah Evening Ledger,* September 2, 1813; *Charleston Courier,* August 30, 1813; Ludlum, *Early American Hurricanes,* 58–59; Spence, *Guide to South Carolina,* 61; Jordan, "History of Storms," 22.

35. Ibid.

36. *Charleston Courier,* August 30, 31, September 2, 1813; Purvis, "Listing of Tropical Cyclones," 12.

37. Wade, "Fort Winyaw at Georgetown"; *Republican and Savannah Evening Ledger,* September 2, 1813.

38. Dunn and Miller, *Atlantic Hurricanes,* 294; Ludlum, *Early American Hurricanes,* 59.

39. Arnow, "History of St. Marys."

40. Bullard, *Robert Stafford,* 190–91; Bullard, *Cumberland Island,* 99–101.

41. Arnow, "History of St. Marys"; Reddick, *Camden's Challenge,* 150.

42. Ibid.

43. Sandrik and Landsea, "Tropical Cyclones," 16.

44. Ludlum, *Early American Hurricanes,* 58; *Charleston Courier,* August 30, 1813.

45. John Floyd to Miss Mary Floyd, October 7, 1813, "Letters of John Floyd, 1813–1838," *Georgia Historical Quarterly* 33 (September 1949): 228–33.

46. Ibid., 228.

47. Quoted in Keber, *Seas of Gold,* 213.

48. Keber, *Seas of Gold,* 213–14, 236, 245.

49. Lash, "Martin Luther Hurlbut," 305–16.

50. Joseph Bennett to Samuel Law, September 18, 1818, Joseph Bennett Letter, South Caroliniana Library, University of South Carolina.

51. Tannehill, *Hurricanes*, 250; Purvis, "Listing of Tropical Cyclones," 13.

52. *Charleston Courier*, September 2, 4, 1815; Tannehill, *Hurricanes*, 250; Spence, *Shipwrecks, Privates and Privateers*, 98.

53. *Charleston Courier*, September 4, 9, 12, 15, 1815.

54. Ibid., September 8, 9, 1815; Ludlum, *Early American Hurricanes*, 112–13.

55. *Savannah Republican*, September 21, 23, 25, 1815.

56. Sandrik and Landsea, "Tropical Cyclones," 16–17.

57. Sullivan, *Early Days on the Georgia Tidewater*, 99–101; Vanstory, *Golden Isles*, 46–48; Purvis, "Listing of Tropical Cyclones," 13; Coulter, *Thomas Spalding*, 43–47, 124.

58. Quoted in Coulter, *Thomas Spalding*, 47; Ludlum, *Early American Hurricanes*, 251; Sandrik and Landsea, "Tropical Cyclones," 17.

59. Ludlum, *Early American Hurricanes*, 113–14.

60. Ibid.

61. *Charleston Mercury*, October 9, 12, 1822; *Charleston Courier*, October 9, 1822.

62. Ibid.

63. *Charleston Courier*, October 7, 1822.

64. Ibid., September 30, October 1, 8, 1822.

65. Ibid., September 30, October 2, 4, 1822.

66. Ibid., September 30, October 17, 1822.

67. Ibid., September 30, October 1, 1822; *Savannah Museum*, October 1, 1822.

68. *Charleston Courier*, September 30, 1822; *Charleston Mercury*, September 30, 1822; Ball, *Slaves in the Family*, 261.

69. *Charleston Courier*, September 30, 1822; *Charleston Mercury*, September 30, 1822; Ludlum, *Early American Hurricanes*, 114–16.

70. M. L. Beach to Elizabeth L. Gilchrist, September 28, 1822, Mary Lamboll Thomas Beach Papers, South Carolina Historical Society; *Charleston Mercury*, September 30, 1822; *Charleston Courier*, September 30, 1822; *Savannah Museum*, October 1, 1822.

71. Catherine McBeth to "My Brother," October 4, 1822, McBeth Family Papers, South Carolina Historical Society.

72. Ralph Izard to Alice Izard, October 9, 1822, Izard Family Papers, South Carolina Historical Society; McBeth to "My Brother," October 4, 1822.

73. *Charleston Mercury*, September 30, 1822; *Charleston Courier*, September 30, 1822; *Savannah Museum*, October 1, 1822; Izard to Izard, October 9, 1822.

74. Ibid.

75. Izard to Izard, October 9, 1822; *Charleston Mercury*, September 30, October 1, 1822.

76. Ibid.

77. *Charleston Mercury*, September 30, October 1, 1822; Izard to Izard, October 9, 1822.

78. *Charleston Mercury*, September 30, October 1, 1822; *Charleston Courier*, September 30, 1822; Izard to Izard, October 9, 1822.

79. Ibid.

80. "Lines Supposed to be written on Sullivan's Island on the night of the 27th September, during the Gale," *Charleston Courier*, October 17, 1822.

81. "Extract of the Logbook of the United States Revenue Cutter, *Gallatin*," *Charleston Courier*, October 1, 2, 1822.

82. Gill, *Reminiscences in Williamsburg County*, 9–11; *Charleston Mercury*, October 1, 2, 1822; *Charleston Courier*, October 3, 4, 14, 1822; *Charleston News and Courier*, October 21, 1893.

83. Ibid. The account of the Withers's home floating out to sea with its lamps lit — perhaps embellished over time by witnesses — is told by Prevost and Wilder in *Pawley's Island*, 52.

84. *Charleston Mercury*, October 3, 1822; *Charleston Courier*, October 3, 12, 1822.

85. "Extract of a letter from Long Bay, Waccamaw, dated Sunday, 29th [1822]," *Charleston Courier*, October 4, 1822.

86. *Charleston Mercury*, September 30, October 2, 4, 1822; *Charleston Courier*, 1, 2, 4, 12, 1822.

87. Izard to Izard, October 9, 1822.

88. *Charleston Mercury*, October 7, 12, 19, 1822; *Charleston Courier*, October 14, 1822.

89. Charles Steadman, "Autobiography of Rear Admiral Charles Steadman," manuscript, South Carolina Historical Society.

90. "The Tempest," *Charleston Courier*, October 1, 1822.

91. Jordan, "Tropical Storms," 2.

92. Rogers, *History of Georgetown County*, 226; Ludlum, *Early American Hurricanes*, 115.

93. Sandrik and Landsea, "Tropical Cyclones," 17.

94. *Daily Georgian*, September 18, October 2, 1824; *Charleston Courier*, September 18, 20, October 8, 11, 1824.

95. Ibid.

96. *Daily Georgian*, September 21, 30, October 2, 9, 19, 1824; *Charleston Courier*, September 25, 30, October 4, 8, 11, 1824.

97. *Charleston Courier*, September 18, 1824.

98. Sandrik and Landsea, "Tropical Cyclones," 17; *Charleston Courier*, September 16, 24, 1824; Ludlum, *Early American Hurricanes*, 116.

99. *Daily Georgian*, October 12, 1824; *Charleston Courier*, September 21, 1824.

100. *Daily Georgian*, September 18, 28, October 19, 1824; *Charleston Courier*, September 21, 24, 25, 28, October 8, 1824.

101. Keber, *Seas of Gold*, 244–45.

102. Sandrik and Landsea, "Tropical Cyclones," 17.

103. *Daily Georgian*, September 25, October 9, 1824; *Charleston Courier*, September 25, 27, 1824; Coulter, *Thomas Spalding*, 100–101, 104–5, 126–27; Keber, *Seas of Gold*, 245.

104. Ibid.

105. Ibid.

106. "Extract of a letter received from a friend in the country, dated Sept. 15," *Charleston Courier*, October 11, 1824.

107. *Charleston Courier*, October 11, 1824; *Daily Georgian*, September 25, October 9, 1824; Coulter, *Thomas Spalding*, 48, 206–7.

108. Ibid.

109. *Daily Georgian*, September 18, 25, 1824; *Charleston Courier*, September 25, 1854.

110. *Daily Georgian*, September 18, 1824; *Charleston Courier*, September 23, 24, 27, October 1, 1824; Sandrik and Landsea, "Tropical Cyclones," 18.

111. Ibid.

112. *Charleston Courier*, September 24, 25, 1824; *Daily Georgian*, September 28, 30, 1824.

113. *Charleston Courier*, September 16, 21, 1824.

114. *Daily Georgian*, September 28, 30, October 2, 1824; *Charleston Courier*, September 27, 29, 1824.

Chapter Four. Last Storms of the Cycle, 1825–1837

1. *Daily Georgian*, September 30, 1824.

2. "Extract of a letter of . . . September 15th," *Daily Georgian*, October 9, 1824.

3. "Extract of another letter from the country, dated September 15th," *Daily Georgian*, October 9, 1824.

4. "Extract of a letter received from a friend in the country, dated September 15th, 1824," *Charleston Courier*, October 11, 1824.

5. James Couper to [John Couper], March 7, 1825; John Couper to [James Couper], May 24, 1828, Couper Family Papers, Coastal Georgia Historical Society.

6. Quoted in Coulter, *Thomas Spalding*, 49.

7. Coulter, Thomas *Spalding*, 44.

8. Keber, *Seas of Gold*, 234–36, 244–46.

9. Coclanis, *Shadow of a Dream*, 111–58; Fraser, *Charleston! Charleston!* 227, 235; Coclanis, introduction to *Seed from Madagascar*, ix–xviii; Fraser, *Savannah*, 254–55.

10. *Charleston Mercury*, August 23, 1822; *Charleston Courier*, October 8, 1824.

11. *Savannah Republican*, June 7, 16, 1825; *Charleston Courier*, June 10, 13, 1825; Sandrik and Landsea, "Tropical Cyclones," 18.

12. *Savannah Republican*, June 16, 1825; *Charleston Courier*, June 6, 9, 10, 1825.

13. Barnes, *North Carolina's Hurricane History*, 36.

14. Tannehill, *Hurricanes*, 150, 251–52; Ludlum, *Early American Hurricanes*, 119; *Charleston Courier*, September 4, 1827.

15. *Charleston Courier*, September 6, 1827.

16. Ibid., August 31, 1827.

17. Ibid., September 8, 1827.

18. Ibid., September 3, 1827; Ludlum, *Early American Hurricanes*, 119–20; Barnes, *North Carolina's Hurricane History*, 36–37.

19. Ludlum, *Early American Hurricanes*, 120–21; *Charleston Courier*, July 16, 17, 24, 27, August 17, 19, 1830.

20. "William Ogilby Journal, 1830–1831," July 29, August 16, 19, 1830, South Carolina Historical Society; see also Gallant, "Recollections," 56–63.

21. *Georgian*, August 21, 26, 1830; *Charleston Courier*, August 19, 1930; "William Ogilby Journal," August 16, 19, 20, 1830.

22. *Charleston Courier*, August 21, 1830.

23. *Georgian*, August 31, 1830; *Charleston Courier*, August 27, 1830.

24. *Georgian*, August 31, 1830; *Charleston Courier*, September 7, 1830.

25. Sandrik and Landsea, "Tropical Cyclones," 18–19.

26. *Georgian*, August 19, 21, September 18, 1830.

27. Ibid.

28. Quoted in *Georgian*, August 24, 1830.

29. "Extract of a Letter from Edingsville, August 19, 1830," quoted in *Georgian*, August 24, 1830.

30. *Georgian*, August 19, 21, September 18, 1830; *Charleston Courier*, August 18, 19, 20, September 6, 1830.

31. *Charleston Courier*, August 17, 1830; *Georgian*, August 19, 1830.

32. "Extract of a Letter dated Crow Island, (North Santee) August 17th, 1830," *Charleston Courier*, August 19, 1830.

33. *Charleston Courier*, August 26, 27, 1830; *Georgian*, August 21, 31, 1830; Ludlum, *Early American Hurricanes*, 120–21.

34. Quoted in Ludlum, *Early American Hurricanes*, 121.

35. Quoted in *Charleston Courier*, August 27, 1830.

36. Tannehill, *Hurricanes*, 153–54, 252; Ludlum, *Early American Hurricanes*, 121–22; Spence, *Shipwrecks, Pirates and Privateers*, 110–11.

37. Quoted in Ludlum, *Early American Hurricanes*, 122.

38. Barnes, *Florida's Hurricane History*, 55–56; Ludlum, *Early American Hurricanes*, 122–23.

39. *Charleston Courier*, September 22, 23, 25, 1835.

40. *Georgian*, September 19, 1835; *Savannah Republican*, September 25, 1835; *Daily Georgian*, September 24, 26, 1835.

41. *Charleston Courier*, September 21, 22, 28, 1835.

42. *Georgian*, September 22, 28, 1835; Ludlum, *Early American Hurricanes*, 123.

43. *Charleston Mercury*, August 4, November 24, 1837; *Savannah Republican*, August 7, 11, 1837.

44. *Savannah Republican*, August 14, 1837; *Charleston Courier*, August 14, 1837.

45. *Charleston Mercury*, August 9, 1837.

46. Sandrik and Landsea, "Tropical Cyclones," 20–21.

47. John Gould, "Shipwreck — Fourteen Lives Lost," *Savannah Republican*, August 16, 1837.

48. *Savannah Republican*, August 11, 16, 1837; "Extract of a Letter from a gentleman in St. Marys to a respectable commercial house in this city, dated 7th August [1837]," *Savannah Republican*, August 14, 1837; Ludlum, *Early American Hurricanes*, 128; Sandrik and Landsea, "Tropical Cyclones," 20–21.

49. Quoted in Ludlum, *Early American Hurricanes*, 126; quoted in *Charleston Mercury*, August 12, 1837; quoted in *Savannah Republican*, August 18, 1837.

50. Quoted in Sandrik and Landsea, "Tropical Cyclones," 21; Ludlum, *Early American Hurricanes*, 126; *Savannah Republican*, August 11, 1837.

51. *Charleston Mercury*, August 12, 1837; *Savannah Republican*, August 11, 1837.

52. *Savannah Republican*, August 7, 1837; *Charleston Mercury*, August 9, 1837; Ludlum, *Early American Hurricanes*, 126.

53. *Savannah Republican*, August 23, 1837.

54. Ibid., August 23, 27, 1837.

55. Ibid., August 30, 1837; Spence, *Shipwrecks, Pirates and Privateers*, 112–13.

56. "Extract of a Letter to the Editors, dated, Combahee, Aug. 19, 1837," *Savannah Republican*, August 25, 1837.

57. "Extract of a Letter from a respectable planter, dated Edingsville, August 28 [1837]," *Charleston Courier*, August 31, 1837.

58. *Charleston Mercury*, August, 21, 25, 1837.

59. Ibid., August 22, 25, 28, 1837; Ludlum, *Early American Hurricanes*, 127.

60. B. H. Hussey's account of the *Home* disaster following the hurricane of October 13, 1893, *Charleston News and Courier*, October 15, 1893; Stick, *Graveyard of the Atlantic*, 23–26; Ludlum, *Early American Hurricanes*, 146–47.

61. Ibid.

62. Ibid.

63. *Charleston Mercury*, October 25, 1837.

64. Stick, *Graveyard of the Atlantic*, 26.

65. *Charleston Mercury*, November 24, 1837.

Chapter Five. Mid-Century Storms, 1840–1857

1. Quoted in Sandrik and Landsea, "Tropical Cyclones," 22.

2. Quoted in House, *Planter Management*, 88.

3. House, *Planter Management*, x, 5–13; Coleman, *History of Georgia*, 163.

4. Pavich-Lindsay, *Anna*, 8n4, 13n1.

5. Ibid., xix–xxiv.

6. Ibid., 17, 18nn2, 3, 4.

7. Rowland, *History of Beaufort County*, 311–26; Edgar, *South Carolina*, 269; Fraser, *Savannah*, 205–6.

8. Edgar, *South Carolina*, 269, 273–77, 287, 323.

9. Sandrik and Landsea, "Tropical Cyclones," 22; *Charleston Courier*, August 30, 1841; Jordan, "History of Storms," 23.

10. House, *Planter Management*, 90–91; Sandrik and Landsea, "Tropical Cyclones," 23; *Charleston Courier*, September 17, 18, 1841.

11. Pavich-Lindsay, *Anna*, 23; House, *Planter Management*, 93.

12. Barnes, *Florida's Hurricane History*, 57–58.

13. Sandrik and Landsea, "Tropical Cyclones," 24–25.

14. "The Late Gale: To the Editors of the Savannah Republican," as quoted in the *Charleston Courier*, October 17, 1842.

15. "Extract of a Letter Received in [Charleston]," *Charleston Courier*, October 18, 1842.

16. House, *Planter Management*, 95; Sandrik and Landsea, "Tropical Cyclones," 23.

17. Ludlum, *Early American Hurricanes*, 149; Jordan, "History of Storms," 25; *Charleston Courier*, October 6, 7, 8, 14, 1842.

18. Ibid.

19. *Charleston Courier*, 10, 11, 12, 1842.

20. Tannehill, *Hurricanes*, 253; Sandrik and Landsea, "Tropical Cyclones," 24; House, *Planter Management*, 95.

21. Barnes, *Florida's Hurricane History*, 59; Sandrik and Landsea, "Tropical Cyclones," 25; House, *Planter Management*, 101.

22. Sandrik and Landsea, "Tropical Cyclones," 25–26; Barnes, *Florida's Hurricane History*, 59–61.

23. *Charleston Courier*, October 17, 21, 1846.

24. Rowland, *History of Beaufort County*, 324–25; House, *Planter Management*, 107; *Daily Georgian*, October 13, 14, 16, 1846; *Charleston Courier*, October 12, 14, 15, 29, 1846.

25. Ibid.

26. A. M. King to "My dearly Beloved husband [Thomas B. King]," July 11, 1848, to "My beloved Lordy [Henry Lord Page King]," September 5, 1848, in Pavich-Lindsay, *Anna*, 39–43.

27. Barnes, *Florida's Hurricane History*, 62–63; House, *Planter Management*, 111–12.

28. *Savannah Republican*, quoted in Sandrik and Landsea, "Tropical Cyclones," 27.

29. Ibid., 28.

30. Rosengarten, *Tombee*, 9–10.

31. Ibid., 582.

32. Sandrik and Landsea, "Tropical Cyclones," 29.

33. Ibid., 29–30; Ludlum, *Early American Hurricanes*, 133. NOAA researchers now rank this storm a category 3 hurricane.

34. *Savannah Daily Morning News*, September 22, 1854.

35. *Charleston Daily Courier*, September 14, 1854.

36. Ibid., September 14, 15, 16, 22, 25, 1854.

37. Ibid.

38. Ibid., September 12, 18, 25, 1854.

39. *Savannah Daily Morning News*, September 11, 1854; *Charleston Daily Courier*, September 14, 1854.

40. Ludlum, *Early American Hurricanes*, 133; Sandrik and Landsea, "Tropical Cyclones," 29–30.

41. A. M. King to "My one dearly beloved husband [Thomas Butler King]," September 7, 1854, in Pavich-Lindsay, *Anna*, 250–52.

42. House, *Planter Management*, 120; Rev. C. C. Jones to Mr. Charles C. Jones Jr., September 11, 1854, in Myers, *Children of Pride*, 95; Rosengarten, *Tombee*, 632.

43. *Savannah Republican*, quoted in *Charleston Daily Courier*, September 16, 1854.

44. House, *Planter Management*, 120.

45. Myers, *Children of Pride*, 95.

46. Ludlum, *Early American Hurricanes*, 133; Fraser, *Savannah*, 299; *Savannah Daily Morning News*, September 8, 9, 1854; *Savannah Republican*, September 9, as printed in the *New York Times*, September 13, 1854.

47. Fraser, *Savannah*, 297–99; *Savannah Daily Morning News*, September 9, 12, 1854; *Charleston Daily Courier*, September 11, 1854.

48. *Savannah Daily Morning News*, September 11, 1854; *Charleston Daily Courier*, 11, 12, 1854.

49. *Charleston Daily Courier*, September 15, 1854.

50. Ibid., September 15, 18, 1854.

51. Ibid., September 15, 1854.

52. Rosengarten, *Tombee*, 632.

53. *Charleston Daily Courier*, September 13, 1854.

54. Fraser, *Charleston! Charleston!* 233–34.

55. *Charleston Daily Courier*, September 9, 11, 1854; Fraser, *Charleston! Charleston!* 217–18.

56. Ibid.

57. *Charleston Daily Courier*, September 12, 1854.

58. "Mother" to John, Elizabeth, and Jane Ann, September 8, 1854, Adger-Smyth[e]-Flynn Family Papers, South Caroliniana Library, University of South Carolina.

59. E. R. to "My Dear Wife," September 16, 1854, Edmund Ravenel Papers, South Carolina Historical Society.

60. *Charleston Daily Courier*, September 9, 11, 1854.

61. Ibid.

62. Adele Petigru Allston to Benjamin Allston, September 20, 1854, in Easterby, *South Carolina Rice Plantation*, 120.

63. *Charleston Daily Courier*, September 9, 13, 15, 16, 1854; Ludlum, *Early American Hurricanes*, 133–34.

64. Sandrik and Landsea, "Tropical Cyclones," 30–31; House, *Planter Management*, 123.

65. Kinder, *Ship of Gold*, 1–41; Coulter, "Steamship *Central America*," 453–57.

66. Kinder, *Ship of Gold*, 43–75, 191–203; Coulter, "Steamship *Central America*," 457–88; Ludlum, *Early American Hurricanes*, 134–35.

67. Ibid.

68. Rowland, *History of Beaufort County*, 326–28; Rogers, *History of Georgetown County*, 300–303.

69. Trapier, *The Hurricane*, 1–24.

Chapter Six. Another Cycle of Tropical Storms and Hurricanes, 1865–1885

1. Rowland, "Alone on the River," 148–49; Edgar, *South Carolina*, 379–80; Pavich-Lindsay, *Anna*, 412–14; Coleman, *History of Georgia*, 225–26.

2. Sandrik and Landsea, "Tropical Cyclones," 32; *New York Times*, August 11, November 30, 2003; *Savannah Morning News*, March 27, 2004.

3. Ibid.

4. Barnes, *Florida's Hurricane History*, 67; Sandrik and Landsea, "Tropical Cyclones," 32–33; Jordan, "History of Storms," 26; *Savannah Morning News*, November 19, 1941.

5. Quoted in Jordan, "Tropical Storms," 27.

6. *Savannah Morning News*, August 21, 1871.

7. Ibid., August 24, 1871; *Charleston Courier*, August 25, 1871.

8. Sandrik and Landsea, "Tropical Cyclones," 33.

9. *Savannah Morning News*, August 19, 1871; Sandrik and Landsea, "Tropical Cyclones," 33.

10. *Savannah Morning News*, August 21, 25, 1871; *Charleston Courier*, August 26, 1871.

11. *Charleston Courier*, August 22, 30, 1871.

12. Ibid., August 21, 1871.

13. Ibid., August 21, 22, 30, 1871.

14. Ibid., October 20, 1873; Sandrik and Landsea, "Tropical Cyclones," 35–36.

15. Ibid.

16. Sandrik and Landsea, "Tropical Cyclones," 37; *Charleston News and Courier*, September 29, October 1, 1874.

17. *Charleston News and Courier*, September 30, October 1, 1874.

18. Ibid., September 29, 1874.

19. Ibid., September 30, 1874.

20. Ibid., September 29, 30, October 1, 1874.

21. Ibid.

22. Ibid., September 30, 1874.

23. [Anonymous], Adger and Bowen Families Bound Volume, 1874, South Caroliniana Library, University of South Carolina.

24. *Charleston News and Courier*, October 8, 1874.

25. Ibid., September 29, October 1, 2, 1874; Jordan, "Tropical Storms," 28.

26. *Charleston News and Courier*, September 29, 1874.

27. Richard Porcher, manuscript in the author's possession, 2005.

28. Humphries, *Journal of Archibald C. McKinley*, xv, xli–xlii; Porcher manuscript.

29. Heyward, *Seed from Madagascar*, xvii; Rowland, "Alone on the River," 149–50.

30. Sandrik and Landsea, "Tropical Cyclones," 37–39; Jordan, "Tropical Storms," 28–29.

31. Barnes, *Florida's Hurricane History*, 70; *Charleston News and Courier*, September 16, 18, 1878; Sandrik and Landsea, "Tropical Cyclones," 39.

32. Sandrik and Landsea, "Tropical Cyclones," 39; *Charleston News and Courier*, September 21, 1878.

33. *Charleston News and Courier*, September 13, 14, 1878.

34. *Savannah Morning News*, September 1, 10, 1881; *Charleston News and Courier*, September 2, 1881.

35. Ibid.

36. Ibid.

37. *Savannah Morning News*, September 10, 1881.

38. Ibid.

39. *New York Times*, September 3, 1881; *Savannah Morning News*, September 5, 1881.

40. *Savannah Morning News*, August 31, 1881.

41. *Charleston News and Courier*, September 2, 5, 1881; *Savannah Morning News*, September 6, 1881; *New York Times*, September 1, 1881.

42. Ibid.

43. Miller, "Tybee Island, Georgia," 107–19; *Savannah Morning News*, August 31, September 5, 1881; Sandrik and Landsea, "Tropical Cyclones," 41; "Hurricane of 1881 Ravages Savannah," newspaper clipping, Hurricane File, Savannah Public Library.

44. Ibid.

45. *Savannah Morning News*, August 29, 1881; *New York Times*, September 3, 1881.

46. *Savannah Morning News*, August 31, 1881; Sandrik and Landsea, "Tropical Cyclones," 41.

47. "Letter from Pauline [Heyward] after her terrible ordeal at Tybee Island, Savannah, August 29, 1881," newspaper clipping, DeCaradeuc Collection, Georgia Historical Society; *Savannah Morning News*, August 29, September 2, 1881.

48. *Savannah Morning News*, August 29, 31, September 5, 1881; *New York Times*, September 3, 1881.

49. *Savannah Morning News*, August 29, 30, September 1, 1881.

50. Ibid.

51. Ibid., August 29, September 1, 1881.

52. Ibid., August 30, September 5, 1881; *Charleston News and Courier*, September 1, 1881.

53. Clara Waring to Charles Waring, August 31, 1881, J. F. Waring Papers, Georgia Historical Society.

54. *Savannah Morning News*, August 29, September 1, 1881.

55. Sandrik and Landsea, "Tropical Cyclones," 41; *Charleston News and Courier*, September 1, 1881.

56. *New York Times*, August 31, 1881; *Savannah Morning News*, August 30, September 5, 1881.

57. *Charleston News and Courier*, August 30, 31, September 5, 1881; *Savannah Morning News*, August 31, 1881; Jordan, "History of Storms," 30.

58. *Charleston News and Courier*, August 31, September 1, 1881.

59. Ibid., August 31, 1881.

60. Ibid., September 9, 1881.

61. Ibid., September 2, 1881.

62. Ibid., August 29, 31, 1881.

63. Ibid., August 29, September 2, 1881.

64. Ibid.

65. Dunn, *Atlantic Hurricanes*, 295.

66. Miller, "Tybee Island, Georgia," 119–34.

67. *Savannah Morning News*, September 3, 1881.

68. *New York Times*, September 14, 19, 1883; *Charleston News and Courier*, September 16, 1883.

69. *Charleston News and Courier*, September 14, 15, 16, 1883.

70. Ibid.

71. Ibid., September 15, 1883.

72. Barnes, *North Carolina's Hurricane History*, 47; *Charleston News and Courier*, September 13, 1883; Purvis, "Listing of Tropical Cyclones," 19.

73. Barnes, *Florida's Hurricane History*, 72; Sandrik and Landsea, "Tropical Cyclones," 43; *Charleston News and Courier*, August 26, 28, 31, September 5, 1885; *New York Times*, August 28, 1885.

74. Ibid.

75. *Charleston News and Courier*, August 28, 1885.

76. Ibid., August 28, September 7, 1885; Rosengarten, *Tombee*, 55.

77. Ibid.

78. *Beaufort Palmetto Post*, September 3, 10, 1885; *Charleston News and Courier*, August 29, September 9, 12, 1885; Jordan, "History of Storms," 30.

79. Kate Walpole Legare diary, vol. 2, August 14, 25, 1885, Duke University, William R. Perkins Library.

80. *Charleston News and Courier*, August 31, September 2, 7, 1885; Jordan, "History of Storms," 30; *New York Times*, August 28, 1885.

81. William Miller to "My Dear Mother," August 26, 1885, William C. Miller Papers, South Carolina Historical Society; McKinley, "August Cyclone," 371–72.

82. McKinley, "August Cyclone," 385–87; *Charleston News and Courier*, August 26, 27, 29, 1885; Miller to "My Dear Mother," August 26, 1885; *New York Times*, August 26, 27, 1885.

83. Ibid.

84. Ibid.

85. *Charleston News and Courier,* August 27, 28, 31, 1885.

86. Ibid., August 26, 28, September 6, 9, 1885.

87. Ibid.

88. Ibid., August 28, 1885; *New York Times,* August 28, 1885.

89. McKinley, "August Cyclone," 383–84; *Charleston News and Courier,* August 27, September 1, 4, 1885.

90. *Charleston News and Courier,* August 30, 1885; McKinley, "August Cyclone," 379.

91. Miller to "My Dear Mother," August 26, 1885; see also *Charleston News and Courier,* August 26, 1885.

92. Jordan, " History of Storms," 30.

93. McKinley, "August Cyclone," 388.

Chapter Seven. Major Hurricanes at Century's End, 1893–1898

1. *Charleston News and Courier,* July 29, 31, August 2, 1877, September 24–25, 1889; *Beaufort Palmetto Post,* September 26, 1889; Barnes, *Florida's Hurricane History,* 72–73; Jordan, "History of Storms," 30–32; Purvis, "Listing of Tropical Cyclones," 19–21.

2. *New York Times,* August 30, 1893; *Charleston News and Courier,* August 26, 1893; *Savannah Morning News,* September 2, 1893; Barnes, *Florida's Hurricane History,* 74; Rosenfeld, "Hurricane," 34–39.

3. Ibid.

4. Stevens, "Great Storm of 1893," 11–12.

5. *New York Times,* August 31, 1893.

6. *Savannah Morning News,* September 2, 1893; Stevens, "Great Storm of 1893," 11.

7. *Savannah Morning News,* August 31, 1893.

8. Ibid., August 30, 1893.

9. *New York Times,* September 1, 1893; *Savannah Morning News,* September 1, 1893.

10. Daily, "Vessels That Have Borne," 167–71; *New York Times,* August 31, 1893.

11. *Charleston News and Courier,* August 30, 1893.

12. *Savannah Morning News,* August 30, 31, 1893; Stevens, "Great Storm of 1893," 11; Douglas, *Hurricane,* 244–45.

13. *Savannah Morning News,* September 3, 1893.

14. Sandrik and Landsea, "Tropical Cyclones," 45; Sullivan, *Georgia Tidewater,* 510–11.

15. *Darien Gazette,* September 2, 1893, quoted in "Hurricane Activity Affecting Georgia Coast," Weather–Savannah file, Savannah Public Library; *Savannah Morning News,* September 1, 1893.

16. *Savannah Morning News,* August 29, 30, 31, September 1, 4, 1893.

17. Ibid.

18. Ibid.

19. Ibid., August 29, 1893.

20. Rosenfeld, "Hurricane," 36; *Savannah Morning News*, August 29, 1893.

21. Ibid.

22. *Savannah Morning News*, August 30, September 2, 3, 1893; *New York Times*, August 31, 1893.

23. Sandrik and Landsea, "Tropical Cyclones," 45; *Savannah Morning News*, August 29, 1893.

24. *New York Times*, August 31, September 3, 1893; Mather, *Storm Swept Coast*, 4–5.

25. Quoted in Carson, "Cyclonic Winds."

26. *New York Times*, September 3, 1893.

27. *Savannah Morning News*, August 30, September 3, 1893; Marscher and Marscher, *Great Sea Island Storm*, 74.

28. Marscher and Marscher, *Great Sea Island Storm*, 28.

29. Quoted in "Beaufort Historic District," sec. 7, p. 1; see also Johnson, *Social History*, 3–4.

30. *Savannah Morning News*, September 2, 3, 1893; *Charleston News and Courier*, September 3, 1893; *New York Times*, August 30, 31, September 3, 1893; Rosenfeld, "Hurricane," 34–39; Marscher and Marscher, *Great Sea Island Storm*, 47; Carson, "Cyclonic Winds."

31. Ibid.

32. *Savannah Morning News*, September 3, 1893.

33. Quoted in the *New York Times*, August 30, 1893.

34. Wall and Wall, "The Storm of 1893," interview with Joe Rivers, October 18, 1970; Mather, *Storm Swept Coast*, 3; *Savannah Morning News*, September 1, 1893; *Charleston News and Courier*, September 3, 1893; *New York Times*, September 2, 3, 1893.

35. Ibid.

36. Susan Hazel Rice diaries, August 27, 28, 29, 1893, Beaufort County Public Library; Susan J. Rice obituary, *Beaufort Gazette*, December 22, 1911.

37. Satterthwait, *Son of the Carolinas*, 238–42.

38. Quoted in Barnes, *Florida's Hurricane History*, 74.

39. Ibid.

40. *Savannah Morning News*, September 1, 2, 3, 6, 1893; *New York Times*, September 2, 3, 1893; Barton, *Red Cross*, 77, 80–81; Mather, *Storm Swept Coast*, 6–19; Wall and Wall, "Storm of 1893."

41. *Savannah Morning News*, August 30, September 3, 1893; *Charleston News and Courier*, September 3, 7, 1893; *New York Times*, September 2, 3, 1893; Wall and Wall, "Storm of 1893"; Carson, "Cyclonic Winds."

42. Ibid.

43. Ibid.

44. Quoted in Thomas Gamble, "Memories of Savannah's Greatest Hurricane," *Savannah Morning News*, August 22, 1943; *Beaufort Gazette*, August 27, 1893; see also Harris, "Sea Island Hurricanes," 231–47.

45. *Charleston News and Courier*, August 31, September 3, 4, 1893.

46. Ibid.

47. Ibid., August 31, September 3, 4, 19, 1893.

48. *Savannah Morning News*, September 3, 1983.

49. *Charleston News and Courier*, September 2, 5, 6, 7, 1893; *Savannah Morning News*, September 1, 1893; *Charleston News and Courier*, September 3, 4, 1893.

50. *Charleston News and Courier*, August 31, September 6, 8, 1893; *Savannah Morning News*, September 1, 1893.

51. Marscher and Marscher, *Great Sea Island Storm*, 22–23, 35; Jesunofsky, "Notes on the Cyclone," 249–96; *Charleston News and Courier*, August 30, September 10, 1893; *New York Times*, August 30, 1893.

52. Rosenfeld, "Hurricane," 35–36; Jesunofsky, "Notes on the Cyclone," 247–56; *Charleston News and Courier*, August 28, 29, 1893; *New York Times*, September 1, 2, 1893.

53. Ibid.

54. Rosenfeld, "Hurricane," 35–36; Jesunofsky, "Notes on the Cyclone," 247–56; *Charleston News and Courier*, August 29, 30, 1893; *New York Times*, September 2, 1893.

55. *Charleston News and Courier*, August 31, 1893.

56. Anne Simons Deas diary, August 28, 29, 1893, South Caroliniana Library, University of South Carolina.

57. *Charleston News and Courier*, August 31, 1893.

58. Ibid., August 29, 30, 31, 1893; Jesunofsky, "Notes on the Cyclone," 249.

59. Ibid.

60. *Charleston News and Courier*, August 31, September 7, 1893; Carson, "Cyclonic Winds."

61. *New York Times*, August 30, 1893; *Savannah Morning News*, August 31, 1893; *Charleston News and Courier*, August 31, September 5, 1893.

62. Ibid.

63. Quoted in Carson, "Cyclonic Winds."

64. Barton, *Red Cross*, 77, 80–81; *New York Times*, September 3, 1893; E. M. Wister Papers, the Quaker Collection, Haverford College Library.

65. *Savannah Morning News*, September 1, 1893.

66. Langdon Cheves to "My Dearest" [Sofia Haskell Cheves], September 5, 1893, Langdon Cheves Papers, South Carolina Historical Society.

67. Jesunofsky, "Notes on the Cyclone," 252; Jordan, "History of Storms," 32; *New York Times*, August 31, 1893; *Savannah Morning News*, September 1, 1893.

68. *Charleston News and Courier*, October 13, 14, 1893; Jesunofsky, "Notes on the Cyclone," 266; Sandrik and Landsea, "Tropical Cyclones," 46.

69. *Charleston News and Courier*, October 19, 1893.

70. Ibid.

71. Ibid.

72. Jesunofsky, "Notes on the Cyclone," 266.

73. Joyner, "October 1893," 4–5, 15; *Charleston News and Courier*, October 16, 17, 18, 21, 1893; Prevost and Wilder, *Pawley's Island*, 51–60.

74. Ibid.

75. Ibid.

76. Ibid.

77. Ibid.

78. *Charleston News and Courier*, October 21, 1893.

79. Barnes, *North Carolina's Hurricane History*, 48.

80. *Savannah Morning News*, September 27, 1894; Sandrik and Landsea, "Tropical Cyclones," 46–47.

81. Barnes, *Florida's Hurricane History*, 77–78; Sandrik and Landsea, "Tropical Cyclones," 47–48.

82. *Charleston News and Courier*, October 1, 2, 1896; *Savannah Morning News*, October 3, 1896.

83. *Charleston News and Courier*, September 30, October 1, 2, 1896.

84. *Savannah Morning News*, October 1, 1896.

85. Quoted in Sullivan, *Georgia Tidewater*, 511.

86. *Savannah Morning News*, October 1, 1896.

87. Ibid., September 30, October 2, 4, 5, 1896; *Charleston News and Courier*, September 30, 1896.

88. Ibid.

89. *Charleston News and Courier*, October 1, 2, 1896; *Beaufort Palmetto Post*, October 1, 8, 1896.

90. *Charleston News and Courier*, October 1, 2, 3, 1896.

91. Barnes, *Florida's Hurricane History*, 79.

92. Sandrik and Landsea, "Tropical Cyclones," 48; *Savannah Morning News*, August 31, 1898; Susan Rice diaries, August 28, 29, 30, 1898.

93. *Savannah Morning News*, August 30, September 1, 1898.

94. Ibid., September 1, 2, 3, 4, 5, 1898; *Beaufort Palmetto Post*, September 1, 1898.

95. Ibid.

96. Ibid.

97. *Savannah Morning News*, August 30, 31, September 1, 2, 1898; Susan Rice diaries, August 31, September 1, 1898; Jordan, "A History of Storms," 34; *Beaufort Palmetto Post*, September 1, 1898.

98. Ibid.

99. *Beaufort Palmetto Post*, September 20, 1898.

100. Barnes, *Florida's Hurricane History*, 80.

101. *Savannah Morning News*, October 5, 8, 1898; *Charleston News and Courier*, October 5, 9, 1898; Sandrik and Landsea, "Tropical Cyclones," 48.

102. Ibid.

103. *Charleston News and Courier*, October 4, 5, 1898.

104. *Savannah Morning News*, October 7, 1898.

105. Sandrik and Landsea, "Tropical Cyclones," 49; Sandrik and Jarvinen, "Reevaluation"; *Savannah Morning News*, October 7, 1898.

106. *Savannah Morning News*, October 5, 7, 1898.

107. Sandrik and Landsea, "Tropical Cyclones," 49; quoted in Sullivan, *Hurricane and Tidal Wave*, 12.

108. *Savannah Morning News*, October 4, 5, 7, 1898.

109. Ibid.

110. [Horace Gould] to "My Dear Sister," October 10, 1898, printed as "A Letter from the Past," *Atlanta Journal and Constitution*, September 13, 1964; *Savannah Morning News*, October 5, 1898.

111. Ibid.

112. [Gould] to "My Dear Sister," October 10, 1898; *Savannah Morning News*, October 7, 1898; Sullivan, *Hurricane and Tidal Wave*, 6. Accounts about Stokeley vary. For instance, some assert that Stokeley came ashore at St. Simons; others say he landed at Darien. Gould's account of this incident and the two printed in the press differ markedly. I've emphasized those portions of the several accounts that are alike in their summary of events.

113. Humphries, *Journal of Archibald C. McKinley*, xxxix; Sullivan, *Hurricane and Tidal Wave*, 2.

114. Humphries, *Journal of Archibald C. McKinley*, 232–37.

115. Ibid.

116. Quoted in Sullivan, *Hurricane and Tidal Wave*, 4, 6, 8; Sullivan, *Georgia Tidewater*, 506; Humphries, *Journal of Archibald C. McKinley*, 237; *Savannah Morning News*, October 7, 1898.

117. Quoted in Sullivan, *Hurricane and Tidal Wave*, 4, 12.

118. Ibid., 14, 16.

119. *Savannah Morning News*, October 3, 1898; *Charleston News and Courier*, October 3, 5, 1898.

120. *Charleston News and Courier*, October 3, 4, 1898; *Beaufort Palmetto Post*, October 6, 1898; Jordan, "History of Storms," 34.

121. *Charleston News and Courier*, October 3, 1898; *Savannah Morning News*, October 3, 1898.

122. Sullivan, *Hurricane and Tidal Wave*, 2–3; Sullivan, *Early Days on the Georgia Tidewater*, 421, 423, 514; "Hurricane Activity Affecting Georgia Coast," n.p.; *Savannah Morning News*, October 3, 1898; *Charleston News and Courier*, October 3, 5, 1898.

Chapter Eight. Hurricanes and Gales of the Twentieth Century, 1904–1979

1. Purvis, "Listing of Tropical Cyclones," 23–24; Jordan, "History of Storms," 36.

2. *Charleston News and Courier*, September 14, 1904.

3. Ibid., September 15, 1904.

4. Ibid., September 16, 1904.

5. Ibid.

6. Ibid., September 15, 1904.

7. Ibid., September 17, 1904.

8. Ibid., September 15, 1904.

9. Ibid., September 16, 1904; Jordan, "History of Storms," 36.

10. *Charleston News and Courier*, September 24, 1906.

11. Ibid., September 20, 1906.

12. Ibid., September 23, 1906.

13. Ibid., September 19, 26, 1906.

14. Ibid.

15. Ibid.

16. Ibid., September 18, 19, 20, 22, 24, 1906; Barnes, *North Carolina's Hurricane History*, 64; Jordan, "History of Storms," 36.

17. Ibid.

18. *Charleston News and Courier*, September 24, 1906.

19. Ibid., October 26, 28, 1906.

20. Ibid., October 21, 22, 1906; Jordan, "History of Storms," 36.

21. *Charleston News and Courier*, October 23, 1906.

22. Barnes, *Florida's Hurricane History*, 92–93; *Charleston News and Courier*, October 18, 1910.

23. Heyward, *Seed from Madagascar*, 241–45; *Charleston News and Courier*, 19, 20, 21, 23, 1910.

24. Ibid.

25. *Savannah Morning News*, August 27, 1911; Jenkins, "Everybody Knows," 23–24; Jordan, "History of Storms," 40; *Charleston News and Courier*, August 27, 1951.

26. *Charleston News and Courier,* September 1, 1911.

27. *Savannah Morning News,* August 30, 1911; *Charleston News and Courier,* August 30, 31, 1911.

28. *Charleston News and Courier,* September 3, 5, 16, 1911.

29. Ibid., August 31, September 1, 3, 7, 1911.

30. Ibid., August 30, September 1, 5, 18, 1911.

31. Jenkins, "Everybody Knows," 23–24; Jordan, "History of Storms," 40; *Savannah Morning News,* August 29, 1911.

32. *Savannah Morning News,* August 29, 30, 1911; *Charleston News and Courier,* September 2, 1911.

33. Ibid.

34. Rosa B. Cooley (Penn School principal) to the Editor, October 1911; "Disaster on the Sea Islands," extensive letter from Grace Bigelow House to Mrs. Jeffries, October 12, 1911, both Penn School Papers, Southern Historical Collection, University of North Carolina; *Savannah Morning News,* August 30, 1911; *Charleston News and Courier,* August 31, 1911; *Beaufort Gazette,* September 8, 15, 1911; *Charleston Evening Post,* August 27, 1951.

35. Ibid.

36. *Charleston News and Courier,* August 31, 1911.

37. Ibid., September 5, 1911.

38. Ibid., August 29, September 6, 4, 10, 17, 1911; *Charleston Evening Post,* August 27, 1951, September 7, 1960; *Savannah Morning News,* August 29, 30, September 1, 2, 1911.

39. Ibid.

40. Ibid.

41. Heyward, *Porgy,* 142–52; Fraser, *Charleston! Charleston!* 367, 375.

42. "Summer of 1911," letter from Mildred A. Kuhr in the possession of Alan S. Gaynor, Savannah, Ga.; *Charleston News and Courier,* August 29, September 4, 6, 10, 17, 1911; *Charleston Evening Post,* August 27, 1951, September 7, 1960; *Savannah Morning News,* August 29, 30, September 1, 2, 1911. The number of deaths in the Charleston area reported at different times varied from seventeen to over twenty.

43. Ibid.

44. Ibid.

45. *Charleston News and Courier,* August 30, 1911.

46. Heyward, *Seed from Madagascar,* xix, xxix, 221, 245–51; Coclanis, *Shadow of a Dream,* 115.

47. Edgar, *South Carolina,* 479.

48. Ibid., 485.

49. Coclanis, *Shadow of a Dream,* 128; Coleman, *History of Georgia,* 258–64; Fraser, *Charleston! Charleston!* 339–41.

50. Heyward, *Seed from Madagascar*, 221.

51. Barnes, *Florida's Hurricane History*, 96; Barnes, *North Carolina's Hurricane History*, 66; *Charleston News and Courier*, July 14, 15, 16, 17, 20, 1916.

52. *Charleston News and Courier*, July 21, 1916.

53. Ibid., July 18, 20, 21, 1916.

54. Ibid.

55. Fishburne, *William Kershaw Fishburne*, 89–91.

56. Barnes, *Florida's Hurricane History*, 127–40; Barnes, *North Carolina's Hurricane History*, 127–66.

57. Dr. Robert Ridgway to "My dear friend," September 28, 1928, James Henry Rice Jr. Correspondence, Special Collections, Duke University; Jenkins, "Everybody Knows," 23–24; *Savannah Morning News*, September 19, 20, 1928; *Charleston News and Courier*, September 22, 1928.

58. Ibid.

59. *Charleston News and Courier*, September 19, 20, 1928.

60. Ibid., September 21, 22, 1928; Jordan, "History of Storms," 43.

61. *Charleston News and Courier*, September 6, 7, 8, 9, 1933; Jordan, "History of Storms," 43.

62. *Charleston News and Courier*, May 30, 1934; Jordan, "History of Storms," 43.

63. *Savannah Morning News*, August 12, 13, 1940; *Charleston News and Courier*, August 13, 1940.

64. Jordan, "History of Storms," 43; *Charleston News and Courier*, September 7, 1960; *Charleston News and Courier*, August 12, 17, 1940.

65. R. R. Ford to Arthur Elting, August 13, 1940; J. King to Miss Cooley, August 12, 1940; "Notes on the Storm, 8/15/40–9/30/40"; "St. Helena in the Path of the Hurricane," all Penn School Papers, Southern Historical Collection, University of North Carolina; *Charleston News and Courier*, August 12, 14, 1940; Douglas, *Hurricane*, 290. Estimates of the dead on the sea islands around Beaufort ranged from ten to thirty-four to fifty. Most authors give the number as thirty-four, and I have used that figure.

66. Ibid.

67. Puckette, *Edisto*, 78, 82–83; *Charleston News and Courier*, August 13, 1940.

68. *Charleston News and Courier*, August 13, 1940; *Savannah Morning News*, August 13, 1940.

69. Jordan, "History of Storms," 43; *Charleston News and Courier*, August 12, 13, 1940; *Savannah Morning News*, August 13, 1940.

70. *Charleston News and Courier*, August 13, 1940; Jordan, "History of Storms," 43.

71. Ibid.

72. C. R. Martin, "Beaufort and the Storm," *Charleston News and Courier*, August 18, 1940.

73. Sullivan, *Georgia Tidewater*, 737; Jordan, "History of Storms," 47; *Charleston News and Courier*, October 20, 21, 1944.

74. *Charleston News and Courier*, June 24, 25, 26, 1945.

75. Ibid., September 18, 1945; Jordan, "History of Storms," 47.

76. Barnes, *Florida's Hurricane History*, 178–79; *Charleston News and Courier*, October 16, 1947.

77. *Savannah Evening Press*, October 15, 1947; *Savannah Morning News*, October 17, 1947; *Atlanta Journal*, October 16, 1947; *Charleston News and Courier*, October 16, 1947.

78. *Charleston News and Courier*, October 16, 1947.

79. Barnes, *Florida's Hurricane History*, 192–95.

80. *Savannah Morning News*, October 19, 1950.

81. Ibid.

82. *Charleston News and Courier*, December 1, 2, 1952; Jordan, "History of Storms," 47.

83. Ibid.

84. Barnes, *North Carolina's Hurricane History*, 80.

85. Ibid., 82–83; Sanders, "September Gale," 33–34.

86. "Red Cross, Committee's Efforts Carry Area through Disaster," newspaper clipping; Jeffrey Collins, "Era of Surprise Storms Like Hazel Is Past," May 18, 2004, newspaper clipping, both Hurricane File, Georgetown Public Library.

87. Sanders, "September Gale," 33–34.

88. "Hurricane Wrecks Island, Small Damage in City," newspaper clipping, Hurricane File, Georgetown Public Library.

89. Collins, "Era of Surprise Storms"; *Charleston News and Courier*, September 16, 19, 21, 1954; Jordan, "History of Storms," 47.

90. Ibid.

91. Barnes, *North Carolina's Hurricane History*, 106–8; *Charleston News and Courier*, October 16, 17, 1954.

92. *Charleston News and Courier*, October 17, 1954 (my italics).

93. Barnes, *North Carolina's Hurricane History*, 108.

94. Sanders, "September Gale," 35; *Charleston News and Courier*, September 28, 29, October 1, 1959.

95. Sanders, "September Gale," 35–37; *Charleston News and Courier*, September 30, October 1, 2, 6, 1959.

96. Ibid.

97. Barnes, *Florida's Hurricane History*, 216–21.

98. Jenkins, "Everyone Knows," 25; Sullivan, *Georgia Tidewater*, 755; *Brunswick News*, September 10, 1964, May 26, 1999; *Savannah Morning News*, September 12, 1964; Barnes, *North Carolina's Hurricane History*, 120.

99. Ibid.

100. Jordan, "History of Storms," 59; Barnes, *Florida's Hurricane History*, 244; Barnes, *North Carolina's Hurricane History*, 120–36.

101. Barnes, *Florida's Hurricane History*, 244–46; Barnes, *North Carolina's Hurricane History*, 136–37.

102. Jenkins, "Everyone Knows," 24–25; *Savannah Morning News*, September 5, 6, 7, 8, 9, 1979; Jordan, "History of Storms," 59; Cashin, *Beloved Bethesda*, 243.

103. Ibid.

104. Ibid.

Chapter Nine. Hugo and After, 1989–2004

1. Fraser, *Charleston! Charleston!* 439; Barnes, *North Carolina's Hurricanes*, 149–50.

2. Jenkins, "Everyone Knows," 25; *Savannah Morning News*, September 21, 23, 1989.

3. *Atlanta Journal and Constitution*, September 23, 24, 25, 1989; *Savannah Morning News*, September 23, 24, 25, 1989; Fraser, *Charleston! Charleston!* 439–40; Fox, *Lunatic Wind*, 86.

4. Ibid.

5. *Savannah Morning News*, September 24, 1989.

6. *State* (Columbia, S.C.), September 24, 1989; *Atlanta Journal and Constitution*, September 24, 25, 26, 27; *Savannah Morning News*, September 23, 24, 1989; Fraser, *Charleston! Charleston!* 439–40.

7. *Savannah Morning News*, September 24, 1989.

8. David Farrow, "Second Half of Hugo Brought Ocean to Our Door," *Charleston Post and Courier*, September 11, 2003.

9. *Atlanta Journal and Constitution*, September 24, 25, 26, 27, 1989; Fox, *Lunatic Wind*, 89; Fraser, *Charleston! Charleston!* 439–40.

10. Ibid.

11. Charles R. Rowe, "200 Years of the *Post and Courier* . . . Hurricane Hugo," *Charleston Post and Courier*, January 10, 2003.

12. Ibid.

13. Judy Watts, "Hugo Survivors Vow They Won't Stick around for Hurricane," *Charleston Post Courier*, September 2, 2004.

14. Tony Bartelme, "Storm a Defining Event for State," *Charleston Post and Courier*, September 19, 1999; Michael Gartland, "Remembering Hugo: Families Cope with Painful Memories of Waters Invading Their Homes, Lives," *Charleston Post and Courier*, September 21, 2003; Bo Peterson, "McClellanville Prepares with Memories of Hugo," *Charleston Post and Courier*, August 14, 2004; Fox, *Lunatic Wind*, 184.

15. Ibid.

16. Ibid.

17. Ibid.

18. *Hilton Head News*, September 28, 1989; Fox, *Lunatic Wind*, 144, 186, 196.

19. Fox, *Lunatic Wind*, 155; Edgar, *South Carolina*, 581–83.

20. Barnes, *North Carolina's Hurricane History*, 220–25; Lynne Langley et al., "City Is Spared Worst: Hurricane Lands at Cape Fear, North Carolina," *Charleston Post and Courier*, September 16, 1999; Brian Hicks, "Surge Puts McClellanville on the Map," *Charleston Post and Courier*, September 19, 1999; Bartelme, "Storm a Defining Event."

21. Ibid.

22. Ibid.

23. *Carolina Morning News* (Hilton Head, S.C.), August 15, 2004; Matthew Mogul, "Charley's Price Tag," August 17, 2004; Tony Bartelme et al., "Charley's Second Strike," August 15, 2004.

24. Ibid.

25. Douglas Pardue, "Power Punch Leaves Thousands in Dark," *Charleston Post and Courier*, August 30, 2004; "The Message from 'Gaston,'" August 30, 2004; Bartelme, "Storm a Defining Event"; Bruce Smith, "Storm Pounds Previously Battered Coastal Village," *Savannah Morning News*, August 30, 2004.

Conclusion

1. Like the South, the coastal regions of Georgia and South Carolina were shaped by the cultural values of caste and class and economic structures such as the "prevalence of plantations, the impact of U.S. and world markets, the lack of capital, and the levels of defense spending." This is part of the story. The weather is another. See Marc Egnal's review of Carlton and Coclanis, *The South, the Nation, and the World*.

2. Edgar, *South Carolina*, 581–82.

3. Sheets and Williams, *Hurricane Watch*, 268–71; Barnes, *North Carolina's Hurricane History*, 288; *Savannah Morning News*, April 28, September 22, 17, October 1, 2004, May 17, 2005.

4. Ibid.

5. Barnes, *North Carolina's Hurricane History*, 286–87.

Bibliography

Manuscript Collections

Beaufort County Public Library (Beaufort, S.C.): Susan Hazel Rice Diaries.
Coastal Georgia Historical Society (St. Simons, Ga.): Couper Family Papers.
Duke University, William R. Perkins Library: Sylvanus Keith and Cary Keith Papers.
  Kate Walpole Legare Diary. James Henry Rice Jr. Correspondence.
Georgetown Public Library (Georgetown, S.C.): Hurricane File.
Georgia Historical Society: Heyward-Hawkins Family Papers. Savannah Historical
  Research Association Collection. J. F. Waring Papers. DeCaradeuc Collection.
Haverford College Library (Haverford, Pa.): E. M. Wister Papers, the Quaker Collection.
Savannah Public Library (Bull Street): Hurricane File. Savannah Weather.
South Carolina Historical Society (Charleston, S.C.): Cochran Family Papers. Mary
  Lamboll Thomas Beach Papers. McBeth Family Papers. Izard Family Papers.

Manuscript Autobiography of Rear Admiral Charles Steadman. Letter, A. Moubray
to William Moubray, Vertical File. William Ogilby Journal, 1830–1831. Edmund
Ravenel Papers. William C. Miller Papers. Langdon Cheves Papers.

University of North Carolina, Southern Historical Collection: John Rutledge Papers.
Penn School Papers.

University of South Carolina, South Caroliniana Library: Joseph Bennett Letter.
Adger-Smyth[e]-Flynn Family Papers. Adger and Bowen Families Bound Volume,
1874. Anne Simons Deas Diary.

Newspapers

Anti-Monarchist and South Carolina Advertiser (Edgefield, S.C.), 1811.
Atlanta Journal and Constitution, 1947, 1964, 1989.
Beaufort Gazette, 1893, 1911, 1960.
Beaufort Palmetto Post, 1885, 1889, 1896, 1898.
Brunswick News, 1964.
Camden County Tribune, 1952.
Carolina Gazette, 1770, 1800.
Carolina Gazette and Country Journal, 1770.
Carolina Morning News (Hilton Head), 2004.
Charleston City Gazette, 1804.
Charleston Courier, 1804, 1811, 1813, 1815, 1824, 1825, 1827, 1830, 1835, 1837, 1841, 1842,
    1846, 1871, 1873.
Charleston Daily Advertiser, 1792
Charleston Daily Courier, 1854.
Charleston Evening Post, 1951.
Charleston Mercury, 1822, 1837.
Charleston News and Courier, 1874, 1877, 1878, 1881, 1883, 1885, 1889, 1893, 1896, 1898,
    1904, 1906, 1910, 1911, 1916, 1928, 1933, 1934, 1938, 1940, 1944, 1945, 1947, 1951, 1952,
    1954, 1959, 1960, 2001.
Charleston Post and Courier, 1989, 1999, 2003, 2004.
Columbian Museum and Savannah Advertiser, 1797, 1804.
Daily Georgian, 1824, 1835, 1846.
Georgia Republican and State Intelligencer, 1804, 1806.
Georgian, 1830, 1835.
Hilton Head News, 1989.
Monitor (Washington, Ga.), 1813.
New York Times, 1854, 1881, 1883, 1885, 1893, 2003.
Republican and Savannah Evening Ledger, 1813.

Savannah Daily Morning News, 1854.

Savannah Evening Press, 1947.

Savannah Gazette, 1797.

Savannah Morning News, 1871, 1881, 1893, 1894, 1896, 1898, 1911, 1928, 1940, 1941, 1943, 1947, 1950, 1964, 1979, 1989, 2004.

Savannah Museum, 1822.

Savannah Republican, 1825, 1835, 1847.

Savannah Republican and State Intelligence, 1804, 1815.

South Carolina and American General Gazette, 1769.

South Carolina Gazette, 1752.

South Carolina Gazette and General Advertiser, 1783.

South Carolina Weekly Gazette, 1783.

State (Columbia, S.C.), 1989.

State Magazine, 1993.

Times (London), 1804.

Books, Articles, and Miscellaneous Writings

Arsenault, Raymond. "The End of the Long Hot Summer: The Air Conditioner and Southern Culture." *Journal of Southern History* 50 (November 1984): 597–628.

Bagwell, James E. *Rice Gold: James Hamilton Couper and Plantation Life on the Georgia Coast*. Macon: Mercer University Press, 2000.

Ball, Edward. *Slaves in the Family*. New York: Farrar, Straus and Giroux, 1998.

Barnes, Jay. *Florida's Hurricane History*. Chapel Hill: University of North Carolina Press, 1998.

———. *North Carolina's Hurricane History*. Chapel Hill: University of North Carolina Press, 1995.

Barton, Clara. *A Story of the Red Cross: Glimpses of Field Work*. New York: D. Appleton, 1928.

Bartram, John. *Diary of a Journey through the Carolinas, Georgia, and Florida from July 1, 1765, to April 10, 1766*. Philadelphia: American Philosophical Society, 1942.

"Beaufort Historic District: Beaufort, South Carolina." Typescript, Historic Beaufort Foundation, Beaufort, S.C., 2000. Draft copy in the author's possession.

Bell, Malcolm, Jr. *Major Butler's Legacy: Five Generations of a Slaveholding Family*. Athens: University of Georgia Press, 1987.

Bullard, Mary R. *Cumberland Island: A History*. Athens: University of Georgia Press, 2005.

———. *Robert Stafford of Cumberland Island: Growth of a Planter*. Athens: University of Georgia Press, 1995.

Bossak, Brian H. "Early Nineteenth-Century U.S. Hurricanes: A GIS Tool and Climate Analysis." PhD diss., Florida State University, 2003.

Calhoun, Jeanne A. *The Scourging Wrath of God: Early Hurricanes in Charleston, 1700–1804.* Leaflet No. 29, Charleston Museum, 1983.

Carlton, David L., and Peter A. Coclanis, *The South, the Nation, and the World: Perspectives on Southern Economic Development.* Charlottesville: University of Virginia Press, 2003.

Carson, Helen Craig. "Cyclonic Winds, High Tides, Bring Destruction to Islands." *New South Carolina State Gazette* 5 (April 1972).

Cashin, Edward. *Beloved Bethesda: A History of George Whitefield's Home for Boys, 1740–2000.* Macon: Mercer University Press, 2001.

Chesnutt, David R., et al., eds. *The Papers of Henry Laurens.* Vol. 11, *Jan. 5, 1776–Nov. 1, 1777.* Columbia: University of South Carolina Press, 1988.

Cochran, Glenda. *Cumberland Island: A National Seashore.* Macon: Island House, 1986.

Coclanis, Peter A. Introduction to *Seed from Madagascar,* by Duncan Clinch Heyward, ix–xviii. Columbia: University of South Carolina Press, 1993.

———. *The Shadow of a Dream.* New York: Oxford University Press, 1989.

Coleman, Kenneth, et al. *A History of Georgia.* Athens: University of Georgia Press, 1991.

Coulter, E. Merton. "The Loss of the Steamship *Central America* in 1857." *Georgia Historical Quarterly* 54 (Winter 1970): 453–57.

———. *Thomas Spalding of Sapelo.* Baton Rouge: Louisiana State University Press, 1940.

Cowdrey, Albert E. *This Land, This South: An Environmental History.* Rev. ed. Lexington: University Press of Kentucky, 1996.

Daily, R. P. "Vessels That Have Borne the Name *Savannah.*" *Georgia Historical Quarterly* 18 (1934): 167–71.

Douglas, Marjory Stoneman. *Hurricane.* New York: Rinehart, 1958.

Dunn, Gordon E., and Banner I. Miller. *Atlantic Hurricanes.* Baton Rouge: Louisiana State University Press, 1964.

Easterby, J. H., ed. *The South Carolina Rice Plantation: As Revealed in the Papers of Robert F. W. Allston.* Chicago: University of Chicago Press, 1945.

Edgar, Walter B., ed. *Biographical Directory of the South Carolina House of Representatives.* Vol. 1, *Sessions Lists, 1692–1973.* Columbia: University of South Carolina Press, 1974.

———. *South Carolina: A History.* Columbia: University of South Carolina Press, 1998.

Egnal, Marc. Review of *The South, the Nation, and the World,* by David L. Carlton and Peter A. Coclanis. *Journal of Southern History* 45 (February 2005): 221–22.

Ellis, Henry. "An Account of the Heat and the Weather in Georgia." *Gentleman's Magazine* 29 (July 1759): 314.

Ferguson, T. Reed. *The John Couper Family at Cannon's Point.* Macon: Mercer University Press, 1994.

Fishburne, Anne Sinkler. *William Kershaw Fishburne: Doctor to Hell Hole Swamp.* Charleston: R. L Bryan, 1969.

Fox, William Price. *Lunatic Wind: Surviving the Storm of the Century.* Chapel Hill: Algonquin Books, 1992.

Fraser, Walter J., Jr. *Charleston! Charleston! The History of a Southern City.* Columbia: University of South Carolina Press, 1989.

———. *Savannah in the Old South.* Athens: University of Georgia Press, 2002.

Gallant, Mary. "Recollections of a Charleston Childhood, 1822–1836." *South Carolina Historical Magazine* 98 (January 1997): 56–63.

Gill, D. Samuel. *Narrative of Reminiscences in Williamsburg County.* Columbia: Bryan, 1897.

Hamer, Philip M., et al., eds. *The Papers of Henry Laurens.* Vol. 2, *Nov. 1, 1755–Dec. 31, 1758.* Columbia: University of South Carolina Press, 1970.

Harris, Joel Chandler. "The Sea Island Hurricanes: The Devastation." *Scribner's Magazine*, February 1894, 231–47.

Hewatt, Alexander. *An Historical Account of the Rise and Progress of the Colonies of South Carolina and Georgia.* Vol. 1. Spartanburg: Reprint Company, 1962.

Heyward, David Clinch. *Seed From Madagascar.* Columbia: University of South Carolina Press, 1993.

Heyward, DuBose. *Porgy.* New York: Grosset & Dunlap, 1925.

House, Albert V., ed. *Planter Management and Capitalism in Ante-Bellum Georgia: The Journal of Hugh Fraser Grant, Ricegrower.* New York: Columbia University Press, 1954.

Humphries, Robert L., ed. *The Journal of Archibald C. McKinley.* Athens: University of Georgia Press, 1991.

Jenkins, Herndon H. "Everybody Knows that Georgia Doesn't Get Many Hurricanes." Typescript in the author's possession, 1997.

Jesunofsky, Lewis N. "Notes on the Cyclone of August 27–28, 1893." In *City of Charleston Yearbook — 1893,* 249–96. Charleston, 1893.

Johnson, Guion Griffis. *A Social History of the Sea Islands.* Chapel Hill: University of North Carolina Press, 1930.

Jordan, Laylon Wayne. "Tropical Storms and Coastal South Carolina." *Coastal Heritage,* bulletin no. 2 (May–June 1982).

Jordan, Laylon Wayne, et al. "A History of Storms of the South Carolina Coast." Typescript, South Carolina Sea Grant Consortium, Charleston, 1979.

Joyner, Charles. "October 1893: Hurricane!" *State Magazine,* January 16, 1993.

Keber, Martha L. *Seas of Gold, Seas of Cotton: Christophe Poulain DuBignon of Jekyll Island.* Athens: University of Georgia Press, 2002.

Kilgo, James. "Tidewater Heritage." In *The New Georgia Guide,* 623–58. Athens: University of Georgia Press, 1996.

Kinder, Gary. *Ship of Gold in the Deep Blue Sea.* New York: Vintage Books, 1999.

Klingberg, Frank J., ed. *The Carolina Chronicle of Dr. Francis Le Jau, 1706–1717.* Berkeley: University of California Press, 1956.

Lash, Jeffrey N. "The Reverend Martin Luther Hurlbut: Yankee President of Beaufort College, 1812–1814." *South Carolina Historical Magazine* 85 (October 1984): 305–16.

"Letters of John Floyd, 1813–1838." Notes and Documents. *Georgia Historical Quarterly* 33 (September 1949): 228–53.

Lovell, Carolina Couper. *The Golden Isles of Georgia.* Boston: Little, Brown, 1932.

Ludlum, David M. *Early American Hurricanes, 1492–1870.* Boston: American Meteorological Society, 1963.

Marscher, Bill, and Fran Marscher. *The Great Sea Island Storm of 1893.* Lincoln, Neb.: Authors Choice Press, 2001.

Mather, R. C. *The Storm Swept Coast of South Carolina.* Beaufort: New South, 1894.

McCusker, John J. "How Much Is That in Real Money? A Historical Price Index for Use as a Deflator of Money Values in the Economy of the United States." *Proceedings of the American Antiquarian Society* 101, pt. 2 (October 1991): 297–373.

McKenna, Kenneth, L. "Formulas for Estimating Cost in Current U. S. Dollars." Paper in author's possession.

McKinley, Carl. "The August Cyclone." In *City of Charleston Year Book — 1885,* 371–88. Charleston, 1885.

Merrens, H. Roy, and George D. Terry. "Dying in Paradise: Malaria, Mortality, and the Perceptual Environment in Colonial South Carolina." *Journal of Southern History* 56 (November 1984): 533–50.

Meyers, Amy R. W., et al. *Empire's Nature: Mark Catesby's New World Vision.* Williamsburg, Va.: Omohundro Institute of Early American History and Culture, 1998.

Miller, Cynthia Ann. "Tybee Island, Georgia: Changing Images and Land-Use, 1733–1895." Master's thesis, University of Georgia, 1984.

Mock, Cary J. "Tropical Cyclone Reconstructions from Documentary Records: Examples for South Carolina, U.S.A.," 1–22. Paper in author's possession.

Myers, Robert M. *The Children of Pride: A True Story of Georgia and the Civil War.* New Haven: Yale University Press, 1972.

Pavich-Lindsay, Melanie, ed. *Anna: The Letters of a St. Simons Island Plantation Mistress, 1817–1859.* Athens: University of Georgia Press, 2002.

Pielke, Roger A., Jr., and Roger A. Pielke Sr. *Hurricanes: Their Nature and Impacts on Society*. New York: John Wiley, 1997.

Prevost, Charlotte K., and Effie L. Wilder. *Pawley's Island, A Living Legend*. Columbia: State, 1972.

Puckette, Clara C. *Edisto: A Sea Island Principality*. Cleveland: Seaforth, 1978.

Purvis, John C., et al. "A Descriptive Listing of Tropical Cyclones That Have Affected South Carolina." Typescript, South Carolina Disaster Preparedness Agency, Columbia, 1973.

Ramsay, David. *Ramsay's History of South Carolina, from Its First Settlement in 1670 to the Year 1804*. Vol. 2. Spartanburg: Reprint Company, 1960.

Reddick, Marguerite, et al. *Camden's Challenge: A History of Camden County, Georgia*. Camden: Camden County Historical Commission, 1976.

Rogers, George C., Jr. *History of Georgetown County, South Carolina*. Columbia: University of South Carolina Press, 1970.

Rogers, George C., Jr., et al., eds. *The Papers of Henry Laurens*. Vol. 7, Aug. 1, 1769–Oct. 9, 1771. Columbia: University of South Carolina Press, 1979.

Rosenfeld, Jeff. "The Hurricane." *Weatherwise* 51 (September–October 1998): 34–39.

Rosengarten, Theodore. *Tombee: Portrait of a Cotton Planter: with the Journal of Thomas B. Chaplin (1922–1890)*. New York: Morrow, 1986.

Rowland, Lawrence S. "Alone on the River: Savannah River Plantations of St. Peter's Parish, South Carolina." *South Carolina Historical Magazine* 88 (July 1987): 121–50.

Rowland, Lawrence S., et al. *The History of Beaufort County, South Carolina*. Vol. 1, 1514–1861. Columbia: University of South Carolina Press, 1996.

Sanders, John. "September Gale." *South Carolina Wild Life*, July–August 1979, 33–37.

Sandrik, Al, and Brian Jarvinen. "A Reevaluation of the Georgia and Northeast Florida Tropical Cyclone of 2 October 1898." Typescript in author's possession.

Sandrik, Al, and Christopher W. Landsea. "Chronological Listing of Tropical Cyclones Affecting North Florida and Coastal Georgia 1565–1899." Typescript in author's possession.

Satterthwait, Elisabeth Carpenter. *A Son of the Carolinas: A Story of the Hurricane Upon the Sea Islands*. Philadelphia: H. Altemus, 1898.

Scotti, R. A. *Sudden Sea: The Great Hurricane of 1938*. Boston: Little, Brown, 2003.

Screven, Frank B. "The Georgia Bryans and Screvens." *Georgia Historical Quarterly* 40 (December 1956): 325–48.

Sheets, Bob, and Jack Williams. *Hurricane Watch: Forecasting the Deadliest Storms on Earth*. New York: Vintage Books, 2001.

Smythe, Augustine T., et al. *The Carolina Low-Country*. New York: Macmillan, 1931.

Spence, E. Lee, ed. *Shipwrecks, Pirates and Privateers: Sunken Treasures of the Upper South Carolina Coast 1521–1865*. Charleston: Narwhal Press, 1995.

———. *Spence's Guide to South Carolina*. N.p.: E. Lee Spence, 1976.

Stegeman, John F., and Janet A. Stegeman. *Caty: A Biography of Catharine Littlefield Greene*. Athens: University of Georgia Press, 1977.

Stevens, Paul. "Great Storm of 1893." *Independent Republic Quarterly* 2 (July 1968): 11–12.

Stewart, Mart A. "'Let Us Begin with the Weather?': Climate, Race, and Cultural Distinctiveness in the American South." In *Nature and Society in Historical Context*, 240–56. Cambridge: Cambridge University Press, 1997.

Stick, David. *Graveyard of the Atlantic*. Chapel Hill: University of North Carolina Press, 1952.

Sullivan, Buddy. *Early Days on the Georgia Tidewater: The Story of McIntosh County and Sapelo*. Darien, Ga.: McIntosh County Board of Commissioners, 1997.

———. "Touring Coastal Georgia." In *The New Georgia Guide*, 659–93. Athens: University of Georgia Press, 1996.

———, ed. *The Hurricane and Tidal Wave of 1898 in McIntosh County, Georgia: A Collection of Contemporary Accounts*. Darien, Ga.: Lower Altamaha Historical Society, 1998.

Tannehill, Ivan Ray. *Hurricanes: Their Nature and History Particularly Those of the West Indies and the Southern Coasts of the United States*. Princeton: Princeton University Press, 1952.

Trapier, Rev. Richard Shubrick. *The Hurricane: A Narrative of Facts*. Charleston: Evans and Cogswell, 1862.

Tresp, Lothar L. "September, 1748 in Georgia, from the Diary of John Martin Bolzius." *Georgia Historical Quarterly* 47 (September 1963): 320–32.

Vanstory, Burnett. *Georgia's Land of the Golden Isles*. Athens: University of Georgia Press, 1956.

Wade, Arthur P. "Fort Winyaw at Georgetown, 1776–1923." *South Carolina Historical Magazine* 84 (October 1983): 214–43.

Wall, Mary J., and W. O. Wall Jr. "The Storm of 1893." Typescript, Beaufort Public Library.

Webber, Mabel L., ed. "Peter Manigault's Letters." *South Carolina Historical and Genealogical Magazine* 32 (April 1931): 115–30.

Wood, Virginia S., and Mary R. Bullard, eds. *Journal of a Visit to the Georgia Islands of St. Catherines, Green, Ossabaw, Sapelo, St. Simons, Jekyll, and Cumberland... in 1753*. Macon: Mercer University Press, 1996.

Wood, Virginia Steele, and Ralph Van Wood, eds. "The Reuben King Journal, 1800–1806." *Georgia Historical Quarterly* 50 (December 1966): 421–58.

Index

Rice, Susan Hazel, family of, 175–76, 191
Riley, Joe, 241, 242
Robinson, Rosa, 215
Rose-in-Bloom, sinking of, 55, 56, 58–60
Rutherford, N. G., family of, 91
Rutledge, John, Jr., 56; aboard Rose-in-
Bloom, 58–60 passim

Saffir-Simpson Hurricane Potential
Damage Scale, 3, 4, 269n37
Sampit River, 82, 103
Sapelo Island, Ga., 96; hurricanes at, 87,
88, 89, 168, 199–200; tropical storm at,
73
Savannah, Ga., 8, 21–22, 25–26, 29, 30,
36–37, 97; tropical storms at, 105, 156,
201, 209, 221–29 passim, 230, 238, 247;
wind gusts reach 96 mph at, 213
—hurricanes at: 1686–1797, 8, 13, 15, 16,
24; 1800–1804, 47–48, 52; 1806–1824, 91;
1825–1837, 101, 107; 1840–1857, 119, 120,
121–22, 126–27; 1865–1885, 137, 150–51;
1893–1898, 171, 189–90, 193; 1904–1979,
224
Savannah River, 11, 13, 33, 47, 91, 127
Screven, Hannah, 46
Screven, John, family of, 46
Shadduck, Theodore, 144
Shepard, Steven A., 246
ships damaged or lost in harbor or at
wharfside: Abbeville, 171; Amazon, 49;
Arago, 155–56; Atlantic, 102; Augusta,
91; Benjamin, 76; Birmingham Packet,
49; Borrows, 92; Canton, 65; Carlotta,
102; Catherine, 174; Charlestonian,
245; Christopher, 49; Collector, 48;
Comet, 104; Commerce, 65; Concord,
49; Cornelia, 65; Daddy's Girl, 244;
Dorchester Packet, 25; Dove, 25; Eagle,

76; Edisto, 245; Eureka, 128–29;
Exchange, 104; Experiment, 25, 102;
Favorite, 49; Florida, 65; Francis
Ann, 104; Fred F. Brown, 171; General
Jackson, 47; Glenlivet, 160; Guilielmi,
48; G. W. Coffee, 129; Hiram, 47;
Island Flower, 189; James Madison, 92;
Jenny Lind, 127; John Kennedy, 174;
John Stoney, 104; Joseph and Benjamin,
26; Jubilee, 219; Liberty, 47; London,
29; Louis V. Chapels, 154; Lucky Lady,
245; Lydia, 49; Maria, 104; Mary, 49;
Mary Ann, 245; Mary G. Reed, 169;
Massasoit, 129; Medbor, 159; Minerva,
47; Montserrat, 49; Moonrise, 245;
Morning Star, 65; Mutual Safety,
118–19; Orange, 49; Oregon, 127;
Othello, 102; Pocahontas, 102; Phoenix,
65; Rasselas, 102; Rebecca M. Wall,
205; Retrieve, 65; Robert Turner, 189;
Sally, 65; Sam Jones, 127; Sarah D.
Fell, 211; Sun Maid, 245; Theis, 29;
Thomas Jefferson, 47; Two Friends,
90; Washington, 102; Wasp, 245;
Winyaw, 34
ships damaged or lost offshore: Africa, 15,
16, 18; Alexander, 38–39; Alibon, 85–86;
Alice Franklin, 136; Alonzo, 75–76;
Angenett, 122; Ann, 57–58; Anna and
Minerva, 106; Anna S. Conants,
165–66; Astoria, 167; Augusta, 50;
Aurora, 76; Banan, 167; Bessie
Whiting, 210–11; Betsey (1783), 31–32;
Betsey (1804), 40; Betty, 24; Big Ella,
204; Brandt, 98–99; Brunswick, 143–44;
Brutus, 72; Carolina Susannah, 156;
Caroline Ann, 87; Caroline Hall, 123;
Central America, 131–33; Chance, 23;
City of Atlanta, 154–55; City of Savan-